THE NEW TESTAMENT

OF

THE INCLUSIVE LANGUAGE

BIBLE

THE NEW TESTAMENT

OF

THE INCLUSIVE LANGUAGE

BIBLE

Cross Cultural Publications, Inc.

CrossRoads Books

Published by **CROSS CULTURAL PUBLICATIONS, INC.**
CROSS ROADS BOOKS
Post Office Box 506
Notre Dame, Indiana, 46556, U.S.A.
Phone: (219) 272-0889
FAX: (219) 273-5973

Editors
Proofreaders
and
Contributors

Many women and a few good men have helped in the preparation of this version. Some of their names are:

Anderson-Smith, Andrews, Asher, Barniskis, Brown, Bryan, Chamberlain, Cox, Ellynn, Ensley, Fure, Grace, Hagberg, Hammargren, Hanssen, Harmon, Holden, Hollifield, Hustver, Jacobus, Johnson, Kaplan, Kerns, Kimbrough, Klug, Knight, Kozelka, Krause, Kunnari, Larson, Lingo, Lyon, McNey, Mattson, Mains, Mason, Murphy, Newell-Anderson, Palumbo, Peck, Peterson, Ray, Rone, Salyers, Satter, Sautter, Spyhalski, Stapek, Stiles, Stinson-Wesley, Stockhausen, Sudman, Sumstine, Valentine, Vassar, Warmanen, Weidendorf, Weinhagen, White, Williams and Windsheimer.

It is the hope of the editors that this version will be critiqued by readers so that improvements may be imcorporated in subsequent editions. Please contact the publisher.

WHY AN INCLUSIVE LANGUAGE VERSION
OF THE BIBLE?

The fundamental purpose of the Biblical message is to prepare us for the heavenly realm. In this realm, according to the Bible, God and the angels and resurrected people are all spirits. Jesus says in Matthew 22:30, "At the resurrection men and women do not marry, they are like the angels in heaven." In this existence, our true and permanent existence, there are no gender differences among persons.

Yet, we should realize that the Bible was written for people still living in this world who do have different gender roles in their earthly existence. These roles, while they may be different, do not make men and women unequal.

However, there arose the practice of male domination, starting with the evolution of the early societies. The emerging media of expression in these societies, their arts and language, inevitably reflected this practice of male domination. When the Biblical messages were first put to writing, what the writers used was this tainted language of the early societies. No change had occurred either in the practice of male dominance or in the use of sexist language by the time the original texts of the Bible were translated into modern languages.

We are fortunate to live today in a culture that is attempting to change the way that society treats women. Therefore, it is proper for us to put the message of the Bible into a language that reflects the values of our culture without changing its basic meaning. To not do so would be counter to the core concepts of the Bible, which hold that men and women are equals before their Creator. Not doing so will also perpetuate the inequalities between the sexes that existed in earlier societies, inequalities which had nothing to do with the message of the Bible and which we recognize as unjust in our modern society.

Thus, there are two imperatives that require us to change the language of the Bible: one that comes from the nature of the Biblical message itself and one that comes from the criteria of our culture today. This version of the New Testament is a response to these imperatives.

It is the hope of the editors and the publisher that this version will bring women and men of all races and nationalities to a closer relationship with God's Word. Please forward your critiques and suggestions to the publisher, who is considering the publication of an Inclusive Language Version of the Old Testament.

The Publishers

Contents

Matthew

THE ANCESTRY OF JESUS

1:1These are the ancestors of Jesus Christ, the descendant of David, the descendant of Abraham:

FROM ABRAHAM TO DAVID

2-16Abraham, Isaac, Jacob (the father of Judah and his brothers), Judah (the father of Perez and Zerah - Tamar was their mother), Perez, Hezron, Ram, Amminadab, Nahshon, Salmon, Boaz (Rahab was his mother), Obed (Ruth was his mother), Jesse and David the king.

FROM DAVID TO THE EXILE IN BABYLON

Solomon (his mother had been the wife of Uriah), Rehoboam, Abijah, Asa, Jehoshaphat, Joram, Uzziah, Jotham, Ahaz, Hezekiah, Manasseh, Amos and Josiah (the father of Jeconiah and his brothers, about the time they were taken away to Babylon).

FROM THE EXILE IN BABYLON TO THE MESSIAH

Jeconiah, Shealtiel, Zerubbabel, Abiud, Eliakim, Azor, Zadok, Achim, Eliud, Eleazar, Matthan, Jacob and Joseph (the husband of Mary, of whom was born Jesus, who is called the Messiah). 17So all the generations from Abraham to David were fourteen generations, and from David till the exile in Babylon were fourteen generations, and from the exile in Babylon to the Messiah were fourteen generations.

THE BIRTH OF JESUS

18Now the birth of Jesus the Messiah happened in this way. His mother Mary was engaged to Joseph, but before they came together she found that she was with child by the Holy Spirit. 19Then Joseph, being reasonable and unwilling to make her a public example, determined to quietly let her go. 20While he was thinking about this, an angel of God appeared to him in a dream and said, "Joseph son of David, do not be afraid to take Mary to be your wife, for what is conceived in her is by the Holy Spirit. 21She will give birth to a Son, and you shall call His name Jesus, for He will save His people from their sins."

22All this happened in order to fulfill what God had said through the prophet: 23"A virgin shall be with child and give birth to a Son and they shall call His name Emmanuel," which means, "God is with us."

24Joseph woke up from sleep and did as the angel of God commanded. He took Mary to himself to be his wife 25but did not have intercourse with her until after she gave birth to a Son. Then Joseph gave Him the name Jesus.

THE VISIT OF THE WISE ONES FROM THE EAST

[2:1]Jesus was born in Bethlehem of Judea during the time when Herod was king. About that time, wise ones from the east came to Jerusalem [2]asking, "Where is He who has been born King of the Jews? We saw His star when it appeared and have come to worship Him."

[3]When King Herod heard of this, he was disturbed, and all Jerusalem with him. [4]He gathered all the chief priests and scribes of the people together and demanded to know where the Messiah would be born. [5]They said to him, "In Bethlehem of Judea, for thus it was written by the prophet: [6]'And you, Bethlehem, in the land of Judah, are by no means least among the rulers of Judah; for out of you will come a Ruler who will shepherd My people Israel.'"

[7]Herod secretly called the wise ones and asked them what time the star had appeared. [8]He sent them to Bethlehem and said, "Go and search diligently for the young child. When you find Him, bring me word, so that I too may come and worship Him." [9]They listened to the king and departed. Then the star they had seen in the east went before them till it came and stood over where the young child was. [10]Seeing the star filled the wise ones with joy.

[11]They came into the house and saw the young child with Mary His mother, and they knelt down and worshiped Him. Then they opened their treasures and presented Him with gifts of gold, frankincense and myrrh. [12]Then, being warned by God in a dream not to return to Herod, they went back to their country another way.

AN ANGEL WARNS JOSEPH TO FLEE TO EGYPT

[13]After they departed, the angel of God appeared to Joseph in a dream and said, "Arise! Take the young child and His mother and flee to Egypt. Stay there until I bring you word, for Herod will seek the young child to destroy Him." [14]He arose and took the young child and His mother by night and departed for Egypt. [15]They were there until the death of Herod, so that what God had spoken by the prophet might be fulfilled, "Out of Egypt I called My Son."

THE LITTLE CHILDREN OF BETHLEHEM ARE KILLED

[16]When Herod saw that he had been misled by the wise ones, he was exceedingly angry. He sent word to kill all the male children two years old and under who were in or near Bethlehem, according to the time he had learned from the wise ones. [17]Then was fulfilled what had been spoken by Jeremiah the prophet, [18]"A voice was heard in Ramah, lamentation and weeping and great mourning, Rachel weeping for her children and refusing to be comforted because they were no more."

THE FAMILY MOVES TO NAZARETH IN GALILEE

[19]After Herod's death, an angel appeared in a dream to Joseph in Egypt [20]and said, "Arise! Take the young child and His mother and go to the land of Israel, for those who sought the young child's life are dead." [21]So Joseph took the young child and His mother and went to the land of Israel. [22]But when Joseph heard that Archelaus was reigning in Judea in the place of his father Herod, Joseph was afraid to go there. Warned in a dream, he went on to Galilee [23]and stayed in a town called Nazareth. Thus what was spoken by the prophets was fulfilled, "He will be called a Nazarene."

JOHN THE BAPTIST

$3{:}1$In those days John the Baptist appeared, preaching in the wilderness of Judea $2$and saying, "Repent, for the heavenly realm is here!" 3This is the one who was spoken of by the prophet Isaiah, "The voice of one calling in the wilderness, 'Prepare the way for Yahweh! Make straight paths for our God!'" 4John had a robe of camel's hair, a leather belt around his waist and his food was locusts and wild honey. 5Jerusalem, all Judea and all the region around the Jordan went out to him. 6Acknowledging their sins, they were baptized by him in the Jordan.

7When John saw many Pharisees and Sadducees come to where he was baptizing, he said, "You generation of snakes! Who warned you to flee from the wrath to come? 8Bear fruit worthy of repentance! 9Do not imagine that you can say to yourselves, 'We have Abraham as our ancestor,' for I say to you that God is able to raise up children for Abraham from these stones. 10Even now the ax is laid to the root of the trees, and every tree that does not bear good fruit will be cut down and thrown into the fire. 11I indeed baptize you with water for repentance, but someone more powerful than me is coming. I am not worthy to carry His sandals. He will baptize you with the Holy Spirit and fire. 12His threshing fork is in His hand, and He is ready to separate the wheat from the straw. He will gather His wheat into the granary, but the straw He will burn up with unquenchable fire."

JESUS IS BAPTIZED AND A VOICE IS HEARD FROM HEAVEN

13Jesus came from Galilee to the Jordan to be baptized by John, 14but John tried to prevent Him, saying, "I have need to be baptized by You, and You come to me?" 15Jesus answered and said, "Let it be so now, for we must do this to fulfill God's righteous plan." So John consented. 16After Jesus was baptized, He immediately came up out of the water. Suddenly the heavens were opened to Him and He saw the Spirit of God descending like a dove and alighting on Him. 17A voice from heaven said, "This is My dearly loved Son, with whom I am well pleased."

THE DEVIL TRIES TO TEMPT JESUS

$4{:}1$Then Jesus was led by the Spirit into the wilderness to be tempted by the devil. 2He fasted forty days and forty nights, and afterward He was hungry. 3The tempter came to Him and said, "If You are the Son of God, command these stones to become bread." 4Jesus answered, "It is written, 'Humans shall not live by bread alone, but by every word that comes out of the mouth of God.'" 5Then the devil took Him to the holy city and had Him stand on the peak of the temple. 6The devil said to Him, "If You are the Son of God, throw Yourself down, for it is written, 'God will command angels concerning you, and they will hold you up in their hands, lest you dash your foot against a stone.'" 7Jesus said to the devil, "It is also written, 'You shall not tempt your God.'" 8Then the devil took Him up a very high mountain and showed Him all the countries of the world and their glory. 9The devil said to Him, "All these I will give You if You will kneel down and worship me." 10Jesus said to the devil, "Get behind Me, Satan! For it is written, 'You shall fear your God and serve God only.'" 11Then the devil left Him, and angels came and cared for Him.

JESUS LEAVES NAZARETH AND MOVES TO CAPERNAUM

[12]When Jesus heard that John had been put in prison, He went back to Galilee. [13]He left Nazareth and came and lived in Capernaum, which is on the seashore in the region of Zebulun and Naphtali. [14]This was so that what was spoken by Isaiah the prophet might be fulfilled: [15]"The land of Zebulun and the land of Naphtali on the road by the sea beyond the Jordan, Galilee of the Gentiles! [16]The people who lived in darkness have seen a great light! A light has shined on those who live in the region of the shadow of death." [17]From that time Jesus began to speak in public, saying, "Repent, for the heavenly realm is at hand."

JESUS CHOOSES FOUR DISCIPLES

[18]As Jesus walked by the Sea of Galilee, He saw two brothers, Simon (called Peter) and his brother Andrew. They were casting a net into the sea, for they were fishers. [19]He said to them, "Follow Me and I will show you how to fish for humans." [20]They immediately left their nets and followed Him. [21]Going on from there, He saw two other brothers, James and John. They were in a boat with Zebedee their father, mending their nets. He called them, [22]and they immediately left the boat and their father and followed Him.

JESUS TELLS THE GOOD NEWS AND HEALS THE SICK

[23]Jesus went through all Galilee teaching in their synagogues, preaching the good news of the realm and healing every sickness and every disease among the people. [24]His fame went throughout all Syria, and the people brought to Him all the sick who were afflicted with all kinds of diseases and pains - the demon-possessed, the epileptics, the paralytics - and He healed them. [25]Great crowds followed Him from Galilee, Decapolis, Jerusalem, Judea and from beyond the Jordan.

THE GREAT TEACHINGS

[5:1]Seeing the crowds, Jesus went up a mountain. He sat down there, and His disciples came to Him. [2]Jesus began to teach them. He said, [3]"Blessed are the poor in spirit, for the heavenly realm is theirs. [4]Blessed are those who mourn, for they will be comforted. [5]Blessed are the humble, for they will inherit the earth. [6]Blessed are those who hunger and thirst for righteousness, for they will be filled. [7]Blessed are the merciful, for they will receive mercy. [8]Blessed are the pure in heart, for they will see God. [9]Blessed are the peacemakers, for they will be called the children of God. [10]Blessed are those who are persecuted for the sake of righteousness, for the heavenly realm is theirs. [11]Blessed are you when they insult you and persecute you and say hurtful lies against you because of Me. [12]Rejoice and be glad, because great is your reward in heaven; for that is the way they persecuted the prophets who were before you.

[13]"You are the salt of the earth, but if the salt loses its flavor, can it be made salty again? From then on it is not good for anything but to be thrown out and trampled on. [14]You are the light of the world. A city that is built on a hill cannot be hidden. [15]Neither do they light a lamp and put it under a basket, but on a lampstand. Then it shines for all who are in the house. [16]Let your light so shine before others that they see your good works and glorify your heavenly Parent.

[17]"Do not think that I have come to destroy the law of Moses or the teachings of the prophets. I have not come to destroy, but to fulfill. [18]For truly I say to you, until the sky and the earth pass away, not one dot or one mark shall pass from the law until all is fulfilled. [19]Therefore anyone who breaks even one of the least of these commandments and teaches others to do so shall be called the least in the heavenly realm, but whoever practices them and teaches them shall be called great in the heavenly realm. [20]For I say to you that, unless your righteousness exceeds that of the scribes and Pharisees, you cannot enter the heavenly realm.

[21]"You have heard that it was said to those of old, 'You shall not kill, and whoever kills shall be in danger of judgment.' [22]But I say to you that anyone who is angry without cause will be in danger of the judgment. Anyone who says to another, 'You are worthless,' will be judged by the council. And anyone who says, 'You are stupid!' shall be in danger of the fires of hell.

[23]"Therefore if you bring your gift to the altar and then remember that another believer has something against you, [24]leave your gift there by the altar and go your way. First be reconciled to your fellow believer; then come and offer your gift. [25]Agree with your adversary quickly while you are on the way to court, lest at any time your adversary deliver you to the judge, and the judge deliver you to the officer and you are thrown into prison. [26]Truly I say to you, you will by no means come out of there until you have paid the last penny.

[27]"You have heard that it was said to those of old, 'You shall not commit adultery.' [28]But I say to you that if you look lustfully at another, you have already committed adultery in your heart.

[29]"If your right eye leads you astray, pluck it out and throw it from you. It is better for you to lose one part of your body than for your whole body to be thrown into hell. [30]If your right hand causes you to offend, cut it off and throw it from you. It is better for you to lose one part of your body than for your whole body to be thrown into hell.

[31]"It was said, 'If you put away your spouse, you shall furnish a bill of divorce.' [32]But I say to you that if you put away your spouse except for the cause of unfaithfulness, you cause your spouse to commit adultery. And anyone who marries a divorced person commits adultery.

[33]"Again, you have heard that it was said to those of old, 'You shall not break your vows, but shall perform your vows to God.' [34]But I say to you: Do not make vows at all! Neither by heaven, for it is God's throne, [35]nor by the earth, for it is God's footstool, nor by Jerusalem, for it is the city of the great God. [36]Neither shall you swear by your head, because you cannot make one hair white or black. [37]Let your 'Yes' mean 'Yes' and your 'No' mean 'No.' Anything more than that is from the evil one.

[38]"You have heard that it was said, 'An eye for an eye and a tooth for a tooth.' [39]But I say to you, do not resist those who wrong you. If they slap you on your right cheek, turn the other to them also. [40]If they see you and take your coat, let them have your shirt also. [41]If they compel you to go a mile, go with them two. [42]Give to the one who asks of you, and do not turn away from the one who would borrow from you.

[43]"You have heard that it was said, 'You shall love your friends and hate your enemies.' [44]But I say to you, love your enemies and pray for those who persecute you [45]so that you may be the children of your heavenly Parent. For God makes the sun rise on the evil and the good, and sends rain on the just and the unjust. [46]If you love those who love you, what reward have you? Even the tax collectors do that. [47]And if you greet only your friends, what do you do more than others? Even the unbelievers do that. [48]Be perfect, therefore, even as your heavenly Parent is perfect.

[6:1]"Beware of practicing your good deeds before others to be noticed by them, for then you will have no reward from your Parent who is in heaven. [2]When you practice good deeds, do not sound a trumpet before you like the hypocrites do in the synagogues and in the streets so that they may be honored by others. Truly I say to you, they have their reward. [3]When you practice good deeds, do not let your left hand know what your right hand is doing [4]so that your good deeds may be a secret. Then your heavenly Parent who sees in secret will reward you openly.

JESUS TEACHES ABOUT PRAYER

[5]"When you pray, do not be like the hypocrites; for they love to pray, standing in the synagogues and on the street corners to be seen by others. Truly I say to you, they have their reward. [6]But you, when you pray, go into a room by yourself and shut the door and pray to your heavenly Parent who is unseen. Then your heavenly Parent who sees in the unseen will reward you openly. [7]When you pray, do not go on and on like the pagans. They think they will be heard because of their many words. [8]Do not be like them, for your heavenly Parent knows what you need before you ask.

[9]Therefore pray in this way: Our heavenly Parent, I pray that Your holy name is honored. [10]May Your realm come, may Your will be done, on earth as it is in heaven. [11]Give us this day our daily bread; [12]and forgive us our offenses, as we forgive those who offend us. [13]And lead us not into hard testing, but rescue us from evil.

OTHER REVELATIONS

[14]"If you forgive others their offenses, your heavenly Parent will also forgive you. [15]But if you do not forgive others their offenses, neither will your heavenly Parent forgive your offenses.

[16]"When you fast, do not put on a sad face like the hypocrites do, for they look gloomy to show others they are fasting. Truly I say to you, they have their reward. [17]But you, when you fast, dress as usual and wash your face. [18]Then you will not appear to be fasting to others, but only to your heavenly Parent who is unseen. And your heavenly Parent who is unseen will reward you.

[19]"Do not lay up treasures for yourselves on earth, where moth and rust corrupt, and where thieves break in and steal. [20]But lay up treasures for yourselves in heaven, where neither moth nor rust corrupt, and where thieves do not break in or steal. [21]For where your treasure is, there will your heart be also.

[22]"The light of the body is the eye. If your eye is clear, your whole body will be full of light. [23]But if your eye is bad, your whole body will be full of darkness. If the light that is in you is dark, how great is that darkness.

24"No one can work for two bosses. You will either hate the one and love the other, or you will be loyal to the one and despise the other. And you cannot serve God and money.

25"Therefore I say to you, do not worry about what you should eat or what you should drink; or about your body, what you should put on. Is not life more than for food and the body more than for clothing? 26Look at the birds of the air. They do not sow or reap or gather into granaries, and yet your heavenly Parent feeds them. Are you not worth more than they?

27"Which of you by worrying can add one cubit to your stature? 28And why do you worry about clothing? Consider the lilies of the field, how they grow. They do not toil, nor do they spin. 29But I say to you that even Solomon in all his glory was not arrayed like one of these. 30If this is how God clothes the plants of the field today, which tomorrow are thrown into the oven, how much more you, O you of little faith? 31Therefore do not worry and say, 'What will we eat?' or 'What will we drink?' or 'What will we wear?' 32All these the unbelievers seek. Your heavenly Parent knows that you need all these things. 33Seek first God's realm and God's righteousness and all these will be added to you. 34Therefore do not worry about tomorrow, for tomorrow can worry about itself. Each day has trouble enough of its own.

7:1"Judge not, lest you be judged. 2For with the judgment you judge, you will be judged; and the measure you use will be used on you in return. 3Why do you stare at the speck of sawdust in your friend's eye, but pay no attention to the log that is in your own eye? 4Or how can you say to your friend, 'Let me pull the speck out of your eye,' when there is a log in your own eye? 5You hypocrite! First take the log out of your own eye, and then you can see clearly to take the speck out of your friend's eye.

6"Do not give what is holy to the dogs or throw your pearls before swine, lest they trample them under their feet and turn and attack you.

7"Ask and it will be given to you, seek and you will find, knock and it will be opened to you. 8For everyone who asks receives, and everyone who seeks finds, and to everyone who knocks it will be opened. 9Which of you, if your children ask for bread, will give them a stone? 10Or if they ask for a fish, will give them a snake? 11If you then, being evil, know how to give good gifts to your children, how much more will your heavenly Parent give good gifts to those who ask? 12Do unto others as you would have them do unto you. This is the law and the prophets.

13"Enter in at the narrow gate. For wide is the gate and broad is the way that leads to destruction, and many are those who go in that way. 14But narrow is the gate and difficult is the way that leads to life, and few are those who find it.

15"Beware of false prophets who come to you in sheep's clothing but inwardly are preying wolves. 16You will know them by their fruits. Are grapes gathered from thorn bushes or figs from thistles? 17Every good tree brings forth good fruit, but a worthless tree brings forth bad fruit. 18A good tree cannot bring forth bad fruit, nor can a worthless tree bring forth good fruit. 19Every tree that does not bring forth good fruit is cut down and thrown into the fire. 20Therefore by their fruits you will know them.

21"Not everyone who says to Me, 'Rabbi! Rabbi!' will enter the heavenly realm, but only those who do the will of My heavenly Parent. 22Many will say to Me in that day, 'Rabbi! Rabbi! Did we not prophesy in Your name and in Your name cast out demons and in Your name do many miracles?' 23Then I will say to them, 'You were not My followers. Depart from Me, you who work iniquity.'

24"All those who hear these words of Mine and put them into practice are like the wise who build their house upon the rock. 25The rain descends, the floods come and the winds blow and beat upon that house, but it does not fall, for it is built upon the rock. 26All those who hear these words of Mine and do not put them into practice are like the foolish who build their house upon the sand. 27The rain descends, the floods come and the winds blow and beat upon that house, and it falls - and great is its fall."

28When Jesus was finished with this message, the people were astonished at His teaching, 29for He taught them as one having authority, and not as the scribes.

JESUS HEALS A LEPER

8:1When Jesus came down from the mountain, great crowds followed Him. 2Just then a man who had leprosy came and bowed down to Him, saying, "Rabbi! If You are willing, You can make me clean." 3Jesus put out His hand, touched him and said, "I am willing, be clean." Immediately the man was healed. 4Jesus said to him, "See that you tell no one. Go show yourself to the priest and offer the gift that Moses commanded as proof that you are healed."

A FOREIGNER'S SERVANT IS HEALED AT A DISTANCE

5When Jesus entered Capernaum, a centurion came to Him and pleaded, 6"Rabbi, my servant lies at home paralyzed and badly tormented." 7Jesus said to him, "I will come and heal him." 8The centurion said, "Rabbi, I am not worthy to have You come under my roof, but say the word and my servant will be healed. 9For I am a man under authority and have soldiers under me. I say to this one, 'Go,' and he goes, and to another, 'Come,' and he comes, and to my servant, 'Do this,' and he does it." 10Jesus was amazed when He heard this, and He said to those who followed, "Truly I say to you, I have never found so great a faith, not even in Israel. 11And I say to you, many will come from the east and the west and sit at the table with Abraham, Isaac and Jacob in the heavenly realm. 12But the subjects of the realm will be thrown out into outer darkness, and there will be weeping and gnashing of teeth." 13Then Jesus said to the centurion, "Go your way! As you believe, so will it be done for you." And his servant was healed that same hour.

JESUS HEALS PETER'S MOTHER-IN-LAW

14When Jesus arrived at Peter's house, He saw Peter's mother-in-law lying down, burning with fever. 15He touched her hand and the fever left her. Then she got up and ministered to them.

OLD TESTAMENT PROPHECY FULFILLED

16When evening came, they brought to Him many who had demons. He cast out the spirits with a word and healed all who were sick. 17This was to fulfill what was spoken by the prophet Isaiah, "He took our sicknesses and bore our diseases."

THE COMMITMENT REQUIRED OF A DISCIPLE

[18]When Jesus saw the crowd around Him, He gave a command to go across to the other side of the sea. [19]One of the scribes came and said to Him, "Teacher, I will follow You wherever You go." [20]Jesus said to him, "Foxes have dens and the birds of the air have nests, but the Son of Humanity has nowhere to lay His head." [21]Another of His disciples said to Him, "Rabbi, let me go and bury my father first." [22]But Jesus said to him, "Follow Me, and let the dead bury their dead."

JESUS CALMS THE STORM

[23]Jesus went aboard a boat, and His disciples went with Him. [24]Suddenly a violent wind arose on the sea and the waves came over the boat, but Jesus was asleep. [25]His disciples came and woke Him, saying, "Rabbi! Save us! We are going to be swept away!" [26]He said to them, "Why are you fearful, O you of little faith?" Then He stood up and rebuked the winds and the sea and there was a great calm. [27]The disciples were astonished and said, "Who is this, that even the winds and the sea obey Him!"

THE DEMONS THAT WENT INTO THE PIGS

[28]When He arrived at the other side in the country of the Gadarenes, two men came out to meet Him from the tombs. The men had demons in them. They were exceedingly fierce and no one could pass by that way. [29]They cried out, "What have we to do with You, You Son of God? Have You come here to torment us before the time?" [30]Some distance away from them a herd of pigs was feeding. [31]The demons begged Him, "If You cast us out, send us into the herd of pigs." [32]He said to them, "Go!" and they came out and went into the herd of pigs. Immediately the whole herd of pigs ran down the steep bank into the sea and drowned. [33]Those who took care of the pigs ran into town and told everything that had happened to those who had demons in them. [34]Then the whole town came out to meet Jesus. When they saw Him, they pleaded with Him to depart from their country.

JESUS IS REBUKED FOR FORGIVING SIN

[9:1]Jesus went aboard a boat, crossed over and came to His own town. [2]Just then some people brought a paralytic to Him, lying on a bed. Seeing their faith, Jesus said to the paralytic, "Have courage, son, your sins are forgiven." [3]Some scribes thought to themselves, "This is blasphemy!" [4]But Jesus, knowing their thoughts, said, "Why do you think evil in your hearts? [5]Which is easier to say: 'Your sins are forgiven,' or to say, 'Arise and walk'? [6]But so you know that the Son of Humanity has authority on earth to forgive sins, I say to this man: Get up, pick up your mat and go home." [7]The man got up and went to his home. [8]When the crowds saw this, they were afraid; and they praised God for giving such authority to humans.

A TAX COLLECTOR IS CHOSEN AS A DISCIPLE

[9]As Jesus went on from there, He saw a man named Matthew sitting at the tax collector's booth. Jesus said to him, "Follow Me," and Matthew got up and followed Him. [10]Later, as Jesus was eating at Matthew's house, many tax collectors and sinners came and sat down with Him and His disciples. [11]When the Pharisees saw

this, they said to His disciples, "Why does your Teacher eat with tax collectors and sinners?" [12]Jesus heard them and said, "It is not the healthy who need a physician, but the sick. [13]Now go and learn what this means: 'I desire mercy and not sacrifice.' I have not come to call the righteous, but sinners."

THERE IS A TIME TO FAST

[14]Then the disciples of John came to Him and said, "Why do we and the Pharisees fast, but Your disciples do not fast?" [15]Jesus said to them, "Can the guests of the bridegroom mourn while the bridegroom is with them? But the day is coming when the bridegroom will be taken away from them. Then they will fast.

THE PARABLE OF THE WINESKINS

[16]"No one patches a piece of new cloth on an old garment, for the patch will pull away from the garment and the tear will be made worse. [17]Nor does anyone put new wine into old wineskins, lest the wineskins break and the wine run out and the wineskins be ruined. Instead, they put new wine into new wineskins and both are preserved."

A FATHER PLEADS FOR LIFE FOR HIS DAUGHTER

[18]As Jesus was saying these things to them, a leader of the synagogue came and knelt before Him, saying, "My daughter has just died; but come and lay Your hand upon her and she will live." [19]Jesus stood up and followed him, and so did His disciples.

A WOMAN IS HEALED BECAUSE OF HER FAITH

[20]Just then a woman who had suffered with hemorrhages for twelve years came up behind Him and touched the edge of His cloak, [21]for she said to herself, "If I but touch His cloak, I will be healed." [22]Jesus turned, and when He saw her, He said, "Daughter, be encouraged. Your faith has healed you." And the woman was healed from that hour.

JESUS BRINGS A GIRL BACK TO LIFE

[23]When Jesus came into the leader's house and saw the flute players and the people making a clamor, [24]He said to them, "Go out! The girl is not dead; she is just sleeping." They laughed at Him. [25]But when the people were put out, He went in and took her by the hand. The girl got up. [26]The fame of this spread through all that land.

TWO BLIND MEN RECEIVE THEIR SIGHT

[27]As Jesus departed from there, two blind men followed Him, calling loudly, "Son of David, have mercy on us!" [28]When He went into a house, the blind men came to Him. Jesus said to them, "Do you believe that I am able to do this?" They said to Him, "Yes, Rabbi." [29]Touching their eyes, He said, "Let it be done to you as you have believed," [30]and their eyes were opened. Jesus sighed and said to them, "Make sure that not even one person knows!" [31]But they departed and spread His fame through all that land.

THE PHARISEES ACCUSE JESUS OF BEING EMPOWERED BY THE DEVIL

[32]As they were going out, a man who had a demon in him and who could not talk was brought to Jesus. [33]When the demon was cast out, the man started talking. The crowds marveled and said, "Nothing like this has ever been seen in Israel!" [34]But the Pharisees said, "He casts out demons by the prince of demons."

JESUS' LOVE FOR THE PEOPLE

^{35}Jesus went through all the towns and villages, teaching in their synagogues, preaching the good news of God's realm and healing every sickness and every disease. ^{36}As He looked at the crowds, He felt compassion for them; for they were harassed and scattered, like sheep without a shepherd. ^{37}He said to His disciples, "The harvest is truly large, but the workers are few. ^{38}Pray therefore that the Overseer of the harvest will send out laborers to bring in the harvest."

JESUS SENDS OUT THE TWELVE

$^{10:1}$Jesus called His twelve disciples and gave them authority to cast out unclean spirits and to heal every sickness and every disease. ^{2}These are the names of the twelve apostles: first Simon (called Peter), Andrew his brother, James the son of Zebedee, John his brother, ^{3}Philip, Bartholomew, Thomas, Matthew the tax collector, James the son of Alphaeus, Thaddaeus, ^{4}Simon the Zealot and Judas Iscariot (who betrayed Him).

^{5}These twelve Jesus sent out with the command: "Do not go to the Gentiles and do not enter any Samaritan town. ^{6}Rather, go to the lost sheep of the house of Israel. ^{7}As you go, call out, 'The heavenly realm is here!' ^{8}Heal the sick, raise the dead, cleanse the lepers, cast out demons. Freely you have received, now freely give. ^{9}Do not take gold, silver or copper in your money-belts. ^{10}Do not take a knapsack for your journey or two coats or sandals or a walking stick. Workers should be given what they need to live on. ^{11}In whatever city or town you enter, inquire in it who is worthy and stay there till you go. ^{12}When you come into a home, embrace them. ^{13}If the home is worthy, let your peace come upon it. If it is not worthy, let your peace return to you. ^{14}If no one will welcome you or listen to your words, leave that house or city and shake the dust off your feet. ^{15}Truly I say to you, on the day of judgment it will be worse for that city than for the land of Sodom and Gomorrah.

^{16}"Beware! I send you out like sheep in the midst of wolves. Therefore be as wise as serpents and as gentle as doves. ^{17}But beware of humans, for they will hand you over to councils and flog you in their synagogues. ^{18}You will be brought before powerful rulers for My sake, and you will testify to them and to the nations. ^{19}When they hand you over, do not think about what you will say. What you are to say will be given to you at that time, ^{20}for it will not be you speaking, but the Spirit of your heavenly Parent speaking through you. ^{21}Brother will hand over brother to death, and the parent the child; and the children will rise up against their parents and cause them to be put to death. ^{22}You will be hated by everyone because of My name, but those who endure to the end will be saved. ^{23}When they persecute you in one town, flee to another. Truly I say to you, you will not go through all the towns of Israel before the Son of Humanity comes.

^{24}"The student is not above the teacher, nor the novice above the expert. ^{25}It is enough for the student to be like the teacher and the novice like the expert. If they call the Head of the house the dung-god, how much more those of His family?

^{26}"Therefore do not fear them. Nothing is concealed that will not be revealed, or hidden that will not be known. ^{27}What I tell you in darkness, speak in the light. And what is whispered in your ear, shout from the housetops. ^{28}Do not fear those who kill the body but are not able to kill the soul. Rather, fear the One who is able to destroy both soul and body in hell. ^{29}Are not two sparrows sold for a penny? Yet not one of them will fall to the ground without your heavenly Parent knowing. ^{30}Indeed, the very hairs of your head are all numbered. ^{31}Therefore do not fear. You are of more value than many sparrows.

^{32}"If you acknowledge Me before humans, I will also acknowledge you before My heavenly Parent. ^{33}But if you deny Me before humans, I will deny you before My heavenly Parent.

^{34}"Do not think that I have come to bring peace upon the earth. I have not come to bring peace, but a sword. ^{35}I have come to alienate 'a man from his father, a daughter from her mother and a daughter-in-law from her mother-in-law. ^{36}Your enemies will be those of your own family.' ^{37}If you love your father or mother more than Me, you are not worthy of Me. And if you love your son or daughter more than Me, you are not worthy of Me. ^{38}And if you do not take your cross and follow Me, you are not worthy of Me. ^{39}If you find your life, you will lose it. But if you lose your life for My sake, you will find it.

^{40}"Those who welcome you welcome Me, and those who welcome Me welcome the One who sent Me. ^{41}Those who welcome a prophet in the name of a prophet will receive a prophet's reward. And those who welcome the righteous in the name of righteousness will receive the reward of the righteous. ^{42}And if any of you give a cup of cold water to one of these little ones because you are My disciple, you will in no way lose your reward."

JOHN THE BAPTIST WONDERS IF JESUS IS REALLY THE MESSIAH

$^{11:1}$When Jesus finished instructing His twelve disciples, He went on from there to teach and preach in their towns. ^{2}When John heard in prison of the works of the Messiah, he sent his disciples ^{3}to say to Him, "Are You the One who is to come, or should we look for another?" ^{4}Jesus said to them, "Go and tell John what you have heard and seen: ^{5}The blind receive their sight, the lame walk, the lepers are cleansed, the deaf hear, the dead are raised and the poor are told good news. ^{6}And blessed is the one who is not offended by Me."

JESUS TELLS EVERYONE WHO JOHN IS

^{7}When John's disciples had departed, Jesus spoke to the crowds concerning John. "What did you go out into the wilderness to see? A reed shaken by the wind? ^{8}No? Then what did you go out to see? A man dressed in fine clothes? Those who wear fine clothes are in the courts of rulers. ^{9}What then did you go out to see? A prophet? Yes, and I tell you, more than a prophet. ^{10}This is the one of whom it was written, 'Watch! I send My messenger ahead of You to prepare Your way before You.' ^{11}Truly I say to you, among those born of women, not one has ever appeared who is greater than John the Baptist. Yet the one who is least in the heavenly realm is greater than he.

EVERYONE WANTS TO GO TO HEAVEN

[12]"From the days of John the Baptist until now the heavenly realm has been forcefully crowded into, and those full of life seize it. [13]For all the prophets and the law prophesied until John, [14]and if you will believe it, John is the Elijah who was to come. [15]If you have ears to hear, then listen!

JESUS CONDEMNS UNBELIEF

[16]"To what can I compare the people of this generation? They are like children sitting in the marketplace and calling to the others, [17]'We played the flute for you and you did not dance. We mourned and you did not lament.' [18]John came neither eating nor drinking and they say, 'He has a demon.' [19]The Son of Humanity came eating and drinking and they say, 'Look, a glutton, a wine drinker and a friend of tax collectors and sinners.' But wisdom is justified by its consequences."

[20]Then Jesus began to chide the towns where most of His miracles had been done because they did not repent. [21]"Woe to you, Chorazin! Woe to you, Bethsaida! If the miracles that were done in you had been done in Tyre and Sidon, they would have repented long ago in sackcloth and ashes. [22]But I tell you, it will be more tolerable for Tyre and Sidon on the day of judgment than for you. [23]And you, Capernaum! Will you be exalted to heaven? No, you will be brought down to hell. If the miracles that were done in you had been done in Sodom, it would remain till this day. [24]But I say to you that it will be more tolerable for the land of Sodom on the day of judgment than for you."

[25]At that time Jesus said, "I thank You, My dear Parent, God of heaven and earth, because You hid these things from those who think they are wise and revealed them to children, [26]for this was pleasing in Your sight. [27]Everything has been entrusted to Me by You. No one fully knows the Son but You. And no one fully knows You but the Son and those to whom the Son chooses to reveal His heavenly Parent.

ALL ARE INVITED TO COME TO JESUS

[28]"Come to Me, all you who are weary and have heavy loads, and I will give you rest. [29]Take My yoke upon you and learn from Me, for I am gentle and lowly in heart and you will find rest for your souls. [30]For My yoke is easy and My burden is light."

JESUS HAS AUTHORITY OVER THE SABBATH

[12:1]One Sabbath Jesus walked through some grain fields. His disciples were hungry and began to pick the heads of grain and eat them. [2]When the Pharisees saw this, they said to Him, "Look! Your disciples are doing what is unlawful on the Sabbath." [3]Jesus said to them, "Have you not read what David and his companions did when they were hungry? [4]They went into the house of God and ate the showbread, which was not lawful for them to eat, but was only for the priests. [5]Or have you not read in the law that on the Sabbath the priests in the temple may work and be innocent? [6]But I say to you that there is something here greater than the temple. [7]If you had known what this means: 'I desire mercy and not sacrifice,' you would not have condemned the innocent. [8]For the Son of Humanity has authority over the Sabbath."

JESUS IS CONDEMNED FOR HEALING ON THE SABBATH

[9]When He departed from there, He went into their synagogue. [10]A man with a withered hand was there. They hoped to accuse Him, so they asked, "Is it lawful to heal on the Sabbath?" [11]He said to them, "What one of you who has a sheep that falls into a pit on the Sabbath will not take hold of it and lift it out? [12]And how much more is a person worth than a sheep? Therefore it is lawful to do good on the Sabbath." [13]Then He said to the man, "Stretch out your hand." The man stretched it out, and it was restored to wholeness like the other. [14]Then the Pharisees went out and plotted how to destroy Him.

JESUS FULFILLS PROPHECY

[15]Jesus knew of this, and He withdrew from there. Many followed Him, and He healed them all. [16]But He warned them not to make Him known. [17]This was to fulfill what was spoken by Isaiah the prophet: [18]"Here is My Servant whom I have chosen, My beloved in whom My Soul is well pleased. I have put My Spirit on Him, and He will show judgment to the nations. [19]He will not argue or shout, nor will His voice be heard in the streets. [20]A bruised reed He will not break, and smoking flax He will not quench. He will faithfully bring divine law, [21]and in His name will the nations trust."

JESUS IS ACCUSED OF BEING SATAN'S DISCIPLE

[22]Then some people brought a man who was blind and could not speak because he had a demon in him. Jesus healed him and the blind man was then able to both speak and see. [23]All the people were amazed and said, "Could this be the Son of David?" [24]But when the Pharisees heard this, they said, "He casts out demons with the help of the dung-god, the prince of the demons." [25]Jesus knew their thoughts and said to them, "Every realm divided against itself will come to nothing, and every town or family divided against itself will fall. [26]If a demon casts out a demon, they are divided against themselves. How then can their realm stand? [27]And if I cast out demons by the dung-god, by whom do your own people cast them out? Therefore your own people will be your judges. [28]But if I cast out demons by the Spirit of God, then the realm of God has come upon you. [29]Furthermore, how can one enter a strong person's house and plunder the goods, unless one first binds the strong one? Then that house can be plundered.

[30]"If you are not with Me, you are against Me. If you do not gather with Me, you scatter. [31]Therefore I say to you, people will be forgiven every offense and blasphemy, but blasphemy against the Spirit will not be forgiven. [32]Whoever speaks a word against the Son of Humanity will be forgiven, but whoever speaks against the Holy Spirit will not be forgiven, either in this world or in the one to come.

[33]"If a tree is good, then its fruit will be good; but if a tree is bad, its fruit will be bad. A tree is known by its fruit. [34]O generation of snakes, how can you, being evil, speak good? From the many things in the heart the mouth speaks. [35]Good people bring good out of the good stored in their hearts, and evil people bring evil out from the evil stored in theirs. [36]And I say to you, you will have to give an account on the day of judgment for every idle word you have spoken. [37]For by your words you will be justified, and by your words you will be condemned."

SOME OF THE LEADERS ASK JESUS FOR MORE PROOF

[38]Then certain scribes and Pharisees said, "Teacher, we would like to see a sign from You." [39]He answered them, "An evil and adulterous generation seeks a sign, but no sign will be given to it but the sign of the prophet Jonah. [40]For as Jonah was three days and three nights in the belly of the whale, so will the Son of Humanity be three days and three nights in the heart of the earth. [41]The people of Ninevah will rise with this generation at the judgment and condemn them. For Ninevah repented at the preaching of Jonah, and now something greater than Jonah is here. [42]The Queen of the South will rise up with this generation at the judgment and condemn it. For she came from the ends of the earth to hear the wisdom of Solomon, and now something greater than Solomon is here!

A DEMON IS CAST OUT BUT RETURNS WITH SEVEN MORE

[43]"When an unclean spirit comes out of a person, it goes through dry places seeking rest and finds none. [44]Then it says, 'I will return to my house from which I came,' and it comes and finds it empty and swept and in order. [45]Then it goes and takes with it seven other spirits more wicked than itself, and they go in and live there. In the end that person is worse off than at the first. That is how it will be for this wicked generation."

JESUS EXPLAINS WHO HIS REAL FAMILY IS

[46]While He was still talking to the people, His mother and His brothers stood outside seeking to speak to Him. [47]Someone said to Him, "Your mother and Your brothers are standing outside and they want to speak to You." [48]Jesus answered, "Who is My mother? And who are My brothers?" [49]He stretched out His hand toward His disciples and said, "Here are My mother and My brothers! [50]For whoever does the will of God is My brother and sister and mother."

THE PARABLE OF THE SEEDS

[13:1]That same day Jesus went out of the house and sat by the seashore. [2]Such great crowds gathered around Him that He got into a boat and sat down. The whole crowd stood on the shore, [3]and He spoke many things to them in parables. He said, "Listen! A farmer went out to sow. [4]Some of the seeds fell by the roadside, and the birds came and ate them. [5]Some fell on rocky ground where they did not have much soil. They sprang up quickly because they had no depth of soil. [6]When the sun came up they were scorched, and they withered because they had no root. [7]Some fell among thistles, and the thistles sprang up and choked them. [8]But others fell on good ground and produced fruit, some a hundred times as much, some sixty and some thirty. [9]If you have ears to hear, then listen."

THE REASON FOR PARABLES

[10]The disciples came to Him and asked, "Why do You speak to them in parables?" [11]He replied, "To you it is given to understand the mysteries of the heavenly realm, but not to them. [12]Those who have will be given more and they will have an abundance. But those who do not have, from them will be taken even what they have. [13]That is why I speak to them in parables, because seeing they do not see, and hearing they do not hear; nor do they understand. [14]The prophecy of Isaiah is fulfilled in them that

says, 'By hearing you will hear and not understand, and seeing you will see but not comprehend. [15]For this people's hearts have become hard; their ears are dull of hearing and their eyes are closed, lest at any time they see with their eyes, hear with their ears, understand with their hearts and turn and be healed.' [16]But blessed are you, for your eyes see and your ears hear. [17]Truly I say to you, many prophets and godly persons longed to see what you see and have not seen, and to hear what you hear and have not heard.

THE EXPLANATION OF THE PARABLE OF THE SEEDS

[18]"Now listen to what the parable of the farmer means. [19]When people hear an explanation of the heavenly realm and do not understand it, the evil one comes and snatches away the words that were sown in their hearts. That is the seed sown by the roadside. [20]Those who received the seed in rocky ground are the ones who hear the words and immediately receive them with joy, [21]but they have no roots. They endure for a while, but when tribulation or persecution comes, they immediately stumble. [22]Those who receive the seed among the thistles are the ones who hear the words, but the cares of this world and the deceitfulness of riches choke the words and they become unfruitful. [23]But those who receive the seed into good ground are the ones who hear the words and understand and bear fruit and yield, some a hundred times as much, some sixty and some thirty."

THE PARABLE OF THE WEEDS IN THE WHEAT

[24]Then He told them another parable: "The heavenly realm is like a farmer who sowed good seed in a field. [25]But while everyone was asleep, an enemy came and sowed weeds among the wheat and went away. [26]When the wheat came up and ripened, the weeds could be seen also. [27]The farmer's servants came and asked, 'Didn't you sow good seed in your field? Where did these weeds come from?' [28]The farmer replied, 'An enemy did this.' The servants asked, 'Do you want us to go and pull them up?' [29]But the farmer said, 'No, for when you pull up the weeds, you might uproot the wheat with them. [30]Let both grow together until the harvest, and at harvest time I will tell the reapers: First gather the weeds and bind them in bundles to burn, then gather the wheat into my granary.'"

THE PARABLE OF THE MUSTARD SEED

[31]Then He told them another parable: "The heavenly realm is like a mustard seed that a farmer took and sowed in a field. [32]It is the smallest of all seeds, but when it is grown it is a large plant. It becomes a tree, and the birds of the air come and nest in its branches."

THE PARABLE OF THE YEAST

[33]He spoke another parable to them: "The heavenly realm is like yeast that a cook hid in three measures of flour until it was all fermented."

JESUS FULFILLS PROPHECY

[34]All these things Jesus spoke to the crowd in parables. He did not speak to them without a parable, [35]so that what was spoken by the prophet might be fulfilled: "I will open my mouth in parables; I will utter mysteries from the creation of the world."

JESUS EXPLAINS THE PARABLE ABOUT THE WEEDS IN THE WHEAT

36Jesus left the crowds and went into the house. His disciples came to Him and said, "Explain to us the parable of the weeds in the field." 37He replied, "The sower of the good seed is the Son of Humanity. 38The field is the world, the good seed is the children of the realm and the weeds are the children of the evil one. 39The enemy who sows them is the devil, the harvest is the end of the age and the reapers are the angels. 40Just as the weeds are gathered and burned in the fire, so will it be at the end of the age. 41The Son of Humanity will send out His angels and gather out of His realm all who cause others to go astray and those who break the law. 42They will throw them into the blazing furnace, and there will be wailing and gnashing of teeth. 43Then the righteous will shine like the sun in the realm of their heavenly Parent. If you have ears to hear, then listen.

MORE PARABLES ILLUSTRATING THE HEAVENLY REALM

44"The heavenly realm is like treasure hidden in a field. Those who found it covered it up. Then they joyfully went and sold all they had and bought that field.

45"Again, the heavenly realm is like a trader searching for beautiful pearls 46who found one pearl of great value and went and sold every possession and bought it.

47"Again, the heavenly realm is like a net thrown into the sea that gathered many different kinds of fish. 48When it was full, they drew it to shore and sat down and gathered the good into baskets, but threw the bad away. 49So shall it be at the end of the age. The angels will come and pick out the wicked from among the godly 50and throw them into the blazing furnace, where there will be wailing and gnashing of teeth."

51Jesus asked them, "Do you understand all this?" They replied, "Yes, Rabbi." 52Then He said to them, "Therefore every reader of the law who becomes a disciple in the heavenly realm is like a homeowner who brings things new and old out of the storehouse."

THE PEOPLE OF NAZARETH ARE OFFENDED

53When Jesus had finished these parables, He departed from there 54and went to His hometown. He taught the people in their synagogue in such a way that they were astonished. They asked, "Where did this man get this wisdom and these miracles? 55Isn't this the carpenter's son? Isn't His mother's name Mary? Aren't His brothers James, Joseph, Simon and Judas? 56Don't His sisters live here? Where did He get all this?" 57They were offended at Him, but Jesus said to them, "Prophets are honored everywhere but in their own town and in their own family." 58He did very few miracles there because of their unbelief.

JOHN THE BAPTIST IS BEHEADED

14:1At that time Herod the tetrarch heard of the fame of Jesus 2and said to his servants, "This is John the Baptist! He has risen from the dead, and these miracles are done by him." 3For Herod had arrested John and bound him and put him in prison because of Herodias, his brother Philip's wife. 4John had said to Herod, "It is not lawful for you to have her." 5Herod would have put John to death, but he feared the people, for they considered John a prophet. 6On Herod's birthday, the daughter of

Herodias danced at his court. Herod was pleased, [7]and he promised with an oath to give her whatever she asked. [8]Forced forward by her mother, she said, "Give me the head of John the Baptist here on a platter." [9]The king was sorry, but because of the oath he had taken, and because of those who sat with him, he gave the command [10]and had John beheaded in the prison. [11]John's head was carried on a platter and given to the girl, and she carried it to her mother. [12]John's disciples came and took the body and buried it. Then they went and told Jesus.

A LARGE CROWD IS FED WITH FIVE LOAVES AND TWO FISH

[13]When Jesus heard about this, He left there by boat and went to a deserted place to be alone. When the people heard that He had left, they followed Him on foot out of the towns. [14]Jesus went out and saw the great crowds and felt compassion for them and healed their sick. [15]As evening approached, His disciples came to Him and said, "This is a deserted place and the time is slipping away. Send the people into the villages so they may buy themselves food." [16]"They need not leave," Jesus said. "You give them something to eat!" [17]They said to Him, "We have nothing here but five loaves and two fish." [18]He said, "Bring them here to Me." [19]He asked the people to sit down on the grass. Taking the five loaves and the two fish, He looked up toward heaven and blessed them. Then He broke the loaves, gave them to the disciples, and the disciples gave them to the people. [20]They all ate and were filled. Afterward they picked up twelve baskets full of pieces that were left over. [21]More than five thousand had eaten.

JESUS AND PETER WALK ON WATER

[22]Jesus made His disciples get into a boat and go on ahead of Him to the other side while He sent the people away. [23]When He had sent the people away, He went up on the mountain alone to pray. As the evening grew dark, He was there alone. [24]The boat was now far out on the sea and tossed by the waves, for the wind was against them. [25]Sometime after midnight Jesus went to them, walking on the sea. [26]When the disciples saw Him walking on the sea, they were startled. "It's a ghost!" they said, and cried out in fear. [27]At once Jesus spoke to them and said, "Have courage! It is I, do not be afraid." [28]Peter answered Him and said, "Rabbi, if it is You, command me to come to You on the water." [29]Jesus said, "Come," and Peter stepped down out of the boat and walked on the water toward Jesus. [30]But when he saw how fierce the wind was, he was afraid and began to sink. He cried out, "Rabbi! Save me!" [31]At once Jesus reached out His hand and held on to him. Jesus said, "O you of little faith, why did you waver?" [32]When they stepped into the boat, the wind ceased. [33]Then those who were in the boat worshiped Him and said, "Truly, You are the Son of God!"

MANY ARE HEALED BY A TOUCH

[34]When they had crossed over, they came to land at Gennesaret. [35]When the people of that place recognized Him, they sent word to everyone who lived in that country, and they brought to Him all who were sick. [36]They begged Him to let them touch the edge of His garment, and as many as touched Him were healed.

THE TRADITION OF HAND WASHING

15:1Then some scribes and Pharisees from Jerusalem came to Jesus, saying, 2"Why do Your disciples go contrary to the tradition of the elders? They do not wash their hands properly before they eat." 3Jesus replied, "And why do you go contrary to the commandment of God by your tradition? 4For God commanded, 'Honor your father and mother,' and 'Those who despise their father or mother must be put to death.' 5But you say that your needy father or mother may be told, 'Anything of mine that you might have been helped by has been set apart for God,' 6and that you need not honor your father or mother with that. Thus you make the commandment of God ineffective by your tradition. 7You hypocrites! Rightly did Isaiah prophesy about you when he said, 8'These people honor Me with their words, but their hearts are far from Me. 9In vain they worship Me, for they teach their own doctrines as though they were the commandments of God.'"

JESUS EXPLAINS WHAT UNCLEAN REALLY MEANS

10Jesus called the people to Him and said, "Listen and understand! 11It is not what goes into the mouth that makes a person unclean, but what comes out of the mouth." 12Then His disciples came and said to Him, "Do You know that the Pharisees were offended when they heard You say that?" 13He replied, "Every plant that My heavenly Parent did not plant will be rooted up. 14Don't be concerned about them; they are blind leaders of the blind. And if the blind lead the blind, both will fall into the ditch."

15Then Peter said, "Explain this parable to us." 16Jesus said, "Are you still without understanding? 17Do you not yet understand that whatever enters in at the mouth goes into the stomach and passes out of the body? 18But what comes out of the mouth comes forth from the heart and makes a person unclean. 19For out of the heart comes evil thoughts, murder, adultery, sexual sins, theft, lying and verbal abuse. 20These are the things that make a person unclean; but to eat with unwashed hands does not make a person unclean."

THE FAITH OF A NON-JEWISH WOMAN

21Jesus left that place and went to the region of Tyre and Sidon. 22A Canaanite woman from there came to Him, crying out, "Have mercy on me, Rabbi, Son of David! My daughter is greatly tormented by a demon!" 23Jesus did not answer her a word. His disciples came and urged Him, "Send her away, for she rails at us." 24Jesus replied, "I was sent only to the lost sheep of the house of Israel." 25Then she came and knelt before Him and said, "Rabbi, help me!" 26He replied, "It is not right to take the children's bread and toss it to the dogs." 27She said, "Yes, Rabbi, but the dogs eat the crumbs that fall from the table." 28Jesus replied, "O woman, great is your faith. You shall have your request." And her daughter was restored from that very hour.

A CROWD IS FED WITH SEVEN LOAVES AND A FEW LITTLE FISH

29Jesus departed from there. Near the Sea of Galilee He went up a mountain and sat down. 30Great crowds came to Him, bringing with them the lame, the crippled, the blind, the dumb and many others. They laid them at Jesus' feet and He healed them.

[31]The people were amazed to see the dumb speak, the crippled healed, the lame walk and the blind see; and they praised the God of Israel. [32]Jesus called His disciples and said, "I feel sorry for these people. They have been with Me three days now and have nothing to eat. I do not want to send them away hungry, lest they faint on the way." [33]His disciples said, "Where could we get enough food in this uninhabited place to satisfy so great a crowd?" [34]Jesus said to them, "How many loaves do you have?" They said, "Seven, and a few little fish." [35]He told the people to sit down on the ground. [36]Then He took the seven loaves and the fish and gave thanks. He broke the loaves and gave to His disciples. The disciples gave to the people, [37]and they all ate and were filled. Afterward they picked up seven baskets full of pieces. [38]More than four thousand had eaten. [39]Then He sent the people home and took a boat to the region of Magadan.

SOME OF THE LEADERS ASK JESUS FOR MORE PROOF

[16:1]The Pharisees and Sadducees came, and to test Him they asked Him to show them a sign from heaven. [2]Jesus said to them, "In the evening you say, 'It will be fair weather,' for the sky is red. [3]And in the morning you say, 'It will be rainy today,' for the sky is red and threatening. You can recognize the appearance of the sky, but can you recognize the signs of the times? [4]A wicked and adulterous generation seeks a sign, but no sign will be given to it but the sign of Jonah." Then He left them.

JESUS CAUTIONS AGAINST FOLLOWING THE LEADERS

[5]His disciples crossed over to the other side but forgot to take bread. [6]Jesus said to them, "Watch carefully! Beware of the yeast of the Pharisees and Sadducees." [7]They talked among themselves and said, "It is because we brought no bread." [8]Jesus knew what they were thinking, and He said to them, "O you of little faith! Why do you talk among yourselves because you have no bread? [9]Don't you understand yet? Don't you remember the five loaves for the five thousand and how many basketfuls you picked up? [10]Or the seven loaves for the four thousand and how many basketfuls you picked up? [11]How is it that you do not understand that I was not speaking to you about bread? Beware of the yeast of the Pharisees and Sadducees!" [12]Then they understood that He was not telling them to beware of the yeast in bread, but to beware of the doctrine of the Pharisees and Sadducees.

GOD REVEALS TO THE DISCIPLES THAT JESUS IS THE MESSIAH

[13]When Jesus came to the region of Caesarea Philippi, He asked His disciples, "Who do people say that the Son of Humanity is?" [14]They said, "Some say John the Baptist, some Elijah and others Jeremiah or one of the prophets." [15]He said to them, "But who do you say I am?" [16]Simon Peter answered and said, "You are the Messiah, the Son of the living God." [17]Jesus said to him, "Blessed are you, Simon son of Jonah, for this was not revealed to you by flesh and blood, but by My heavenly Parent. [18]And I say to you that you are Peter, and upon this Rock I will build My church, and the gates of hell will not prevail against it. [19]I will give you the keys of the heavenly realm, and whatever you bind on earth will be bound in heaven, and whatever you loose on earth will be loosed in heaven." [20]Then He warned His disciples not to tell anyone that He was the Messiah.

JESUS REBUKES PETER

^{21}From that time on Jesus began to tell His disciples that He must go to Jerusalem and endure much suffering from the elders and chief priests and scribes and be killed and be raised the third day. ^{22}Then Peter took Him aside and began to rebuke Him, saying, "God forbid! This must not happen to You." ^{23}Jesus turned and said to Peter, "Get behind Me, Satan! You are a hindrance to Me! You are not interested in Godly things, but in human things."

THE IMPORTANCE OF THE SOUL

^{24}Then Jesus said to His disciples, "If any of you want to come after Me, you must deny yourselves and take up your cross and follow Me. ^{25}If you want to save your life, you must lose it. But if you lose your life for My sake, you will find it. ^{26}What profit is it to you if you gain the whole world but lose your soul? What can you give in exchange for your soul? ^{27}The Son of Humanity will come with His angels in His heavenly Parent's glory, and then He will reward everyone according to what has been done. ^{28}Truly I say to you, there are some standing here who will not taste of death till they see the Son of Humanity coming in His realm."

THE TRANSFIGURATION: JESUS BECOMES A BEING OF LIGHT

$^{17:1}$Six days later Jesus took Peter and the brothers James and John and they went up on a high mountain where they could be alone. ^{2}Jesus was transfigured before them. His face shone like the sun, and His clothing became as white as the light. ^{3}Suddenly Moses and Elijah appeared and talked with Him. ^{4}Then Peter said to Jesus, "Rabbi, it is good for us to be here. If You wish, I will put up three tents here, one for You, one for Moses and one for Elijah." ^{5}While he was still speaking, a bright cloud flowed over them. A voice from the cloud said, "This is My beloved Son in whom I am well pleased. Listen to Him." ^{6}When the disciples heard this, they were terrified and fell with their faces to the ground. ^{7}Jesus came and touched them and said, "Get up, do not be afraid." ^{8}When they looked up, they saw no one except Jesus. ^{9}As they came down the mountain, Jesus warned them, "Tell the vision to no one until the Son of Humanity is raised from the dead." ^{10}His disciples asked Him, "Why do the scribes say that Elijah must come first?" ^{11}Jesus replied, "Elijah does come, and will restore all things. ^{12}But I tell you that Elijah has already come and they did not know him, but did to him whatever they wanted. The Son of Humanity will suffer in a similar way at their hands." ^{13}Then the disciples understood that He spoke to them of John the Baptist.

THE STUBBORN DEMON THAT WOULD NOT COME OUT

^{14}When they got back to the crowd, a man came and knelt before Him and said, ^{15}"Rabbi, have mercy on my son, for he is an epileptic and in much pain. He often falls into the fire or water. ^{16}I brought him to Your disciples, but they could not heal him." ^{17}Jesus said, "O unbelieving and perverse generation, how long must I be with you? How long must I put up with you? Bring him here to Me." ^{18}Jesus rebuked the demon and it came out of him. The boy was healed from that very hour. ^{19}Then the disciples came to Jesus in private and said, "Why couldn't we cast it out?" ^{20}Jesus said to them, "Because of your unbelief. For truly I say to you, if you have faith like a mustard seed, you will say to this mountain, 'Move from here to there,' and it will move. Nothing will be impossible for you. [21]However, this kind does not go out except by prayer and fasting."

THE DISCIPLES ARE AGAIN TOLD OF FUTURE EVENTS

[22]They returned to Galilee and Jesus said to them, "The Son of Humanity will be betrayed into human hands. [23]They will kill Him, and the third day He will be raised again." The disciples were greatly distressed.

THE MIRACLE OF THE COIN IN THE MOUTH OF A FISH

[24]When they arrived at Capernaum, the collectors of the temple tax came to Peter and said, "Doesn't your Teacher pay the temple tax?" [25]He said, "Yes." When he came into the house, Jesus anticipated him and said, "What do you think, Simon? From whom do the rulers of the earth take taxes, from their own people or from strangers?" [26]Peter answered, "From strangers." Jesus said, "Then their own people are exempt. [27]But lest we offend them, go down to the sea and cast out a hook. Take the first fish you catch, open its mouth and you will find a coin. Take it and give it to them for both of us."

JESUS TEACHES ABOUT HUMILITY

[18:1]At that time the disciples came to Jesus and said, "Who is the greatest in the heavenly realm?" [2]Jesus called a little child and held the child up among them. [3]He said, "Truly I say to you, unless you change and become like little children, you will not enter the heavenly realm. [4]Whoever becomes humble like this little child is the greatest in the heavenly realm. [5]And whoever welcomes one little child like this in My name welcomes Me. [6]But if you lead one of these little ones who believe in Me astray, it would be better for you to have a millstone hung around your neck and be drowned in the depths of the sea. [7]Woe to the world for causing people to sin. It is necessary that stumbling blocks come, but woe to that person through whom they come!

[8]"If your hand or your foot leads you astray, cut it off and throw it away. It is better for you to enter life limping or maimed than to have two hands or two feet and be thrown into everlasting fire. [9]And if your eye leads you astray, pluck it out and throw it away. It is better to enter life with one eye than to have two eyes and be thrown into the fires of hell. [10]Be careful that you do not despise one of these little ones; for I tell you that in heaven their angels can always look at the face of God.

[11]THE SON OF HUMANITY CAME TO SAVE THE LOST

[12]"What do you think about this? If a shepherd has a hundred sheep, and one of them goes astray, will not the shepherd leave the ninety-nine and go into the mountains to seek the one that strayed? [13]And if the shepherd finds it, I tell you, the shepherd rejoices more over that one than over the ninety-nine that did not stray. [14]Therefore it is not the will of your heavenly Parent that one of these little ones perish.

DISAGREEMENTS BETWEEN BELIEVERS

[15]"If your friend wrongs you, go and tell your friend about the matter just between the two of you. If your friend listens to you, you have gained your friend. [16]But if your friend will not listen, take with you one or two others, so that every word may be supported by two or three witnesses. [17]If your friend will not listen to them, tell it to the believers. If your friend will not listen to the believers, then treat your friend like an unbeliever and a tax collector.

IF TWO AGREE TOGETHER

[18]"Truly I say to you, whatever you bind on earth will be bound in heaven, and whatever you loose on earth will be loosed in heaven.

[19]"Again I tell you, if two of you agree on earth in regard to anything you ask, it will be done for you by My heavenly Parent. [20]For where two or three are gathered in My name, there am I in the midst of them."

FORGIVING OTHERS

[21]Peter came to Him and said, "Rabbi, how often should I forgive someone who wrongs me? Seven times?" [22]Jesus said to him, "I say to you, not seven times, but seventy times seven times. [23]The heavenly realm may be compared to a king who decided to examine the accounts of his managers. [24]As they began the audit, one man was brought in who owed ten thousand talents. [25]Since he didn't have enough to pay, the king ordered that he and his wife and children and everything that he had be sold to repay the debt. [26]Then the man got down on his knees and pleaded and said, "Please! Have patience with me and I will repay you everything." [27]The king was sympathetic and let him go and forgave the debt. [28]But that same manager went out and found another manager who owed him a hundred coins. He seized him by the throat and said, 'Pay me what you owe!' [29]The other manager got down on his knees and begged him, 'Be patient with me and I will repay you everything!' [30]But he was not inclined to, and he had the other manager thrown into jail until he paid the debt. [31]When the other managers saw what had been done, they were quite shocked and went and told the king everything that had been done. [32]Then the king called that manager in and said, 'You worthless good-for-nothing! I forgave you all that debt because you pleaded with me. [33]Shouldn't you have had compassion on that other manager, even as I had compassion on you?' [34]The king was furious with him and sent him to the torturers until he paid back all that was owed. [35]And that is what My heavenly Parent will do to each of you if you do not forgive other believers from your heart."

THE PHARISEES TRY TO TRAP JESUS WITH A QUESTION ABOUT DIVORCE

[19:1]When Jesus finished saying these things, He departed from Galilee and went to the region of Judea beyond the Jordan. [2]Great crowds followed Him and He healed them. [3]The Pharisees came there to test Him and said, "Is it lawful for a man to divorce his wife for just any reason?" [4]He replied, "Have you not read that at the beginning the Creator made them male and female [5]and said, 'For this cause shall a man leave his father and mother and be bonded to his wife and the two shall be one flesh'? [6]Therefore they are no longer two, but one. What God has joined together, humans must not separate." [7]They said to Him, "Then why did Moses command that a written divorce is sufficient for dismissal?" [8]Jesus said to them, "Moses allowed you to divorce your spouses because of the hardness of your hearts. But from the beginning it was not so. [9]And I say to you that whoever divorces, except for unfaithfulness, and marries another commits adultery." [10]His disciples said to Him, "If that is the way it is between husbands and wives, it is better not to marry." [11]He said to them, "Not everyone can accept this teaching, only those who have the gift. [12]For some are born unable to marry, some were made unable to marry by humans and some do not marry for the sake of the heavenly realm. Let those who are able to enter in do so."

CHILDREN: THE ESSENCE OF THE HEAVENLY REALM

[13]Little children were brought to Jesus so that He could put His hands on them and pray for them. The disciples rebuked the people, [14]but Jesus said, "Let the little children come and do not forbid them, for the heavenly realm belongs to such as these." [15]Then Jesus laid His hands on the children and went on His way.

POSSESSIONS

[16]A young man came and said to Him, "Good Teacher, what good thing may I do in order to have eternal life?" [17]Jesus said to him, "Why do you call Me good? No one is good but God. If you choose to enter life, obey the commandments." [18]"Which ones?" the young man asked. Jesus said, "Do not murder, do not commit adultery, do not steal, do not give false testimony, [19]honor your father and your mother and love your neighbor as yourself." [20]The young man said to Him, "All these I have obeyed. What do I still lack?" [21]Jesus said to him, "If you want to be perfect, go and sell your possessions, give the money to the poor and you will have treasure in heaven. Then come and follow Me." [22]When the young man heard this, he went sadly away, for he had many possessions.

[23]Then Jesus said to His disciples, "Truly I say to you, it is hard for a rich person to enter the heavenly realm. [24]Again I say to you, it is easier for a camel to go through the eye of a needle than for a rich person to enter the realm of God." [25]When His disciples heard this, they were greatly amazed and said, "Who then can be saved?" [26]Jesus looked intently at them and said, "With humans this is impossible, but with God all things are possible."

REWARDS IN HEAVEN

[27]Peter said to Jesus, "Look, we have forsaken all to follow You. What will we get?" [28]Jesus said to them, "Truly I say to you, when nature is renewed and the Son of Humanity sits on His glorious throne, you who have followed Me will also sit upon twelve thrones judging the twelve tribes of Israel. [29]Everyone who has forsaken houses or brothers or sisters or father or mother or children or land for the sake of My

name will receive a hundred times as much and will inherit everlasting life. ^{30}But many who are first will be last, and the last first.

THE PARABLE OF THE WORKERS WHO WERE ALL PAID THE SAME

$^{20:1}$"The heavenly realm may be compared to the owner of a vineyard who went out at dawn to hire laborers to work in the vineyard. ^{2}The owner agreed to pay them a silver coin for the day and sent them into the vineyard. ^{3}The owner went out to the town square about mid-morning and saw others standing around ^{4}and said to them, 'Go out to the vineyard, and I will pay you whatever is fair,' and they went. ^{5}The owner went out again about noon and at mid-afternoon and did the same. ^{6}In the late afternoon the owner went out and found others standing around and said to them, 'Why do you stand here doing nothing all day?' ^{7}They answered, 'Because no one has hired us.' The owner said to them, 'You may go and work in the vineyard also.' ^{8}When evening came, the owner of the vineyard said to the manager, 'Call the laborers and pay them their wages, beginning with the last and ending with the first.' ^{9}Those who came in the late afternoon each received a silver coin. ^{10}When those hired first came, they supposed that they would receive more, but they each received a silver coin also. ^{11}After they received it, they grumbled against the owner, ^{12}saying, 'These last worked only one hour, and you have made them equal to those of us who endured the burden and heat of the day.' ^{13}The owner answered one of them and said, 'Friend, I do you no wrong. Did you not agree to work for me for a silver coin? ^{14}Take what is yours and go. I choose to give to these last ones the same as to you. ^{15}Do I not have the right to do what I choose with what belongs to me? Are you hurt because I am kind?' ^{16}Thus the last will be first, and the first last."

JESUS TELLS HIS DISCIPLES HE WILL BE CRUCIFIED

^{17}As Jesus was going up to Jerusalem, He took His twelve disciples aside on the way and said to them, ^{18}"Beware! We are going up to Jerusalem and the Son of Humanity will be betrayed to the chief priests and the scribes. They will condemn Me to death ^{19}and hand Me over to the unbelievers to be mocked, whipped and crucified. The third day I will rise again."

THE DISCIPLES LOOK FORWARD TO HEAVEN

^{20}Then the mother of the sons of Zebedee came to Him with her sons. She knelt down before Him and desired something from Him. ^{21}Jesus said to her, "What would you like?" She said to Him, "Grant that these two sons of mine may sit on Your right and on Your left in Your realm." ^{22}Jesus said to them, "You don't know what you are asking. Are you able to drink of the cup that I must drink?" They said, "We are able." ^{23}Jesus said, "You will indeed drink of My cup, but to sit on My right and on My left is not Mine to give, but is for those for whom it has been prepared by My heavenly Parent."

THE GREAT ONES IN THE OTHER WORLD ARE THE HUMBLE

^{24}When the others heard of this, they were indignant with the two brothers. ^{25}But Jesus called them and said, "You know that the rulers of the nations and those who are great exercise authority over them, ^{26}but it must not be that way with you. Whoever chooses to be great among you must be your servant, [27]and whoever chooses to be foremost among you must be your slave; [28]just as the Son of Humanity did not come to be served, but to serve and to give His life as a ransom for many."

TWO BLIND MEN ARE HEALED NEAR JERICHO

[29]As they departed from Jericho, a great crowd followed Him. [30]Two blind men were sitting by the roadside. When they heard that Jesus was passing by, they cried out, "Rabbi! Son of David! Have mercy on us!" [31]The crowd rebuked them and told them to be quiet; but they cried out louder, "Rabbi! Son of David! Have mercy on us!" [32]Jesus stopped and called to them. He said, "What do you want Me to do for you?" [33]They said to Him, "Rabbi! We want our eyes opened!" [34]Jesus felt compassion for them and touched their eyes. Immediately their eyes recovered their sight, and they followed Him.

JESUS RIDES A DONKEY AND FULFILLS PROPHECY

[21:1]When they came near Jerusalem and had reached Bethphage and the Mount of Olives, Jesus sent two disciples, [2]saying, "Go into that next village and you will find a donkey and a colt tied there. Untie them and bring them to Me. [3]If a man says anything to you, you are to say, 'The Teacher needs them,' and he will send them at once."

[4]All this happened to fulfill what was spoken by the prophet: [5]"Tell the daughter of Zion: Watch! Your king comes to you, gentle and riding on a donkey, and a colt, the foal of a donkey." [6]The disciples went and did as Jesus directed them. [7]They brought the donkey and the colt, laid their garments on them and Jesus sat on them.

THE MESSIAH'S TRIUMPHANT ENTRY INTO JERUSALEM

[8]A great crowd spread their garments on the road, and others cut down branches from the trees and strewed them on the road. [9]The crowds that went in front and behind cried out, "Hosanna to the Son of David! Blessed is He who comes in the name of Yahweh! Hosanna in the highest!"

[10]When He came into Jerusalem, the whole city was stirred up. They asked, "Who is this?" [11]and the crowd answered, "This is Jesus, the prophet from Nazareth in Galilee."

JESUS DRIVES THE MERCHANTS OUT OF THE TEMPLE

[12]Jesus went into the temple and drove out all those who were buying and selling there. He overturned the tables of the money changers and the seats of those who sold doves. [13]He said to them, "It is written, 'My house shall be called a house of prayer,' but you have made it a 'den of thieves.'"

[14]The blind and the lame came to Him in the temple and He healed them. [15]When the chief priests and the scribes saw the wonderful things He did and the children crying out in the temple, "Hosanna to the Son of David!" they were indignant. [16]They said to Him, "Do You hear what these are saying?" "Yes," Jesus said to them, "and have you never read, 'Out of the mouths of babes and sucklings God has perfected praise'?" [17]Then He left them and went out of the city to Bethany. He spent the night there.

JESUS LOOKS FOR FOOD ON A FIG TREE

18At dawn as He returned to the city, Jesus was hungry. 19He saw a fig tree by the road and went to it. He found nothing on it but leaves, so He said to it, "No more fruit will grow on you forever!" Instantly the fig tree withered. 20The disciples saw and marveled. They said, "How quickly the fig tree withered!" 21Jesus said to them, "Truly I say to you, if you have faith and do not doubt, you will not only do this to a fig tree, but even if you say to this mountain, 'Be lifted up and thrown into the sea!' it will be done. 22And whatever you ask in believing prayer, you will receive."

THE LEADERS QUESTION JESUS' AUTHORITY

23After He came into the temple, the chief priests and the elders of the people came to Him as He was teaching and said, "By what authority do You do these things? Who gave You this authority?" 24Jesus said, "I will ask you a question also. If you answer Me, then I will tell you by what authority I do these things. 25Who gave John the authority to baptize? Was it from heaven or from humans?" They talked it over among themselves, saying, "If we say, 'From heaven,' He will say to us, 'Then why didn't you believe John?' 26But if we say, 'From humans,' we fear the people, for they all consider John a prophet." 27So they answered, "We don't know." Jesus said to them, "Then neither will I tell you by what authority I do these things.

THE LEADERS AND THE PEOPLE COMPARED

28"What do you think? A man had two sons. He went to the first and said, 'Son, go work today in my vineyard.' 29The son answered, 'I won't,' but afterward he changed his mind and went. 30The father went to the second son and said the same thing. He answered, 'I will go, sir,' but did not go. 31Which of the two did the will of his father?" They answered, "The first." Jesus said to them, "Truly I say to you, the tax collectors and the prostitutes will enter God's realm before you. 32For John came to show you a righteous way and you did not believe him; but the tax collectors and prostitutes believed him. And even when you saw this, you would not repent and believe him.

THE VINEYARD AND THE UNGRATEFUL TENANTS

33"Listen to another parable: A landowner planted a vineyard, put a fence around it, dug a winepress in it, built a watchtower, rented it to tenants and then went to a far country. 34At harvest time the owner sent servants to the tenants for a share of the fruit. 35The tenants took hold of the servants and beat one and killed one and stoned one. 36Again the owner sent servants, more than at first, and the tenants did the same to them. 37Last of all, the owner said, 'I will send my son to them,' thinking, 'Surely they will respect my son.' 38But when the tenants saw the son, they said among themselves, 'This is the heir! Come, let's kill him and keep his inheritance.' 39So they killed him and threw him out of the vineyard. 40Now when the owner of the vineyard comes, what will the owner do to those tenants?" 41They said to Jesus, "The owner will destroy those worthless wretches and rent the vineyard to other tenants who will give the owner a share of the fruit at the proper time." 42Jesus said to them, "Have you never read in the Scriptures, 'The stone that the builders rejected has become the head of the corner. Yahweh has done this and it is marvelous in our eyes'? [43]Therefore I tell you, God's realm will be taken from you and given to a people who will give God a share of the fruit. [44]Whoever falls on this stone will be broken, and it will grind to a powder anyone on whom it falls." [45]The chief priests and Pharisees heard His parables, and they knew He was speaking about them. [46]They considered ways to arrest Him, but they were afraid, for the crowds considered Him a prophet.

HEAVEN COMPARED TO A WEDDING BANQUET

[22:1]Jesus again spoke to them in parables and said, [2]"The heavenly realm may be compared to a king who arranged a wedding banquet for his son. [3]He sent his servants to tell those who had been invited to the wedding banquet to come, but they would not come. [4]Then he sent other servants and said, 'Tell those who have been invited that I have prepared a feast. My grain-fed oxen have been butchered and everything is ready. Come to the wedding banquet!' [5]But they made light of it and went their ways, one to a farm and another to a business. [6]The rest seized the king's servants and abused them and killed them. [7]When the king heard, he was angry. He sent his army to destroy those murderers and burn their town. [8]Then he said to his servants, 'The wedding banquet is ready, but those who were invited were not worthy. [9]Now go out to the street corners and invite as many as you find to the wedding banquet.' [10]So those servants went out to the street corners and gathered all the people they could find, both bad and good, and the wedding banquet was filled with guests. [11]The king came in to look at the guests and saw a man who did not have on a wedding garment. [12]He said to him, 'Friend, how did you get in here without a wedding garment?' The man was speechless. [13]Then the king said to his servants, 'Bind him hand and foot and throw him into outer darkness, where there will be weeping and gnashing of teeth.' [14]For many are called, but few are chosen."

THE LEADERS TRY TO TRAP JESUS INTO OPPOSING CAESAR

[15]Then the Pharisees went and made plans to try to trap Jesus by what He said. [16]They sent their disciples to Him, along with the Herodians, saying, "Teacher, we know that You are honest and teach the way of God truthfully and are not partial to any, for You are not swayed by people's opinion of You. [17]Tell us, therefore, what do You think? Is it lawful to pay taxes to Caesar, or not?" [18]Jesus was aware of their hostility and said, "Why do you test Me, you hypocrites? [19]Show Me the coin used for paying taxes!" They brought Him a coin [20]and He asked them, "Whose likeness and inscription is this?" [21]They said to Him, "Caesar's." Then He said to them, "Give to Caesar the things that are Caesar's and to God the things that are God's." [22]They heard this and they marveled. Then they left Him and went away.

JESUS GIVES THE SADDUCEES A GLIMPSE INTO HEAVEN

[23]That same day the Sadducees, who say there is no resurrection, came to Him and asked Him, [24]"Teacher, Moses said that if a man dies without any children, his brother must marry the widow and raise up children for his brother. [25]Once there were seven brothers. The first married and died, and having no children, left his wife to his brother. [26]The same thing happened to the second and to the third, and eventually to

all seven. [27]Last of all, the woman died also. [28]Now at the resurrection, whose wife will she be, since all seven married her?" [29]Jesus answered, "You stray from the truth because you don't know the Scriptures or the power of God. [30]For at the resurrection men and women do not marry; they are like the angels in heaven. [31]As for the resurrection of the dead, have you not read what God spoke to you, [32]'I am the God of Abraham, the God of Isaac and the God of Jacob.' God is not the God of the dead, but of the living!" [33]When the crowds heard this, they were astonished at His teaching.

THE MOST IMPORTANT COMMANDMENT

[34]When the Pharisees heard that He had silenced the Sadducees, they met together. [35]Then one of them, a lawyer, tested Him by asking, [36]"Teacher, what is the most important commandment in the law?" [37]Jesus said to them, "'You shall love Yahweh your God with all your heart, with all your soul and with all your mind.' [38]This is the first and great commandment. [39]And the second is like it: 'You shall love others as you love yourself.' [40]On these two commandments hang the whole law of Moses and the teachings of the prophets."

THE MESSIAH IS THE CHILD OF GOD

[41]While the Pharisees were gathered together, Jesus asked them, [42]"What do you think about the Messiah? Whose son is He?" They answered, "The son of David." [43]He said to them, "Why then does David, inspired by the Spirit, call Him God? David said, [44]'Yahweh said to God: Sit at My right hand till I make Your enemies Your footstool.' [45]If David calls the son 'God,' how can He be David's son?" [46]No one was able to answer Him a word, nor from that day did anyone dare ask Him any further questions.

BEWARE OF HYPOCRISY

[23:1]Then Jesus said to the crowd and to His disciples, [2]"The scribes and the Pharisees interpret the law of Moses, [3]therefore observe what they tell you and do it. But do not live as they live, for they do not practice what they preach. [4]They tie up burdensome duties to lay on people's shoulders, but they won't lift a finger to help bear them. [5]They do everything in their lives for the eyes of humans. They make their phylacteries large and their fringes long; [6]they love the places of honor at banquets and the seats of honor in the synagogues; [7]they love greetings in the market and having people call them 'Teacher.' [8]But you are not to be called 'Teacher,' for you are all disciples and have only one Teacher. [9]And call no one on earth your parent, for you have one Parent, and that Parent is in heaven. [10]Neither are you to be called guides, for you have one Guide, the Messiah. [11]The greatest among you will be your servant. [12]Those who exalt themselves will be humbled, and those who humble themselves will be exalted. [13]But woe to you hypocritical scribes and Pharisees, for you close the heavenly realm to humans. You do not go in, nor do you allow others to enter who want to.

[14]"Woe to you hypocritical scribes and Pharisees! You cheat widows out of their homes, and pretend to make long prayers. Therefore you will receive a more severe judgment.

[15]"Woe to you hypocritical scribes and Pharisees! You travel around together over land and sea to make one disciple, and when you obtain one, you make that one twice the child of hell that you are.

[16]"Woe to you blind guides who say, 'If anyone swears by the temple, that is nothing. But if you swear by the gold in the temple, you are obligated.' [17]Blind fools! Which is greater - the gold, or the temple that sanctifies the gold? [18]And you say, 'If anyone swears by the altar, it is nothing; but if you swear by the sacrifice that is on it, you are obligated.' [19]Blind fools! Which is greater - the sacrifice, or the altar that sanctifies the sacrifice? [20]Therefore anyone who swears by the altar swears by it and by everything on it. [21]And anyone who swears by the temple swears by it and by the One who resides in it. [22]And anyone who swears by heaven swears by the throne of God and by the One who sits on it.

[23]"Woe to you hypocritical scribes and Pharisees! For you tithe of your mint and dill and cummin, but you neglect the weightier matters of the law: justice and mercy and faithfulness. These you ought to have done and not neglected the others. [24]Blind guides! You strain at a gnat and swallow a camel.

[25]"Woe to you hypocritical scribes and Pharisees! For you clean the outside of the cup and dish, but inside they are full of spoil and self-indulgence. [26]Blind Pharisees! First clean the inside of the cup and dish, then the outside may be cleaned also.

[27]"Woe to you hypocritical scribes and Pharisees! You are like whitewashed tombs that look beautiful on the outside, but inside are full of the bones of the dead and every uncleanness. [28]You appear righteous to people on the outside, but inside you are full of hypocrisy and wickedness.

[29]"Woe to you hypocritical scribes and Pharisees! You build tombs for the prophets and decorate the graves of the righteous. [30]Then you say, 'If we had lived in the days of our ancestors, we would never have taken part with them in the murder of the prophets.' [31]Therefore you are witnesses against yourselves that you are the children of those who killed the prophets. [32]Complete then what your ancestors started!

[33]"Serpents! Generation of vipers! How will you avoid being sentenced to hell? [34]Beware! I will send you prophets and sages and scribes. Some you will kill, some you will crucify and some you will whip in your synagogues and persecute from city to city. [35]Therefore there will come upon you all the righteous blood shed upon the earth, from the blood of righteous Abel to the blood of Zechariah the son of Berachiah, whom you murdered between the temple and the altar. [36]Truly I say to you, all this will come upon this generation.

JESUS MOURNS OVER ALL THE HARDHEARTED REBELS

[37]"O Jerusalem, Jerusalem! You who kill the prophets and stone those who are sent to you, how often I have longed to gather your children together, even as a hen gathers her chicks under her wings, but you would not let Me. [38]Look! Your house is left to you deserted. [39]Now you will not see Me again until you say, 'Blessed is the One who comes in the name of Yahweh.'"

JESUS FORETELLS THE DESTRUCTION OF THE TEMPLE

24:1As Jesus went out from the temple, His disciples came to point out the buildings of the temple to Him. 2Jesus said to them, "Do you see all these? Truly I say to you, not one stone will be left here in its place; they will all be thrown down."

FUTURE TRIBULATIONS

3As Jesus sat on the Mount of Olives, the disciples came to Him privately and asked, "Tell us, when will these things happen? And what will be the sign of Your coming and the end of the age?" 4Jesus said to them, "Watch out that no one deceives you. 5For many will come in My name, saying, 'I am the Messiah,' and will deceive many. 6You will hear of wars and rumors of wars, but see to it that you are not frightened. Such things must be, but the end is yet to come. 7Nation will rise against nation, and country against country. There will be famines and earthquakes in many places. 8These will be just the beginning of the birth pains. 9Then you will be handed over to be persecuted and killed, and all the people will hate you because of My name. 10At that time many will be offended and will betray one another and will hate one another. 11Many false prophets will arise and deceive many people. 12And because wickedness will increase, the love of many will grow cold. 13But those who endure to the end will be saved. 14This good news of God's realm will be preached in all the world for a witness to all nations; then the end will come.

15"So when you see the abomination of desolation standing in the holy place of which Daniel the prophet spoke (let the reader understand), 16then those in Judea must flee to the mountains. 17Those on the housetops must not go down to take anything out of their houses, 18nor should those in the field turn back to get their coats. 19Woe to those who are pregnant and those with nursing babies in those days. 20Pray that your flight is not in winter or on the Sabbath. 21For there will be great tribulation, such as has never been from the beginning of the world to this time, nor will there ever be again. 22If those days had not been shortened, no flesh would survive. But for the sake of the chosen, those days will be cut short.

23"In those days, if anyone says to you, 'Look, here is the Messiah!' or 'There the Messiah is!' do not believe it. 24For false Messiahs and false prophets will appear and show great signs and wonders to deceive, if possible, even the chosen. 25Remember, I have told you before it happens. 26So if they say to you, 'Look! He is in the desert!' do not believe it. 27For as the lightning comes from the east and shines even to the west, so shall the coming of the Son of Humanity be. 28Wherever the carcass is, there the vultures will gather.

THE SPECTACULAR RETURN OF JESUS

29"Immediately after the tribulation of those days, the sun will be darkened, the moon will not give its light, the stars will fall from the sky and the powers in the sky will be shaken. 30Then the sign of the Son of Humanity will appear in the sky and all the nations of the earth will mourn when they see the Son of Humanity coming among the clouds of heaven with power and great glory. 31The Son of Humanity will send angels with the great sound of a trumpet, and they will gather God's chosen from every direction from all over the earth.

THE TIME OF JESUS' RETURN

[32]"Now learn a lesson from the fig tree: When its branch is still tender and leaves start growing, you know that summer is near. [33]So, when you see all these things, you will know that it is near, at the very door. [34]Truly I say to you, this generation will not pass away until all this has happened. [35]The sky and the earth will pass away, but My words will not pass away. [36]But of that day and hour no one knows, not even the angels of heaven, nor the Son. Only My heavenly Parent knows. [37]As the days of Noah were, so will be the coming of the Son of Humanity. [38]In the days before the flood, people were eating and drinking and marrying until the day that Noah entered the ark. [39]They did not know what would happen until the flood came and took them all away. That is how it will be at the coming of the Son of Humanity. [40]Two will be in the field; one will be taken and the other left. [41]Two will be grinding at the mill; one will be taken and the other left. [42]Watch, therefore, for you do not know at what hour your Owner will come. [43]But know this: If the head of the house had known at what hour the thief would come, the householder would have watched and not allowed the house to be broken into. [44]Therefore be ready, for the Son of Humanity will come in the hour you do not expect.

ALWAYS BE READY!

[45]"Who then is the faithful and wise servant, whom the owner of the house puts in charge of the household to give the others food at the proper time? [46]Blessed is that servant who is found doing so when the owner comes. [47]Truly I say to you, the owner will make that servant ruler over everything. [48]But if that servant is worthless and says, 'The owner is not coming back for a long time,' [49]and begins to beat the other servants and eats and drinks with drunkards, [50]the owner will return on a day not looked for and in an hour not expected. [51]Then that servant will be whipped and assigned a portion with the hypocrites, where there will be weeping and gnashing of teeth.

THE PARABLE OF THE TEN VIRGINS

[25:1]"The heavenly realm may be compared to ten virgins, who took their lamps and went out to meet the bridegroom. [2]Five of them were wise and five were foolish. [3]Those who were foolish took their lamps, but they took no extra oil. [4]But the wise took oil in their flasks, as well as in their lamps. [5]The bridegroom was late, and they all nodded off to sleep. [6]At midnight there was a shout, 'Look! The bridegroom is coming! Go out to meet him!' [7]Then all the virgins got up and trimmed their lamps. [8]The foolish virgins said to the wise, 'Give us some of your oil, for our lamps are going out.' [9]The wise answered, 'There may not be enough for all of us. Go instead to those who sell oil and buy some for yourselves.' [10]While they were on their way to buy oil, the bridegroom came. Those who were ready went in with him to the wedding banquet, and the door was shut. [11]After awhile the other virgins came and said, 'Bridegroom! Bridegroom! Open up for us!' [12]But he replied, 'Truly I say to you, I do not know you.' [13]Watch, therefore, for you do not know the day nor the hour.

THE PARABLE OF THE SERVANTS WHO WERE GIVEN DIFFERENT GIFTS

14"It will be like a landowner traveling to a far country, who called the servants and put them in charge of the property. 15One received five thousand coins, another two thousand and another one thousand, each according to ability. Then the owner went on the journey. 16The servant who was given five thousand engaged in business and made five thousand more. 17In the same way, the servant who was given two thousand gained another two thousand. 18But the servant who was given one thousand went and dug a hole and hid the owner's coins in the ground. 19After a long time, the owner came to settle accounts. 20The one who had received five thousand came and brought five thousand more and said, 'You put me in charge of five thousand coins. Look, I have gained five thousand more.' 21The owner said, 'Well done, you good and faithful servant. You have been faithful over a little, I will make you ruler over much. Enter into the joy of your owner!' 22The one who had received two thousand coins came and said, 'You put me in charge of two thousand coins. Look, I have gained two thousand more.' 23The owner said, 'Well done, you good and faithful servant. You have been faithful over a little, I will make you ruler over much. Enter into the joy of your owner!' 24Then the one who had received one thousand coins came and said, 'I always knew you were a hard person, reaping where you have not sown and gathering where you have not winnowed. 25Therefore I was afraid and went and hid your coins in the ground. Here, take what is yours.' 26The owner said, 'You lazy good-for-nothing! So you knew that I reap where I have not sown and gather where I have not winnowed! 27Well then, you should have put my money in the bank, so that when I came back I could have received what was mine with interest. 28Take the thousand coins from that servant and give them to the one who has ten thousand. 29For to those who have, more will be given, and they will have an abundance. But from those who do not have, even what they have will be taken from them. 30Now throw that worthless servant into outer darkness, where there will be weeping and gnashing of teeth.'

JESUS WILL SEPARATE THE SHEEP FROM THE GOATS

31"When the Son of Humanity comes in glory with all God's angels, I will sit on My glorious throne. 32Before Me will be gathered all the people. I will separate them one from another as a shepherd separates the sheep from the goats. 33I will put the sheep on My right and the goats on My left. 34Then I will say to those on My right, 'Come, you who are blessed by My heavenly Parent, take your inheritance, the realm prepared for you since the creation of the world. 35For I was hungry and you gave Me food, I was thirsty and you gave Me a drink, I was a stranger and you invited Me in, 36I was naked and you clothed Me, I was sick and you took care of Me, I was in prison and you visited Me.' 37Then the righteous will ask Me, 'When did we see You hungry and feed You? Or thirsty and give You a drink? 38When did we see You a stranger and invite You in? Or needing clothes and give You something to wear? 39When did we see You sick or in prison and come to visit You?' 40Then I will answer, 'Truly I say to you, that which you have done for one of the least of these, My family, you have done for Me.'

[41] "Then I will say to those on the left, 'Depart from Me, you who are cursed, into the everlasting fire prepared for the devil and the devil's angels. [42] For I was hungry and you gave Me no food, I was thirsty and you gave Me no drink, [43] I was a stranger and you did not invite Me in, I needed clothes and you gave Me nothing to wear, I was sick and in prison and you did not visit Me.' [44] Then they will answer and say, 'When did we see You hungry or thirsty or a stranger or needing clothes or sick or in prison and not help You?' [45] I will answer them and say, 'Truly I say to you, that which you did not do for one of the least of these, you did not do for Me.' [46] Then the wicked will go away into everlasting punishment, but the righteous into everlasting life."

JESUS TELLS HIS DISCIPLES THAT HE WILL BE CRUCIFIED

[26:1] When Jesus had finished all these teachings, He said to His disciples, [2] "You know that in two days it will be Passover. Then the Son of Humanity will be betrayed and crucified."

THE LEADERS PLAN TO KILL JESUS

[3] The chief priests and the elders of the people assembled together in the court of Caiaphas the high priest [4] and plotted how to overcome Jesus secretly and kill Him. [5] "But not during the Feast," they said, "or there will be a riot among the people."

A WOMAN PUTS OIL ON JESUS' HEAD

[6] While Jesus was in Bethany in the home of Simon the leper, [7] a woman with an alabaster jar of perfumed oil came to Him and poured it on His head as He sat at the table. [8] When His disciples saw this, they were indignant and said, "What is the purpose of this waste? [9] This perfume could have been sold and the money given to the poor." [10] Jesus was aware of this and said to them, "Why do you criticize this woman? She has done a charitable thing for Me. [11] The poor you have with you always, but you will not always have Me. [12] She has poured this perfume on Me to prepare My body for burial. [13] Truly I say to you, wherever this good news is proclaimed throughout the world, what she has done will be told in memory of her."

JUDAS GOES TO THE LEADERS AND OFFERS TO BETRAY JESUS

[14] Then Judas Iscariot, one of the twelve, went to the chief priests [15] and said, "How much will you give me if I hand Jesus over to you?" They counted out thirty silver coins for him. [16] From that time on he sought an opportunity to betray Jesus.

PREPARATIONS FOR THE PASSOVER

[17] On the first day of unleavened bread the disciples came to Jesus and asked, "Where do You want us to make preparations for You to eat the Passover?" [18] He said, "Go into the city to a certain person and say, 'The Teacher says: My time is at hand. I will keep the Passover at your house with My disciples.'" [19] The disciples did as Jesus had directed them, and they prepared the Passover.

JESUS SHOWS WHO WILL BETRAY HIM

[20] When evening came, He sat down with the twelve. [21] As they were eating, He said, "Truly I say to you, one of you will betray Me." [22] This made them very sad, and they began to ask Him, one after another, "Rabbi, is it I?" [23] He replied, "One who has eaten with Me from this dish will betray Me. [24] The Son of Humanity will go as it is

written of Him, but woe to that man by whom the Son of Humanity is betrayed! It would have been better for that man if he had never been born." [25]Then Judas, who was to betray Him, said, "Rabbi, is it I?" Jesus said to him, "So you say."

THE PASSOVER

[26]As they were eating, Jesus took bread and blessed it. Then He broke it and gave it to His disciples, saying, "Take and eat, this is My body." [27]Then He took the cup and gave thanks. He gave it to them, saying, "Drink from it, all of you. [28]This is My blood of the covenant which is poured out for many for the forgiveness of sins. [29]And I tell you, I will not drink of this fruit of the vine again until that day when I drink it anew with you in the realm of My heavenly Parent." [30]Then they sang a psalm and went out to the Mount of Olives.

JESUS WARNS THEM ALL ABOUT THE COMING NIGHT

[31]Jesus said to them, "You will all be offended because of Me this night, for it is written, 'I will strike the Shepherd and the sheep of the flock will be scattered.' [32]But after I am raised, I will go ahead of you into Galilee."

PETER IS TOLD HE WILL DENY JESUS THREE TIMES

[33]Peter said to Him, "Even if everyone is embarrassed because of You, I will never be embarrassed." [34]Jesus said to him, "Truly I say to you, before the rooster crows this night you will deny Me three times." [35]Peter said to Him, "Even if I have to die with You, I will never deny You!" And all the other disciples said the same.

THE GARDEN OF GETHSEMANE

[36]Jesus went with the disciples to a place called Gethsemane. He said to them, "Sit here while I go over there and pray." [37]Taking Peter and the two sons of Zebedee with Him, He began to be sorrowful and filled with troubling thoughts. [38]He said to them, "My Soul is overwhelmed with sorrow; it is almost killing Me. Stay here with Me and keep awake." [39]He went a little farther and flung Himself face down on the ground. He prayed, "O My dear Parent, if it be possible, spare Me from drinking this cup. Nevertheless, not My will but Yours be done."

[40]Jesus returned to the disciples and found them asleep. He said to Peter, "What? Could you not watch with Me one hour? [41]Be watchful, and pray not to have to go through testing. The spirit is willing, but the flesh is weak." [42]He went away a second time and prayed, "O My dear Parent, if this cup will not go away from Me unless I drink it, Your will be done." [43]Again He returned and found the disciples asleep, for their eyes were heavy. [44]He left them and went away and prayed the third time, saying the same thing. [45]Then He returned to His disciples and said to them, "Sleep now and rest? Look! The time has come! The Son of Humanity is betrayed into the hands of sinners! [46]Get up, let us be going! Look! My betrayer is approaching!"

JESUS IS ARRESTED TO FULFILL GOD'S PLAN

[47]Jesus was still speaking when Judas, one of the twelve, came. With him was a large crowd armed with swords and clubs. They had been sent by the chief priests and elders of the people. [48]The betrayer gave the crowd a sign: "The man I kiss is the one - seize Him." [49]Going up to Jesus, he said, "Peace to You, Rabbi," and kissed Him.

[50]Jesus said to him, "Friend, what are you here for?" Then they came and laid hands on Jesus and took Him. [51]One of those with Jesus reached for his sword and struck the servant of the high priest, cutting off his ear. [52]Jesus said to him, "Put your sword back in its place, for all who use the sword will die by the sword. [53]Don't you know that I could pray to My heavenly Parent, who would immediately give Me more than twelve legions of angels? [54]But then, how would the Scriptures be fulfilled that say this is the way it must be?" [55]Then Jesus said to the crowd, "Am I a thief, that you come out against Me with swords and clubs to capture Me? I sat daily teaching in the temple and you did not arrest Me. [56]But all this has taken place so that what the prophets wrote may be fulfilled." Then all His disciples left Him and fled.

JESUS ADMITS BEFORE THE SANHEDRIN THAT HE IS THE SON OF GOD

[57]Those who arrested Jesus took Him to Caiaphas, the high priest, where the scribes and the elders had gathered. [58]Peter followed Him at a distance as far as the courtyard of the high priest and went in and sat with the servants to see the end.

[59]The chief priests and the whole council sought false testimony against Jesus so that there would be a reason to put Him to death. [60]They found none, though many came and told lies. At last two false witnesses came [61]and testified, "He said, 'I am able to destroy the temple of God and rebuild it in three days.'" [62]The high priest stood up and said to Jesus, "Have You no answer to these charges against You?" [63]But Jesus was silent. The high priest said to Him, "I place You under oath and ask You before the living God to tell us whether You are the Messiah, the Son of God." [64]Jesus said to him, "So you say. And furthermore, I say to you, you will soon see the Son of Humanity sitting at the right hand of the Almighty and coming on the clouds of heaven." [65]Then the high priest tore his clothes and said, "He has spoken blasphemy! What further need do we have of witnesses? There! Now you have heard His blasphemy. [66]What do you think?" They answered, "He deserves death!" [67]Then they spit in His face and hit Him with their fists. Others slapped Him [68]and said, "Prophesy to us, You Messiah! Who is the one who hit You?"

PETER DENIES KNOWING JESUS THREE TIMES

[69]Now Peter was sitting outside in the courtyard. A servant girl came up to him and said, "You also were with Jesus of Galilee." [70]He denied it before everyone, saying, "I don't know what you mean." [71]He went out into the entrance. Another servant girl saw him and said to those who were there, "This one was with Jesus of Nazareth." [72]Again he denied it with an oath: "I don't know the man!" [73]After a while one of those standing about came and said to Peter, "Surely you are one of them, for the way you talk betrays you." [74]Then Peter began to curse and swear: "I don't know the man!" Immediately a rooster crowed. [75]Then Peter remembered what Jesus had said to him: "Before the rooster crows, you will deny Me three times." And he went out and wept bitterly.

JESUS IS TAKEN TO THE ROMAN GOVERNOR

27:[1]Early in the morning, all the chief priests and elders of the people made plans to put Jesus to death. [2]After tying His hands, they led Him away and handed Him over to Pontius Pilate, the governor.

JUDAS KILLS HIMSELF

[3]When Judas, who betrayed Him, saw that Jesus was condemned, he remorsefully returned the thirty pieces of silver to the chief priests and the elders, [4]saying, "I have sinned by betraying innocent blood." They said, "What is that to us? See to it yourself." [5]Then Judas threw down the silver coins in the temple and went out and hanged himself.

[6]The chief priests took the silver coins and said, "It is not lawful to put this into the treasury; it is blood money." [7]So they decided to use it to buy the potter's field to bury foreigners in. [8]That is why it is called the Field of Blood to this day. [9]Then was fulfilled what was spoken of by Jeremiah the prophet: "They took the thirty silver coins - the price He was valued at by the people of Israel - [10]and purchased the potter's field as Yahweh directed."

JESUS BEFORE PILATE

[11]Jesus stood before the governor, and the governor asked Him, "Are You the King of the Jews?" "So you say," Jesus answered. [12]But when Jesus was accused by the chief priests and the elders, He did not reply. [13]Then Pilate said to Him, "Don't You hear all the things they are testifying against You?" [14]Jesus did not answer a single accusation, and the governor was greatly amazed.

[15]At Passover it was the governor's custom to release a prisoner chosen by the people. [16]They had there a notorious prisoner called Barabbas. [17]Since the people were gathered together, Pilate asked them, "Which one do you want me to release to you: Barabbas, or Jesus, who is called the Messiah?" [18]Pilate knew that they had handed Jesus over out of envy.

THE UNBELIEVERS WANT JESUS CRUCIFIED

[19]As Pilate sat on the judge's seat, his wife sent him this message: "Have nothing to do with that godly man, for I suffered greatly in a dream last night because of Him." [20]But the chief priests and the elders persuaded the crowd to ask for Barabbas and to have Jesus put to death. [21]The governor asked, "Which of the two do you want me to release to you?" They cried, "Barabbas!" [22]Pilate asked, "Then what shall I do with Jesus, who is called the Messiah?" They all answered, "Crucify Him!" [23]The governor asked, "Why? What harm has He done?" But they shouted all the more, "Crucify Him!" [24]When Pilate saw that he could not prevail, but that a riot was starting instead, he took water and washed his hands before the crowd. He said, "I am innocent of this man's blood. See to it yourselves." [25]All the people answered, "His blood be on us and on our children!" [26]Pilate released Barabbas to them, but he had Jesus whipped. Then he handed Jesus over to be crucified.

THE SOLDIERS MOCK JESUS

[27]Then the soldiers took Jesus into the palace, and the whole band of soldiers gathered around Him. [28]They stripped Him and put a scarlet robe on Him. [29]They plaited a crown of thorns and put it on His head. They put a stick in His right hand and kneeled before Him, saying, "Hail, King of the Jews!" [30]Then they spit on Him and took the stick and beat Him on the head. [31]After they had mocked Him, they took the robe off Him, put His clothes on Him and led Him away to be crucified.

SIMON OF CYRENE IS FORCED TO CARRY THE CROSS

32As they were going out of the city, they met a man from Cyrene named Simon, and they forced him to carry Jesus' cross.

JESUS IS CRUCIFIED

33When they came to a place called Golgotha, which is also called Calvary, 34they offered Jesus vinegar mixed with gall to drink. He tasted it but would not drink it. 35They crucified Him and divided His garments by casting lots, so that the word that was spoken by the prophet might be fulfilled: "They divided My garments among them and cast lots for My clothing." 36Sitting down, they kept watch over Him there.

37Over His head they put the written accusation against Him: THIS IS THE KING OF THE JEWS. 38Two thieves were crucified with Him, one on the right and one on the left. 39Those who passed by blasphemed Him and wagged their heads. 40They said, "You who would destroy the temple and rebuild it in three days, save Yourself! If You are the Son of God, come down from the cross!" 41The chief priests, the scribes and the elders also mocked Him. They said, 42"He saved others, but He can't save Himself! He is the King of Israel? Let Him come down from the cross now and we will believe Him. 43He trusted in God; let God rescue Him now if God delights in Him; for He said, 'I am the Son of God.'" 44In the same way, the robbers who were crucified with Him also hurled insults at Him.

JESUS YIELDS UP HIS SPIRIT

45At noon, darkness came over the whole land for three hours. 46About mid-afternoon Jesus cried out with a loud voice, "Eli, Eli, lama sabachthani?" which means, "My God, My God, why have You forsaken Me?" 47Some of those standing there heard Him and said, "He is calling Elijah." 48Immediately one of them ran and filled a sponge with vinegar, put it on a stick and gave it to Jesus to drink. 49The rest said, "Wait, let's see whether Elijah will come to save Him." 50But Jesus cried out again with a loud voice and yielded up His Spirit. 51And the veil of the temple was torn in two from the top to the bottom. The earth quaked and the rocks split.

THE RELEASE OF THE HOLY ONES

52The graves were opened and the bodies of many holy ones who slept awoke. 53They came out of their graves after Jesus' resurrection, went into the holy city and appeared to many. 54The centurion and those with him who were keeping watch over Jesus saw the earthquake and everything that happened. They were filled with awe and said, "Truly, this was the Son of God."

THE WOMEN WHO CARED FOR JESUS

55Many women who had followed Jesus from Galilee and looked after His needs were there, watching from a short distance away. 56Among them were Mary Magdalene, Mary the mother of James and Joses, and the mother of Zebedee's sons.

JESUS IS BURIED IN A NEW TOMB BY A COURAGEOUS LEADER

57Evening came, and a rich man from Arimathea named Joseph, who was himself a disciple of Jesus, 58went to Pilate and asked for the body of Jesus. Pilate ordered the body given to him. 59Joseph took the body, wrapped it in a clean linen cloth 60and laid it in his own new tomb that had been cut out of the rock. He rolled a great stone across the entrance of the tomb and departed. [61]Mary Magdalene and the other Mary were there, sitting across from the tomb.

THE TOMB IS SEALED AND GUARDED

[62]The next day, which is the day after Preparation Day, the chief priests and the Pharisees went to Pilate [63]and said, "Sir, we remember that while He was yet alive, that deceiver said, 'After three days I will rise again.' [64]Therefore command that the tomb be made secure until the third day, lest His disciples come and steal Him and say to the people, 'He is risen from the dead!' This last lie would be worse than the first." [65]Pilate said to them, "You have a guard, go and make it as secure as you can." [66]So they went and made the tomb secure by putting a seal on the stone and posting the guard.

THE WOMEN GO TO SEE THE TOMB

28:1[After the Sabbath, as it began to grow light on the first day of the week, Mary Magdalene and the other Mary went to see the tomb. [2]Suddenly there was a great earthquake, for an angel from God descended from heaven, came and rolled back the stone and sat on it. [3]The angel's appearance was like lightning, and the angel's clothing was as white as snow. [4]The guards shook with fear and fell down like the dead.

THE ANGEL TELLS THE WOMEN THAT JESUS HAS RISEN

[5]The angel said to the women, "Do not be afraid! I know that you seek Jesus who was crucified. [6]He is not here, for He is risen as He said. Come see the place where He was lying, [7]then go quickly and tell His disciples that He is risen from the dead and is going ahead of you into Galilee. There you will see Him. Now I have told you."

JESUS APPEARS TO THE WOMEN AND GIVES THEM A MESSAGE

[8]They departed quickly from the tomb, afraid, yet filled with great joy. They ran to tell His disciples. [9]As they were going, suddenly Jesus met them and said, "Greetings!" They came and held Him by the feet and worshiped Him. [10]Jesus said to them, "Do not be afraid! Go tell My disciples to go to Galilee; there they will see Me."

THE CHIEF PRIESTS PAY THE GUARDS TO SAY THEY WERE SLEEPING

[11]While they were going on their way, some of the guards went into the city and told the chief priests everything that had happened. [12]The chief priests met with the elders, and they decided to give some money to the soldiers. [13]They said, "You are to say, 'His disciples came by night and stole Him away while we slept.' [14]And if this comes to the governor's ears, we will pacify him and you won't need to worry." [15]So they took the money and did as they were told. This story is still told among the Jews to this very day.

JESUS COMMISSIONS THE DISCIPLES IN GALILEE

[16]The eleven disciples went to Galilee to the mountain where Jesus had told them to go. [17]They saw Him and worshiped Him; but some doubted. [18]Then Jesus came and said to them, "All authority has been given to Me in heaven and on earth. [19]Therefore go and teach disciples in all nations, baptizing them in the name of God and the Son and the Holy Spirit. [20]And teach them to observe everything I have commanded you. Watch! I am with you always, even to the end of the age."

Mark

THE ELIJAH WHO WAS TO COME [Mark 9:11]

1:1This is the beginning of the good news about Jesus the Messiah, the Child of God, 2as it is written in the prophets: "Watch! I send My messenger ahead of You who will prepare Your way, 3the voice of one calling in the wilderness: Prepare the way for Yahweh! Make straight paths for our God."

JOHN THE BAPTIST

4John the Baptist appeared in the wilderness proclaiming a baptism of repentance for the forgiveness of sins. 5People from Jerusalem and from all over the land of Judea went out to him and were baptized by him in the River Jordan, acknowledging their sins. 6John wore a robe of camel's hair with a leather belt around his waist, and he ate locusts and wild honey. 7He preached, "After me there is One coming who is mightier than I. I am not worthy to stoop down and untie His sandals. 8I baptize you with water, but He will baptize you with the Holy Spirit."

JESUS IS BAPTIZED AND A VOICE IS HEARD FROM HEAVEN

9In those days Jesus came from Nazareth in Galilee and was baptized by John in the Jordan. 10As soon as Jesus came up out of the water, He saw the heavens open and the Spirit descend upon Him like a dove. 11A voice from heaven said, "You are My dearly loved Child. I am pleased with You." 12Then the Spirit sent Him away into the wilderness. 13He was there among the animals of the wilderness for forty days being tempted by Satan, and the angels took care of Him.

JESUS MOVES TO CAPERNAUM AND CHOOSES FOUR DISCIPLES

14After John was put in prison, Jesus went to Galilee and told them the good news of God's realm. 15Jesus proclaimed, "The time is fulfilled! God's realm is at hand! Repent and believe the good news!" 16As He walked by the Sea of Galilee, He saw Simon and his brother Andrew casting a net into the sea, for they were fishers. 17Jesus said to them, "Follow Me and I will show you how to fish for humans." 18They immediately left their nets and followed Him. 19He walked a little farther and saw James the son of Zebedee and his brother John in a boat, mending their nets. 20Immediately He called them, and they left their father Zebedee in the boat with the hired help and followed Him.

JESUS CASTS OUT A DEMON AT CAPERNAUM

21They went to Capernaum, and on the Sabbath Jesus went into the synagogue and began to teach. 22The people were astonished at His teaching. He did not teach like the scribes did; He taught them with authority. 23A man in their synagogue with an unclean spirit cried out, [24]"What do You want with us, Jesus of Nazareth? Have You come to destroy us? I know who You are, the Holy One of God!" [25]Jesus rebuked the spirit, saying, "Be quiet and come out of him!" [26]The unclean spirit shook the man with a loud cry and came out of him. [27]They were all amazed and said among themselves, "What is this? What new teaching is this? With authority He commands even the unclean spirits and they obey Him!" [28]Soon His fame spread throughout all the region around Galilee.

JESUS HEALS PETER'S MOTHER-IN-LAW

[29]After Jesus left the synagogue, He went with James and John to the home of Peter and Andrew. [30]Peter's mother-in-law lay sick with a fever, and they immediately told Jesus about her. [31]He came and took her by the hand and woke her up. Immediately the fever left her and she got up and ministered to them.

AN OLD PROPHECY FULFILLED

[32]That evening after sunset the people brought to Him all of the sick and those who were possessed by demons. [33]All of the people of the town were gathered at the door. [34]He healed many who were sick with various diseases and cast out many demons. He did not allow the demons to speak, because they knew Him.

JESUS PRAYS BEFORE DAWN

[35]In the darkness before dawn, Jesus got up and went out to a place where He could be alone, and there He prayed. [36]Simon and the others went looking for Him. [37]When they found Him, they said to Him, "Everyone is looking for You." [38]He said to them, "Let's go on to the other towns so that I can tell the good news there also, for that is why I came." [39]And He went throughout Galilee telling the good news in their synagogues and casting out demons.

JESUS HEALS A LEPER AND HIS FAME GROWS

[40]A man with leprosy came to Jesus, knelt down before Him and pleaded, "If You will, You can make me clean." [41]Moved with compassion, Jesus put out His hand and touched him, saying, "I am willing; be clean." [42]Immediately the leprosy left him and he was clean. [43]Jesus sent him away with a stern warning, [44]"See that you don't say anything to anyone, but go and show yourself to the priest. Offer for your cleansing what Moses commanded, then everyone will know that you are healed." [45]But the man went out and began publishing it everywhere and divulging it to everyone to such an extent that Jesus could no longer enter a town openly. He stayed outdoors, away from the towns, yet the people came to Him from every direction.

JESUS IS REBUKED FOR FORGIVING SIN

[2:1]After a while He returned to Capernaum. The news spread that He was at home; [2]and so many gathered together that there was hardly room to hold them, even outside the door. As He explained the message to them, [3]four people came carrying a paralyzed boy. [4]They could not get near Him because of the crowds, so they separated the roof. They removed it over where Jesus was and let down the mat on which the paralyzed boy was lying. [5]When Jesus saw their faith, He said to the paralytic, "Son, your sins are forgiven." [6]Some of the scribes who were sitting there thought to themselves, [7]"Why speak blasphemy? Who can forgive sins but God alone?" [8]Immediately Jesus knew in His Spirit what they were thinking and He said to them, "Why do you think these things in your hearts? [9]Is it easier to say to this paralytic, 'Your sins are forgiven,' or to say, 'Get up, pick up your mat and walk'? [10]But so that you know that the Son of Humanity has authority on earth to forgive sins, I now say to this paralytic, [11]'Get up! Pick up your mat and go home.'" [12]Immediately he got up, picked up his mat and went out before them all. They were all amazed and glorified God, saying, "We have never seen anything like this!"

A TAX COLLECTOR IS CHOSEN AS A DISCIPLE

[13]Once again Jesus went out to the seashore. Crowds of people came to Him and He taught them. [14]As He walked along, He saw Levi the son of Alphaeus sitting at the tax collector's booth. He said to him, "Follow Me," and Levi got up and followed Jesus.

[15]Later, as Jesus was eating at Levi's house, many tax collectors and sinners were eating together with Jesus and His disciples, for there were many who followed Him. [16]When the scribes and Pharisees saw Him eating with tax collectors and sinners, they asked His disciples, "Why does He eat with tax collectors and sinners?" [17]Jesus heard them and said, "It is not the healthy who need a physician, but the sick. I have not come to call the righteous, but sinners."

THERE IS A TIME TO FAST

[18]John's disciples and the Pharisees were fasting. Some people came and asked Jesus, "Why do John's disciples and the Pharisees fast, but Your disciples do not fast?" [19]Jesus said to them, "Do the guests of the bridegroom fast while he is with them? As long as they have the bridegroom with them, they don't fast. [20]But the days are coming when the bridegroom will be taken away from them. In those days they will fast.

THE PARABLE OF THE WINESKINS

[21]No one sews a piece of new cloth on an old garment. If one does, the patch will pull away from the garment and the tear will be made worse. [22]And no one puts new wine into old wineskins, lest the new wine burst the wineskins and be spilled and the wineskins ruined. New wine must be put into new wineskins."

JESUS HAS AUTHORITY OVER THE SABBATH

[23]One Sabbath as Jesus and His disciples were walking by some fields of grain, His disciples began to pick off heads of grain. [24]The Pharisees said to Jesus, "Look! Why are they doing what is unlawful on the Sabbath?" [25]Jesus said to them, "Have you never read what David and those who were with him did when they were hungry and had nothing to eat? [26]David went into the house of God in the time of Abiathar the high priest and ate the showbread, which only the priests are allowed to eat. And he also gave some to those who were with him." [27]Then Jesus said to them, "The Sabbath was made for the good of people, not people for the good of the Sabbath. [28]So the Son of Humanity has authority even over the Sabbath."

JESUS IS CONDEMNED FOR HEALING ON THE SABBATH

[3:1]On another occasion He went to the synagogue, and a man was there who had a withered hand. [2]They hoped to accuse Him, so they watched to see if He would heal the man on the Sabbath. [3]He said to the man with the withered hand, "Stand up among them." [4]Then He asked them, "Is it lawful to do good or to do evil on the Sabbath, to save life or to destroy?" But they would not answer. [5]Jesus was angry as He looked around at them. He was grieved over the hardness of their hearts, and He said to the man, "Stretch out your hand." The man stretched it out and his hand was restored. [6]The Pharisees immediately went and made plans with the Herodians to destroy Him.

VAST CROWDS OF PEOPLE LISTEN TO JESUS BY THE SHORE

[7]Jesus withdrew with His disciples to the sea, and a great crowd from Galilee and Judea followed Him. [8]From Jerusalem, from Idumea, from beyond the Jordan and from Tyre and Sidon great crowds came to Him when they heard of the great things He had done. [9]He asked the disciples to have a boat ready for Him, lest the crowds crush Him, [10]for all those who had diseases pressed toward Him to touch Him because of the many He had healed. [11]When unclean spirits saw Him, they fell down before Him and cried out, "You are God's Child!" [12]But He strictly ordered them not to make Him known.

JESUS CHOOSES TWELVE DISCIPLES

[13]Jesus went up on the mountain and called to Himself those He wanted. They came to Him [14]and He appointed twelve to be with Him. They were to be sent out to preach [15]and to have authority to cast out demons. [16]He appointed Simon, whom He called Peter; [17]James the son of Zebedee, and John the brother of James, whom Jesus called "Sons of Thunder"; [18]and Andrew, Philip, Bartholomew, Matthew, Thomas, James the son of Alphaeus, Thaddeus, Simon the Zealot [19]and Judas Iscariot, who betrayed Him.

THE CRITICISM OF JESUS GROWS

They returned to the house, [20]and such a large crowd gathered again that Jesus and His disciples could not even eat. [21]When His family heard, they went out to get Him, for they said, "He has gone crazy."

[22]The scribes who came down from Jerusalem said, "He has the dung-god in Him! The ruler of the demons gives Him the power to cast out demons."

[23]Then Jesus called the people to Him and used parables to teach them. He said, "How can Satan cast out Satan? [24]If a realm is divided against itself, that realm cannot stand. [25]And if a family is divided against itself, that family cannot stand. [26]And if Satan has risen up and is divided, Satan cannot stand, but is finished. [27]No one can enter the house of a strong one and steal the goods unless they first bind the strong one. Then that house can be plundered. [28]Truly I say to you, humans can be forgiven every sin and every evil thing they say. [29]But anyone who says evil things against the Holy Spirit will never be forgiven, but is guilty of an eternal sin." [30]This was because they said He had an unclean spirit.

JESUS' REAL FAMILY

[31]His mother and His brothers came and stood outside. They sent someone in to call Him, [32]but a crowd was sitting around Him. Someone said to Him, "Rabbi! Your mother and Your brothers are outside asking for You." [33]He answered, "Who are My mother and My brothers?" [34]Then He looked around at those who sat there and said,

"Look! My mother and My brothers! [35]Whoever does the will of God is My mother and My sister and my brother."

THE PARABLE OF THE SEEDS

[4:1]On another occasion Jesus began to teach by the seashore. Great crowds gathered around Him, and He got into a boat. Jesus sat out on the sea, and the whole crowd was there on the shore. [2]He taught them many things by parables, and as He taught them He said, [3]"Listen, and think about this! A farmer went out to sow. [4]As the farmer sowed, some seed fell by the roadside and the birds came and ate it up. [5]Some fell on stony ground where it did not have much soil. It sprang up immediately because it had no depth of soil. [6]But when the sun came up it was scorched, and it withered because it had no root. [7]Some fell among thistles. The thistles grew up and choked it, and it yielded no harvest. [8]But some fell on good ground and grew up and increased and yielded a harvest, some thirty times as much, some sixty and some a hundred." [9]Then He said, "If you have ears to hear, then listen."

THE REASON FOR PARABLES

[10]When He was alone, some of those around Him and the twelve asked Him about the parable. [11]He said to them, "To you it is given to understand the mysteries of God's realm, but to those who are outside, everything is said in parables [12]so that, 'Seeing they may see and not comprehend, and hearing they may hear and not understand, lest at any time they turn and be forgiven.'"

THE EXPLANATION OF THE PARABLE OF THE SEEDS

[13]Jesus said to them, "You don't understand this parable? How then will you understand any parable? [14]The farmer sows the words. [15]When the people along the roadside hear the words, Satan comes immediately and takes away the words that were sown in their hearts. [16]The people on stony ground hear the words and immediately receive them with joy. [17]But they have no root and only last a little while. Afterward, when affliction or persecution comes because of the words, they are immediately offended. [18]When the people among the thistles hear the words, [19]the cares of this world, the deceitfulness of riches and all kinds of longings enter in and choke the words. Then the words do not produce anything. [20]The seeds that are sown on good ground are the people who hear the words, accept them and yield a harvest, some thirty times as much, some sixty and some a hundred."

OTHER PARABLES

[21]Jesus said to them, "Is a lamp brought in and put under a bushel basket or under a bed? No, it is put on a lampstand. [22]Nothing is hidden that will not be revealed, nor is there any secret that will not be made public. [23]If you have ears to hear, then listen. [24]Pay attention to what you hear.

"The way you treat others will determine how you are treated in return. [25]For to those who have, more will be given; but to those who do not have much, from them will be taken even what little they do have.

[26]"God's realm is like a farmer who scatters seed on the ground. [27]The farmer lies down at night and gets up each day, and all the while the seed sprouts and grows.

How? The farmer doesn't know. [28]By itself the earth brings forth fruit: first the blade, then the ear, then the kernel on the ear. [29]As soon as the grain is ripe, the farmer puts in the sickle, because harvest time has come."

THE PARABLE OF THE MUSTARD SEED

[30]Jesus said, "To what can we compare God's realm? To what shall we compare it? [31]It can be compared to a mustard seed, which is the smallest of all the seeds that you plant in the ground. [32]But after it is planted, it sprouts and becomes greater than all the garden plants; and it grows such big branches that the birds of the air can nest in its shade."

[33]With many such parables He spoke the word to them, to the extent that they were able to understand. [34]He did not speak to them without a parable. But when He was alone with His disciples, He explained everything.

JESUS CALMS THE STORM

[35]That same day when evening had come, Jesus said to them, "Let's go over to the other side." [36]Jesus was already in the boat, so they left the crowds and departed. Other small boats were with them. [37]A great windstorm arose, and the waves beat against the boat so that it was being swamped. [38]Jesus was asleep in the stern on a pillow. They woke Him and said to Him, "Teacher! Don't You care that we are about to drown?" [39]Jesus, now fully awake, rebuked the wind and said to the waves, "Be calm! Be still!" Then the wind weakened and there was a great calm. [40]He said to them, "Why are you afraid? Do you still have no faith?" [41]They were very frightened and said to one another, "Who is this, that even the wind and the waves obey Him?"

THE DEMONS THAT WENT INTO THE PIGS

[5:1]When they got to the other side of the sea in the country of the Gadarenes, [2]Jesus got out of the boat. A man with an unclean spirit came out from the tombs to meet Him. [3]The man lived among the tombs. No one could bind him any more, even with a chain. [4]He had often been bound with shackles and chains, but he broke the chains apart and no one could restrain him. [5]Night and day he was continually in the mountains and in the tombs, crying out and cutting himself with stones. [6]When he saw Jesus from a distance, he ran and kissed Him [7]and cried out with a loud voice, "What do You want with me, Jesus, Child of the Most High God? Swear to God that You won't torment me," [8]for Jesus was saying, "Unclean spirit, come out of the man!" [9]Jesus asked, "What is your name?" The spirit said, "My name is Legion, for we are many." [10]The spirit pleaded with Jesus repeatedly not to be sent out of the country. [11]There was a large herd of pigs feeding on the hillside nearby, [12]and the demons pleaded with Jesus, "Send us into the pigs; let us go into them." [13]Jesus gave them permission. Then the unclean spirits came out and went into the pigs. Immediately the herd of about two thousand dashed down the steep bank into the sea and drowned. [14]Those who tended the pigs fled and told it in the town and in the country, and the people went out to see what had happened. [15]They came to Jesus and saw the man who had been possessed by the legion of demons. He was sitting there clothed and in his right mind, and they were afraid. [16]Those who had seen everything told them what had happened to the man possessed by the demons and what had happened to the pigs. [17]Then they began to plead with Jesus to depart from their country. [18]As Jesus was getting into the boat, the man possessed by the demons begged to go with Him. [19]Jesus did not let him, but said to him, "Go home to your family and tell them how much God has done for you and what compassion God has had on you." [20]So the man departed and began to tell in the Ten Towns everything that Jesus had done for him. And everyone marveled.

A FATHER PLEADS FOR LIFE FOR HIS DAUGHTER

[21]Jesus crossed over again by boat to the other side, and many people gathered around Him. While He was there by the sea, [22]one of the leaders of the synagogue, Jairus by name, saw Him and came and bowed down at His feet. [23]Jairus pleaded desperately, "My little daughter lies dying! Come and lay Your hands on her so that she will get well and live." [24]So Jesus went with him. Many people followed Him and crowded around Him.

A WOMAN IS HEALED BECAUSE OF HER FAITH

[25]A woman was there who had suffered hemorrhages for twelve years. [26]She had endured much from many physicians and had spent all her money, yet instead of getting better, she got worse. [27]She heard about Jesus and came up behind Him in the crowd and touched His cloak, [28]for she thought, "If I but touch His cloak, I will be healed." [29]Immediately the source of the hemorrhage dried up and she felt in her body that she was healed of the disease. [30]Jesus immediately knew that power had gone out of Him. He turned in the crowd and said, "Who touched My cloak?" [31]His disciples said, "You see the crowds thronging You; how can You ask, 'Who touched Me?'" [32]But He looked around to see who had done this. [33]Then the woman, frightened and trembling because she knew what had been done in her, came and fell down before Him and told Him the whole truth. [34]He said to her, "Daughter, your faith has made you whole. Go in peace and be healed of your affliction."

JESUS BRINGS THE DAUGHTER BACK TO LIFE

[35]While Jesus was still speaking, someone came from the synagogue leader's house and said, "Your daughter is dead. Why bother the Teacher any further?" [36]Hearing what was said, Jesus said to the synagogue leader, "Do not be alarmed, only believe." [37]He allowed no one to follow Him except Peter, James and John the brother of James. [38]Arriving at the house of the synagogue leader, He observed the clamor of those who were weeping and loudly wailing. [39]He went in and said to them, "Why are you crying and making such a commotion? The child is not dead, but sleeping." [40]They laughed scornfully at Him. But when He had put them all out, He took the father and mother of the child and those who were with Him and went in where the child was lying. [41]He took the child by the hand and said to her, "Talitha, koum," which means, "Awaken, little girl." [42]Immediately the girl stood up and walked. She was twelve years old. They were beside themselves with amazement. [43]Jesus ordered them not to tell anyone what had been done. Then He told them to give the girl something to eat.

THE PEOPLE OF NAZARETH ARE OFFENDED

6:1Jesus went from there to His home town with His disciples. 2On the Sabbath He began to teach in the synagogue, and many who heard Him were astonished. They wondered, "Where does He get this from? What is this wisdom that has been given Him so that even miracles like these are done by His hands? 3Is not this the carpenter, the son of Mary, and the brother of James, Joses, Judas and Simon? Are not His sisters here with us?" They were embarrassed by Him; 4but Jesus said to them, "Prophets are honored everywhere but in their home town and among their own relatives and in their own family." 5He was unable to do any miracles there, except lay His hands on a few sick people and heal them. 6And He marveled at their unbelief.

SIX PAIRS OF DISCIPLES ARE SENT OUT

Jesus went around to the villages teaching. 7Then He called the twelve, sent them out two by two and gave them authority over unclean spirits. 8He instructed them, "Take nothing for your journey except a walking stick. No bag for food, no bread, no coppers in your money belts. 9Wear sandals, but do not take an extra shirt. 10Whenever you enter a house, stay there until you leave that place. 11And wherever they do not receive you or listen to you, depart from there and shake the dust off your feet as a testimony against them." 12They went out and preached repentance, 13cast out many demons and anointed many of the sick with oil and healed them.

JOHN THE BAPTIST IS BEHEADED

14King Herod heard of this, for the name of Jesus had spread widely. He said, "John the Baptist has risen from the dead, and these miracles are done by him." 15Others said, "He is Elijah." Others said, "He is a prophet, like one of the prophets of old." 16When Herod heard this, he said, "He is John, whom I beheaded. He has risen from the dead." 17For Herod himself had given orders to have John bound and put in prison to please Herodias, his brother Philip's wife. Herod had married her, 18even though John had said to Herod, "It is not lawful for you to have your brother's wife." 19Herodias had a grudge against John and wanted to kill him; but she could not, 20for Herod feared John. He listened to John and protected him. He knew that John was a just and holy man, and he liked to listen to him. 21Herodias finally found an opportunity on Herod's birthday, when he gave a banquet for his political officials, military commanders and the leading citizens of Galilee. 22The daughter of Herodias came in and danced, and she pleased Herod and his guests. The king said to the girl, "Ask me for anything you want, and I will give it to you." 23And Herod swore to her, "Whatever you ask of me I will give you, up to half of my realm." 24She went and asked her mother, "What shall I ask for?" and her mother answered, "The head of John the Baptist." 25Immediately she hurried back in to the king and said, "I want you to give me the head of John the Baptist on a platter right now." 26The king was exceedingly sorry; but because of his oath and because of those who sat with him, he could not refuse her. 27So the king sent an executioner and ordered that John's head be brought. The executioner beheaded John in prison 28and brought his head on a platter and gave it to the girl. The girl gave it to her mother.

^{29}When John's disciples heard, they came and took his body and laid it in a tomb.

A LARGE CROWD IS FED WITH FIVE LOAVES AND TWO FISH

^{30}The apostles returned to Jesus and told Him all they had done and taught. ^{31}He said to them, "Come away by yourselves to a place where we can be alone and rest awhile." There were so many coming and going that they didn't even have time to eat. ^{32}They got into a boat and went away by themselves to an uninhabited place. ^{33}Many of the people who saw them leaving knew them and ran on foot from all the towns and got there ahead of them. ^{34}When Jesus got out of the boat, He saw a large crowd of people. He was moved with compassion toward them because they were like sheep without a shepherd. He began teaching them many things, ^{35}and the time slipped away. His disciples came to Him and said, "This is an uninhabited place and the time is slipping away. ^{36}Send them away so that they can go into the country villages around here and buy themselves something to eat." ^{37}Jesus said, "You give them something to eat." They said to Him, "It would take a lot of money to buy food for all these people." ^{38}He said to them, "How many loaves do you have? Go and see." When they found out, they said, "Five, and two fish." ^{39}Jesus told the people to sit in groups on the green grass, ^{40}so they sat down group by group in hundreds and in fifties. ^{41}Jesus took the five loaves and two fish, looked up toward heaven and blessed them. Then He broke the loaves and handed them to His disciples to serve to the people. He also divided the two fish among them all. ^{42}They all ate and were filled. ^{43}Afterward they picked up twelve baskets full of pieces of bread and fish. ^{44}More than five thousand had eaten.

JESUS WALKS ON WATER

^{45}Immediately Jesus made His disciples get into the boat to go ahead of Him across the sea to Bethsaida. Jesus remained there to send the people home. ^{46}After He sent them on their way, He went up on the mountain to pray. ^{47}When evening came, the boat was far out on the sea and Jesus was alone on the land. ^{48}He saw the disciples toiling at the oars, for the wind was against them. Around midnight He went out to them, walking on the sea. He would have passed by them, ^{49}but they saw Him and thought it was a ghost walking on the sea. They cried out, ^{50}for they saw Him and were terrified. Immediately He spoke to them. "Have courage," He said, "It is I. Don't be afraid." ^{51}Then He got into the boat with them, and the wind let up. They were utterly amazed, ^{52}for they did not understand about the loaves. Their hearts were hardened.

MANY ARE HEALED BY A TOUCH

^{53}When they had crossed over, they landed at Gennesaret and moored there. ^{54}When they got out of the boat, the people immediately recognized Jesus. ^{55}They ran throughout that whole region and began to carry the sick on mats to where they heard He was. ^{56}Wherever He went in the villages, the towns or the countryside, people laid their sick in the streets and begged Him to let them touch even the edge of His garment. And as many as touched Him were healed.

THE TRADITION OF HAND-WASHING

7:1The Pharisees and some of the scribes who had come from Jerusalem gathered around Jesus. 2They saw some of His disciples eating food with unclean, that is, with unwashed hands. 3The Pharisees and the Jews who keep the tradition of the elders do not eat without washing. 4When they come from the market, they do not eat unless they wash. And they hold to many other traditions they have received, such as the washing of cups, pots, bowls and tables. 5The Pharisees and scribes asked Him, "Why don't Your disciples follow the tradition of the elders more closely, instead of eating their food with unwashed hands?" 6Jesus answered, "How well Isaiah prophesied about you hypocrites! As it is written, 'This people honor Me with their words, but their hearts are far from Me. 7In vain they worship Me, for their teachings are the mere commandments of humans.' 8For you lay aside the commandments of God to follow the traditions of humans, such as the washing of pots and cups. 9You virtuously lay aside the commandments of God so that you can keep your own traditions. 10Moses said, 'Honor your father and your mother,' and 'Those who despise their father or mother must be put to death.' 11But you let them tell their needy father or mother, 'Anything of mine that you might have been helped by is Corban' (set apart for God), 12and you don't allow them to do any more for their needy father or mother. 13Thus you go against the word of God by the tradition you have handed down. And you do many other things like that."

JESUS EXPLAINS WHAT UNCLEAN REALLY MEANS

14Jesus again called the people to Him and said to them, "Listen to Me, all of you, and understand. 15Nothing from the outside can make you unclean by going into you. But the bad words and actions that come out of you, those are what make you unclean. 16If you have ears to hear, then listen."

17After He left the people and went into the house, His disciples asked Him about the parable. 18He said to them, "Are you so uncomprehending that you do not understand this? Whatever enters you from the outside cannot make you unclean, 19because it does not go into your mind but into your stomach and then passes out of the body." Thus Jesus declared all food "clean." 20He said, "It is what comes out of a person that makes a person unclean. 21For from within a person's mind come evil thoughts, adulteries, sexual sins, murder, 22theft, covetousness, perversity, deceit, lack of restraint, envy, verbal abuse, haughtiness and recklessness. 23All these evil things come from within and make a person unclean."

THE FAITH OF A NON-JEWISH WOMAN

24Jesus left that place and went to a house on the border of Tyre. He did not want anyone to know where He was, but He could not remain unnoticed. 25A woman whose young daughter had an unclean spirit heard of Him and came and fell at His feet. 26The woman was Gentile, a Syrophoenician by birth, and she begged Him to cast the demon out of her daughter. 27But Jesus said to her, "Let the children be filled first. It is not right to take the children's bread and toss it to the dogs." 28She answered, "Yes,

Rabbi, but the dogs under the table eat the children's crumbs." [29]He said to her, "Because you have said this, you may go. The demon is gone out of your daughter." [30]She went home and found her daughter lying on the bed. The demon was gone.

JESUS HEALS A DEAF-MUTE IN A GENTILE COUNTRY

[31]Jesus departed from the region of Tyre and Sidon and went to the Sea of Galilee by way of the Ten Towns. [32]They brought to Him a deaf man who could hardly talk, and they begged Jesus to touch him. [33]Jesus took him to one side away from the crowd and put His fingers into the man's ears. Then He spit and touched the man's tongue. [34]He looked up to heaven, sighed, and said to the man, "Ephphatha," which means, "Be opened." [35]Immediately his ears were opened, his tongue was loosened and he spoke plainly. [36]Jesus instructed them not to tell anyone. But the more He warned them, the more they told it everywhere. [37]The people were astonished beyond measure and said, "He does all things well; He makes the deaf hear, and those who can't talk speak!"

A CROWD IS FED WITH SEVEN LOAVES AND A FEW LITTLE FISH

[8:1]Once again a large crowd gathered. Since they had nothing to eat, Jesus called His disciples and said to them, [2]"I feel sorry for these people, for they have been with Me three days now and have nothing to eat. [3]If I send them away hungry to their homes, they will faint on the way, for some of them have come a long way." [4]His disciples said, "Where could anyone get food for all these people in this deserted place?" [5]Jesus asked them, "How many loaves do you have?" and they said, "Seven." [6]He told the people to sit down on the ground. Then He took the seven loaves, gave thanks, broke them and gave them to His disciples to serve to the people. [7]They also had a few small fish. He blessed the fish and told the disciples to serve them also. [8]The people ate and were filled, and the disciples picked up seven baskets full of broken pieces that were left. [9]More than four thousand had eaten. Jesus sent them on their way. [10]Then He got into a boat with His disciples and went to the district of Dalmanutha.

SOME OF THE LEADERS ASK JESUS FOR MORE PROOF

[11]The Pharisees came and began to question Him. To test Him, they asked Him for a sign from heaven. [12]He sighed deeply in His Spirit and said, "Why does this generation crave a sign? Truly I say to you, no sign will be given to this generation." [13]Then He left them.

JESUS CAUTIONS AGAINST FOLLOWING THE LEADERS

Getting into the boat again, He departed for the other side. [14]They had forgotten to bring bread, and they had only one loaf with them in the boat. [15]Jesus warned them, "Beware of the yeast of the Pharisees; be careful of the yeast of Herod." [16]They continued to discuss the fact that they had no bread. [17]Jesus knew what they were saying and asked, "Why are you talking about not having any bread? Do you not yet perceive or understand? Are your hearts hardened? [18]Having eyes, do you not see? And having ears, do you not hear? Don't you remember? [19]When I broke the five loaves among the five thousand, how many basketfuls of pieces did you pick up?" They said to Him, "Twelve." [20]"And when I broke the seven loaves for the four thousand, how many basketfuls of pieces did you pick up?" They said, "Seven." [21]Then He said to them, "How is it that you do not yet understand?"

A BLIND MAN NEEDS A SECOND TOUCH

[22]They went to Bethsaida, where some people brought a blind man and begged Jesus to touch him. [23]He took the blind man by the hand and led him out of town. Jesus put spit on the man's eyes and laid His hands on him. When He asked him if he saw anything, [24]the man looked up and said, "I see people. They look like trees walking." [25]Jesus put His hands on the man's eyes again. As the man opened his eyes wide, he was restored and saw everything clearly. [26]Jesus sent him to his home, saying, "Don't go into the town or tell anyone."

PETER AFFIRMS THAT JESUS IS THE MESSIAH

[27]Jesus and His disciples went on to the towns around Caesarea Philippi. On the way He asked His disciples, "Who do people say I am?" [28]They answered, "Some say John the Baptist, some Elijah, and others say one of the prophets." [29]"But who do you say I am?" He asked. Peter answered, "You are the Messiah." [30]Then He warned them not to tell anyone about Him.

JESUS REBUKES PETER

[31]He began to teach them that the Son of Humanity must suffer many things and be rejected by the elders, the chief priests and the scribes. Then He would be killed, but after three days would rise again. [32]Jesus freely spoke of these things. Then Peter took Jesus aside and began to disagree with Him. [33]Jesus turned around, looked at His disciples, and rebuked Peter. "Get behind Me, Satan. Your opinions are not from God, but are human."

THE IMPORTANCE OF THE SOUL

[34]Jesus called the people and His disciples and said to them, "If any of you want to come after Me, you must deny yourself and take up your cross and follow Me. [35]If you want to save your life, you must lose it; but if you lose your life for My sake and for the sake of the gospel, you will save it. [36]What profit is it to you if you gain the whole world and lose your soul? [37]What can you give in exchange for your soul? [38]If you are ashamed of Me and My words in this adulterous and sinful generation, the Son of Humanity will be ashamed of you when He comes in the glory of His heavenly Parent with the holy angels."

[9:1]And He said to them, "Truly I say to you, there are some of those standing here who will not taste death until they have seen God's realm come with power."

THE TRANSFIGURATION: JESUS BECOMES A BEING OF LIGHT

[2]Six days later Jesus took Peter, James and John and led them up a high mountain apart by themselves. Jesus was transfigured before them. [3]His clothes glistened bright and white like snow, whiter than anyone on earth could whiten them. [4]Elijah and Moses appeared and talked to Jesus. [5]Then Peter said to Jesus, "Rabbi, it is good for us to be here. Let us put up three tents, one for You, one for Moses and one for Elijah." [6]He didn't know what to say, for they were terribly afraid. [7]Then a cloud flowed over them, and a voice from the cloud said, "This is My beloved Son! Listen to Him!" [8]Suddenly, when they looked around, they saw no one with them any more but Jesus.

[9]As they came down the mountain, Jesus warned them not to tell anyone what they had seen until the Son of Humanity had been raised from the dead. [10]They kept the matter to themselves, but they questioned one another about what being raised from the dead meant. [11]Then they asked Him, "Why do the scribes say that Elijah must come first?" [12]Jesus replied, "Yes, it is true that Elijah comes first to put everything in order. But why is it written that the Son of Humanity must suffer many things and be despised? [13]But I tell you that Elijah has already come! And they did to him whatever they wanted, as it is written of him."

THE STUBBORN DEMON THAT WOULD NOT COME OUT

[14]When they got back to the other disciples, they saw a great crowd around them and the scribes questioning them. [15]As soon as the people saw Jesus, they were greatly relieved and ran to welcome Him. [16]Jesus asked the disciples, "What are you arguing with them about?" [17]Someone in the crowd answered, "Teacher, I brought my son to You. He has a spirit that prevents him from talking. [18]Whenever it seizes him, it convulses him. Then he foams at the mouth, gnashes his teeth and becomes stiff. I asked Your disciples to cast it out, but they could not." [19]Jesus said, "O faithless generation, how long must I be with you? How long must I put up with you? Bring him here to Me." [20]They brought the boy to Jesus. When the spirit saw Jesus, it immediately convulsed the boy and he fell on the ground, wallowing and foaming. [21]Jesus asked his father, "How long has he been falling like this?" He replied, "Since he was a little boy. [22]It often throws him into the fire or into the water to destroy him. If You can do anything, have compassion on us and help us." [23]"How can you say, 'If You can?'" Jesus asked. "All things are possible to those who believe." [24]Immediately the boy's father cried out, "I believe! Help me to fully believe!" [25]When Jesus saw that the crowd was running toward them, He rebuked the unclean spirit and said to it, "Dumb and deaf spirit, I command you to come out of him! And do not go into him any more!" [26]It cried out, convulsed him repeatedly and came out of him. The boy looked like he was dead, and many said, "He is dead." [27]But Jesus took him by the hand and helped him stand up.

[28]Jesus went into the house, and His disciples asked Him privately, "Why couldn't we cast it out?" [29]He said to them, "This kind will only come out by prayer."

THE DISCIPLES ARE AGAIN TOLD OF FUTURE EVENTS

[30]They departed from there and walked through Galilee. Jesus did not want anyone to know where they were [31]because He was teaching His disciples. He said, "The Son of Humanity will be betrayed into human hands and they will kill Him. After He has been killed, He will rise on the third day." [32]They did not understand what He was saying, and they were afraid to ask Him.

JESUS TEACHES ABOUT HUMILITY

[33]When they arrived at Capernaum, they went into a house. He asked them, "What was it you were talking about along the way?" [34]They remained silent, because along the way they had been wondering among themselves who would be the greatest. [35]He sat down, called the twelve and said to them, "Anyone who desires to be first must be last of all and the servant of all." [36]Jesus invited a child to stand among them.

He took the child in His arms and said to them, [37]"Whoever receives a child like this in My name receives Me. And whoever receives Me, receives not only Me, but the One who sent Me."

FURTHER TEACHINGS

[38]John said, "Teacher, we saw someone casting out demons in Your name, and we stopped him because he was not one of us." [39]Jesus said, "Do not forbid anyone. No one who does a miracle in My name can readily speak evil of Me. [40]Those who are not against us are for us. [41]Truly I say to you, whoever gives you a cup of water to drink in My name because you belong to the Messiah will certainly be rewarded. [42]But if any of you were to lead one of these little ones who believe in Me astray, it would be better for you to have a millstone hung around your neck and to be thrown into the sea. [43]If your hand leads you astray, cut it off. It is better for you to enter life maimed than to have two hands and to go into the fire of hell that will never be quenched, [44]where 'their worm will not die, and their fire will not be quenched.' [45]And if your foot leads you astray, cut if off. It is better for you to enter life limping than to have two feet and to be thrown into the fire of hell that will never be quenched, [46]where 'their worm will not die, and their fire will not be quenched.' [47]And if your eye leads you astray, pluck it out. It is better for you to enter God's realm with one eye than to have two eyes and to be thrown into the fire of hell, [48]where 'their worm will not die, and their fire will not be quenched.' [49]Everyone will be salted with fire. [50]Salt is good, but if the salt loses its saltiness, how can you make it salty again? Have salt within yourselves, and be at peace with one another."

THE PHARISEES TRY TO TRAP JESUS WITH A QUESTION ABOUT DIVORCE

[10:1]Jesus left there, went down to Judea and then crossed the Jordan. The people gathered to Him again, and as usual, He taught them. [2]The Pharisees came to Him and tested Him by asking, "Is it lawful for a man to divorce his wife?" [3]He answered, "What did Moses command you?" [4]They said, "Moses allowed us to write a bill of divorce and to send her away." [5]Jesus replied, "Moses wrote you this injunction because of the hardness of your hearts. [6]But from the beginning of creation, 'God made them male and female.' [7]'For this reason a man shall leave his mother and father and be bonded to his wife, [8]and the two shall become one flesh.' Thus they are no longer two, but one. [9]Therefore, what God has joined together, humans must not separate."

[10]Returning to the house, His disciples asked Him again about this. [11]He said to them, "If a man divorces his wife and marries another, he commits adultery. [12]And if a woman divorces her husband and marries another, she commits adultery."

CHILDREN: THE ESSENCE OF THE HEAVENLY REALM

[13]People brought young children to Jesus to have Him touch them, and His disciples rebuked those who brought them. [14]When Jesus became aware of this, He was displeased and said to them, "Let the little children come to Me and do not forbid them, for God's realm belongs to such as these. [15]Truly I say to you, if you cannot accept God's realm like a little child, you will never enter it." [16]Then He took the little children in His arms and put His hands on them and blessed them.

POSSESSIONS

[17]As Jesus was going out to the road, a man came running and knelt before Him. He asked, "Good Teacher, what must I do to inherit eternal life?" [18]Jesus said to him, "Why do you call Me good? No one is good but God. [19]You know the commandments: 'Do not murder, do not commit adultery, do not steal, do not lie about others, do not cheat, honor your father and mother.'" [20]He answered, "Teacher, all these I have kept since my youth." [21]Jesus looked at him and felt love for him. He said to him, "You still lack one thing. Go and sell everything you have and give to the poor; then you will have treasure in heaven. Then come and follow Me." [22]The man hated to hear this and went sadly away, for he had many possessions. [23]Jesus looked around and said to His disciples, "How hard it is for a rich person to enter God's realm." [24]The disciples were astonished at His words, but Jesus said again, "Children, how hard it is for some to enter God's realm. [25]It is easier for a camel to go through the eye of a needle than for a rich person to enter God's realm." [26]They were even more astonished and said among themselves, "Who then can be saved?" [27]Jesus looked at them and said, "With humans it is impossible, but not with God. With God all things are possible."

REWARDS OF DISCIPLESHIP

[28]Peter said to Him, "Look, we have left everything and followed You." [29]Jesus answered, "Truly I say to you, anyone who has left home or sisters or brothers or mother or father or children or lands for My sake and for the gospel [30]will get back a hundred times as much in this life - homes and sisters and brothers and mothers and children and lands, and with them persecutions - and in the world to come, eternal life. [31]But many who are first will be last, and the last first.

JESUS AGAIN TELLS HIS DISCIPLES THAT HE WILL BE KILLED

[32]They were on the road going up to Jerusalem, and Jesus was ahead of them. The disciples were overwhelmed, and those who followed were afraid. He again took the twelve and began to tell them what would happen to Him. [33]"Even now we are going up to Jerusalem. The Son of Humanity will be handed over to the chief priests and the scribes. They will condemn Him to death and hand Him over to unbelievers. [34]They will mock Him, whip Him, spit on Him and kill Him. On the third day He will rise again."

THE DISCIPLES LOOK FORWARD TO HEAVEN

[35]James and John, the sons of Zebedee, came to Him and said, "Teacher, we want You to do us a favor." [36]He said, "What do you want Me to do for you?" [37]They said, "Grant that we may sit on Your right and on Your left in Your glory." [38]Jesus said, "You don't know what you are asking. Can you drink the cup that I drink or be baptized as I shall be baptized?" [39]They said, "We can." Then Jesus said, "You will indeed drink from the cup that I drink and be baptized as I am baptized. [40]But to sit at My right and My left is not Mine to give, but is for whom it has been prepared."

[41]When the other ten heard about this, they were indignant with James and John. [42]But Jesus called them and said, "You know that those who are considered the rulers of the nations have power over them. Their great leaders exercise authority over them,

[43]but it must not be so among you. Whoever wishes to be great among you must be your servant, [44]and whoever wishes to be foremost among you must be the servant of all. [45]For even the Son of Humanity did not come to be served, but to serve and to give His life as a ransom for many."

BLIND BARTIMAEUS IS HEALED

[46]They came to Jericho. As He was leaving Jericho with His disciples and a great number of people, a blind beggar named Bartimaeus was sitting by the roadside. [47]When he heard that it was Jesus of Nazareth, he began to cry out and say, "Jesus! Son of David! Have mercy on me!" [48]Many told him to keep quiet, but he cried out even louder, "Son of David! Have mercy on me!" [49]Jesus stopped and said, "Call him." They called the blind man and said to him, "Have courage! Get up! He is calling you." [50]He threw aside his coat, jumped up and went to Jesus. [51]Jesus said to him, "What do you want Me to do for you?" The blind man said to Him, "Rabbi! I want to see." [52]Jesus said, "Go your way. Your faith has saved you." Immediately he received his sight and followed Jesus along the road.

JESUS BORROWS A DONKEY AND FULFILLS PROPHECY

[11:1]When they came near Jerusalem and were approaching Bethphage and Bethany on the Mount of Olives, He sent two of His disciples [2]and said to them, "Go to that village over there. As you enter it, you will find a colt tied there that has never been ridden. Untie it and bring it here. [3]If anyone asks you, 'Why are you doing this?' say, 'The Teacher has need of it and will send it back soon.'" [4]They went and found the colt tied by an outside door in the street. As they untied it, [5]some people standing there asked them, "Why are you untying that colt?" [6]They answered just as Jesus had told them to. The people let them take the colt, [7]and the disciples brought it to Jesus. They put their garments on it and He sat on it.

THE MESSIAH'S TRIUMPHANT ENTRY INTO JERUSALEM

[8]Many people spread their garments in the road, and others cut branches off trees and strewed them in the road. [9]Those who were ahead and those who followed cried out, "Hosanna! Blessed is He who comes in the name of Yahweh! [10]Blessed is the coming realm of our ancestor David! Hosanna in the highest!" [11]Jesus entered Jerusalem and went into the temple. He looked around at everything, but since it was late in the day, He went out to Bethany with the twelve.

THE UNFRUITFUL FIG TREE

[12]The next day as they were coming from Bethany, Jesus was hungry. [13]Seeing a fig tree in the distance with leaves on it, He went to see if perhaps He might find some fruit on it. When He got to it, He found nothing but leaves, because it was not the season for figs. [14]Jesus said to it, "May no one ever eat fruit from you again." His disciples heard this.

JESUS DRIVES THE MERCHANTS OUT OF THE TEMPLE

[15]When they got to Jerusalem, Jesus went into the temple and began driving out those who were selling and buying there. He overturned the tables of the money changers and the seats of those who sold doves, [16]and He would not allow anyone to carry anything through the temple courts. [17]He taught them, "Is it not written, 'My

house shall be called a house of prayer for all nations'? But you have made it a den of thieves." [18]The chief priests and scribes heard about this and continued to look for a way to kill Him. But they feared Him, because all the people marveled at His teachings. [19]When evening came, He went out of the city.

JESUS TEACHES ABOUT FAITH

[20]In the morning when they walked by they saw the fig tree dried up from the roots. [21]Peter remembered and said to Jesus, "Rabbi, look! The fig tree You cursed is withered!" [22]Jesus said to them, "Have faith in God! [23]Truly I say to you, if you say to this mountain, 'Get up and throw yourself into the sea,' and do not doubt in your heart, but believe that what you say will happen, you shall have whatever you say. [24]Therefore I say to you, whatever you ask in prayer, believe that you have received it and you will have it. [25]And when you are praying, if you have anything against anyone, forgive that person. Then your heavenly Parent will forgive you your offenses. [26]But if you do not forgive, your heavenly Parent will not forgive your offenses."

THE LEADERS QUESTION JESUS' AUTHORITY

[27]They returned to Jerusalem. As Jesus was walking in the temple, the chief priests, the scribes and the elders came to Him [28]and said to Him, "By what authority are You doing these things? Who gave You the authority to do these things?" [29]Jesus said, "I will ask you a question also. If you answer Me, then I will tell you by what authority I do these things. [30]The baptism of John: was it from heaven or from humans? Answer Me!" [31]They talked it over among themselves and said, "If we say, 'From heaven,' He will say, 'Why then didn't you believe him?' [32]But if we say, 'From humans....'" (They feared the people, for everyone considered John a prophet.) [33]So in answer they said to Jesus, "We don't know." Then Jesus said to them, "Neither will I tell you by what authority I do these things."

THE VINEYARD AND THE UNGRATEFUL TENANTS

[12:1]Then Jesus began to speak to them in parables. "A landowner planted a vineyard, set a hedge around it, dug a place for a winepress, built a watchtower, rented the vineyard out to some tenants and then went to a far country. [2]At harvest time the owner sent a servant to the tenants for a share of the fruit from the vineyard. [3]But the tenants seized the servant, beat him and sent him away empty-handed. [4]Then the owner sent another servant to them. They insulted him and wounded him in the head. [5]The owner sent another, and they killed him. The owner sent many others, and they beat some and killed some. [6]The owner had only one left to send, a beloved son. The owner sent him to them last, thinking, 'They will respect my son.' [7]But the tenants said among themselves, 'This is the heir! Come, let's kill him; then the inheritance will be ours.' [8]So they killed him and threw him out of the vineyard. [9]Now what will the owner of that vineyard do? The owner will come and kill those tenants and give the vineyard to others. [10]Surely you have read this Scripture: 'The stone the builders rejected has become the head of the corner. [11]This was God's doing, and it is marvelous in our eyes.'"

[12]The Jewish leaders knew that He had spoken the parable against them, and they considered ways to arrest Him. But they feared the people, so they left Him and went

away.

THE LEADERS TRY TO TRAP JESUS INTO OPPOSING CAESAR

[13]Later they sent some Pharisees and Herodians to Him to trap Him with a question. [14]They came to Him and said, "Teacher, we know that You are impartial and unswayed by people. You don't look at mere appearances, but teach the ways of God honestly. Tell us, is it lawful to pay taxes to Caesar or not?" [15]Jesus was aware of their hypocrisy and said, "Why do you tempt Me? Bring Me a coin and let Me see it." [16]They brought it and He asked, "Whose likeness and inscription are on it?" "Caesar's," they said. [17]Then Jesus said to them, "Give to Caesar the things that are Caesar's and to God the things that are God's." They marveled at His reply.

JESUS GIVES THE SADDUCEES A GLIMPSE INTO HEAVEN

[18]Then the Sadducees, who say there is no resurrection, came and asked Him, [19]"Teacher? Moses wrote that if a man dies and leaves a widow without children, his brother should marry the widow and raise up children for his brother. [20]Once there were seven brothers. The first married and died and left no children. [21]The second married the widow and died and left no children. And the third did the same. [22]All seven married her and left no children. Last of all, the woman died also. [23]Now at the resurrection when the dead come to life, whose wife will she be, since all seven married her?" [24]Jesus answered and said to them, "You stray from the truth because you don't know the Scriptures or the power of God. [25]When the dead rise, they do not marry, but are like the angels in heaven. [26]As to whether the dead are awakened, have you never read in the Book of Moses how God spoke to Moses from the burning bush? God said, 'I am the God of Abraham, the God of Isaac and the God of Jacob.' [27]God is not the God of the dead, but the God of the living. You have strayed far from the truth."

THE MOST IMPORTANT COMMANDMENT

[28]One of the scribes who had listened to them reasoning together came forward. Perceiving that Jesus had answered them well, he asked Him, "Which is the most important commandment of all?" [29]Jesus answered, "The most important of all the commandments is, 'Hear, O Israel: Yahweh our God is one God. [30]You shall love Yahweh your God with all your heart, with all your soul, with all your mind and with all your strength.' [31]The second is like it: 'You shall love others as you love yourself.' There is no commandment greater than these." [32]The scribe said to Him, "Well said, Teacher; You have spoken the truth. For there is one God, and no other God exists. [33]And to love God with all your heart and with all your mind and with all your strength and to love your neighbor as yourself is more important than all burnt offerings and sacrifices." [34]Jesus saw that he had answered prudently, and He said to him, "You are not far from God's realm." After that, no one dared ask Him any more questions.

THE MESSIAH

[35]As Jesus taught in the temple, He asked, "Why do the scribes say that the Messiah is the son of David? [36]For David himself, inspired by the Holy Spirit, said, 'Yahweh said to God: Sit at My right hand till I make Your enemies Your footstool.' [37]If David himself calls the son 'God,' how can He be David's son?" The common people listened to all this with sweet attentiveness.

BEWARE OF HYPOCRISY

[38]As He taught them, He said, "Beware of the scribes, who love to stroll about in long robes and receive salutations in the marketplaces. [39]They love the chief seats in the synagogues and the places of honor at banquets. [40]But they cheat widows out of their homes, and for a show make long prayers. They will receive the greater punishment."

JESUS PRAISES A POOR WIDOW

[41]Jesus sat there opposite the temple treasury and watched the people putting coins into the chest. Many who were rich put in much. [42]Then a certain poor widow came along and put in two small coins. [43]Jesus called His disciples together and said to them, "Truly I say to you, this poor widow has put more into the treasury than all those others. [44]For they put in out of their abundance, but she is poor and put in all she had to live on."

JESUS FORETELLS THE DESTRUCTION OF THE TEMPLE

[13:1]As they left the temple, one of His disciples said to Him, "Teacher, look! What huge stones and wonderful buildings!" [2]Jesus answered and said to him, "Look closely at these great buildings, for they will all be thrown down. Not one stone will be left upon another."

FUTURE TRIBULATIONS

[3]As He sat on the Mount of Olives opposite the temple, Peter, James, John and Andrew asked Him privately, [4]"Tell us, when will these things happen? What will be the sign that all these things are about to take place?" [5]Jesus answered, "Watch out that no one deceives you. [6]For many will come in My name saying, 'I Am,' and will deceive many. [7]When you hear of wars and rumors of wars, do not be troubled. Such things must be, but the end is yet to come. [8]For nation will rise against nation and country against country. There will be earthquakes and famines in many places. Those will be just the beginnings of the birth pains. [9]But look carefully to yourselves, for they will hand you over to councils and you will be beaten in synagogues. You will stand before powerful rulers for My sake as a witness to them. [10]The good news must first be told before all nations. [11]When they arrest you and take you away, do not be anxious in advance about what to say. Whatever is given to you in that hour, speak it; for it will not be you speaking, but the Holy Spirit. [12]Friend will hand over friend to death, and the parents their children. Children will rise up against parents and cause them to be put to death. [13]You will be hated by everyone because of My name, but those who endure to the end will be saved.

[14]"When you see the abomination of desolation standing where it ought not to be (let the reader understand), then those who are in Judea must flee to the mountains. [15]Those who are on the housetops must not go down to save anything out of their homes. [16]Those who are in the field must not turn back to pick up their coats. [17]Woe to pregnant women and to those with nursing babies in those days. [18]Pray that your flight is not in the winter. [19]For in those days there will be tribulation such as has not been from the beginning of God's creation until this time, and never will be again. [20]If God had not shortened those days, no one would be saved. But for the sake of the

special ones whom God has chosen, God has shortened those days. [21]"Then, if anyone says to you, 'Look, here is the Messiah!' or 'Look, there He is!' do not believe it. [22]For false Messiahs and false prophets will appear and show signs and wonders to lead astray, if possible, even the chosen. [23]So be careful. Remember, I have told you everything before it happens.

THE SPECTACULAR RETURN OF JESUS

[24]"In those days, and after that tribulation, the sun will be darkened, the moon will not give its light, [25]the stars will fall from the sky and the powers in the sky will be shaken. [26]Then they will see the Son of Humanity coming in the clouds with great power and glory. [27]He will send His angels and gather His chosen from the four winds, from the depths of the earth and to the heights of heaven.

THE TIME OF JESUS' RETURN

[28]"Now learn a lesson from the fig tree: When its branch is yet tender and its leaves start to grow, you know that summer is near. [29]So, when you see these things come to pass, you will know that it is near, at the very door. [30]Truly I say to you, this generation will not pass away until all this has happened. [31]The sky and the earth will pass away, but My words will not pass away. [32]But of that day and that hour no one knows, neither the angels in heaven, nor the Son. Only My Parent in heaven knows. [33]Be careful! Watch and pray, for you do not know when that time will come.

BE READY!

[34]"When homeowners go on a journey, before leaving the house they give authority to their servants, assign everyone their work and command the watchers to watch. [35]Watch therefore! For you do not know when the owner of the house will return. It may be late in the day or at midnight or before dawn or at sunrise. [36]Don't let the owner of the house come suddenly and find you sleeping! [37]And what I say to you, I say to everyone: Watch!"

THE LEADERS CONTINUE TO LOOK FOR A WAY TO KILL JESUS

[14:1]It was two days before the Passover and the Feast of Unleavened Bread. The chief priests and scribes were seeking a way to arrest Jesus secretly and put Him to death, [2]but they said, "Not during the Feast, lest the people riot."

MARY ANOINTS JESUS WITH AN EXPENSIVE PERFUME [John 12:3]

[3]Jesus was in Bethany at the home of Simon the leper. As He sat there, a woman came with an alabaster jar of pure nard, a very expensive perfume. She broke the jar and poured the perfume on His head. [4]Some who were there said indignantly to one another, "What is the purpose of this waste? This perfume [5]could have been sold for more than three hundred silver coins and the money given to the poor." And they were indignant at her. [6]Jesus said, "Let her alone. Why do you trouble her? She has done a beautiful thing for Me. [7]The poor you have with you always; and whenever you wish, you may help them. But you will not always have Me with you. [8]She did what she could. She came beforehand to anoint My body for burial. [9]Truly I say to you, wherever this good news is proclaimed throughout the whole world, what she has done will be told in memory of her."

JUDAS GOES TO THE LEADERS AND OFFERS TO BETRAY JESUS

[10]Then Judas Iscariot, one of the twelve, went to the chief priests and offered to betray Jesus to them. [11]They were pleased when they heard this and promised to give him money. Then Judas looked for an opportunity to betray Him.

PREPARATIONS FOR THE PASSOVER

[12]On the first day of the Feast of Unleavened Bread, the day when the Passover lambs were killed, His disciples asked Him, "Where do You want us to make preparations for You to eat the Passover?" [13]He sent two of His disciples, saying to them, "Go into the city and you will meet a man carrying a jar of water. Follow him. [14]When he enters a house, say to the householder, 'The Teacher asks: Where is the guest room where I may eat the Passover with My disciples?' [15]He will show you a large upper room, furnished and prepared. Make it ready for us there." [16]His disciples went out and entered the city and found everything as Jesus had said. And they prepared the Passover.

JESUS SHOWS WHO WILL BETRAY HIM

[17]In the evening, Jesus came with the twelve. [18]As they sat and ate, Jesus said, "Truly I say to you, one of you who is eating with Me will betray Me." [19]This made them sad, and they said to Him one after another, "Is it I?" [20]He replied, "It will be one of you twelve who dip bread into the dish with Me. [21]The Son of Humanity will go as it is written of Him, but woe to that man by whom the Son of Humanity is betrayed. It would be better for that man if he had never been born."

THE PASSOVER

[22]As they were eating, Jesus took bread and blessed it. Then He broke it and gave it to them, saying, "Take and eat; this is My body." [23]Then He took the cup and gave thanks. He gave it to them and they all drank from it. [24]Jesus said to them, "This is My blood of the covenant which is poured out for many. [25]Truly I say to you, I will not drink again from the fruit of the vine until that day I drink it anew in God's realm." [26]Then they sang a psalm and went out to the Mount of Olives.

JESUS WARNS THEM ALL ABOUT THE COMING NIGHT

[27]Jesus said to them, "You will all forsake Me this night, for it is written, 'I will strike the shepherd and the sheep will be scattered.' [28]But after I am raised, I will go ahead of you into Galilee."

PETER IS TOLD THAT HE WILL DENY JESUS THREE TIMES

[29]Peter said to Jesus, "Although everyone else leaves You, I will not." [30]Jesus said to him, "Truly I say to you, this very night before the rooster crows twice you will deny Me three times." [31]But Peter strongly protested, "Even if I die with You, I will not deny You." And they all said the same.

THE GARDEN OF GETHSEMANE

[32]Jesus went with His disciples to a place called Gethsemane. He said to them, "Sit here while I pray." [33]Then He took Peter, James and John with Him. He became distressed and greatly troubled [34]and said to them, "My Soul is overwhelmed with sorrow to the point of death. Stay here and keep awake." [35]He went a little farther, fell

to the ground and prayed that, if possible, the hour might pass Him by. [36]He said, "O My dear Parent, all things are possible for You! Please take this cup from Me. Nevertheless, not My will but Yours be done." [37]Then He went back and found them sleeping. He said to Peter, "Simon, are you sleeping? Couldn't you keep awake for one hour? [38]Keep watch and pray that you will not be tested. The spirit is willing, but the flesh is weak." [39]Again He went away and prayed, saying the same words. [40]When He returned, He found them asleep again, for their eyes were heavy. They did not know what to say to Him. [41]He went back the third time and said to them, "Sleep now and rest? It is enough. The hour has come. Look! The Son of Humanity is betrayed into the hands of sinners. [42]Get up! Let us go! Look! Here comes My betrayer." [43]He was still speaking when Judas, one of the twelve, came. With him was a large crowd armed with swords and clubs. They had been sent by the chief priests, scribes and elders.

JESUS IS ARRESTED TO FULFILL GOD'S PLAN

[44]The betrayer had arranged this signal: "The one I kiss is the one. Arrest Him and lead Him away under guard." [45]As soon as he came, he went straight to Jesus and said, "Rabbi!" and kissed Him. [46]Then they took hold of Jesus and arrested Him. [47]One of those standing there drew a sword and struck a servant of the high priest, cutting off his ear. [48]Jesus said to them, "Did you have to come out with swords and clubs to capture Me as though I were a thief? [49]I was with you daily in the temple and you didn't arrest Me. But the Scriptures must be fulfilled."

[50]Then His disciples all forsook Him and fled. [51]A certain young man wearing only a linen garment had followed Him. They took hold of the young man, [52]but he left the linen garment behind and fled from them naked.

JESUS ON TRIAL BEFORE THE UNBELIEVERS

[53]They led Jesus away to the high priest. All the chief priests and scribes and elders were assembled there. [54]Peter followed Jesus at a distance and went as far as the courtyard of the high priest. He sat with the servants and warmed himself at the fire. [55]The chief priests and the whole council sought testimony against Jesus so that they could put Him to death, but they found none. [56]Many gave false testimony against Him, but their testimonies did not agree. [57]Then some others stood up and gave false testimony against Him, saying, [58]"We heard Him say, 'I will destroy this temple made with hands, and within three days I will build another not made with hands.'" [59]Yet these witnesses did not agree either. [60]Then the high priest stood up in the council and asked Jesus, "Aren't You going to answer? What are these charges against You?" [61]But Jesus remained silent and did not answer. Then the high priest asked Him, "Are You the Messiah, the Son of the Blessed One?" [62]Jesus answered, "I Am. And you will see the Son of Humanity sitting at the right hand of the Almighty and coming on the clouds of heaven." [63]Then the high priest tore his clothes and said, "Why do we need any further witnesses? [64]You have heard this blasphemy! What's your decision?" They all judged Him to be worthy of death. [65]Then some began to spit on Him. They blindfolded Him, beat Him with their fists and said to Him, "Prophesy!" The guards also struck Him.

PETER DENIES KNOWING JESUS THREE TIMES

[66]Peter was down in the courtyard. One of the high priest's servant girls came [67]and saw Peter warming himself. She looked at him and said, "You also were with Jesus of Nazareth." [68]He denied it, saying, "I don't know what you're talking about." He went out into the entrance. [69]The servant girl saw him again and said to those standing there, "He is one of them." [70]Again Peter denied it. A little later those standing there said to Peter, "Surely you are one of them, for you are a Galilean." [71]Then he began to curse and swore an oath, saying, "I don't know the man you are talking about." [72]Immediately the rooster crowed, and Peter remembered what Jesus had said to him: "Before the rooster crows, you will deny Me three times." And he broke down and wept.

JESUS IS TAKEN TO THE ROMAN GOVERNOR

[15:1]Early in the morning, the chief priests consulted with the elders and the scribes and the whole council. They bound Jesus, led Him away and handed Him over to Pilate. [2]Pilate asked Him, "Are You the king of the Jews?" "So you say," Jesus answered. [3]Then the chief priests made accusations against Him, but He did not answer. [4]Pilate again questioned Him, saying, "You won't answer anything? Look at all of the accusations against You!" [5]But Jesus still did not answer, and Pilate was amazed.

THE UNBELIEVERS WANT JESUS CRUCIFIED

[6]Now at Passover it was the custom to release one prisoner, whomever the people requested. [7]Among the rioters in the prison was one named Barabbas, who had committed murder in the uprising. [8]The crowd came up and asked Pilate to release a prisoner, as was the custom. [9]Pilate answered them, "Do you want me to release the king of the Jews to you?" [10]Pilate knew that the chief priests had handed Jesus over out of envy, [11]but the chief priests incited the crowd to ask for the release of Barabbas. [12]Pilate asked, "What do you want me to do with the one you call the king of the Jews?" [13]They cried out, "Crucify Him!" [14]Then Pilate asked, "Why? What harm has He done?" But they cried out even louder, "Crucify Him!" [15]And so Pilate, wanting to appease the people, released Barabbas to them. Then he had Jesus whipped and handed Him over to be crucified.

THE SOLDIERS MOCK JESUS FOR CLAIMING TO BE A KING

[16]The soldiers took Jesus into the palace and the whole band of soldiers gathered around Him. [17]They clothed Him with purple and put a crown of thorns on Him. [18]Then they began to salute Him, saying, "Hail, King of the Jews!" [19]They struck Him on the head with a stick, spit on Him and bent their knees and bowed down to Him. [20]When they finished mocking Him, they took off the purple robe and put His own clothes back on Him. Then they led Him out to crucify Him.

SIMON OF CYRENE IS FORCED TO CARRY THE CROSS

[21]Simon of Cyrene, the father of Alexander and Rufus, was coming in from the country. As he passed by, they forced him to carry Jesus' cross. [22]They brought Jesus to the place called Golgotha, which is also called Calvary.

JESUS IS CRUCIFIED AS THE PROPHET PREDICTED

[23]They offered Him wine mixed with myrrh to drink, but He didn't take it. [24]When they crucified Him, they divided up His clothing, casting lots to decide see what each would take. [25]It was mid-morning when they crucified Him. [26]The words of His accusation read: THE KING OF THE JEWS. [27]They crucified two thieves with Him, one on His right and one on His left. [28]Thus the Scripture was fulfilled that said, "He was counted among the lawless ones." [29]Those who passed by shook their heads and spoke abusively to Him, saying, "Aha! So You would destroy the temple and rebuild it in three days! [30]Save Yourself and come down from the cross!" [31]The chief priests and the scribes also mocked Him. Among themselves they said, "He saved others, but He can't save Himself. [32]If He is the Messiah and the King of Israel, let Him descend from the cross now so that we may see and believe." Those who were crucified with Him also reviled Him.

JESUS YIELDS UP HIS SPIRIT

[33]At noon, darkness came over the whole land for three hours. [34]At mid-afternoon Jesus cried out with a loud voice, "Eloi, Eloi, lama sabachthani?" which means, "My God, My God, why have You forsaken Me?" [35]Some of those standing there heard Him and said, "Listen! He is calling Elijah." [36]One ran and filled a sponge with vinegar, put it on a stick and gave it to Him to drink, saying, "Wait! Let's see if Elijah comes to take Him down." [37]But Jesus cried out with a loud voice and yielded up His Spirit. [38]At that moment, the veil of the temple was torn in two from top to bottom. [39]When the centurion who stood facing Jesus saw the way He died, he said, "Truly, this man was the Son of God."

THE WOMEN WHO CARED FOR JESUS

[40]Some women were there watching from a distance. Among them were Mary Magdalene, Salome and Mary (the mother of James the younger and Joses.) [41]When Jesus was in Galilee, these women had been His followers and looked after Him, as did many other women who came up to Jerusalem with Him.

JESUS IS BURIED IN A NEW TOMB BY A COURAGEOUS LEADER

[42]Evening came. Because it was Preparation Day, the day before the Sabbath, [43]Joseph of Arimathea, a respected member of the council who was also waiting for God's realm, boldly went to Pilate and asked for the body of Jesus. [44]Pilate marveled that He was already dead. He called the centurion and asked if Jesus was already dead. [45]When the centurion confirmed the fact, Pilate gave Joseph permission to take the body. [46]Joseph bought linen, took Jesus down, wrapped Him in the linen, laid Him in a tomb hewn out of the rock and rolled a stone across the entrance of the tomb. [47]Mary Magdalene and Mary the mother of Joses saw where He was laid.

THE WOMEN DISCOVER THE EMPTY TOMB

[16:1]When the Sabbath was past, Mary Magdalene, Mary the mother of James, and Salome bought spices so that they could go and anoint Him. [2]Before dawn on the first day of the week, they went to the tomb as the sun was rising. [3]They asked each other, "Who will roll the stone away from the entrance of the tomb for us?" [4]But when they looked, they saw that the huge heavy stone had been rolled away.

AN ANGEL TALKS TO THE WOMEN

[5]Entering the tomb, they saw a youth sitting on the right side, clothed in a white garment. They were astonished, [6]but the youth said to them, "Don't be astonished. You are looking for Jesus of Nazareth, who was crucified. He has risen; He is not here. Look, here is the place where they laid Him. [7]Now go tell His disciples and Peter that He goes before you to Galilee. There you will see Him, as He told you." [8]Then they began to tremble. They quickly went out and fled from the tomb, for they were beside themselves with fear. They did not say anything to anyone.

THE FOLLOWING DOES NOT APPEAR IN THE OLDEST MANUSCRIPTS

THE RESURRECTED JESUS APPEARS TO MARY MAGDALENE

[9]After Jesus was raised before dawn on that first day of the week, He appeared first to Mary Magdalene, out of whom He had cast seven demons. [10]She went and told those who had been with Him. They were mourning and weeping. [11]When they heard that He was alive and that she had seen Him, they did not believe it. [12]Later He appeared with a changed appearance to two of them as they walked in the country. [13]They went and told the others, but the others did not believe them either.

JESUS COMMISSIONS THE ELEVEN

[14]Still later He appeared to the eleven as they were eating. He chided them for their unbelief and stubborn refusal to believe those who had seen Him after He was awakened. [15]He said to them, "Go into all the world and tell the good news to the whole creation. [16]Those who believe and are baptized will be saved, but those who do not believe will be judged. [17]These signs shall follow those who believe: In My name they will cast out demons, they will speak in new tongues, [18]they will pick up snakes, if they drink anything deadly it will not hurt them and when they lay their hands on the sick they will recover."

JESUS IS TAKEN UP TO HEAVEN

[19]After Jesus spoke to the disciples, He was taken up to heaven and sat at the right hand of God. [20]Then the disciples went out and told about these things everywhere. God helped them and confirmed the message with the miracles that followed.

Luke

THE BELOVED PHYSICIAN [Colossians 4:14] WRITES TO A FRIEND

^{1:1}Whereas many have endeavored to set in order an account of those things that have been accomplished among us ²as they were passed on to us by those who were from the beginning eyewitnesses and guardians of the message, ³it seemed good that I also, having carefully followed all these things from the first, should write to you in my turn, most excellent Theophilus, ⁴so that you know the truth concerning the things about which you have been instructed.

THE EVENTS LEADING TO THE BIRTH OF JOHN THE BAPTIST

⁵In the days when Herod was king of Judea, there was a certain priest named Zechariah of the Abijah division. His wife was a descendant of Aaron. Her name was Elizabeth. ⁶They were both virtuous in God's sight, walking blamelessly in all the commandments and ordinances of God. ⁷Elizabeth and Zechariah had been unable to have children, and both of them were quite old.

⁸Once when Zechariah was serving as priest before God in the succession of his division ⁹according to the custom of the priesthood, he was chosen by lot to enter the temple to burn incense. ¹⁰As the whole crowd of people prayed outside at the time of the incense offering, ¹¹an angel of God appeared to him, standing at the right side of the altar of incense. ¹²When Zechariah saw the angel, he trembled and was seized with fear. ¹³But the angel said to him, "Don't be afraid, Zechariah, for your prayer has been heard. Your wife Elizabeth will have a son, and you are to name him John. ¹⁴You will have joy and gladness, and many will rejoice at his birth, ¹⁵for he will be great in the sight of God. He must never drink wine or strong drink, and he will be filled with the Holy Spirit, even from within his mother's womb. ¹⁶Many of the people of Israel will return to Yahweh their God because of him. ¹⁷He will go before Yahweh in the spirit and power of Elijah to turn the hearts of the parents to their children and the disobedient to the wisdom of the righteous to make ready a people prepared for God." ¹⁸Zechariah said to the angel, "How can I be sure of this? My wife and I are both quite old." ¹⁹The angel answered, "I am Gabriel! I stand in the presence of God. I have been sent to speak to you and tell you this good news. ²⁰But now you will be silent and unable to speak until the day this is fulfilled, because you did not believe my words, which will be fulfilled in their time."

²¹The people waited for Zechariah and wondered why he took so long in the temple. ²²When he came out, he could not speak, but he motioned to them with his

hands. He remained speechless, and they realized that he had seen a vision in the temple. [23]When the days of his service were completed, he returned home. [24]During that time Elizabeth conceived, and remained secluded for five months. She said, [25]"What God has done for me will make my name a blessing among the people."

THE ANGEL GABRIEL APPEARS TO MARY

[26]In Elizabeth's sixth month, the angel Gabriel was sent from God to a town in Galilee named Nazareth [27]with a message for a girl named Mary. She was engaged to a man named Joseph of the house of David. [28]The angel came into her room and said, "Rejoice, O favored one, for God is with you!" [29]Mary was startled by the angel's words and wondered what kind of greeting this might be. [30]"Do not be afraid, Mary," the angel said, "for you have found favor with God. [31]Listen! You will become pregnant and bear a son, and you shall name Him Jesus. [32]He will be great and will be called the Son of the Most High. God will give Him the throne of His ancestor David. [33]He will reign over the house of Jacob forever, and His realm will never end." [34]Mary said to the angel, "How can this be, since I am a virgin?" [35]The angel replied, "The Holy Spirit will come upon you, and the power of the Most High will overshadow you. Therefore the Holy One who will be born will be called the Son of God. [36]You will also find that your cousin Elizabeth has conceived a son in her old age. She whom people said couldn't have children is in her sixth month, [37]for with God nothing is impossible." [38]Mary said, "I am God's servant. May it happen as you have said." Then the angel left her.

MARY VISITS ELIZABETH AND HEARS A PROPHECY

[39]Mary quickly got ready and went to a town in the mountains of Judah. [40]She went to the house of Elizabeth and Zechariah and greeted Elizabeth. [41]When Elizabeth heard Mary's greeting, the baby leaped within her, and Elizabeth was filled with the Holy Spirit. [42]She exclaimed with a loud voice, "Blessed are you among women, and blessed is the child within you. [43]What an honor this is to me, that the mother of my God should come to me! [44]As soon as I heard the sound of your greeting, the baby inside me leaped for joy. [45]How blessed you are because you believe that what was spoken to you from God will happen!"

MARY'S PROPHECY

[46]Mary said, "My soul magnifies God, [47]my spirit rejoices in God my Savior. [48]God has looked upon this insignificant servant, and from now on all generations will call me blessed. [49]Almighty God has done great things for me; holy is God's name. [50]God shows mercy from generation to generation to those who are reverent. [51]God has shown great strength and has scattered those who have proud thoughts in their hearts. [52]God has brought down the mighty from their thrones and has exalted those in humble circumstances. [53]God has filled the hungry with good things and sent the rich away empty. [54]God has always helped Israel, God's servant, [55]as was promised to our ancestor Abraham and his descendants forever."

[56]Mary stayed with Elizabeth about three months and then returned to her home.

THE BIRTH OF JOHN THE BAPTIST

57The time finally came, and Elizabeth gave birth to a son. 58Her neighbors and relatives heard that God had shown great compassion to her, and they rejoiced with her. 59On the eighth day they came to circumcise the child. They were going to name him Zechariah after his father, 60but his mother spoke up and said, "No, he will be named John." 61They said to her, "But none of your relatives has this name." 62Then they made signs to the baby's father, asking what he wanted to name him. 63He asked for a writing tablet and wrote, "His name is John," and they were all astonished.

ZECHARIAH IS ENABLED TO SPEAK

64Immediately Zechariah's mouth was opened, his voice returned and he praised God. 65Awe came upon all those who lived around them, and all that had happened was talked about throughout the hills of Judea. 66All who heard of it remembered it in their hearts and said, "What sort of child will this be?" For surely the hand of God was upon him.

ZECHARIAH'S PROPHECY ABOUT THE MESSIAH TO COME

67John's father Zechariah was filled with the Holy Spirit and prophesied: 68"Blessed be the God of Israel, who has visited and redeemed the people. 69God has raised up a mighty savior for us in the house of God's servant David 70as was promised through the mouth of the holy prophets from of old. 71Therefore we will be saved from our enemies and from the power of all those who hate us. 72God has dealt mercifully with our ancestors by remembering the holy covenant, 73the oath God swore to our ancestor Abraham. 74God has rescued us from the power of our enemies, so that we may serve God fearlessly 75in holiness and righteousness before God all the days of our life. 76And you, my child, will be called the prophet of the Most High; for you will go on before God to prepare the way 77by giving the knowledge of salvation to God's people through the forgiveness of their sins. 78Because of the tender mercy of our God, the sunrise from on high will visit us 79to give light to those who sit in darkness and the shadow of death and to guide our feet into the way of peace."

80The child grew and became strong in spirit. He lived in the wilderness until the time he appeared to Israel.

JESUS IS BORN IN BETHLEHEM

2:1Now it came to pass in those days that a decree went out from Caesar Augustus that the whole empire must be registered. 2This was the first registration while Quirinius was governor of Syria. 3All the people went to be registered in the town of their birth. 4Joseph went up from the town of Nazareth in Galilee to Bethlehem, the town of David in Judea, since he was of the house and lineage of David. 5He went to be registered with Mary, his betrothed, and she was great with child. 6While they were there the time came for her to have her baby 7and she gave birth to a son, her firstborn. They wrapped Him in swaddling cloths and laid Him in a manger because there was no place for them in the inn.

AN ANGEL TELLS THE SHEPHERDS ABOUT JESUS

[8]In the countryside nearby there were shepherds out in the fields, keeping watch over their flock by night. [9]An angel of God stood before them, the glory of God shone around them and they were exceedingly afraid. [10]The angel said to them, "Do not be afraid! Look! I bring you good tidings of great joy which will be for all people. [11]For to you this day in the town of David is born a Savior who is God's Messiah. [12]This will prove to you that what I say is true: You will find the baby wrapped in cloth and lying in a manger." [13]Suddenly there was with the angel a multitude of the heavenly host praising God and saying, [14]"Glory to God in the highest, and on earth peace to the people whom God has favored." [15]As the angels went away from them into heaven, the shepherds said to one another, "Let us go to Bethlehem and see this thing that has taken place which God has made known to us." [16]They quickly went and found Mary and Joseph and the baby lying in a manger. [17]After they saw Him, they told what the angel had said to them about this child. [18]All who heard it were amazed by what the shepherds told them. [19]Mary pondered all these things in her heart and remembered them. [20]The shepherds returned, glorifying and praising God; for all that they had heard and seen was just as the angel had told them.

JESUS IS PRESENTED IN THE TEMPLE

[21]When eight days had gone by and it was time for Him to be circumcised, He was named Jesus, which is the name the angel gave Him before He was conceived. [22]When the days of their purification according to the law of Moses were accomplished, Mary and Joseph took Him to Jerusalem to present Him to God, [23]for it is written, "Every firstborn male is sanctified to Yahweh." [24]They also went to offer a sacrifice in accordance with what it says in God's law: "A pair of turtledoves or two young pigeons."

GOD ALLOWS SIMEON TO SEE THE MESSIAH

[25]There was a man in Jerusalem whose name was Simeon. He was godly and devout and waiting for the Consolation of Israel. The Holy Spirit was upon him, [26]and it had been revealed to him by the Holy Spirit that he would not see death before he had seen God's Messiah. [27]Simeon came by the Spirit into the temple courts, and when the parents brought in the child Jesus to do for Him as was the custom of the law, [28]Simeon took Jesus in his arms and praised God, saying, [29]"O God, now your servant is free to depart in peace as You promised, [30]for my eyes have seen Your salvation [31]which You have prepared for all people to see: [32]A light to enlighten the nations and the glory of Your people Israel." [33]Joseph and Mary were amazed at the things Simeon said about Jesus. [34]Simeon blessed them and said to Mary His mother, "This child is destined to cause the fall and rise of many in Israel and to be a sign that will be spoken against [35]so that the thoughts of many hearts will be revealed. And a sword will pierce through your soul also."

GOD ALLOWS ANNA TO SEE JESUS

[36]There was also the prophet Anna, the daughter of Phanuel of the tribe of Asher. She was of a great age, having lived with a husband for seven years after they were married. [37]She was now a widow of eighty-four years and never departed from the

temple, but worshiped night and day with fasting and prayer. [38]She came up to them just then, gave thanks to God and spoke about Jesus to all those who were looking for the redemption of Jerusalem.

[39]When Mary and Joseph had performed everything required by God's law, they returned to Galilee to their own town of Nazareth. [40]The child grew and became strong. He was filled with wisdom, and the favor of God was upon Him.

TWELVE YEAR OLD JESUS IN THE TEMPLE

[41]Every year Mary and Joseph went to Jerusalem for the Feast of Passover. [42]When Jesus was twelve years old, they went up to Jerusalem as usual for the Feast. [43]When the Feast was over, they started for home. The boy Jesus stayed behind in Jerusalem, but Joseph and Mary did not know it. [44]Supposing Him to be in the caravan, they traveled a day's journey. Then they started looking for Him among their relatives and acquaintances. [45]When they could not find Him, they went back to Jerusalem to search for Him. [46]After three days they found Him in the temple sitting among the teachers, listening to them and asking them questions. [47]Everyone who heard Him was astonished at His understanding and His answers. [48]When His parents saw Him, they were astonished. His mother said to Him, "Son, why have You done this to us? Look how anxiously Your father and I have searched for You." [49]He said to them, "Why were you searching for Me? Didn't you know that I must be about My heavenly Parent's business?" [50]They didn't understand what He meant when He said this. [51]But He went down to Nazareth with them and was obedient to them.

His mother kept all these things in her heart. [52]And Jesus increased in wisdom, in stature and in favor with God and with humans.

JOHN THE BAPTIST PREPARES THE WAY

[3:1]In the fifteenth year of the reign of Tiberius Caesar, when Pontius Pilate was governor of Judea, Herod was ruler of Galilee, Herod's brother Philip was ruler of Iturea and the region of Trachonitis, Lysanias was ruler of Abilene [2]and Annas and Caiaphas were the high priests, the word of God came to John the son of Zechariah in the wilderness. [3]Then he went out into all the country around the Jordan telling about a baptism of repentance for the forgiveness of sins [4]as it is written in the book of the words of Isaiah the prophet: "The voice of one crying out in the wilderness, 'Prepare the way for Yahweh! Make straight paths for our God. [5]Every valley shall be filled and every mountain and hill shall be brought low. The crooked will be made straight and the rough ways made smooth. [6]And all flesh will see the salvation of God.'"

[7]John said to the crowds who came out to be baptized by him, "You brood of snakes! Who warned you to flee from the wrath to come? [8]Bear fruit worthy of repentance! Do not even begin to say to yourselves, 'We have Abraham as our ancestor,' for I say to you that God is able to raise up children for Abraham from these stones. [9]Even now the ax is laid to the root of the trees. Every tree that does not bear good fruit will be cut down and thrown into the fire." [10]The people asked him, "What then should we do?" [11]John replied, "Those who have two coats should share with those who have none, and those who have food should do likewise."

[12]Tax collectors also came to be baptized, and they said to him, "Teacher, what

should we do?" [13]He said to them, "Extract no more than you are supposed to." [14]Some soldiers asked him, "What should we do?" He said to them, "Intimidate no one, don't accuse anyone falsely and be content with your wages."

[15]The people were anticipating the Messiah, and everyone wondered about John. Could he be the Messiah? [16]John said, "I baptize you with water, but One who is mightier than I is coming. I am not worthy to unloose the strap of His sandals. He will baptize you with the Holy Spirit and with fire. [17]His winnowing fork is in His hand and He will thoroughly winnow His threshing floor. He will gather His wheat into the granary, but the chaff He will burn with unquenchable fire." [18]And He called the people near to hear the good news.

[19]But Herod the ruler, when he was reproved by John for marrying Herodias, his brother's wife, and for many other evil deeds, [20]added to his crimes by shutting John up in prison.

JESUS IS BAPTIZED AND A VOICE IS HEARD FROM HEAVEN

[21]When all the people had been baptized, and when Jesus was baptized and was praying, heaven was opened [22]and the Holy Spirit descended in a bodily shape like a dove upon Him. A voice came from heaven, saying, "You are My dearly loved Son. In You I am well pleased."

THE ANCESTRY OF JESUS

[23]Jesus was about thirty years old when He began to teach. He was the son, so people thought, of Joseph, who was descended from [24-38]Heli, Matthat, Levi, Melchi, Jannai, Joseph, Mattathias, Amos, Nahum, Esli, Naggai, Maath, Mattathias, Semein, Josech, Joda, Joanan, Rhesa, Zerubbabel, Shealtiel, Neri, Melchi, Addi, Cosam, Elmodam, Er, Joshua, Eliezer, Jorim, Matthat, Levi, Simeon, Judah, Joseph, Jonam, Eliakim, Melea, Menna, Mattatha, Nathan, David, Jesse, Obed, Boaz, Sala, Nahshon, Amminadab, Admin, Aram, Hezron, Perez, Judah, Jacob, Isaac, Abraham, Terah, Nahor, Serug, Reu, Peleg, Eber, Shelah, Cainan, Arphaxad, Shem, Noah, Lamech, Methuselah, Enoch, Jared, Mahalaleel, Cainan, Enos, Seth, Adam and God.

THE DEVIL TEMPTS JESUS

[4:1]Jesus returned from the Jordan full of the Holy Spirit and was led by the Spirit into the wilderness. [2]For forty days He was tempted by the devil. He ate nothing during those days, and when they were over, He was hungry. [3]The devil said to Him, "If You are God's Son, command this stone to become bread." [4]Jesus replied, "It is written, 'Humans shall not live by bread alone.'" [5]Then the devil took Him up and showed Him all the countries of the world in a moment of time. [6]The devil said to Him, "I will give You control of all this and all the glory, for it has been given to me, and I give it to anyone I please. [7]If You will worship me, it will all be Yours." [8]Jesus answered, "It is written, 'You must worship and serve only God!'" [9]The devil took Him to Jerusalem and set Him on top of the temple. The devil said to Him, "If You are God's Son, throw Yourself down, [10]for it is written, 'God will command the angels concerning You to guard You, [11]and in their hands they will hold You up, lest You dash your foot against a stone.'" [12]Jesus answered, "It is written, 'You shall not tempt your God.'" [13]Having finished every temptation, the devil departed from Him until another time.

THE PEOPLE OF CAPERNAUM WELCOME JESUS [Matthew 4:12]

[14]Jesus returned to Galilee in the power of the Spirit, and news of Him went out through the whole region. [15]He taught in their synagogues and everyone thought well of Him.

THE PEOPLE OF NAZARETH TRY TO THROW JESUS OVER A CLIFF

[16]He went to Nazareth where He had been brought up, and, as was His custom, went into the synagogue on the Sabbath day and stood up to read. [17]The scroll of the prophet Isaiah was handed to Him, and He opened the scroll and found the place where it is written: [18]"The Spirit of God is upon Me, because God has anointed Me to tell the good news to the poor. God has sent Me to heal the brokenhearted, proclaim liberty to the captives and recovery of sight to the blind, to set free those who are oppressed [19]and to proclaim the year of God's favor." [20]Jesus closed the scroll, gave it back to the attendant and sat down. The eyes of all those in the synagogue were on Him, [21]and He said to them, "Today this Scripture was fulfilled as you listened to it." [22]They were amazed at the gracious words that came out of His mouth and all spoke well of Him. They said, "Can this be Joseph's son?"

[23]Jesus said to them, "You will undoubtedly quote this proverb to Me: 'Physician, heal yourself. What we have heard that You did in Capernaum, do also here in Your own town.' [24]Truly I say to you, no prophet is accepted in the prophet's own town. [25]Truly I tell you, many widows were in Israel in the days of Elijah when the heavens were shut up for three and a half years and great famine was throughout the land. [26]Elijah was sent to none of them, but only to a widow in Zarephath of Sidon. [27]And many lepers were in Israel in the days of Elisha the prophet, but none of them were healed except Naaman the Syrian."

[28]All those in the synagogue were filled with wrath when they heard these things. [29]They jumped up, drove Him out of town and led Him to the brow of the hill on which the town was built, intending to throw Him over the cliff. [30]But He walked through their midst and went His way.

JESUS CASTS OUT A DEMON AT CAPERNAUM

[31]Jesus went down to Capernaum, a town in Galilee, and taught them on the Sabbath. [32]They were astonished at His teaching, for His words were spoken with authority. [33]In the synagogue there was a man who had the spirit of an unclean demon, and it cried out with a loud voice, [34]"What do You want with us, Jesus of Nazareth? Have You come to destroy us? I know who You are - the Holy One of God!" [35]Jesus rebuked the spirit, saying, "Be quiet, and come out of him!" The demon threw the man down among them and came out of him without hurting him. [36]They were all amazed and said among themselves, "What a word this is! For with authority and power He commands the unclean spirits! And they come out!" [37]And His fame went out everywhere in that country.

JESUS HEALS PETER'S MOTHER-IN-LAW

[38]Jesus left the synagogue and went to Peter's house. Peter's mother-in-law had a high fever, and they asked Him to help her. [39]He stood over her and rebuked the fever and it left her. She immediately got up and ministered to them.

AN OLD PROPHECY IS FULFILLED [Matthew 8:17]

40As the sun was setting, people with all kinds of diseases were brought to Jesus, and He laid His hands on each one of them and healed them. 41Demons came out of many, crying out, "You are the Son of God!" He rebuked them and did not allow them to speak, for they knew that He was the Messiah.

JESUS PRAYS, THEN ANNOUNCES THE GOOD NEWS

42At daybreak Jesus departed to a secluded place. The people searched for Him, and when they found Him, they urged Him not to leave them. 43But He said to them, "I must tell the good news of God's realm in other towns as well. That is why I was sent." 44And He preached in the synagogues of Judea.

THE MIRACULOUS CATCH OF FISH

5:1One day as Jesus stood by the Sea of Galilee with the people pressed around Him to hear the message of God, 2He saw two boats on the seashore. The fishers had left them there while they cleaned their nets. 3He got into one of the boats, the one that was Peter's, and asked him to put out a little from the shore. Then He sat down and taught the people from the boat. 4When He finished speaking, He said to Peter, "Launch out into the deep and let down your nets for a catch." 5Peter said to Him, "Rabbi! We toiled all night and caught nothing! But since You say so, I will let down the nets." 6When they did so, they netted such a large number of fish that their nets were about to break. 7They beckoned their partners in the other boat to come and help them. They came and filled both boats so full that they began to sink. 8When Simon Peter saw this, he fell at Jesus' knees and said, "Depart from me, Rabbi, for I am a sinful man." 9Peter and all who were with him were astonished at the catch of fish they had taken, 10and so were Simon's partners James and John, the sons of Zebedee. Jesus said to Simon, "Do not be afraid; from now on you will catch humans." 11They brought their boats to shore, forsook everything and followed Him.

JESUS HEALS A LEPER AND HIS FAME GROWS

12When Jesus was in a certain town, a man came who was covered with leprosy. Seeing Jesus, he fell to the ground and begged Him, "Rabbi! If You are willing, You can make me clean!" 13Jesus put out His hand, touched him and said, "I am willing; be clean." Immediately the leprosy left him. 14Jesus said, "Don't tell anyone, but go show yourself to the priest. Offer for your cleansing what Moses commanded as proof that you are healed." 15Yet His fame spread continually, and great multitudes came to hear and be healed by Him of their weaknesses. 16But He would often withdraw to an isolated place and pray.

A PARALYTIC IS LOWERED THROUGH THE ROOF

17One day as Jesus was teaching, Pharisees and teachers of the law were sitting there who had come from all the towns of Galilee, Judea and Jerusalem. Power from God was there for Him to heal people. 18Just then some men brought a paralyzed boy on a mat, and they looked for a way to bring him into the house to lay him before Jesus. 19When they couldn't find a way to bring him in because of the crowd, they went up on the roof and let him and the mat down through the roof into the middle of the crowd in front of Jesus. [20]When Jesus saw their faith, He said to the boy, "Your sins are forgiven!" [21]Then the scribes and the Pharisees began to wonder, "Who is this? He speaks blasphemy! Who can forgive sins but God alone?" [22]Jesus knew their thoughts and said to them, "What are you thinking in your hearts? [23]Which is easier to say, 'Your sins are forgiven you,' or to say, 'Rise up and walk'? [24]But so you may know that the Son of Humanity has power on earth to forgive sins, I now say to this paralytic: Get up, pick up your mat and go home." [25]Immediately he got up, picked up his mat and went to his home glorifying God. [26]Everyone was amazed and glorified God. They were filled with awe and said, "We have seen things today that are hard to understand."

A TAX COLLECTOR IS CHOSEN AS A DISCIPLE

[27]After this, Jesus went out and saw a tax collector named Levi sitting at the tax collector's booth. Jesus said to him, "Follow Me." [28]Levi abandoned everything, got up and followed Jesus.

THERE IS A TIME TO FAST

[29]Levi prepared a sumptuous feast in his home for Jesus, and there were many rich tax collectors and others who sat down with them. [30]The Pharisees and their scribes complained to His disciples, "Why do you eat and drink with tax collectors and sinners?" [31]Jesus answered them, "It is not those who are healthy who need a physician, but those who are sick. [32]I did not come to call the righteous to repent, but sinners." [33]They asked Him, "Why do the disciples of John often fast and pray, and so do the Pharisees, but Your disciples eat and drink?" [34]Jesus said to them, "Can you make the wedding guests fast while the bridegroom is with them? [35]But the days are coming when the bridegroom will be taken away from them. In those days they will fast."

THE PARABLE OF THE WINESKINS

[36]Jesus told them a parable: "No one tears a piece of cloth from a new garment to patch an old one, because the new garment would be ruined and the patch from the new would not match the old. [37]And no one puts new wine into old wineskins, because the new wine would burst the wineskins and be spilled and the wineskins would be ruined. [38]New wine must be put into new wineskins. [39]And no one after drinking old wine desires new. 'The old is better,' they say."

JESUS HAS AUTHORITY OVER THE SABBATH

[6:1]One Sabbath Jesus walked through some grain fields. His disciples picked off heads of grain, rubbed the hulls off with their hands and ate them. [2]Some Pharisees said to them, "Why do you do what is unlawful on the Sabbath?" [3]Jesus answered them, "Have you not read what David did when he and those who were with him were hungry? [4]He went into the house of God and ate the showbread and gave it to those who were with him, even though only the priests were allowed to eat it." [5]Then Jesus said to them, "The Son of Humanity has authority over the Sabbath."

JESUS IS CONDEMNED FOR HEALING ON THE SABBATH

⁶On another Sabbath Jesus went into the synagogue and taught. A man was there whose right hand was withered. ⁷The scribes and Pharisees watched Him to see if He would heal on the Sabbath so that they might find an accusation against Him. ⁸Jesus knew their thoughts and said to the man with the withered hand, "Get up and stand among them," and he got up and stood. ⁹Then Jesus said to them, "I will ask you something. Is it lawful on the Sabbath to do good or to do evil, to save life or to destroy?" ¹⁰After looking at each one of them, He said to the man, "Stretch out your hand." The man did so, and his hand was restored. ¹¹Then they were filled with rage and discussed among themselves what to do to Jesus.

AFTER PRAYING ALL NIGHT, JESUS CHOOSES TWELVE

¹²On one of those days Jesus went out to a mountain to pray and continued all night in prayer to God. ¹³When it was daylight, He summoned His disciples and chose twelve of them, whom He also called apostles: ¹⁴Simon (whom He called Peter) and Andrew his brother, James and John, Philip and Bartholomew, ¹⁵Matthew and Thomas, James (the son of Alphaeus) and Simon (who was called the Zealot), ¹⁶Judas (the son of James) and Judas Iscariot, who became the traitor.

JESUS TELLS THE GOOD NEWS AND HEALS THE SICK

¹⁷Jesus came down with them and stood on a level place. A large group of His disciples and a great multitude of people from all Judea and Jerusalem and the seacoast of Tyre and Sidon were there. They had come to hear Him and be healed of their diseases. ¹⁸Those who were harassed by unclean spirits came and were healed. ¹⁹The whole multitude sought to touch Him, for power was coming out of Him and healing them all.

THE GREAT TEACHINGS

²⁰Jesus looked at His disciples and said, "Blessed are you if you are poor, for God's realm is yours. ²¹Blessed are you who hunger now, for you will be filled. Blessed are you who weep now, for you will laugh. ²²Blessed are you when others hate you, when they exclude you and slander you and reject your very name as evil because of the Son of Humanity. ²³Rejoice in that day and leap for joy! Look! Great is your reward in heaven! Their ancestors treated the prophets the same way. ²⁴But woe to you who are rich, for you have received your consolation. ²⁵Woe to you who are full, for you will hunger. Woe to you who laugh now, for you will mourn and weep. ²⁶Woe to you when everyone speaks well of you, for that is how their ancestors spoke of the false prophets.

²⁷"But I say to you who hear: Love your enemies. Do good to those who hate you. ²⁸Bless those who curse you and pray for those who abuse you. ²⁹If anyone strikes you on the cheek, offer the other also. If anyone takes your coat, do not withhold your shirt. ³⁰Give to anyone who asks you; and if anyone takes your goods, do not ask for them back. ³¹Do for others as you wish that they would do for you. ³²If you love those who love you, what credit is that to you? Even sinners love those who love them. ³³If you do good to those who do good to you, what credit is that to you? Even sinners do

that. [34]And if you lend only to those who can repay you, what credit is that to you? For sinners lend to sinners, expecting to be paid back as much. [35]But love your enemies. Do good and lend, expecting nothing in return. Then your reward will be great and you will be children of the Most High, for God is kind to the ungrateful and the wicked. [36]Therefore be compassionate, even as your Parent in heaven is compassionate.

[37]"Do not judge, and you will not be judged. Do not condemn, and you will not be condemned. Forgive, and you will be forgiven. [38]Give, and it will be given to you; good measure, pressed down, shaken together and running over will be given into your hands. For with the same measure that you measure will it be measured to you in return."

[39]Then Jesus told them a parable: "Can the blind lead the blind? Will they not both fall into the ditch? [40]The student is not above the teacher; but when you are mature you will be like your teacher. [41]Why do you stare at the speck of sawdust in your friend's eye but pay no attention to the log in your own eye? [42]How can you say to your friend, 'Let me pull the speck out of your eye,' when you cannot see the log in your own eye? You hypocrite! First take the log out of your own eye, and then you can see clearly to take the speck out of your friend's eye.

[43]"A good tree does not bear bad fruit, nor does a bad tree bear good fruit. [44]Every tree is known by its fruit. One does not gather figs from a thorn bush or grapes from a bramble bush. [45]Good people bring that which is good out of the good stored up in their hearts, and evil people bring that which is evil out of the evil stored up in their hearts. For from the abundance of the heart the mouth speaks.

[46]"Why do you call Me Rabbi when you refuse to do what I say? [47]I will show you what the person is like who comes to Me and listens to My words and does them: [48]You will be like a person building a house, who dug down deep and laid the foundation on a rock. When the flood rose, the river burst against that house but could not shake it, for it was built upon a rock. [49]But the one who hears and does nothing is like the person who built a house upon the ground without a foundation. When the river burst against that house, it was immediately swept away; and great was the destruction of that house."

A FOREIGNER'S SERVANT IS HEALED FROM A DISTANCE

[7:1]When Jesus had finished saying all this to the people, He went to Capernaum. [2]A certain centurion had a servant who was dear to him, and the servant was sick and about to die. [3]When the centurion heard that Jesus was there, he sent some Jewish elders to ask Jesus to come and heal his servant. [4]When they came to Jesus, they earnestly requested that He do this, saying, "This man deserves Your help [5]because he loves our nation and has built us a synagogue." [6]Jesus went with them. He was not far from the house when the centurion sent friends to Him to say, "Rabbi, do not trouble Yourself, for I am not worthy to have You come under my roof. [7]Therefore I did not think myself worthy to come to You. But say a word and my servant will be healed. [8]For I too am a person placed under authority, having soldiers under me. I say to one, 'Go,' and he goes; and to another, 'Come,' and he comes; and to my servant, 'Do this,' and my servant does it." [9]Jesus was amazed when He heard this. He turned to the people following Him and said, "I tell you, I have never found anyone with this much faith, not even in Israel." [10]When the centurion's friends returned to the house, they found the servant well.

A WIDOW'S DEAD SON IS BROUGHT BACK TO LIFE

[11]Soon afterward, Jesus and His disciples went to a town called Nain. Many people went with Him. [12]As He approached the gate of the town, He saw a dead man being carried out. He was the only son of his mother, and she was a widow. Many people from the town were with her. [13]When Jesus saw her, He felt compassion for her and said to her, "Do not weep." [14]He went and touched the bier, and those who carried it stopped. Jesus said, "Young man, I say to you, wake up!" [15]The dead man sat up and began to speak, and Jesus gave him to his mother. [16]Then all were filled with awe and glorified God, saying, "A great prophet has risen among us," and, "God has visited the people." [17]This story about Jesus spread throughout Judea and over all the region.

JOHN THE BAPTIST ASKS IF JESUS IS REALLY THE MESSIAH

[18]John's disciples told John about all these things. Calling two of his disciples, [19]John sent them to Jesus to ask, "Are You the One who is to come, or should we look for another?" [20]The men went to Jesus and said, "John the Baptist sent us to You to ask, 'Are You the One who is to come, or should we look for another?'" [21]At that very hour Jesus was healing many who were sick or in pain or had evil spirits, and many who were blind were given their sight. [22]Jesus answered, "Go and tell John what you have seen and heard: The blind see, the lame walk, lepers are cleansed, the deaf hear, the dead are raised and the poor are told the good news. [23]And blessed is the one who is not offended by Me."

[24]When John's disciples had departed, Jesus began to speak to the crowds about John. "What did you go out into the wilderness to see? A reed shaken by the wind? [25]No? Then what did you go out to see? A man dressed in fine clothes? Beware! Those who are splendidly dressed and living in luxury are in the courts of rulers. [26]What then did you go out to see? A prophet? Yes, I tell you, and more than a prophet. [27]This is the one of whom it is written: 'Watch! I send My messenger ahead of You to prepare Your way before You.' [28]For I say to you, that of all those who have ever been born, there is no one greater than John the Baptist. Yet the one who is least in God's realm is greater than he." [29]When all of the people and the tax collectors heard this, they acknowledged God, having been baptized with the baptism of John. [30]But the Pharisees and lawyers, by refusing to be baptized by John, rejected God's purpose for themselves.

[31]Jesus said, "To what can I compare the people of this generation? What are they like? [32]They are like children sitting in the marketplace and calling to one another, 'We piped the flute for you, and you did not dance. We mourned, and you did not lament.' [33]John the Baptist came neither eating bread nor drinking wine and you say, 'He has a demon.' [34]The Son of Humanity came eating and drinking and you say, 'Look at this

gluttonous man - a wine drinker and a friend of tax collectors and sinners.' [35]But wisdom is justified by what its followers do."

A DESPISED WOMAN IS HONORED BY JESUS

[36]A Pharisee named Simon invited Jesus to eat with him, so He went to the Pharisee's house and sat down to eat. [37]When a certain sinful woman found out that Jesus was eating at the Pharisee's house, she brought an alabaster jar of perfumed oil [38]and stood behind Him at His feet weeping. She began to wash His feet with her tears and wipe them with her hair. Then she kissed His feet and anointed them with the perfumed oil. [39]The Pharisee who had invited Him saw all this, and he thought, "If this man were a prophet, He would know who and what kind of woman this is who is touching Him, for she is a sinner." [40]Jesus answered him, "Simon, I have something to say to you." "What is it, Teacher?" Simon asked. [41]"A certain moneylender had two debtors. One owed five hundred pieces of silver and the other fifty. [42]Neither of them could pay him back, so he forgave them both. Tell Me now, which one will love him more?" [43]Simon answered, "I suppose the one who was forgiven more." Jesus said, "You have judged correctly." [44]Then He turned toward the woman and said to Simon, "Do you see this woman? I came into your home, and you gave Me no water to wash My feet, but she washed My feet with tears and wiped them with her hair. [45]You gave Me no kiss, but this woman has not ceased kissing My feet from the time I came here. [46]You did not anoint My head with oil, but this woman has anointed My feet with perfumed oil. [47]Therefore I tell you that her sins, which are many, are forgiven, for she loves much. But the one who is forgiven little, loves little." [48]Then Jesus said to her, "Your sins are forgiven." [49]Those who sat there by Him began to say among themselves, "Who is this who even forgives sins?" [50]But He said to the woman, "Your faith has saved you. Go in peace."

THE WOMEN WHO HELPED JESUS

[8:1]After this, Jesus went on through many towns and villages, telling the good news about God's realm. The twelve were with Him, [2]and also certain women who had been healed of evil spirits and infirmities: Mary, called Magdalene, from whom seven demons had gone out; [3]Joanna, the wife of Chuza (Herod's steward); Susanna, and many others who provided for Him out of their own resources.

THE PARABLE OF THE SEEDS

[4]Many people from the surrounding towns gathered around Jesus, and He told this parable, [5]"A farmer went out to sow seed. As the farmer sowed, some fell by the roadside and was trampled on and the birds of the air ate it up. [6]Some fell on rocky ground, and as soon as it sprouted, it withered because it lacked moisture. [7]Some fell among thistles, and the thistles grew up with it and choked it. [8]But some fell on good ground and grew up and yielded a hundred times as much." Then He said, "If you have ears to hear, then listen!"

THE REASON FOR PARABLES

[9]When His disciples asked Him what the parable meant, [10]He said, "To you it is given to understand the mysteries of God's realm; but to others they are in parables,

so that 'seeing they might not see, and listening they might not understand.'

JESUS EXPLAINS THE PARABLE OF THE SEEDS

[11]"The parable means this: The seed is the message of God. [12]Those by the roadside are the ones who hear; but then the devil comes and takes the message out of their hearts, lest they believe and be saved. [13]Those on rocky ground are those who hear the message and receive it with joy and believe for a while. But they have no root and in the time of temptation they fall away. [14]Those among thistles are those who hear, but as they grow, they are choked by the cares and riches and pleasures of this life, and they bring no fruit to maturity. [15]But those on the good ground are those with an honest and good heart, who hear the message, grab hold of it and by steadiness of purpose bring forth fruit.

MORE TEACHINGS AND AN ADMONITION TO LISTEN

[16]"No one who lights a lamp covers it up or puts it under a bed, but puts it on a lampstand so that those who come in can see the light. [17]Nothing is hidden that will not be revealed, nor is there any secret that will not be made public. [18]Therefore be careful how you listen. For those who have will be given more. But from those who do not have will be taken even that which they think they have."

JESUS' REAL FAMILY

[19]His mother and His brothers arrived, but they could not get near Him because of the crowds. [20]Someone said to Him, "Your mother and Your brothers are standing out there and want to see You." [21]He replied, "My mother and My brothers are those who hear the message of God and do it."

JESUS CALMS THE STORM

[22]One day He got into a boat with His disciples and said to them, "Let's go over to the other side of the sea." They set out, [23]and as they plunged through the waves, He fell asleep. Just then a windstorm came down the sea and they were being swamped. They were in grave danger; [24]so they woke Jesus, saying, "Rabbi! Rabbi! We are perishing!" He woke up and rebuked the wind and the raging water. Then the wind let up and it became calm. [25]He said to them, "Where is your faith?" Astonished and afraid, they said to one another, "Who can this be? Even the winds and water obey Him!"

THE MAN WHO WAS CHAINED IN A CAVE

[26]They arrived in the country of the Gadarenes, which is across from Galilee. [27]As He stepped ashore, He was met by a man from the town who was possessed by demons. For a long time he had not worn clothes or lived in a house, but lived in the tombs. [28]He fell down before Jesus and cried out with a loud voice, "Jesus! Son of the Most High God! What have I to do with You? I beg You not to torment me!" [29]For Jesus had commanded the unclean spirit to come out of the man. It had often seized him, and though he was bound with chains and fetters and kept under guard, he broke the chains and was driven by the demon into lonesome places. [30]Jesus asked him, "What is your name?" "Legion," he replied, for many demons had entered him. [31]The demons begged Him not to send them into the bottomless pit. [32]There was a large herd of pigs feeding on the hillside, and they pleaded with Him to be allowed to enter

them. Jesus gave them permission. [33]The demons went out of the man and entered the pigs, and the herd ran down the steep bank into the sea and drowned. [34]When those who fed them saw what had happened, they fled and told everyone in the town and in the country. [35]The people came out to see what had happened and found the man from whom the demons had departed sitting at the feet of Jesus, clothed and in his right mind; and they were afraid. [36]Those who had seen everything told the people how the man who had been possessed by demons had been saved. [37]Then all the people from the country of the Gadarenes pleaded with Jesus to depart from them, for they were seized with great fear. So Jesus got into the boat and went back. [38]The man from whom the demons had gone out begged to go with Jesus, but Jesus sent him away, saying, [39]"Return to your home and tell the great things that God has done for you." So he went throughout the town telling of the great things that Jesus had done for him.

A FATHER PLEADS FOR HIS DAUGHTER'S LIFE

[40]When Jesus returned, the crowd welcomed Him, for they were all waiting for Him. [41]A man named Jairus, a leader of the synagogue, came and bowed down at Jesus' feet. He begged Jesus to come to his house, [42]for his only daughter, who was about twelve years old, was dying. The crowds were pressing hard against Jesus as He went.

A WOMAN IS HEALED BECAUSE OF HER FAITH

[43]Just then a woman who had suffered hemorrhages for twelve years and who had spent all her income on physicians but could not be healed [44]came up behind Him and touched the edge of His cloak. Immediately her bleeding stopped. [45]Jesus said, "Who touched Me?" When they all denied it, Peter said, "Rabbi! The multitude crowds and presses You." [46]Jesus said, "Someone touched Me; I felt power go out of Me." [47]When the woman saw that she could not go unnoticed, she came trembling and fell down at His feet. She told Him in front of all the people why she had touched Him and how she was immediately healed. [48]Jesus said to her, "Daughter, your faith has made you whole. Go in peace."

JESUS BRINGS THE DAUGHTER BACK TO LIFE

[49]While Jesus was still speaking, someone came from the synagogue leader's house and said to him, "Your daughter is dead. There is no need to bother the Teacher." [50]But Jesus heard and said to the girl's father, "Don't be afraid. Just believe, and she will be saved." [51]He went to the house and allowed no one to go in with Him except Peter, James, John and the father and mother of the girl. [52]Everyone was weeping and mourning for the girl, but Jesus said, "Stop wailing! She is not dead, but sleeping." [53]They laughed scornfully at Him, because they knew that she was dead. [54]But He took her by the hand and said, "Child, awaken!" [55]and her spirit came back. She immediately stood up, and Jesus told them to give her something to eat. [56]Her parents were astonished. Then He told them not to tell anyone what had happened.

JESUS SENDS OUT THE TWELVE TO TEACH, HEAL AND CAST OUT DEMONS

[9:1]Jesus called His twelve disciples together and gave them power and authority over all demons and to heal diseases. [2]He sent them out to tell the good news about

God's realm and to heal the sick. [3]He said to them, "Take nothing for your journey, neither walking cane, nor knapsack, nor bread, nor money, nor an extra shirt. [4]Whatever house you enter, stay there until you leave. [5]If they will not accept you, then leave that town and shake the dust off your feet as a warning to them." [6]So they departed and went through the towns, telling the good news and healing everywhere.

HEROD WONDERS ABOUT JESUS

[7]Now Herod, the ruler of Galilee, heard about all that was happening. He was perplexed, because it was said by some that John had been raised from the dead, [8]by some that Elijah had appeared and by others that one of the prophets of old had risen again. [9]Herod said, "John I beheaded. Now who is this about whom I hear such things?" And he sought to see Jesus.

A LARGE CROWD IS FED WITH FIVE LOAVES AND TWO FISH

[10]When the apostles returned, they told Jesus all they had done. Then He took them with Him and they went by themselves to a place where they could be alone on the way to a town called Bethsaida. [11]But the crowds found out and followed Him. He let them come and spoke to them about God's realm and healed those who needed healing. [12]The time began to slip away, and the twelve came and said to Him, "Send the crowd away so they can go into the countryside and villages around here and find lodging and food, for we are here in a deserted place. [13]But He said to them, "You give them something to eat!" They said, "We have nothing here but five loaves and two fish, unless we go and buy food for all these people." [14]More than five thousand were there. He said to His disciples, "Have them sit down in groups of fifty." [15]So the disciples had everyone sit down. [16]Taking the five loaves and the two fish, He looked up toward heaven and blessed them. Then He broke them and gave them to the disciples to set before the large crowd of people. [17]They all ate and were filled, and afterward twelve basketfuls of leftover pieces of food were picked up.

PETER AFFIRMS THAT JESUS IS THE MESSIAH

[18]One day Jesus was praying alone, and only the disciples were with Him. "Who do people say I am?" He asked them. [19]They answered, "John the Baptist. But some say Elijah, and others say that one of the prophets of old has risen." [20]Jesus said to them, "But who do you say I am?" Peter said, "God's Messiah." [21]Then He warned them not to tell anyone, [22]saying, "The Son of Humanity must suffer many things and be rejected by the elders, the chief priests and the scribes. He will be killed, and then raised the third day."

THE IMPORTANCE OF THE SOUL

[23]Then Jesus said to them all, "If any of you want to come after Me, you must deny yourselves and take up your cross daily and follow Me. [24]If you want to save your life, you must lose it, but if you lose your life for My sake, you will save it. [25]What profit is it to you if you gain the whole world but lose your soul and waste your life? [26]If you are ashamed of Me and My words, the Son of Humanity will be ashamed of you when I comes in My glory and in the glory of My heavenly Parent and the holy angels. [27]And I tell you the truth, some are standing here who will not taste death before they see God's realm."

THE TRANSFIGURATION: JESUS BECOMES A BEING OF LIGHT

[28]About eight days after saying this, He took Peter, John and James and went up on a mountain to pray. [29]As He prayed, His face changed and His clothing became radiantly white. [30]Suddenly two men were talking with Him! They were Moses and Elijah, [31]appearing in glory. They spoke about His departure, which He would accomplish at Jerusalem. [32]Meanwhile, Peter and those who were with him were drowsy with sleep. When they awoke, they saw His glory and the two men standing with Him. [33]As the men were leaving Jesus, Peter said to Him, "Rabbi, it is good that we are here. Let us put up three tents here - one for You, one for Moses and one for Elijah." He didn't know what he was saying. [34]As he was speaking, a bright cloud flowed over them. Peter, John and James were afraid as the cloud covered them. [35]A voice out of the cloud said, "This is My Son, My Chosen. Listen to Him." [36]After the voice had spoken, Jesus was there alone. They kept quiet and told no one at that time what they had seen.

THE STUBBORN DEMON THAT WOULD NOT COME OUT

[37]When they came down from the mountain the next day, a great crowd of people met Him. [38]One man from the crowd called out, "Rabbi! I beg You! Come here and look at my son, for he is my only child. [39]Look how a spirit takes hold of him! He suddenly cries out, and it convulses and crushes him until he foams at the mouth. It bruises him, hardly ever leaving him. [40]I begged Your disciples to cast it out, but they could not." [41]Jesus said, "O unbelieving and perverse generation, how long must I be with you and put up with you? Bring your son here!" [42]As the boy was coming, the demon threw him down and convulsed him. Jesus rebuked the unclean spirit, healed the boy and gave him back to his father. [43]They were all amazed at the power of God.

THE DISCIPLES ARE AGAIN TOLD OF FUTURE EVENTS

While they were all marveling at everything Jesus did, He said to His disciples, [44]"Pay close attention to what I'm going to tell you: The Son of Humanity will be handed over to humans." [45]They didn't know what He meant. The meaning was hidden from them so that they could not understand it. And they were afraid to ask Him to explain.

JESUS TEACHES ABOUT HUMILITY

[46]An argument arose among them as to which one of them would be the greatest. [47]But Jesus, knowing the thoughts of their hearts, took a little child and stood the child beside Him. [48]Jesus said to the disciples, "Whoever accepts this child in My name accepts Me. And whoever accepts Me accepts the One who sent Me. The one who is least among you is the one who will be the greatest."

THE FRIENDS OF GOD

[49]John said, "Teacher, we saw a man casting out demons in Your name and we stopped him because he was not one of us." [50]Jesus said to him, "Do not forbid anyone; for those who are not against you are for you."

SOME SAMARITANS REJECT JESUS

[51]When the time approached for Him to be taken up, Jesus steadfastly set His face toward Jerusalem. [52]He sent messengers ahead, and they went to a village in Samaria

to get things ready for Him. [53]But the Samaritans would not welcome Him because He was going toward Jerusalem. [54]His disciples James and John saw this, and they said, "Rabbi! Should we command fire to come down from heaven to destroy them?" [55]Jesus turned and rebuked them, saying, "The Son of Humanity did not come to destroy lives, but to save." [56]And they went on to another village.

THE COMMITMENT REQUIRED OF A DISCIPLE

[57]As they went along the road, a man said to Him, "Rabbi, I will follow You wherever You go." [58]Jesus said to him, "Foxes have dens and the birds of the air have nests, but the Son of Humanity has nowhere to lay His head." [59]He said to another, "Follow Me." But the man said, "Rabbi, first allow me to go and bury my father." [60]Jesus said to him, "Let the dead bury their dead. You go and declare God's realm far and wide." [61]Another man said, "Rabbi, I will follow You, but first let me say goodbye to those at home." [62]Jesus said to him, "No one who puts a hand to the plow and looks back is fit for God's realm."

JESUS SENDS OTHER DISCIPLES OUT IN PAIRS

10:1[After this Jesus appointed seventy-two others and sent them ahead of Him two by two to every town and place where He intended to visit. [2]He said to them, "The harvest is truly great, but the workers are few. Pray, therefore, that the God of the harvest sends out workers to the harvest field. [3]Go, but watch out! I am sending you out like lambs among wolves. [4]Carry no moneybag, no knapsack, no sandals; and don't stop to greet anyone along the way. [5]Whenever you enter a house, first say, 'Peace to this house.' [6]If friends of peace are there, your peace will rest upon them; if not, it will return to you. [7]Remain in the same house and eat and drink what is provided, for the workers are worthy of their wages. Do not go from house to house. [8]When you enter a town and they welcome you, eat what is set before you. [9]Heal the sick that are there and say to them, 'God's realm is very near you!' [10]But when you go into a town and they do not welcome you, go out into its streets and say, [11]'Even the dust of your town that sticks to our feet we wipe off against you. Nevertheless, you may be sure of this - God's realm has been near you.' [12]I tell you, it will be more tolerable for Sodom on that day than for that town.

[13]"Woe to you, Chorazin! Woe to you, Bethsaida! If the miracles that were done in you had been done in Tyre and Sidon, they would have repented long ago, sitting in sackcloth and ashes. [14]It will be more tolerable for Tyre and Sidon at the judgment than for you. [15]And you, Capernaum, will you be exalted to heaven? No! You will be thrust down to hell.

[16]"Whoever listens to you, listens to Me; whoever rejects you, rejects Me; and whoever rejects Me, rejects the One who sent Me."

[17]Later the seventy-two returned with joy and said, "Rabbi! Even the demons submit to us when we use Your name!" [18]He said to them, "I saw Satan fall like lightning from heaven! [19]I have given you authority to tread on snakes and scorpions and over all the power of the enemy. Nothing will harm you. [20]Nevertheless do not rejoice that the spirits submit to you, but rejoice because your names are written in heaven."

^{21}In that hour Jesus rejoiced in Spirit and said, "I thank You My dear Parent, God of heaven and earth, that You have hidden these things from those who think they are wise and revealed them to children, for this was pleasing in Your sight. ^{22}Everything has been entrusted to Me by My heavenly Parent. No one knows who God's Son is but the Parent, and no one knows who the Parent is but the Son and those to whom the Son chooses to reveal the Parent." ^{23}Then He turned to His disciples and said privately, "Blessed are the eyes that see the things you see. ^{24}For I tell you, many prophets and kings desired to see what you have seen and did not see it, and to hear what you have heard and did not hear it."

THE GOOD SAMARITAN

^{25}One time a certain lawyer stood up and tested Jesus by asking, "Teacher, what must I do to inherit eternal life?" ^{26}Jesus said to him, "What is written in the law? How do you read it?" ^{27}The lawyer answered, "You shall love your God with all your heart, with all your soul, with all your strength and with all your mind; and you shall love your neighbor as you love yourself." ^{28}Jesus said, "You have answered correctly. Do this and you will live." ^{29}But the lawyer, wanting to justify himself, asked Jesus, "But who is my neighbor?" ^{30}Jesus answered, "A certain man went down from Jerusalem to Jericho and fell among robbers. They stripped him of his clothes and beat him and departed, leaving him half dead. ^{31}A priest came down the same road, and when he saw him, he passed by on the other side. ^{32}Likewise a Levite came to that place, looked at him and passed by on the other side. ^{33}But a Samaritan who was traveling came to where the man was, and when he saw him, he had compassion. ^{34}He went and bound up his wounds, poured on oil and wine, set him on his own donkey, brought him to an inn and took care of him. ^{35}The next day he took out money and gave it to the innkeeper and said to him, 'Take care of him, and if you spend more, I will repay you when I come back.' ^{36}Now which of these three do you think was a neighbor to the man who fell among robbers?" ^{37}The lawyer said, "The one who had compassion on him." Then Jesus said to him, "Go and do likewise."

JESUS VISITS MARY AND MARTHA

^{38}As they continued on their way, Jesus entered a village, and a woman named Martha welcomed Him into her home. ^{39}She had a sister named Mary who sat at Jesus' feet and listened to His teaching. ^{40}Martha was distracted with much serving and came to Him and said, "Rabbi, don't You care that my sister has left me to serve alone? Tell her to help me!" ^{41}Jesus answered her, "Martha, Martha, you are anxious and stirred up about many things, ^{42}but only one thing is needed. Mary has chosen the best part, and it must not be taken from her."

JESUS TEACHES ABOUT PRAYER

$^{11:1}$One day He was praying in a certain place. When He finished, one of His disciples said to Him, "Rabbi, teach us to pray as John taught his disciples." ^{2}Jesus said to them, "When you pray, say, 'Our Parent in heaven, I pray that Your holy name is honored. May Your realm come, may Your will be done, on earth as it is in heaven. ^{3}Give us each day our daily bread; ^{4}and forgive us our offenses, as we forgive those who offend us. And lead us not into hard testing, but rescue us from evil.'"

JESUS ENCOURAGES HIS DISCIPLES TO PRAY

[5]Jesus said to them, "Suppose one of you has a friend, and you go to your friend at midnight and say, 'Friend, lend me three loaves of bread. [6]A friend of mine has arrived from a journey and I have nothing to serve.' [7]And suppose that your friend inside answers, 'Don't make me exert myself. The door is already locked and my children are with me in bed. I cannot get up and give you bread.' [8]I tell you, even if your friend will not get up and give you bread out of friendship, if you keep knocking long enough, your friend will get up and give you as many loaves as you need. [9]So I say to you: Ask and it will be given to you; seek and you will find; knock and it will be opened to you. [10]For everyone who asks receives, and everyone who seeks finds, and to everyone who knocks it will be opened.

[11]"If a son asks his father for a fish, which of you fathers would give your son a snake? [12]If he asked for an egg, would you give him a scorpion? [13]If you then, being evil, know how to give good gifts to your children, how much more will your Parent in heaven give the Holy Spirit to those who ask?"

JESUS IS ACCUSED OF BEING SATAN'S DISCIPLE

[14]Jesus was casting out a demon that had control of speech. When the demon had gone out, the speechless person spoke. The people marveled, [15]but some of them said, "He casts out demons with the help of the dung-god, the prince of demons." [16]Others tested Him by asking Him for a sign from heaven. [17]Jesus knew their intentions and said to them, "Every realm divided against itself will be destroyed, and a family divided against itself will fly apart. [18]If Satan's realm is divided against itself, how will it stand? You say that I cast out demons with the help of the dung-god; [19]but if it is by the dung-god that I cast out demons, by whom do your own people cast them out? Therefore your own people will be your judges. [20]But if I cast out demons by the finger of God, then God's realm has truly come upon you. [21]When a strong person fully armed guards a home, the possessions are not disturbed. [22]But when someone stronger attacks and subdues the strong person, the stronger one takes all the armor in which the strong person trusted and distributes the plunder. [23]Whoever is not with Me is against Me, and whoever does not gather with Me scatters.

A DISPOSSESSED DEMON RETURNS WITH SEVEN MORE

[24]"When an unclean spirit comes out of a person, it goes through dry places seeking rest. Finding none, it says, 'I will go back to the home I left,' [25]and it goes back and finds it swept and in order. [26]Then it goes and takes with it seven other spirits more wicked than itself and they go in and live there. In the end that person is worse off than at the first."

A WOMAN WISHES FOR A CHILD LIKE JESUS

[27]As He spoke these things, a woman in the crowd raised her voice and said to Him, "Blessed is the woman who bore You and nurtured You." [28]Jesus answered, "Yes, but even more blessed are those who hear the message of God and obey it."

PEOPLE ASK JESUS FOR MORE PROOF

[29]The people were gathered together, and Jesus began to speak. "This is an evil generation. They seek a sign, but no sign will be given but the sign of Jonah. [30]For as

Jonah was a sign to the Ninevites, so also will the Son of Humanity be to this generation. [31]The Queen of the South will rise up during the judgment of the people of this generation and condemn them. For she came from the ends of the earth to hear the wisdom of Solomon, and now something greater than Solomon is here. [32]The people of Nineveh will rise up during the judgment of this generation and condemn it. For they repented at the preaching of Jonah, and now something greater than Jonah is here.

[33]"No one lights a lamp and puts it in a hidden place or under a basket, but on a lampstand. Then those who come in may see the light. [34]The light of the body is the eye. If your eyes are good, your whole body will be full of light. But if your eyes are bad, your body will be full of darkness. [35]Therefore be careful that the light in you is not darkness. [36]If your whole body is full of light, with no part dark, the whole will be full of light, as when the bright light of a lamp gives you light."

AN UNDISCERNING PHARISEE INVITES JESUS TO DINNER

[37]As Jesus spoke, a certain Pharisee invited Him to dine with him, and Jesus went in and sat down to eat. [38]When the Pharisee saw that Jesus did not wash before eating, he was surprised. [39]Jesus said to him, "You Pharisees make the outside of the cup and dish clean, but inside you are full of greed and wickedness. [40]Fools! Did not the One who made the outside make the inside also? [41]Rather, give compassionately from what you have; then you will see that all things are clean! [42]Woe to you Pharisees! You tithe mint and rue and other herbs, but you neglect justice and the love of God. These you ought to have done and not neglected the others. [43]Woe to you Pharisees! For you love the seats of honor in the synagogues and greetings in the marketplace. [44]Woe to you! You are like unseen graves that people walk over unaware."

BEWARE OF HYPOCRISY

[45]One of the lawyers answered and said to Him, "Teacher, You insult us also when you say these things." [46]Jesus answered, "Woe to you lawyers too! You load people down with burdens too heavy to bear, but you yourselves will not touch the burdens with one finger. [47]Woe to you! For you build tombs for the prophets that your ancestors killed; [48]therefore you testify that you approve the deeds of your ancestors. They killed them, and you build their tombs. [49]Therefore the Wisdom of God said, 'I will send them prophets and apostles. Some they will kill and some they will persecute.' [50]Therefore this generation will have to answer for the blood of all the prophets that has been shed from the beginning of the world, [51]from the blood of Abel to the blood of Zechariah, who perished between the altar and the temple. Truly I tell you, this generation will have to answer. [52]Woe to you lawyers! You take away the key to knowledge! You won't go in yourselves, and you keep out those who want to go in."

[53]As Jesus was leaving, the scribes and the Pharisees began to argue with Him forcefully, trying to provoke Him to speak of many things [54]so they could catch Him making some incriminating remark.

JESUS CONTINUES TO TEACH THOSE WHO WILL LISTEN

[12:1]In the meantime, a crowd of many thousands had gathered, and they were stepping on one another. Jesus began saying to His disciples, "Beware of the leaven of the Pharisees, which is hypocrisy. [2]Nothing is concealed that will not be revealed or hidden that will not be known. [3]What you say in the dark will be heard in the daylight, and what you whisper in someone's ear in a private room will be shouted from the housetops. [4]I say to you, My friends, do not be afraid of those who kill the body and after that can do nothing more. [5]I warn you, here is the One you should fear: Fear God, who has the power to kill and also the power to cast into hell. Yes, I say to you, fear God. [6]Are not five sparrows sold for two pennies? But not one of them is forgotten by God. [7]Even the hairs of your head are all numbered. Therefore do not fear; you are of more value than many sparrows. [8]I also say to you, if you acknowledge Me before humans, the Son of Humanity will also acknowledge you before the angels of God. [9]But if you deny Me before humans, you will be denied before the angels of God. [10]If you speak a word against the Son of Humanity, you will be forgiven. But if you speak abusively against the Holy Spirit, it will not be forgiven. [11]When they bring you into the synagogues and before the magistrates and authorities, don't worry about how or what you will answer or what you should say; [12]for the Holy Spirit will teach you at that time what you should say."

[13]Someone in the crowd said to Him, "Teacher, tell my brother to divide the inheritance with me!" [14]Jesus answered him, "Friend, who made Me the judge to divide between you?" [15]Then He said to them, "Beware of covetousness. A person's life is not in the abundance of possessions."

[16]Then Jesus told them this parable: "The land of a certain rich man produced bountifully, [17]and he thought to himself, 'What will I do? I have no room to store my harvest.' [18]Then he said, 'I will do this: I will pull down my granaries and build bigger ones. There I will store all my produce and my goods. [19]Then I will say to my soul, "Soul, you have plenty of goods laid up for many years. Take it easy! Eat, drink, and be merry."' [20]But God said, 'You fool! This night your soul will be demanded back from you. Then who will get all these things you have prepared?' [21]That is how it will be for you if you store up things for yourself but are not rich in the things of God."

[22]And He said to His disciples, "Therefore I say to you, don't worry about your life and what you will eat, or your body and what you will wear. [23]Life is more than for eating, and the body more than for clothing. [24]Consider the ravens. They neither sow nor reap. They have neither storehouse nor granary, and yet God feeds them. And you are much more valuable than birds! [25]Which of you by worrying can add one cubit to your stature? [26]If you are not able to do this little thing, why are you anxious about the rest? [27]Consider the lilies, how they grow. They do not toil or spin. But I say to you that not even Solomon in all his glory was arrayed like one of these. [28]If this is how God clothes the plants of the field today, which tomorrow are thrown into the oven, how much more you, O you of little faith? [29]Do not keep wondering what you will eat and what you will drink; don't be anxious about that. [30]All these the unbelievers seek. Your Parent in heaven knows that you need all these things. [31]Rather, seek God's realm, and all these things will be added to you.

³²"Do not be afraid, little flock. It is your heavenly Parent's pleasure to give you the realm. ³³Sell what you have and give to the poor. Provide yourselves purses that will not wear out, an unfailing treasure in heaven, where no thief approaches or moth destroys. ³⁴For where your treasure is, there will your heart be also.

³⁵"Be dressed and have your light lit, ³⁶like servants awaiting the homeowner's return from a wedding banquet, so that when the owner comes and knocks, you may open immediately. ³⁷Blessed are those servants who are watching when the owner comes. Truly I say to you, the owner will take a towel, have them sit down and will come and serve them. ³⁸If the owner comes at nine at night or at midnight and finds them waiting, blessed are those servants. ³⁹Remember, if the owner of the house had known what hour the thief would come, guards would have been employed who would not have allowed the house to be broken into. ⁴⁰Therefore be ready, for the Son of Humanity will come at an hour you do not expect."

⁴¹Peter asked, "Are You telling this parable just for us, or is it for everyone?" ⁴²Jesus said, "Who is the faithful and wise servant whom the owner of the house puts in charge of the household to give the others food at the proper time? ⁴³Blessed is that servant who is found doing that when the owner comes. ⁴⁴Truly I say to you, the owner will make that servant ruler over everything. ⁴⁵But if that servant says, 'The owner is not coming back for a long time,' and begins to beat the other servants and eats and drinks and becomes drunk, ⁴⁶the owner will return on a day not looked for and in an hour not expected and will whip that servant and assign that servant a place among the unbelievers. ⁴⁷That servant who knew the owner's will and did not prepare or act accordingly will be beaten with many blows. ⁴⁸But the one who did not know and who committed something deserving a beating will be whipped with just a few blows. For of those to whom much is given, much will be required. And of those to whom the owner has committed much, even more will be required.

⁴⁹"I have come to throw fire upon the earth, and how I wish it were already kindled! ⁵⁰But I have a baptism to be baptized with, and how distressed I am until it is accomplished. ⁵¹Do you suppose that I came to bring peace on earth? No, not peace, but division. ⁵²From now on there will be five in one house divided - three against two and two against three. ⁵³They will be divided, father against son and son against father, mother against daughter and daughter against mother, mother-in-law against daughter-in-law and daughter-in-law against mother-in-law."

⁵⁴He also said to the people, "When you see a cloud rise from the west, you immediately say, 'Here comes a shower,' and so it happens. ⁵⁵And when the south wind blows, you say, 'It's going to be hot,' and it comes to pass. ⁵⁶You hypocrites! You know how to interpret the sky and the earth; how is it that you cannot interpret the times?

⁵⁷"Why can't you judge for yourselves what is right? ⁵⁸When you go with your adversary to the magistrate, try diligently along the way to be reconciled, lest your adversary drag you before the judge, and the judge hand you over to the officer, and the officer throw you into prison. ⁵⁹I tell you, you will not get out of there until you have paid the last cent."

13:1About that time someone told Jesus about the Galileans whose blood Pilate had mingled with their sacrifices. 2Jesus said to them, "Do you suppose that these Galileans were worse sinners than every other Galilean because they suffered this? 3No, I tell you. But unless you repent, you also will perish. 4Or those eighteen upon whom the tower in Siloam fell, killing them; do you think they were worse sinners than all the rest living in Jerusalem? 5No, I tell you. But unless you repent, you also will perish."

6Jesus also spoke this parable: "A man had a fig tree planted in his vineyard. He went and looked for fruit on it and found none. 7He said to the pruner of his vineyard, 'Look, for three years I have come seeking fruit on this fig tree and have found none. Cut it down! Why let it use up the soil?' 8The pruner answered, 'Sir! Let's leave it one more year and I will dig around it and fertilize it. 9Then if it bears fruit, good. If not, then you can cut it down.'"

A WOMAN CRIPPLED BY A DEMON IS HEALED ON THE SABBATH

10One Sabbath Jesus was teaching in one of the synagogues. 11A woman was there who had a spirit of weakness. She had been stooped over for eighteen years and could never entirely straighten up. 12When Jesus saw her, He called and said to her, "Woman, you are loosed from your weakness!" 13He laid His hands on her, and immediately she straightened up and praised God. 14But the leader of the synagogue was indignant because Jesus had healed on the Sabbath, and he said to the people, "Six days are for work! Come and be healed on those days, not on the Sabbath!" 15Jesus answered him, "You hypocrite! Do not each of you loose your ox or donkey from the stall on the Sabbath and lead it to water? 16Should not this woman, a daughter of Abraham whom Satan kept bound for eighteen years, be loosed on the Sabbath from what bound her?" 17When He said this, all His adversaries were ashamed. But the people were delighted at all of the wonderful things He was doing.

THE PARABLE OF THE MUSTARD SEED

18Then Jesus asked, "What is God's realm like? To what can I compare it? 19It is like a mustard seed that a farmer took and sowed in a garden. It grew and became a large tree, and the birds of the air nested in its branches."

THE PARABLE OF THE YEAST

20Once more He asked, "What is God's realm like? 21It is like yeast that a baker hides in a large batch of flour. Eventually the whole batch is affected.

ENTER AT THE NARROW GATE!

22Jesus continued on through the towns and villages, teaching as He went on toward Jerusalem. 23Someone asked Him, "Rabbi, are only a few going to be saved?" Jesus answered, 24"Strive to go in at the narrow gate; for many, I tell you, will plot to get in and will not be able to. 25Once the Owner of the house gets up and shuts the door, you will be left standing outside knocking. You will say, 'Rabbi! Rabbi! Open to us!' and the Owner will say, 'I don't know you or where you come from.' 26You will say, 'We ate and drank before Your eyes, and You taught in our streets.' 27But the Owner will say, 'I tell you, I don't know you or where you come from. Depart from Me, all of you who do unjust things.' 28There will be weeping and gnashing of teeth when you see Abraham, Isaac and Jacob and all the prophets in God's realm, and yourselves thrown out. [29]They will come from the east and from the west, from the north and from the south, and will sit down at the Feast in God's realm. [30]But beware! Some who are last here will be first there, and some who are first here will be last there."

JESUS MOURNS OVER THE REBELS

[31]That same day some Pharisees said to Him, "Go away and leave this place, for Herod wants to kill You." [32]Jesus said to them, "Go and tell that fox, 'Think about this: I cast out demons and do healing today and tomorrow, and on the third day I will be finished.' [33]Nevertheless I must travel on today and tomorrow and the following day, for it would not be acceptable for a prophet to die anywhere but Jerusalem. [34]O Jerusalem, Jerusalem, you who kill the prophets and stone those who are sent to you - how often I have longed to gather your children together, even as a hen gathers her chicks under her wings, but you would not let Me. [35]Look, your temple is deserted. Now you will not see Me again until the day you say, 'Blessed is the One who comes in the name of Yahweh.'"

JESUS ADMONISHES THE LEADERS

[14:1]One Sabbath Jesus went to eat in the house of one of the chief Pharisees, and everyone watched Him. [2]There in front of Him was a man who had dropsy. [3]Jesus asked the lawyers and Pharisees, "Is it lawful to heal on the Sabbath?" [4]But they were silent. Jesus healed the man and let him go. [5]He said to them, "If your ox falls into a pit on the Sabbath, will you not immediately pull it out?" [6]They could not answer Him.

LESSONS IN HUMILITY

[7]When Jesus noticed how the guests chose for themselves the places of honor, He told them this parable: [8]"When someone invites you to a wedding feast, do not sit down at the place of honor, for someone more honorable than you may have been invited. [9]The person who invited you both may have to come and say to you, 'Please give this person your place.' Then you would be embarrassed and have to sit in the last place. [10]But when you are invited, go and sit in the last place. Then the person who invited you may come and say to you, 'Friend, go up higher,' and you will be honored in the presence of those who sit with you. [11]Those who exalt themselves will be humbled, and those who humble themselves will be exalted." [12]Then Jesus said to the Pharisee who had invited Him, "When you put on a lunch or a dinner, do not invite your friends or your fellow Jews or your relatives or your rich neighbors, lest you be repaid when they invite you in return. [13]Instead, when you put on a feast, invite the poor, the crippled, the lame and the blind. [14]Then you will be blessed, for they cannot repay you. But you will be repaid at the resurrection of the righteous."

EXCUSES FOR NOT COMING TO THE BANQUET

[15]One of those who sat at the table with Jesus said to Him, "Blessed are those who will eat at the Feast in God's realm." [16]Jesus answered, "A certain man prepared a great banquet and invited many. [17]He sent his servant at dinnertime to say to those who were invited, 'Come, for everything is ready.' [18]But they all began to make excuses. The first said, 'I have bought a field, and I need to go see it. I pray you excuse

me.' [19]Another said, 'I have bought five yoke of oxen, and I am on my way to try them out. I pray you excuse me.' [20]Another said, 'I was recently married; therefore I cannot come.' [21]The servant returned and reported all this to his employer. The owner of the house became angry and said to his servant, 'Go quickly out into the streets and crowded places of the town and bring back the poor, the maimed, the lame and the blind.' [22]The servant said, 'It has been done as you ordered, sir, but there is still room.' [23]Then the owner of the house said to the servant, 'Go out into the highways and byways and compel them to come in so that my house may be full. [24]I tell you, none of those who were invited shall taste of my banquet.'"

JESUS TEACHES THE PEOPLE WHAT THEY MUST DO

[25]Great crowds were following Jesus. He turned and said to them, [26]"If any of you come to Me and do not hate your father and mother, wife and children, brothers and sisters and even your own life, then you cannot be My disciple. [27]If you will not bear your cross and come after Me, you cannot be My disciple. [28]Which of you, intending to build a tower, does not first sit down and calculate the cost to finish it? [29]Otherwise, after you have laid the foundation and are not able to finish, all who see it will begin to mock you, [30]saying, 'This one began to build but isn't able to finish!' [31]Or what king, going to make war against another king, does not sit down first and consider whether he is able with ten thousand soldiers to counter the one coming against him with twenty thousand. [32]If not, then while the other king is still a long way off he will send ambassadors to ask for terms of peace. [33]Likewise, none of you can be My disciple unless you give up everything you have. [34]Salt is good, but if the salt loses its flavor, how can it be made salty again? [35]It is fit for neither the soil nor the manure pile and it is thrown out. If you have ears to hear, then listen."

THE JOY OVER ONE SINNER WHO REPENTS

[15:1]The tax collectors and sinners all gathered around Jesus to listen to Him. [2]The Pharisees complained, "This fellow associates with sinners and even eats with them." [3]Then He spoke this parable to them: [4]"What one of you, having a hundred sheep and losing one of them, will not leave the other ninety-nine in the wilderness and go search for the lost one until you find it? [5]And when you find it, you lay it across your shoulders and rejoice. [6]When you get home, you call together your friends and neighbors and say to them, 'Rejoice with me, for I have found my sheep that was lost.' [7]In the same way, I tell you, there will be more joy in heaven over one sinner who repents than over ninety-nine righteous who do not need to repent. [8]Or what one of you, having ten silver coins and losing one of them, will not light a lamp, sweep the house and search diligently until you find it? [9]And when you find it, you call friends and neighbors together and say, 'Rejoice with me, for I have found the coin that I lost.' [10]In the same way, I tell you, there is joy among the angels of God over one sinner who repents."

THE PRODIGAL SON

[11]Then Jesus said, "A certain man had two sons. [12]The younger one said to his father, 'Father, give me the portion of your property that will belong to me.' So he divided his livelihood between them. [13]A few days later the younger son gathered everything together and took his journey to a far country and there wasted his

substance on wanton living. [14]After he had spent it all, a severe famine occurred in that country and he began to go hungry. [15]He went and attached himself to a citizen of that country. The man sent him out to his fields to feed the pigs. [16]He longed to fill his belly with the pods the pigs were eating, but no one gave him anything. [17]Then he came to his senses and thought, 'How many of my father's hired servants have food enough, and then some, and here I am dying from hunger! [18]I will get up and go back to my father and say to him, "Father, I have sinned against heaven and you. [19]I am no longer worthy to be called your son; treat me like one of your hired servants."' [20]So he got up and went to his father. But when he was still a long way off, his father saw him. Filled with compassion for him, his father ran to meet him and hugged him and kissed him. [21]The son said, 'Father, I have sinned against heaven and against you, and I am no longer worthy to be called your son.' [22]But his father said to the servants, 'Bring the best robe and put it on him! And put a ring on his finger and sandals on his feet. [23]Fetch the fatted calf and butcher it; let's eat and be merry! [24]For this son of mine was dead and is alive again! He was lost and now is found!' And they began to celebrate.

[25]"Now the older son was in the field, and as he came near the house, he heard music and dancing. [26]He called one of the servants and asked what this meant. [27]The servant said, 'Your brother has returned, and your father has killed the fatted calf because he has him back safe and sound.' [28]The older brother was angry and would not go in. Then his father came out and pleaded with him. [29]The older brother said to his father, 'Look, all these years I have worked for you. I have never once disobeyed your orders, but you never gave me even a little goat so that I could celebrate with my friends. [30]Now as soon as this son of yours comes who ate up your livelihood with harlots, you kill the fatted calf for him!' [31]The father said, 'Son, you are always with me and all that I have is yours; [32]but it is right for us to rejoice and be glad. Your brother was dead and is alive again! He was lost and now is found!'"

THE PARABLE ABOUT THE WORLDLY-WISE MANAGER

[16:1]Jesus said to His disciples, "There was once a rich man whose manager was accused of wasting his goods. [2]He called him and said to him, 'What is this I hear about you? Give an account of your management, for you are no longer my manager.' [3]The manager said to himself, 'What will I do? My employer is taking away my position! I can't dig, and I'm ashamed to beg. [4]I know what I'll do! When I'm put out of my position, they will welcome me into their homes!' [5]Then he called each of his employer's debtors one by one. He said to the first, 'How much do you owe my employer?' [6]He answered, 'A hundred barrels of oil.' He said to him, 'Take your bill and sit down quickly and write fifty.' [7]Then he said to another, 'How much do you owe?' He answered, 'A thousand bushels of wheat.' He said to him, 'Take your bill and write eight hundred.' [8]Then the employer praised the dishonest manager because he had acted shrewdly.

BE WISE ABOUT RECEIVING THE RICHES OF GOD

"The people of this world are more shrewd in dealing with their generation than the children of the light. [9]And I say to you, make friends with worldly riches, so that when that fails, you will be welcomed into an eternal home. [10]Whoever is trustworthy with a little will be trustworthy with much, and whoever is dishonest with a little will be dishonest with much. [11]If you have not been trustworthy with the riches of unrighteousness, who will trust you with true riches? [12]And if you have not been trustworthy with what is someone else's riches, who will give you that which is your own? [13]No one can follow two pipers. You will either hate the one and love the other, or you will be loyal to the one and despise the other. You cannot serve God and money."

[14]The Pharisees heard all this and sneered at Him, for they loved money. [15]Jesus said to them, "You are those who justify yourselves before humans, but God knows your hearts. What is highly esteemed among humans is detestable in the sight of God.

EVERYONE WANTS TO GO TO HEAVEN

[16]"The law of Moses and the writings of the prophets guided you until John. Since that time the realm of God is being declared and everyone tries hard to get in. [17]But it is easier for the sky and the earth to pass away than for one bit of the law to be changed.

DIVORCE

[18]"If you divorce your spouse and marry another, you commit adultery. And anyone who marries a divorced person commits adultery.

THE RICH MAN AND LAZARUS

[19]"There was once a rich man who was clothed in purple and fine linen and who fared sumptuously every day. [20]At his gate lay a beggar named Lazarus, covered with sores. [21]As Lazarus thought about what fell from the rich man's table, the dogs came and licked his sores. [22]After a while the beggar died and was carried by the angels to be in the arms of Abraham. The rich man also died and was buried. [23]He was in torment in hell, and he looked and saw Abraham far away, with Lazarus by his side. [24]He called out, 'Father Abraham! Have mercy on me! Send Lazarus to dip the tip of his finger in water and cool my tongue, for I am in agony in this fire.' [25]But Abraham said, 'Son, remember that in your lifetime you received the good and Lazarus the bad. But now he is comforted here and you are in agony. [26]Besides all that, between us and you a great gulf has been fixed, so that those who long to go from here to you cannot, nor can anyone go from there to us.' [27]Then the rich man said, 'Then I beg you to send Lazarus to my family home, [28]for I have five brothers. Let him testify to them, lest they also come into this place of torment.' [29]Abraham said, 'They have Moses and the prophets; let your brothers listen to them.' [30]The rich man said, 'They won't, father Abraham. But if someone rose from the dead and went to them, they would repent.' [31]Abraham said, 'If they won't listen to Moses and the prophets, neither will they be persuaded by someone who rises from the dead.'"

TEACHINGS ABOUT INNOCENCE, FORGIVENESS, FAITH, HUMILITY

[17:1]Jesus said to His disciples, "Occasions to fall are sure to come, but woe to you through whom they come. [2]It would be better for you to have a millstone tied around your neck and be thrown into the sea than for you to cause one of these little ones to sin.

[3]"Be careful. If other believers sin against you, rebuke them. If they repent, forgive them. [4]If they sin against you seven times in a day and seven times in a day come back to you and say, 'I repent,' you must forgive them."

[5]The apostles said to Jesus, "Increase our faith!" [6]Jesus said, "If you have faith the size of a mustard seed, you can say to this sycamore tree, 'Be uprooted and planted in the sea,' and it will obey you.

[7]"Which of you would say to your servant who has just come in from plowing the field or tending the sheep, 'Come, sit down and eat'? [8]Rather, you would say, 'Put on an apron and prepare my dinner and serve me. After I eat and drink, you may eat and drink.' [9]Would you thank that servant for doing what was commanded? [10]So you also, when you have done everything you were commanded, should say, 'We are just servants, we have only done our duty.'"

A SAMARITAN LEPER IS THANKFUL

[11]As Jesus traveled toward Jerusalem, He went through the region between Samaria and Galilee. [12]As He entered a village, ten men who were lepers met Him. They stood at a distance [13]and called out loudly, "Jesus! Rabbi! Have mercy on us!" [14]When Jesus saw them, He said, "Go and show yourselves to the priests." As they were going, they were cleansed. [15]One of them, when he saw that he was healed, turned back. With a loud voice he praised God. [16]He fell on his face at Jesus' feet and thanked Him. And he was a Samaritan! [17]Jesus asked, "Were not ten cleansed? Where are the nine? [18]Could none be found to return and give praise to God but this foreigner?" [19]Jesus said to him, "Stand up and go your way; your faith has healed you."

THE COMING OF GOD'S REALM

[20]Some Pharisees asked Him when God's realm would come, and He said, "The coming of God's realm is not visible to the eye, [21]nor will people say, 'Look! Here it is!' or 'Look! There it is!' Look closely, for God's realm is within you."

[22]Then He said to His disciples, "The days will come when you will long to see one of the days of the Son of Humanity, but you will not. [23]People will say to you, 'Look! There He is!' or 'Look! Here He is!' Don't go, and do not follow them. [24]For as the lightning flashing out of the sky illuminates the sky from one end to the other, so will the Son of Humanity be in that day. [25]But first I must suffer much and be rejected by this generation. [26]As it was in the days of Noah, so will it be in the days of the Son of Humanity. [27]Men and women were eating and drinking and marrying until the day that Noah entered the ark. Then the flood came and destroyed them all. [28]It was the same in the days of Lot. They were eating and drinking, buying and selling, planting and building. [29]But on the day Lot went out of Sodom, fire and brimstone rained from heaven and destroyed them all. [30]It will be the same on the day the Son of Humanity is revealed. [31]On that day those who are on the housetop with their belongings in the house should not go down to get them. And those who are in the field should not turn back. [32]Remember Lot's wife. [33]Those who try to save their lives will lose them, but those who lose their lives will save them. [34]I tell you, on that night two will be in one bed; one will be taken and the other will be left. [35]Two will be grinding grain together;

one will be taken and the other left. [36]Two will be in the field; one will be taken and the other left." [37]They asked Him, "Where, Rabbi?" and He said to them, "Where the body is, there the vultures will gather."

THE PARABLE ABOUT THE PERSISTENT WIDOW

[18:1]Jesus told them a parable to show that they should always pray and not be discouraged. [2]He said, "In a certain town there was a judge who did not fear God or care about people. [3]A certain widow in that town kept coming to him and saying, 'Grant me protection from my adversary!' [4]For a long time he refused, but at last he said to himself, 'Though I do not fear God or care what people think, [5]yet because this widow keeps bothering me, I will grant her wish, lest by her continual coming she wear me out.'" [6]Then Jesus said, "Hear what the unjust judge says! [7]Will not God protect God's chosen ones who cry out to God day and night? Will not God be patient with them? [8]I tell you, God will vindicate them speedily. Nevertheless, when the Son of Humanity comes, will the Son of Humanity find faith on the earth?"

THE SELF-RIGHTEOUS AND THE HUMBLE

[9]Then He told this parable to certain ones who trusted in themselves and their own righteousness and despised everyone else: [10]"Two men went up to the temple to pray. One was a Pharisee and the other was a tax collector. [11]The Pharisee stood up and prayed this to himself: 'God, I thank You that I am not like other people who are greedy, unjust and immoral, or even like that tax collector. [12]I fast twice a week, and I tithe of everything I get.' [13]But the tax collector stood at a distance and would not so much as look up to heaven. He beat his breast and said, 'God, be merciful to me a sinner.' [14]I tell you, this man went down to his house forgiven rather than the other. For those who exalt themselves will be humbled, and those who humble themselves will be exalted."

CHILDREN: THE ESSENCE OF THE HEAVENLY REALM

[15]People brought their babies for Jesus to touch; but when the disciples saw this, they rebuked the people. [16]But Jesus gathered the disciples together and said, "Let the children come to Me and do not forbid them, for God's realm belongs to such as these. [17]Truly I say to you, if you cannot accept God's realm like a little child, you will never get in."

POSSESSIONS

[18]A certain leader asked Him, "Good Teacher, what must I do to inherit eternal life?" [19]Jesus said to him, "Why do you call Me good? No one is good but God. [20]You know the commandments, 'Do not commit adultery, do not kill, do not steal, do not lie about others, honor your father and mother.'" [21]The man said, "All these I have kept since my youth." [22]When Jesus heard this, He said to him, "You still lack one thing! Go and sell everything you have, give the money to the poor and you will have treasure in heaven. Then come and follow Me." [23]When the man heard this, he was sad, for he was very rich. [24]Jesus saw that he was sad and said, "How hard it is for a rich person to enter God's realm. [25]It is easier for a camel to go through the eye of a needle than for the rich to enter God's realm." [26]Those who heard this said, "Who then can be saved?" [27]Jesus said, "What is impossible with humans is possible with God."

REWARDS

28Then Peter said, "Look, we have left everything and followed You." 29Jesus said to them, "Truly I say to you, no one has left home or parents or brothers or sisters or spouse or children for the sake of God's realm 30who will not receive much more in this age, and in the world to come eternal life."

JESUS AGAIN TELLS HIS DISCIPLES ABOUT COMING THINGS

31Jesus took the twelve aside and said to them, "We are going up to Jerusalem, and everything that was written by the prophets concerning the Son of Humanity will be accomplished. 32He will be handed over to the unbelievers and be mocked, mistreated and spit on. 33After they have whipped Him, they will put Him to death. On the third day He will rise again." 34They understood none of this. The meaning was concealed from them, and they didn't comprehend what was meant.

A BLIND MAN IS HEALED NEAR JERICHO

35As Jesus came near Jericho, a certain blind man was sitting by the roadside begging. 36Hearing the crowd passing by, he asked what it meant. 37They told him that Jesus of Nazareth was passing by. 38He cried out, "Jesus! Son of David! Have mercy on me!" 39The people in front told him to be quiet, but he cried out even louder, "Son of David! Have mercy on me!" 40Jesus stopped and told them to bring the man to Him. When he came near, Jesus asked him, 41"What do you want Me to do for you?" He said, "Rabbi! I want to see!" 42Jesus said, "Receive your sight; your faith has saved you." 43Immediately he received his sight and followed Jesus, giving thanks to God. And all the people who saw gave thanks to God.

ZACCHAEUS REPENTS

19:1As Jesus was going through Jericho, 2a man named Zacchaeus, a chief tax collector and a rich man, 3wanted to see what sort of person Jesus was. But he could not because he was too short to see over the crowds. 4So he ran ahead and climbed up into a sycamore tree to see Jesus, for Jesus was coming that way. 5When Jesus came to the place, He looked up and said to him, "Zacchaeus, come down at once! Today I must stay at your house." 6He quickly came down and received Him joyfully. 7When other people saw this, they all complained that He had gone to be the guest of a sinner. 8Zacchaeus stood up and said, "Look, Rabbi! Today I give half my possessions to the poor; and if I have cheated anyone out of anything, I restore it fourfold." 9Jesus said to him, "This day salvation has come to this house, for he too is a child of Abraham. 10For the Son of Humanity has come to seek and to save the lost."

THE SERVANTS WHO WERE GIVEN DIFFERENT GIFTS

11As the people listened, He went on to tell them a parable because He was approaching Jerusalem and because they thought that God's realm was about to appear. 12He said, "A certain prince went to a far country to be made king and then return. 13He called ten of his servants, gave each one a coin and said to them, 'Use this to make more money until I return.' 14But his citizens hated him and sent messengers after him to say, 'We do not want this man to reign over us.' 15Later he returned, having been made king, and he commanded those servants to be called to whom he had given the money so that he might find out how much each servant had earned. [16]The first came and said, 'Sir, your coin has increased to ten coins.' [17]He said to him, 'Well done, my good servant! Because you have been faithful in little, I give you authority over ten cities.' [18]The second servant came and said, 'Sir, your coin yielded five coins.' [19]He said to him, 'You will be over five cities.' [20]Then another servant came and said, 'Look, sir, here is your coin. I have kept it preserved in a napkin [21]because I was afraid of you. You are a harsh person. You pick up what you did not lay down and reap what you did not sow.' [22]The king said to him, 'Out of your own mouth I will judge you, you wicked servant. You knew that I was a harsh person, picking up what I did not lay down and reaping what I did not sow? [23]Then why didn't you put my money into the bank, so that when I returned, I could have collected it with interest?' [24]Then he said to those who stood by, 'Take the coin from him and give it to the one who has ten coins.' [25]'Sir!' they said, 'He already has ten coins!' [26]The king said, 'To everyone who has, more will be given. But to those who do not have, even what they have will be taken from them. [27]Now as for my enemies who did not want me to be king over them, bring them here and slay them before me.'"

JESUS RIDES A DONKEY AND FULFILLS PROPHECY

[28]After saying this, Jesus went on ahead up toward Jerusalem. [29]As He approached Bethphage and Bethany at the mountain called the Mount of Olives, He sent two of His disciples, [30]saying, "Go to that village over there. As you are entering it, you will find a colt tied there that has never been ridden. Untie it and bring it. [31]If anyone asks you, 'Why are you untying it?' say to them, 'Because God needs it.' [32]They went and found the colt there just as He had told them they would. [33]As they were untying the colt, the owners asked them, "Why are you untying that colt?" [34]They said, "God needs it." [35]They brought the colt to Jesus, threw their garments across its back and seated Jesus on it.

THE MESSIAH'S TRIUMPHANT ENTRY INTO JERUSALEM

[36]As He rode along, the people spread their garments in the road. [37]As He came near the descent of the Mount of Olives, the whole company of disciples began loudly and joyfully to praise God for all the miracles they had seen. [38]They shouted, "Blessed is the king who comes in the name of Yahweh! Peace in heaven and glory in the highest!" [39]Some of the Pharisees in the crowd said to Him, "Teacher, rebuke Your disciples!" [40]But He answered them and said, "I tell you, if they kept quiet, the very stones would shout."

[41]When He came near and looked at the city, He wept over it [42]and said, "If only you had known, even on this your day, what would bring you peace! But now it is hidden from your eyes. [43]The days will come when your enemies will put a mound against you and surround you and close you in on every side. [44]They will throw you to the ground and your children with you. They will not leave one stone upon another, because you did not recognize the time when God visited you."

JESUS DRIVES THE MERCHANTS OUT OF THE TEMPLE

[45]Jesus went into the temple and began to drive out those who were buying and selling there. [46]He said to them, "It is written! 'My house is the house of prayer,' but you have made it 'a den of thieves!'" [47]Then He taught daily in the temple. The chief

priests and the scribes and the leaders of the people sought to destroy Him, [48]but they could not find a way, because all the people listened to Him attentively.

THE LEADERS QUESTION JESUS' AUTHORITY

[20:1]On one of those days as Jesus was teaching the people in the temple and telling the good news, the chief priests and the scribes and the elders came [2]and said to Him, "Tell us by what authority You do these things. Who gave You this authority?" [3]He answered, "I will ask you a question also. Tell me, [4]who gave John the authority to baptize? Was it from heaven or from humans?" [5]They talked it over among themselves, saying, "If we say, 'From heaven,' He will say, 'Then why didn't you believe John?' [6]But if we say, 'From humans,' all the people will stone us, for they are convinced that John was a prophet." [7]So they answered, "We don't know." [8]Then Jesus said to them, "Then neither will I tell you by what authority I do these things."

THE VINEYARD AND THE UNGRATEFUL TENANTS

[9]Jesus told the people this parable: "A landowner planted a vineyard, rented it to tenants and went to a far country for a long time. [10]At harvest time the owner sent a servant to the tenants for a share of the fruit from the vineyard, but the tenants beat him and sent him away empty-handed. [11]The owner sent another servant; and they also beat him and treated him shamefully and sent him away without a thing. [12]The owner sent a third, and they wounded him and threw him out. [13]Then the owner of the vineyard said, 'What should I do? Should I send my beloved son? Surely they will respect him.' [14]But when the tenants saw him, they said among themselves, 'This is the heir! Let's kill him, then the inheritance will be ours.' [15]So they killed him and threw him out of the vineyard. Now what will the owner of the vineyard do to them? [16]The owner will come and destroy those tenants and give the vineyard to others." When the people heard this, they said, "God forbid!" [17]Jesus looked at them and said, "What does the Scripture mean that says, 'The stone that the builders rejected has become the head of the corner'? [18]Whoever falls on that stone will be broken, but it will grind to a powder anyone on whom it falls."

THE LEADERS TRY TO TRAP JESUS INTO OPPOSING CAESAR

[19]The chief priests and the scribes sought to lay hands on Him, but they were afraid of the people. They knew that He had spoken this parable against them, [20]so they sent spies who pretended to be sincere. The spies watched to see if they could trip Him up with His own words so that they could hand Him over to the power and authority of the governor. [21]They asked Him, "Teacher, we know that what You say and teach is right and that You are impartial and honestly teach God's ways. [22]Is it lawful to pay taxes to Caesar or not?" [23]Jesus saw through their trickery and said, [24]"Show Me a coin. Whose picture and name are on it?" They answered, "Caesar's." [25]Then He said to them, "Give to Caesar the things that are Caesar's and to God the things that are God's." [26]They could not trap Him by His words in front of the people, and they were surprised by His answer. So they held their peace.

JESUS GIVES THE SADDUCEES A GLIMPSE INTO HEAVEN

[27]The Sadducees, who say there is no resurrection, came to Jesus and asked Him, [28]"Teacher, Moses wrote that if a man dies and leaves a widow without children, his

brother should marry the widow and raise up children for his brother. [29]Once there were seven brothers. The first married and died and left no children. [30]The second married the widow and died and left no children. [31]And the third did the same. All seven married her and died and left no children. [32]Last of all, the woman died also. [33]Now at the resurrection, whose wife will she be, since all seven married her?" [34]Jesus said to them, "The men and women of this world marry, [35]but the men and women who are considered worthy and are ready for that other world and the resurrection from the dead do not marry. [36]They cannot die anymore, for they are like the angels. They are the children of God, since they are children of the resurrection. [37]As to whether the dead are awakened, Moses proved at the bush when he called God the God of Abram, the God of Isaac and the God of Jacob [38]that God is not the God of the dead, but of the living. For all are alive before God." [39]One of the scribes said, "Teacher, You have answered well." [40]After that they did not venture to ask Him anything.

THE MESSIAH

[41]Jesus said to them, "How can you say that the Messiah is David's son? [42]David himself says in the book of Psalms, 'Yahweh said to God: Sit at My right hand [43]till I make Your enemies Your footstool.' [44]If David calls the son 'God,' how can He be David's son?"

BEWARE OF HYPOCRISY

[45]There in front of all the people He said to His disciples, [46]"Beware of the scribes. They like to walk around in fringed robes and love to be greeted in the marketplaces. They want the front seats at synagogues and the places of honor at banquets. [47]But they cheat widows out of their homes and for a show make long prayers. They will receive the greater punishment."

JESUS PRAISES A POOR WIDOW

21:1[Jesus looked up and saw the rich putting their gifts into the treasury. [2]He also saw a certain needy widow put in two small coins. [3]He said, "Truly I say to you, this impoverished widow has put in more than all the others. [4]For they put in offerings out of their abundance, but she in her poverty put in all she had to live on."

JESUS FORETELLS THE DESTRUCTION OF THE TEMPLE

[5]As some spoke about the temple and how it was adorned with beautiful stones and gifts offered to God, Jesus said, [6]"As for these things you are looking at, the day will come when not one stone will be left upon another. They will all be thrown down."

FUTURE TRIBULATIONS

[7]They asked Him, "Teacher, when will these things happen? What will be the sign that all these things are about to take place?" [8]Jesus said, "Watch out that you are not deceived. For many will come in My name and say, 'I am the Messiah!' and 'The time is near!' Do not follow them. [9]When you hear of wars and riots, do not be frightened. These must come first, but the end is yet to come. [10]Nation will rise against nation and country against country. [11]There will be great earthquakes, famines, plagues, fearful sights and great signs in the sky. [12]But before all this, they will lay their hands on you and persecute you. They will take you to synagogues and prisons and bring you

before rulers and governors for My name's sake. [13]But it will turn out to be a chance to testify. [14]Make up your mind beforehand not to ponder about your answer, [15]for I will give you words and wisdom that your adversaries will not be able to refute or stand against. [16]You will be betrayed by parents, sisters, brothers, relatives and friends. They will put some of you to death. [17]You will be hated by everyone because of My name, [18]but not a hair of your head will perish. [19]By continuing strong you will save your soul.

[20]"When you see Jerusalem surrounded by armies, then know that its destruction is near. [21]Those in Judea must flee to the mountains, those in the city must go out and those in the country must not come in. [22]For those will be the days of vindication when all the things that are written will be fulfilled. [23]Woe to pregnant women and those with nursing babies in those days, for there will be great distress in the land and wrath upon this people. [24]They will fall by the edge of the sword and will be led captive to all nations. Jerusalem will be trampled by the unbelievers until the times of the unbelievers are fulfilled.

THE SPECTACULAR RETURN OF JESUS

[25]"There will be signs in the sun and the moon and the stars. On the earth nations will be distressed and perplexed by the sea and the roaring waves. [26]Human hearts will fail from apprehension because of what is coming upon the earth, for the forces in the sky will be shaken. [27]Then they will see the Son of Humanity coming in a cloud with power and great glory. [28]When these things begin to come to pass, be elated and lift your heads high, for your liberation is drawing near."

THE TIME OF JESUS' RETURN

[29]Jesus told them this parable: "Observe the fig tree and all the trees. [30]When their leaves start growing, you know and can see that summer is near. [31]In the same way, when you see these things come to pass, you will know that God's realm is near at hand. [32]Truly I say to you, this generation will not pass away until all this has happened. [33]The sky and the earth will pass away, but My words will not pass away. [34]Take care, lest at any time your hearts become heavy with overindulgence and drunkenness and the cares of this life and that day catch you unaware. [35]For it will come like a snare upon all those who live on the earth. [36]Therefore watch and always pray that you will have the strength to escape all these things that will happen and that you will be able to stand before the Son of Humanity."

[37]In the daytime He was teaching in the temple, and at night He went out and stayed on the Mount of Olives. [38]Early in the morning all the people came to Him in the temple to hear Him.

JUDAS GOES TO THE LEADERS AND OFFERS TO BETRAY JESUS

22:1Now the Feast of Unleavened Bread called the Passover was near. [2]The chief priests and scribes were looking for a way to kill Him, but they were afraid of what the people would do. [3]Then Satan entered Judas Iscariot, one of the twelve, [4]and he went and talked to the chief priests and temple officers about how he might betray Jesus to them. [5]They were pleased and agreed to give him money. [6]Then he promised to look for an opportunity to betray Jesus to them when the crowds were not present.

PREPARATIONS FOR THE PASSOVER

[7]The day came for the Feast of Unleavened Bread when the Passover lamb must be killed. [8]Jesus sent Peter and John, saying, "Go and make preparations so that we may eat the Passover." [9]They asked, "Where do You want us to prepare it?" [10]He said, "As you enter the city, a man will meet you carrying a jar of water. Follow him into the house that he enters [11]and say to the owner of the house, 'Our Teacher asks where the guest room is where He may eat the Passover with His disciples.' [12]He will show you a large furnished upper room. Make everything ready there." [13]They went and found everything as Jesus had said. And they prepared the Passover.

THE PASSOVER

[14]When the hour came, Jesus and the twelve apostles sat down together. [15]Jesus said to them, "With all My heart I have desired to eat this Passover with you before I suffer; [16]for I say to you, I will not eat it again until it is fully realized in God's realm." [17]He took the cup, gave thanks, and said, "Take this and share it among yourselves; [18]for I say to you, I will not drink of the fruit of the vine again until God's realm comes." [19]Then He took bread, gave thanks, broke it and gave it to them, saying, "This is My body, given for you. This do in remembrance of Me." [20]In the same way He took the cup after supper, saying, "This cup is the new covenant in My blood that is shed for you. [21]But be careful, for My betrayer is with Me, and his hand is with Mine on the table. [22]Truly, the Son of Humanity is going as it was determined; but woe to that man by whom He is betrayed." [23]Then they began to inquire among themselves which of them would do this.

JESUS PATIENTLY EXPLAINS TRUE GREATNESS

[24]They also disputed among themselves about which of them would be considered the greatest. [25]Jesus said to them, "The rulers of the nations control their people, and those who exercise this authority are called good. [26]But with you it is not so. Rather, let the one who is greatest among you become like the least important, and the one who is leader like one who serves. [27]For who is greater, the one who sits at the table or the one who serves? Is it not the one who sits at the table? But I am among you as one who serves. [28]You are those who have remained with Me in My adversities. [29]I confer upon you a realm, even as My heavenly Parent conferred one upon Me, [30]so that you may eat and drink at My table in My realm and sit on thrones judging the twelve tribes of Israel.

PETER IS TOLD THAT HE WILL DENY JESUS THREE TIMES

[31]"Simon, Simon, Satan has demanded to sift all of you like wheat. [32]But I have prayed for you, that your faith not fail. When you turn back to Me, strengthen the others." [33]Peter said to Him, "Rabbi! I am ready to go with You to prison and to death!" [34]Jesus said, "I tell you, Peter, the rooster will not crow today before you deny three times that you know Me."

BE PREPARED

[35]Jesus asked them, "When I sent you out without moneybag or knapsack or sandals, did you lack anything?" "Nothing," they said. [36]Then He said to them, "But

now, whoever has a moneybag or knapsack should take it. And if you have no sword, sell your garment and buy one. [37]For I say to you that what is written must yet be fulfilled concerning Me: 'He was reckoned among the transgressors.' For the things concerning Me must come true." [38]They said, "Rabbi, look! Here are two swords." He said to them, "Enough!"

THE GARDEN OF GETHSEMANE

[39]Jesus left the house and went as usual to the Mount of Olives. His disciples followed Him. [40]When He reached the place, He said to them, "Pray that you do not submit to temptation." [41]Then He withdrew about a stone's throw from them and kneeled down and prayed, [42]"O My dear Parent, if You are willing, remove this cup from Me. Nevertheless, not My will but Yours be done." [43]An angel appeared to Him from heaven and strengthened Him. [44]Being in agony, He prayed more earnestly, and His sweat was like drops of blood falling down upon the ground. [45]When He rose from prayer and went back to His disciples, He found them asleep, exhausted by sorrow. [46]He said to them, "Why are you sleeping? Get up and pray that you don't submit to temptation."

JUDAS BRINGS THE PEOPLE WHO ARREST JESUS

[47]While He was still speaking, a crowd appeared. Judas, one of the twelve, was leading them. The one called Judas went over to Jesus to kiss Him. [48]Jesus said to him, "Judas, would you betray the Son of Humanity with a kiss?" [49]When those who were with Jesus became aware of what was happening, they asked Him, "Rabbi, should we strike them with the sword?" [50]One of them struck the high priests's servant, cutting off his right ear. [51]Jesus said, "Let him be," and He touched the servant's ear and healed him. [52]Then Jesus said to the chief priests, the elders and the officers from the temple who had come for Him, "Have you come out against Me with swords and clubs as though I were a thief? [53]I was with you daily in the temple, and you did not raise your hand against Me. But this is your hour, and the darkness is your strength."

PETER DENIES KNOWING JESUS THREE TIMES

[54]They arrested Jesus and brought Him to the high priest's house. Peter followed at a distance. [55]They kindled a fire in the middle of the courtyard and sat down together. Peter sat down among them. [56]A servant girl saw him sitting by the fire. She looked intently at him and said, "This one was also with Him." [57]He denied it and said, "Woman, I don't know Him!" [58]After a while another servant saw him and said, "You are also one of them." Peter said, "Man, I am not!" [59]About an hour later someone else confidently affirmed, "It's true! This fellow was with Him also, for he is a Galilean." [60]Peter said, "Man, I don't know what you're talking about!" Immediately, even as he was speaking, the rooster crowed. [61]Jesus turned and looked at Peter. Then Peter remembered the words Jesus had said: "Before the rooster crows today, you will deny Me three times." [62]Peter went out and wept bitterly.

[63]The men who had arrested Jesus began mocking and hitting Him. [64]They blindfolded Him and struck Him on the face and asked, "Who struck You? Prophesy!"

65And they said many other abusive things against Him.

JESUS ON TRIAL BEFORE THE UNBELIEVERS

66When it became daylight, the elders of the people, the chief priests and the scribes met together, and Jesus was brought before them. They asked, 67"Are You the Messiah? Tell us!" He said to them, "If I tell you, you will not believe. 68And if I question you, you will not answer. 69But from now on the Son of Humanity will be seated at the right hand of Almighty God." 70Then they said, "Then You are descended from God?" Jesus answered, "You say that I am." 71They said, "What need have we of further testimony? We have heard it from His own mouth!"

JESUS IS TAKEN TO THE ROMAN GOVERNOR

23:1The whole assembly stood up and led Him to Pilate. 2They began to accuse Him, saying, "We found this man perverting our nation and forbidding the payment of taxes to Caesar. He says that He is the Messiah, a king." 3Pilate asked Him, "Are You the King of the Jews? Jesus answered, "So you say." 4Then Pilate said to the chief priests and the crowd, "I find no reason to condemn this man." 5But they fiercely insisted, "He stirs up the people by teaching throughout all Judea, beginning from Galilee and now spreading here." 6When Pilate heard this, he asked if the man was a Galilean. 7As soon as he found out that He belonged to Herod's jurisdiction, he sent Him to Herod, who was also in Jerusalem at that time.

8Herod was very glad to see Jesus. He had been wanting to see Jesus for a long time. He hoped to see Jesus perform some miracle. 9He questioned Jesus at great length, but Jesus made no answer. 10The chief priests and scribes stood and forcefully accused Him. 11Herod and his soldiers belittled and mocked Him. Then they put a bright-colored robe on Him and sent Him back to Pilate. 12That day Pilate and Herod became friends. Before that they had been enemies.

PILATE YIELDS TO THE DEMANDS OF THE MOB

13Pilate called together the chief priests, the leaders and the people 14and said to them, "You have brought this man to me and you claim that He makes trouble among the people. Beware! I have examined Him before you and have found no reason to condemn this man regarding those things of which you accuse Him. 15Neither has Herod, for he sent Him back to us. Clearly, this man has done nothing deserving death. 16Therefore I will discipline Him and release Him."

17Every year at the Feast the governor was obliged to release one person to them. 18They all cried out at once, "Away with this man! Release Barabbas to us!" 19Barabbas was in the prison for taking part in an uprising in the city and for murder. 20Pilate wanted to release Jesus, so he spoke to them again, 21but they cried out, "Crucify Him! Crucify Him!" 22Pilate spoke to them the third time, "Why? What harm has He done? I have found no reason for Him to die. Therefore I will discipline Him and let Him go." 23But with loud voices they kept on demanding that Jesus be crucified. Their shouts prevailed 24and Pilate passed sentence as they demanded. 25He released the man who was in prison because of an uprising and murder, the one they wanted, and he handed Jesus over to their will.

SIMON IS FORCED TO CARRY THE CROSS

[26]As they led Jesus away, they seized one Simon from Cyrene who was coming in from the country. They laid the cross on him, and he carried it behind Jesus.

JESUS SPEAKS TO THE WOMEN OF JERUSALEM

[27]A great crowd of people followed Jesus, and the women were distressed and weeping for Him. [28]Jesus turned to them and said, "Daughters of Jerusalem, do not weep for Me; weep for yourselves and your children. [29]For the days are coming when they will say, 'Blessed are the women who never gave birth.' [30]They will say to the mountains, 'Fall on us,' and to the hills, 'Cover us.' [31]For if they do these things when the tree is green, what will they do when it is dry?"

JESUS IS CRUCIFIED WITH CRIMINALS

[32]Two others, both criminals, were led away with Jesus to be put to death. [33]When they came to the place that is called Calvary, there they crucified Him and the criminals, one on the right and the other on the left. [34]Jesus said, "Forgive them, My dear Parent, for they do not know what they are doing."

THE SOLDIERS CAST LOTS FOR JESUS' CLOTHING

They divided up His garments by casting lots. [35]The people stood watching, but the leaders sneered and said, "He saved others; let Him save Himself if He is the Messiah, the chosen One of God."

[36]The soldiers also mocked Him. They came up to Him and offered Him sour wine. [37]They said, "If You are the King of the Jews, save Yourself." [38]A sign was above Him written in Greek, Latin and Hebrew which read, THIS IS THE KING OF THE JEWS. [39]One of the criminals hanging there spoke abusively to Him: "If You are the Messiah, save Yourself and us!" [40]But the other rebuked him and said, "Don't you fear God? You are under the same sentence! [41]We are rightly receiving what we deserve for our deeds, but this man has done nothing wrong." [42]Then he said, "Jesus, remember me when You come into Your realm." [43]Jesus said to him, "Truly I say to you, today you will be with Me in Paradise."

JESUS YIELDS UP HIS SPIRIT

[44]At noon, darkness came over the whole land for three hours. [45]The sun was darkened and the veil of the temple was torn in two. [46]Then Jesus cried out with a loud voice, "Heavenly Parent! Into Your hands I commit My Spirit," and yielded up His Spirit. [47]The centurion who saw what had happened glorified God and said, "Certainly this was a righteous man." [48]All the people who had come to see this sight saw what happened. After they saw it, they returned home deeply sorrowful. [49]All of His friends, including the women who had followed Him from Galilee, stood at a distance and watched everything.

JESUS IS BURIED IN A NEW TOMB BY A COURAGEOUS LEADER

[50]A member of the council, a good and honorable man named Joseph [51]of Arimathea in Judea, was waiting for God's realm. He had not consented to the council's decision. [52]He went to Pilate and asked for the body of Jesus. [53]He took it down, wrapped it in linen and laid it in a tomb hewn out of the rock in which no one

had ever been laid. [54]It was Preparation Day, and the Sabbath was about to dawn. [55]The women who had come with Him from Galilee followed Joseph and saw the tomb and how His body was laid. [56]They went home, prepared spices and perfumed oil, then rested on the Sabbath according to the commandment.

THE WOMEN DISCOVER THE EMPTY TOMB

24:1[1]At sunrise on the first day of the week they brought the spices they had prepared to the tomb. [2]They found the stone rolled away from the tomb. [3]They went in, but they did not find the body of Jesus. [4]They were baffled by this, but when they looked around, two youths in shining garments were standing near them.

TWO ANGELS TELL THE WOMEN THAT JESUS HAS RISEN

[5]The women were afraid and bowed their faces to the ground. The two said to them, "Why do you seek the living among the dead? [6]He is not here; He has risen. Remember what He told you while He was still in Galilee: [7]'The Son of Humanity must be given into the hands of sinful humans, be crucified and on the third day be raised.'" [8]They remembered His words. [9]Then the women returned from the tomb and told all this to the eleven and to all the rest. [10]It was Mary Magdalene, Joanna, Mary the mother of James and others with them who told this to the apostles; [11]but what the women said seemed too incredible, and the apostles did not believe them. [12]Peter, however, got up and ran to the tomb. Stooping down, he saw the linen wrappings by themselves. Then he departed, wondering to himself what had happened.

TWO DISCIPLES MEET A STRANGER ON THE ROAD TO EMMAUS

[13]That same day two of them were going to a village called Emmaus, about seven miles from Jerusalem. [14]They were talking together about all the things that had taken place. [15]While they talked and discussed the happenings, Jesus Himself approached and walked with them, [16]but their eyes were kept from recognizing Him. [17]He said to them, "What is it that you are talking about as you sadly walk along?" [18]One of them, whose name was Cleopas, answered, "You must be the only visitor to Jerusalem who doesn't know the things that have happened there these last few days!" [19]He asked them, "What things?" They said, "Concerning Jesus of Nazareth, who was a mighty prophet in word and deed before God and all the people. [20]The chief priests and our leaders handed Him over to be condemned to death and have crucified Him. [21]We were hoping that He was the one who was going to redeem Israel. Besides all this, today is the third day since these things happened. [22]And now some of the women in our group have surprised us out of our wits. At daybreak they went to the tomb [23]but they didn't find His body! They came and told us they had seen a vision of angels who said that He was alive. [24]Then some of our people went to the tomb and found it just as the women had said; but they did not see Him."

[25]Then Jesus said to them, "How foolish and dull-minded you are! Won't you believe all the things the prophets spoke? [26]Should not the Messiah have suffered these things and entered glory?" [27]Then, beginning with Moses and all the prophets, He explained to them what the Scriptures meant concerning Himself. [28]As they came near the village where the two were going, He acted as though He were going farther;

[29]but they persuaded Him to stay with them. They said, "It is nearly evening, and the daylight is slipping away." So He went in and stayed with them. [30]As He sat at the table with them, He took bread, blessed it and broke it and gave it to them. [31]Then their eyes were opened and they recognized Him. But He vanished from their sight.

[32]They said to one another, "Did not our hearts burn within us when He talked with us on the road and opened the Scriptures to us?" [33]They set out that same hour and returned to Jerusalem. They found the eleven and those who were with them gathered together. [34]They were saying, "It's true! Jesus has risen and has appeared to Peter!" [35]Then the two told what had happened on the road to Emmaus and how they recognized Jesus when He broke the bread.

JESUS APPEARS TO THE DISCIPLES

[36]As they spoke, Jesus appeared in their midst and said to them, "Peace to you!" [37]They sprang back terrified, supposing that they were seeing a ghost. [38]Jesus said to them, "Why are you disturbed, and why do doubts arise in your minds? [39]Look at My hands and My feet. It is I. Touch Me and see. A ghost does not have flesh and bones as you see that I have." [40]Then Jesus said, "Here are the marks in My hands and My feet to prove it." [41]They could still not believe it for joy and wonder. Jesus said to them, "Have you anything to eat?" [42]They gave Jesus a piece of broiled fish, [43]and Jesus took it and ate it in front of them. [44]Then Jesus said to them, "This is the reality of which I spoke to you while I was still with you: that all things must be fulfilled which were written about Me in the law of Moses and in the writings of the prophets and in the Psalms." [45]Thus Jesus opened their minds to understand the Scriptures. [46]Jesus said to them, "This is what is written: The Messiah will suffer and rise from the dead the third day; [47]and repentance and forgiveness of sins will be published in the Messiah's name among all the nations, beginning at Jerusalem. [48]You are witnesses of these things. [49]I will send the promise of My heavenly Parent upon you; but stay here in the city until you are clothed with power from on high."

JESUS IS TAKEN TO HEAVEN IN FRONT OF THE DISCIPLES

[50]Jesus led them out as far as Bethany, then lifted up both hands and blessed them. [51]Jesus blessed them, stood apart from them and was taken up into heaven. [52]They worshiped Jesus and returned to Jerusalem with great joy. [53]And they were continually in the temple praising God.

John

$^{1:1}$In the beginning was the Word, and the Word was with God, and the Word was God. ^{2}The Word was with God in the beginning. ^{3}All things were made by the Word, and apart from the Word nothing came into being. ^{4}In the Word was life, and that life was the light of all people. ^{5}The light shines in the darkness, but the darkness has not grasped it.

^{6}There was a man sent from God whose name was John. ^{7}He came as a witness to testify about the light, so that all might believe through him. ^{8}He was not the light, but witnessed about that light. ^{9}The true light which enlightens all people was coming into the world.

BELIEVE IN JESUS AND BE BORN OF GOD

^{10}He was in the world, and the world was made by Him, but the world did not know Him. ^{11}He came to His own, but His own did not accept Him. ^{12}But to all who accepted Him and believed in His name, to them He gave the power to become the children of God. ^{13}They were not born of blood or of the will of the flesh or of the will of man, but of God. ^{14}The Word became flesh and lived among us and we gazed at His glory, the glory of the only begotten Son of God, full of grace and truth. ^{15}John testified about Him and cried out, "This is He of whom I said, 'He who comes after me is ordained to be first, for He was before me.'" ^{16}From His abundance we have all received favor and goodwill. ^{17}The law was given through Moses; favor and truth come through Jesus Christ. ^{18}No one has ever seen God. But the only begotten Son, who is close to God's heart, has made God known.

JOHN THE BAPTIST PREPARES THE WAY

^{19}This was the testimony of John when the Jews sent priests and Levites from Jerusalem to ask him, "Who are you?" ^{20}Without hesitation he declared, "I am not the Messiah." ^{21}They asked him, "Who are you then? Are you Elijah?" He said, "I am not." "Are you the Prophet?" "No," he answered. ^{22}Then they asked him, "Who are you, that we may give an answer to those who sent us? What do you have to say for yourself?" ^{23}He said, "I am the voice of one calling in the wilderness, 'Make straight the way of our God,' as the prophet Isaiah said."

^{24}Some of those who had been sent were Pharisees, ^{25}and they asked him, "Why are you baptizing if you are not the Messiah or Elijah or the Prophet?" ^{26}John answered, "I baptize with water, but standing among you is One whom you do not know, ^{27}One who comes after me. I am not worthy to untie the strap of His sandal." ^{28}This took place in Bethany beyond the Jordan where John was baptizing.

JOHN TELLS WHY JESUS CAME TO EARTH

[29]The next day John saw Jesus coming to him, and he said, "Look! The Lamb of God who takes away the sin of the world! [30]This is He of whom I said, 'After me comes One who is ordained to be first, for He was before me.' [31]I did not know who He was, but I came baptizing with water to make Him known to Israel. [32]I saw the Spirit descend from heaven as a dove and remain on Him. [33]I did not know Him, but the One who sent me to baptize with water said to me, 'You will see the Spirit descend and remain on someone. He is the One who baptizes with the Holy Spirit.' [34]I have seen and I testify that this is the Son of God."

TWO OF JOHN'S DISCIPLES FOLLOW JESUS

[35]The next day John was standing there again with two of his disciples. [36]Seeing Jesus walk by, he said, "Look! The Lamb of God!" [37]The two disciples heard him say this and they followed Jesus. [38]Jesus turned and saw them following and asked, "What are you looking for?" They said to Him, "Rabbi (which means teacher), where do You stay?" [39]He said to them, "Come and see." They came and saw where He was staying and remained with Him that day. It was then about four in the afternoon. [40]One of the two who heard John and followed Jesus was Andrew, Simon Peter's brother. [41]The first thing Andrew did was to find his brother Simon and say to him, "We found the Messiah!" (which means Christ). [42]Then Andrew brought Simon Peter to Jesus. Jesus looked at him and said, "You are Simon the son of John. You will be called Cephas" (which means Peter).

PHILIP AND NATHANAEL

[43]The next day Jesus decided to go to Galilee. Finding Philip, He said to him, "Follow Me." [44]Philip was from Bethsaida, Andrew and Peter's town. [45]Philip found Nathanael and said to him, "We have found the One Moses wrote about in the law and about whom the prophets wrote! It is Jesus of Nazareth, the son of Joseph!" [46]Nathanael said, "Can any good come out of Nazareth?" Philip answered, "Come and see." [47]Jesus saw Nathanael coming to Him and said of him, "Look, a true Israelite - and there is no deceit in him!" [48]Nathanael said to Him, "How do You know me?" Jesus answered, "Before Philip called you, I saw you under the fig tree." [49]Nathanael said, "Rabbi! You are the Son of God! You are the King of Israel!" [50]Jesus said to him, "You believe because I said that I saw you under the fig tree? You will see greater things than that. [51]Truly I say to you, you will see heaven open and the angels of God ascending and descending upon the Son of Humanity."

JESUS TURNS WATER INTO WINE

[2:1]On the third day there was a wedding at Cana in Galilee. Jesus' mother was there. [2]Jesus and His disciples were also invited to the wedding. [3]When they ran out of wine, Jesus' mother said to Him, "They have no wine." [4]Jesus said to her, "Mother, why do you ask this of Me? My hour has not yet come." [5]His mother said to the servants, "Do whatever He tells you." [6]Six stone water jars were standing there for the Jewish ceremonial cleansing, each capable of holding over twenty gallons. [7]Jesus said to them, "Fill the water jars with water," and they filled them to the brim. [8]Then He said to them, "Now draw some out and take it to the one in charge of the feast." The servants took it [9]and the one in charge tasted the water that had become wine. He did not know where it came from, though the servants who had drawn the water knew. Then he called the bridegroom [10]and said to him, "Usually hosts serve the good wine first, and then when the guests have drunk well, the lesser quality. But you have kept the good wine until now." [11]This, the first of His signs, Jesus did at Cana in Galilee. Jesus revealed His glory there, and His disciples believed in Him. [12]After this He went down to Capernaum with His mother, His brothers, and His disciples and they stayed there a few days.

JESUS DRIVES THE MERCHANTS OUT OF THE TEMPLE

[13]It was nearly time for the Jewish Passover, and Jesus went up to Jerusalem. [14]In the temple courtyard He saw people selling oxen, sheep and doves, and also money-changers sitting at tables. [15]He made a whip out of cords and drove them all out of the temple, including the sheep and oxen. He poured out the coins of the money changers and overturned their tables. [16]He said to those who sold doves, "Take these away! Do not make My heavenly Parent's house a market place!" [17]Then His disciples remembered that it was written: "Zeal for Your house will burn in Me like fire."

THE JEWS LOOK FOR PROOF

[18]The Jews said to Him, "What sign can You do to show us that You have the right to do this?" [19]Jesus answered them, "Destroy this temple, and in three days I will raise it up." [20]The Jews said, "It took forty-six years to build this temple! Are You going to rebuild it in three days?" [21]But the temple He spoke of was His body. [22]When He had risen from the dead, His disciples remembered that He had said this. Then they believed the Scripture and the words that Jesus had spoken.

[23]While He was in Jerusalem at the Feast of the Passover, many believed in His name after seeing the signs He did. [24]But Jesus did not trust Himself to them, because He understood them all. [25]Jesus did not need any testimony about people, for He understood people.

A LEADER NAMED NICODEMUS SECRETLY SEEKS OUT JESUS

[3:1]A Pharisee named Nicodemus, a leader of the Jews, [2]came to Jesus at night and said to Him, "Rabbi, we know that You are a teacher who has come from God, for no one could do the miracles You do without God's help." [3]Jesus said to him, "Truly I say to you, unless you are born again, you cannot see God's realm." [4]Nicodemus said to Him, "How can people be born when they are old? Can they enter a second time into their mother's womb and be born?" [5]Jesus answered, "Truly I say to you, unless you are born of water and the Spirit, you cannot enter God's realm. [6]What is born of flesh is flesh, and what is born of Spirit is spirit. [7]Do not be surprised that I said to you, 'You must be born again.' [8]The wind blows where it chooses. You hear the sound of it, but you cannot tell where it comes from or where it is going. So it is with everyone who is born of the Spirit." [9]Nicodemus asked, "How can this be?" [10]Jesus answered, "You are a teacher of Israel and are not aware of these things? [11]Truly I say to you, we speak what we know and testify to what we have seen, but you do not accept our testimony. [12]If I tell you of earthly things and you do not believe, how can you believe if I tell you of heavenly things? [13]No one has gone up to heaven but the One who came down from heaven, the Son of Humanity. [14]And as Moses lifted up the serpent in the wilderness, so must the Son of Humanity be lifted up, [15]so that whoever believes in Him may have eternal life. [16]For God so loved the world that God gave the only begotten Son, that whoever believes in Him would not perish but have everlasting life. [17]God did not send the Son into the world to condemn the world, but that the world might be saved through Him. [18]Those who believe in Him are not judged. But those who do not believe are judged already because they have not believed in the name of the only begotten Son of God. [19]And this is the judgment: Though the light has come into the world, people loved darkness rather than light because their deeds were evil. [20]Those who do foul things hate the light and will not come to the light lest their deeds be seen. [21]But those who are true come to the light so that it is apparent that their deeds are done through God."

JESUS' DISCIPLES BAPTIZE MANY

[22]After this, Jesus and His disciples went out to the countryside of Judea. He stayed with them there and baptized. [23]John also was baptizing at Aenon near Salim, because there was plenty of water there. [24]John had not yet been put in prison.

JOHN TESTIFIES ABOUT JESUS

[25]A question arose between John's disciples and the Jews about ceremonial cleansing. [26]They came to John and said, "Rabbi, that man who was with you on the other side of the Jordan about whom you testified - are you aware that He is baptizing and that everyone is going to Him?" [27]John answered, "No one can have anything except what is given from heaven. [28]You yourselves are my witnesses that I said, 'I am not the Messiah but have been sent before Him. [29]He who has the bride is the bridegroom. The friend of the bridegroom who stands by and listens for Him rejoices greatly to hear the bridegroom's voice. [30]He must increase, but I must decrease. [31]He who comes from above is above all. Anyone who is of the earth is earthly and speaks of earthly things. He who comes from heaven is above all. [32]He testifies to what He has seen and heard, but no one accepts His testimony. [33]Those who accept His testimony certify that God is truthful. [34]He whom God sent speaks the words of God, for God does not give the Spirit by measure. [35]God loves the Son and gives everything into His hand. [36]Those who believe in the Son have everlasting life. Those who will not be persuaded by the Son will not see life, and the wrath of God remains on them."

JESUS FINDS IT NECESSARY TO LEAVE JUDEA

[4:1]The Pharisees heard that Jesus was making and baptizing more disciples than John. When Jesus became aware of this - [2]although Jesus Himself did not baptize, but His disciples did - [3]He left Judea and went back to Galilee. [4]He had to go through Samaria, [5]and He came to a town in Samaria called Sychar near the parcel of ground that Jacob gave to his son Joseph. [6]Jacob's well was there. It was about noon, and Jesus, weary from the journey, sat down beside the well.

THE SAMARITAN WOMAN AT THE WELL

[7]A Samaritan woman came to draw water and Jesus said to her, "Give Me a drink." [8]His disciples had gone into the town to buy food. [9]The woman said to Him, "How is it

that You, a Jew, ask a drink of me, a Samaritan woman?" [10]Jesus answered her, "If you knew what God can give and who it is that says to you, 'Give Me a drink,' you would ask Him and He would give you living water." [11]The woman said to Him, "Sir, You have nothing to get water with and the well is deep. Where will You get this living water? [12]Are You greater than our ancestor Jacob, who gave us the well and drank from it himself, along with his children and his cattle?" [13]Jesus said to her, "Everyone who drinks this water will thirst again. [14]But whoever drinks the water that I give will never thirst. For the spring of water I give will become in them a spring of water flowing out for eternal life." [15]The woman said to Him, "Sir, give me this water! Then I won't get thirsty or have to come here for water." [16]Jesus answered, "Go call your husband and come here." [17]The woman replied, "I have no husband." Jesus said to her, "You answered well when you said, 'I have no husband,' [18]for you have had five husbands, and the man you have now is not your husband. You spoke the truth."

[19]The woman said, "Sir, I perceive that You are a prophet. [20]Our ancestors worshiped on this mountain, but you Jews say that Jerusalem is the place where people ought to worship." [21]Jesus said to her, "Woman, believe Me, the hour is coming when you will worship God neither on this mountain nor in Jerusalem. [22]You do not know what you worship. We know what we worship, for salvation is from the Jews. [23]But the hour is coming, and now is, when the true worshipers will worship God in spirit and in truth. These are the worshipers that God is seeking. [24]God is Spirit, and those who worship God must worship in spirit and in truth." [25]The woman said, "I know that the Messiah, the Anointed One, is coming. When the Messiah comes, everything will be explained." [26]Jesus said to her, " I, the One speaking to you now, am the One."

[27]Just then His disciples came back. They were surprised to find Him talking with a woman, yet no one asked, "What do You want?" or "Why are You talking with her?" [28]The woman left her water jar, went into the town, and said to the people, [29]"Come see a man who told me everything I have ever done. Could this be the Messiah?" [30]Then they came out of the town to see Him.

[31]In the meantime His disciples urged Him, "Rabbi, eat." [32]But He said to them, "I have food to eat that you don't know about." [33]The disciples said to one another, "Has someone brought Him food?" [34]Jesus said to them, "My food is to do the will of the One who sent Me and to finish God's work. [35]Don't you have a saying, 'There are yet four months, and then the harvest'? But I tell you, open your eyes! Open your eyes and look closely at the fields, for they are white and ready to harvest! [36]Even now the reaper receives wages and gathers a harvest for eternal life, so that the sower and the reaper may rejoice together. [37]The proverb is certainly true: 'One sows and another reaps.' [38]I sent you to reap a crop for which you did not labor. Others labored, and you have reaped the benefits of their labors."

[39]Many of the Samaritans in that town believed in Him because of the woman who testified, "He told me everything I ever did." [40]When the Samaritans came to Him, they urged Him to stay with them. Jesus remained there two days. [41]Many more believed because of what He said. [42]They said to the woman, "Now we believe! Not because of

what you said, but now we have heard and know for ourselves that this is indeed the savior of the world."

JESUS HEALS FROM A DISTANCE

[43]After two days He left that place and went to Galilee. [44]Jesus Himself had testified that prophets have no honor in their own country. [45]When He came into Galilee, the Galileans welcomed Him because of all that He had done in Jerusalem at the Feast; for they also had been at the Feast.

[46]Once again Jesus came to Cana of Galilee where He had changed the water into wine. A certain royal official was there whose son was sick at Capernaum. [47]When he heard that Jesus had come from Judea to Galilee, he went to Him and asked Him to come down and heal his son, for his son was at the point of death. [48]Jesus said to him, "Unless you people see signs and wonders, you do not believe!" [49]The official said to Him, "Sir, come down before my little boy dies." [50]Jesus said to him, "You may go, your son lives." The man believed the word that Jesus spoke to him and went. [51]As he was returning home, his servants met him and said, "Your son lives!" [52]He asked the hour when his son had begun to recover, and they said to him, "The fever left him yesterday at one in the afternoon." [53]The father knew this was the same hour that Jesus had said to him, "Your son lives." So he and all his family believed. [54]This was the second sign Jesus did after He returned from Judea to Galilee.

JESUS HEALS A MAN BY THE POOL OF BETHESDA

[5:1]Later on there was a Feast of the Jews, and Jesus went up to Jerusalem. [2]There in Jerusalem by the Sheep Gate is a pool, which in Hebrew is called Bethesda, and it has five covered walkways. [3]A great many sick people were lying there: the blind, the lame, the paralyzed. [4-5]One man was there who had been sick for thirty-eight years. [6]Jesus saw him lying there and knew he had been there a long time. He said to him, "Do you want to be well?" [7]The sick man replied, "Sir, I have no one to put me into the pool when the water is stirred. While I am going, another steps down before me." [8]Jesus said to him, "Stand up! Pick up your mat and walk!" [9]Immediately the man was made whole, and he picked up his mat and walked.

THE LEADERS PROTEST THE HEALING ON THE SABBATH

That day was the Sabbath. [10]Therefore the Jews said to the man who had been healed, "It is the Sabbath! It is not lawful for you to carry a mat." [11]He answered them, "The man who made me whole said to me, 'Pick up your mat and walk.'" [12]They asked him, "Who is the man who said to you, 'Pick up your mat and walk'?" [13]But the man who had been healed did not know who it was, for Jesus had disappeared in the crowd.

[14]Later Jesus found him at the temple and said to him, "See, you have become well! Sin no more, lest something worse happen to you." [15]The man departed and told the Jews that it was Jesus who had healed him.

JESUS TELLS THE LEADERS THAT HE IS FROM GOD

[16]The Jews persecuted Jesus because He had done this on the Sabbath. [17]But Jesus answered them, "My heavenly Parent goes on working, and I also work." [18]Then the Jews sought all the more to kill Him, because He not only broke the Sabbath, but

also said that God was His heavenly Parent, making Himself equal with God. [19]Jesus answered them and said, "Truly I say to you, the Son can do nothing by Himself, but only what He sees His heavenly Parent doing; for whatever the Parent does, the Son does likewise. [20]The Parent loves the Son and shows Him everything that is done. And My heavenly Parent will show Me greater things than these. You will be amazed. [21]For as My heavenly Parent raises the dead and gives life, even so the Son gives life to whom He will. [22]My heavenly Parent judges no one but has committed all judgment to the Son, [23]so that all will honor the Son, even as they honor My heavenly Parent. Anyone who does not honor the Son, does not honor My heavenly Parent who sent Me. [24]Truly I say to you, those who hear what I say and believe My heavenly Parent who sent Me have eternal life. They will not be condemned, but have crossed over from death to life. [25]Truly I say to you, the hour is coming, and now is, when the dead will hear the voice of the Son of God. And those who hear will live. [26]Even as My heavenly Parent has the power to give life, so also the Son has been granted life in Himself, [27]and also the authority to pass judgment because He is the Son of Humanity. [28]Do not be amazed at this. The hour is coming when all who are in the grave will hear the voice of the Son of God [29]and come out. Those who have done good will rise to life, and those who have done evil will rise to the judgment. [30]I can do nothing by Myself. As I hear, I judge. And My judgment is just, because I do not seek My own will, but the will of the One who sent Me.

[31]"If I witness for Myself, My witness is not valid. [32]There is another who witnesses for Me, and I know that what My heavenly Parent testifies about Me is true. [33]You sent messengers to John, and he testified to the truth. [34]Not that I must have a human witness, but I say this so you may be saved. [35]For John was a bright and shining light, and you were willing, for a season, to rejoice in his light. [36]But I have a greater witness than John. For the works that My heavenly Parent gave Me to complete, the very works that I do, witness that My heavenly Parent sent Me. [37]My heavenly Parent who sent Me witnesses for Me.

"You have never heard the voice nor seen the shape of My heavenly Parent. [38]You do not have God's word living in you, for you do not believe the One God sent. [39]You search the Scriptures, for in them you think you have eternal life. Even though these are the Scriptures that witness about Me, [40]you will not come to Me to have life. [41]I do not accept honor from humans, [42]but I know that you have no love for God within you. [43]I have come in My heavenly Parent's name and you do not accept Me; but if others come in their own names, you accept them. [44]How can you believe? You accept honor from one another, but do not seek the honor that is from the one God. [45]Do not think that I will accuse you before My heavenly Parent. The one who accuses you is Moses, in whom you hope. [46]If you believed Moses, you would believe Me, for he wrote about Me. [47]But if you do not believe his writings, how can you believe My words?"

A LARGE CROWD IS FED WITH FIVE LOAVES AND TWO FISH

[6:1]After this, Jesus went to the other side of the Sea of Galilee, which was also known as the Sea of Tiberias. [2]A large crowd followed Him, because they saw the signs He performed for those who were sick. [3]Jesus went up a mountain and sat down there with His disciples. [4]The Passover Feast of the Jews was near. [5]Jesus looked up and saw a great crowd coming to Him. He said to Philip, "Where shall we buy food for these people to eat?" [6]He said this to test Philip, for He knew what He was going to do. [7]Philip answered, "It would take a lot of money to buy enough food for each of them to have even a little!" [8]Another of His disciples, Simon Peter's brother Andrew, said to Him, [9]"A lad is here who has five barley loaves and two small fish, but what are they among so many?" [10]Jesus said, "Tell the people to sit down." There were more than five thousand. There was much grass in that place, so they sat down. [11]Jesus took the loaves, gave thanks and distributed them to those who were sitting down; and likewise the fish, as much as they wanted. [12]When they were full, He said to His disciples, "Gather up the fragments that remain so that nothing is lost." [13]They gathered twelve baskets full of fragments from what was left over of the five barley loaves. [14]The people who had seen the miracle that Jesus did said, "This is truly the Prophet who was to come into the world." [15]Jesus knew that they wanted to come and take Him by force and make Him king, so He once again went into the mountains alone.

JESUS WALKS ON WATER
[16]When evening came, His disciples went down to the sea, [17]got into a boat and started across toward Capernaum. It was now dark, and Jesus had not come to them. [18]A strong wind was blowing and stirring up the sea. [19]When they had rowed more than half way, they saw Jesus walking on the sea and approaching the boat. They were afraid, [20]but He said to them, "Don't be afraid, it is I." [21]Then they gladly allowed Him to get into the boat; and immediately the boat reached the shore where they were going.

JESUS TEACHES IN THE SYNAGOGUE AT CAPERNAUM
[22]The next day the people who were standing on the other side of the sea saw that only one boat had been there and that Jesus had not entered the boat with His disciples, but that His disciples had gone away alone. [23]However, other boats from Tiberias were around that place where they ate the bread. [24]So when the people saw that neither Jesus nor His disciples were there, they also got into boats and went to Capernaum seeking Jesus. [25]They found Him on the other side of the sea and said to Him, "Rabbi, when did You come here?" [26]Jesus answered, "Truly I say to you, you don't seek Me because you saw the signs, but because you ate the loaves and were filled. [27]Do not work for food that doesn't last, but work for food that endures for eternal life. The Son of Humanity will give you this, for My heavenly Parent has put the mark of approval on Me." [28]They asked Him, "What is the work of God that we should do?" [29]Jesus answered, "This is the work of God: that you believe in the One whom God sent." [30]Then they asked Him, "What sign will You show us, that we may see it and believe You? What can You do? [31]Our ancestors ate manna in the wilderness, just as it is written: 'He gave them bread from heaven to eat.'" [32]Then Jesus said to them, "Truly I say to you, it was not Moses who gave you the bread from heaven, but it is My heavenly Parent who gives you the true bread from heaven. [33]For the bread of God is the One who comes down from heaven and gives life to the world." [34]They said

to Him, "Sir, give us this bread always!" [35]Jesus said to them, "I am the bread of life. Anyone who comes to Me will never be hungry, and anyone who believes in Me will never be thirsty. [36]But as I told you, though you have seen Me, you do not believe. [37]Everyone whom My heavenly Parent gives Me will come to Me. I will never turn away anyone who comes to Me. [38]For I have not come down from heaven to do My will, but the will of the One who sent Me. [39]And this is My heavenly Parent's will: that of all those My heavenly Parent gives Me, I lose none, but raise them up on the last day. [40]And this is the will of the One who sent Me: that all who look to Me and believe in Me may have eternal life. I will raise them up on the last day."

[41]Then the Jews murmured against Him because He said, "I am the bread that came down from heaven." [42]They said, "Is this not Jesus the son of Joseph, whose father and mother we know? How is it then that He says, 'I came down from heaven'?" [43]Jesus answered them and said, "Stop murmuring among yourselves. [44]No one can come to Me unless drawn by My heavenly Parent who sent Me. And I will raise that person up on the last day. [45]It is written in the prophets: 'They will all be taught by God.' Therefore everyone who listens to God and learns from God comes to Me. [46]Not that anyone has seen God except the One who has come from God. I have seen God. [47]Truly I say to you, those who believe have everlasting life. [48]I am the bread of life. [49]Your ancestors ate manna in the wilderness and are dead. [50]This is the bread that comes down from heaven which one may eat and not die. [51]I am the living bread that came down from heaven. Those who eat this bread will live forever. The bread that I will give for the life of the world is My flesh."

[52]Then the Jews argued among themselves, saying, "How can He give us His flesh to eat?" [53]Jesus said to them, "Truly I say to you, unless you eat the flesh of the Son of Humanity and drink His blood, you have no life in you. [54]If you eat My flesh and drink My blood you have eternal life and I will raise you up on the last day. [55]For My flesh is real food and My blood is real drink. [56]If you eat My flesh and drink My blood, you are present in Me, and I in you. [57]Just as My living heavenly Parent sent Me, and I live because of My heavenly Parent, so also whoever feeds on Me will live because of Me. [58]This is that bread that came down from heaven. It is not like the manna your ancestors ate and later died. Those who eat this bread will live forever."

[59]Jesus said these things as He taught in the synagogue at Capernaum. [60]Many of His disciples heard these things and said, "This is a hard teaching. Who can listen to it?" [61]Jesus knew that His disciples were murmuring about this, and He said to them, "Does this offend you? [62]What if you see the Son of Humanity go up to where He was before? [63]It is the Spirit who gives life; the flesh is of no use. The words that I speak to you are Spirit and life, [64]but some of you do not believe."

Jesus knew from the beginning which ones would not believe and who would betray Him, [65]so He said, "This is why I said to you that no one can come to Me unless they are allowed to by My heavenly Parent."

MANY DISCIPLES TURN AWAY BECAUSE OF THE DIFFICULT TEACHINGS

[66]From that time on, many of His disciples turned back and no longer walked with Him. [67]Then Jesus asked the twelve, "Do you also wish to go away?" [68]Simon Peter

answered Him, "Rabbi, to whom would we go? You have the words of eternal life. [69]We believe and know that You are the Holy One of God." [70]Jesus answered them, "Did I not choose you twelve? Yet one of you is a devil." [71]He was speaking of Judas' Iscariot, one of the twelve, who was going to betray Him.

THE UNBELIEVING BROTHERS

[7:1]After this, Jesus went from place to place in Galilee. He would not go on the roads of Judea because the Jews sought to kill Him. [2]Now the Jews' Feast of Tabernacles was near [3]and His brothers said to Him, "You should leave here and go to Judea so that Your disciples may see the works You do, [4]for no one seeking publicity does things in secret. If You are going to do these things, show Yourself to the world." [5]His brothers did not believe in Him either. [6]Jesus said to them, "My time has not yet come, but you are ready any time. [7]The world cannot hate you, but it hates Me because I give evidence that its deeds are evil. [8]You go up to the Feast. I am not going up to the Feast yet, for My time has not fully come."

[9]After He said this to them, He remained in Galilee.

[10]But when His brothers had gone up to the Feast, He also went up; not openly, but, as it were, in secret. [11]The Jews sought Him at the Feast and said, "Where is He?" [12]There was much murmuring among the people concerning Him. Some said, "He is good," but others said, "No, He is deceiving the people." [13]No one spoke openly about Him for fear of the Jews.

JESUS TEACHES IN THE TEMPLE AT THE FEAST OF TABERNACLES

[14]Halfway through the Feast, Jesus went up to the temple and began to teach. [15]The Jews were amazed and said, "How can this man be so learned when He has never been educated?" [16]Jesus answered, "My teaching is not Mine, but God's who sent Me. [17]Anyone who chooses to do the will of God will know whether this teaching comes from God or whether I am speaking on My own. [18]Those who speak of themselves seek their own glory. But He who seeks the glory of the One who sent Him is true, and nothing deceptive is in Him. [19]Did not Moses give you the law? But none of you keep the law! Why are you trying to kill Me?"

[20]The people answered, "You have a demon! Who is trying to kill You?" [21]Jesus said to them, "I did one work and you all marveled. [22]Moses gave you circumcision, although it came from your ancestors and not from Moses, and on the Sabbath you circumcise a man. [23]If a man can be circumcised on the Sabbath and the law of Moses is not broken, why are you angry with Me because I made a man completely well on the Sabbath? [24]Do not judge according to appearances, but judge fairly."

[25]Then some of the people of Jerusalem said, "Isn't this the man they are seeking to kill? [26]Look, He is speaking openly, and they say nothing to Him. Have the authorities found that this is indeed the Messiah? [27]But we know where this man is from. When the Messiah comes, no one will know where He is from."

[28]Jesus called out from the temple where He was teaching, "You know Me and know where I come from? I have not come on My own! But the One who sent Me is true. You do not know God, [29]but I do, for I am from God. God sent Me!" [30]Then they sought to arrest Him, but no one laid hands on Him, because His hour had not yet

come. [31]Many of the people believed in Him. They said, "When the Messiah comes, will He do more signs than this man has done?"

THE LEADERS SEND OFFICERS TO ARREST JESUS

[32]The Pharisees heard the people saying these things about Him, so they and the chief priests sent officers to arrest Him. [33]Jesus said, "I will be with you only a little longer; then I will go to the One who sent Me. [34]You will seek Me, but you will not find Me. Where I am, you cannot come." [35]Then the Jews said among themselves, "Where will He go that we cannot find Him? Will He go to the dispersed Jews among the Greeks and teach the Greeks? [36]And what did He mean when He said, 'You will seek Me, but will not find Me,' and 'Where I am, you cannot come'?"

JESUS CONVINCES MANY

[37]On the last day, that great day of the Feast, Jesus stood and said in a loud voice, "If anyone is thirsty, come to Me and drink. [38]If you believe in Me, as the Scripture says, 'Out of your inner being will flow rivers of living water.'" [39]He spoke this about the Spirit, who would be given to those who believed in Him. The Spirit had not yet been given, because Jesus was not yet glorified.

[40]After hearing these words, some of the people said, "Surely this is the Prophet." [41]Some said, "This is the Messiah!" But others said, "Will the Messiah come out of Galilee? [42]Does not Scripture say that the Messiah comes from the seed of David and out of the town of Bethlehem where David was?" [43]So there was a division among the people because of Him. [44]Some wanted Him arrested, but no one laid a hand on Him.

[45]Then the officers went back, and the chief priests and Pharisees said to them, "Why haven't you brought Him?" [46]The officers answered, "Never has a man spoken like this man!" [47]Then the Pharisees said, "You also are deceived! [48]Have any of the authorities or the Pharisees believed in Him? [49]These people who do not know the law are cursed." [50]Nicodemus, a member of the council and the one who came to Jesus by night, said to them, [51]"Does our law judge people before it hears them and knows what they did?" [52]They said to him, "Are you from Galilee too? Search the Scriptures and you will see that no prophet ever comes from Galilee."

THE LEADERS BRING A WOMAN TO JESUS

[8:1]Jesus went to the Mount of Olives. [2]At dawn He came back to the temple. All the people came to Him, and He sat down and taught them. [3]The scribes and Pharisees brought a woman caught committing adultery. They made her stand in front of everyone [4]and they said to Him, "Teacher, this woman was caught committing adultery, in the very act. [5]Now in the law, Moses commanded us to stone such. But what do You say?" [6]They said this to test Him so they could accuse Him. But Jesus stooped down and wrote in the dirt with His finger. [7]When they continued to ask Him, He stood up and said to them, "Let the one who is without sin among you be the one to throw the first stone at her." [8]Then He stooped down again and wrote in the dirt. [9]When they heard this, they began to leave one by one, beginning with the oldest. Jesus was left alone, with the woman still standing there. [10]He stood up and said to her, "Woman, where are they? Did no one condemn you?" [11]She said, "No one, Sir." Then Jesus said to her, "Neither do I condemn you. Go, and sin no more."

JESUS AGAIN TELLS THE LEADERS WHO HE IS

¹²Then Jesus spoke again to the people and said, "I am the light of the world. Whoever follows Me will not walk in darkness, but will have the light of life." ¹³At this the Pharisees said to Him, "You testify about Yourself; Your testimony is not valid." ¹⁴Jesus answered, "Even if I testify about Myself, My testimony is valid because I know where I came from and where I am going. But you do not know where I came from or where I am going. ¹⁵You judge according to the flesh; I judge no one. ¹⁶But if I judge, My judgment is valid because I am not alone; I am with My heavenly Parent who sent Me. ¹⁷It is written in your law that the testimony of two persons is valid. ¹⁸I am One who testifies about Myself, and My heavenly Parent who sent Me also testifies about Me." ¹⁹Then they said to Him, "Where is Your heavenly Parent?" Jesus answered, "You don't know Me or My heavenly Parent. If you knew Me, you would know My heavenly Parent also." ²⁰Jesus spoke these words as He taught in the temple near the treasury. No one laid hands on Him, for His hour had not yet come.

²¹Jesus said to them again, "I am going away. You will seek Me, but you will die in your sins. Where I go, you cannot come." ²²Then the Jews said, "Is He going to kill Himself? For He said, 'Where I go, you cannot come.'" ²³Jesus said to them, "You are from below; I am from above. You are from this world; I am not from this world. ²⁴That is why I said to you that you will die in your sins, for if you don't believe that I Am, you will die in your sins." ²⁵Then they said to Him, "Who are You?" Jesus said to them, "I am what I told you from the beginning. ²⁶I have many things to say and to judge concerning you. But the One who sent Me is true, and I speak to the world what I have heard from My heavenly Parent." ²⁷They were not sure that He spoke to them about God. ²⁸Then Jesus said to them, "When you lift up the Son of Humanity, then you will know that I Am. I do nothing by Myself, but speak those things My heavenly Parent taught Me. ²⁹My heavenly Parent who sent Me is with Me. My heavenly Parent has not left Me alone, for I always do those things that please My heavenly Parent." ³⁰As He was saying this, many believed in Him.

³¹Jesus said to those Jews who believed in Him, "If you remain in My word, then you are truly My disciples. ³²You will know the truth, and the truth will make you free." ³³They answered, "We are descendants of Abraham and were never slaves to anyone, so why do You say, 'You will be made free?'" ³⁴Jesus answered, "Truly I say to you, whoever commits sin is the slave of sin. ³⁵A slave does not remain in the household forever. God's Son remains forever. ³⁶Therefore if the Son makes you free, you will be free indeed. ³⁷I know that you are descendants of Abraham. But you seek to kill Me because you will not accept My message. ³⁸I speak those things I have heard from My heavenly Parent, and you do that which you have heard from your parent." ³⁹They answered Him, "Abraham is our parent." Jesus said to them, "If you were Abraham's children, you would do the works of Abraham. ⁴⁰But now you seek to kill Me, a man who told you the truth that I heard from God. Abraham did not do these things. ⁴¹You do the deeds of your parent."

They said to Him, "We were not conceived in adultery. We have one Parent, God." ⁴²Jesus said to them, "If God were your Parent, you would love Me, for I came from

God. I did not come of My own accord, but God sent Me. [43]Why do you not understand what I say? It is because you cannot accept My message. [44]You are the children of your parent the devil, and you choose to carry out the wishes of your parent. Your parent was a murderer from the beginning and did not stand for the truth, because there is no truth in your parent. When your parent speaks a lie, it is the devil speaking, for the devil is a liar and the parent of liars. [45]But because I tell the truth, you do not believe Me. [46]Which of you can convict Me of sin? If I speak the truth, why do you not believe Me? [47]The Son of God hears God's words. You do not hear, because you are not of God."

THE UNBELIEVERS ACCUSE JESUS OF BEING DEMON-POSSESSED

[48]The Jews answered and said to Jesus, "Aren't we right when we say that You are a Samaritan and that You have a demon?" [49]Jesus answered, "I do not have a demon. I honor My heavenly Parent, but you dishonor Me. [50]I do not seek honor for Myself. There is One who seeks it and judges. [51]Truly I say to you, those who obey My words will never die." [52]Then the Jews said to Him, "Now we know that You have a demon. Abraham is dead and so are the prophets. But You say, 'Those who obey My words will never die.' [53]Are You greater than our ancestor Abraham? He died, and the prophets are also dead. Who do You think You are?" [54]Jesus answered, "If I honor Myself, My honor means nothing. My heavenly Parent, whom you say is your God, is the One who honors Me. [55]You do not know God, but I know God. If I were to say I do not know God, I would be a liar like you. But I know God and obey God's words. [56]Your father Abraham rejoiced because he saw My day. He saw and was glad." [57]Then the Jews said to Him, "You are not yet fifty years old, and You have seen Abraham?"

JESUS TELLS THE UNBELIEVERS THAT HE IS GOD

[58]Jesus said to them, "Truly I say to you, before Abraham was, I Am." [59]Then they picked up stones to throw at Him, but Jesus hid Himself and went out of the temple.

JESUS PUTS MUD ON A BLIND MAN'S EYES

9:1[1]As Jesus walked along, He saw a man who was blind from birth. [2]His disciples asked Him, "Rabbi, who sinned, this man or his parents, that he was born blind?" [3]Jesus answered, "Neither this man nor his parents sinned. It was to display the power of God in him. [4]We must be engaged in the work of God who sent Me while it is day. The night is coming when no one can work. [5]As long as I am in the world, I am the light of the world." [6]After He said this, He spat on the ground, made mud with the saliva and smeared it over the eyes of the blind man. [7]Then He said, "Go wash in the Pool of Siloam." The blind man went and washed, and his sight was restored. [8]The neighbors and those who had seen him before when he was blind said, "Is not this the man who sat and begged?" [9]Some said that he was the one, but others said it was someone who looked like him. But he said, "I am the one!" [10]"How were your eyes opened?" they asked. [11]He said, "A man named Jesus made mud, smeared it on my eyes and said to me, 'Go wash in the Pool of Siloam.' I went and washed and recovered my sight." [12]"Where is He?" they asked. "I don't know," he answered.

[13]They brought the man who had been blind to the Pharisees. [14]It was on the

Sabbath that Jesus made the mud and opened his eyes. [15]The Pharisees asked the man how he had recovered his sight, and he said again, "He put mud on my eyes, I washed and now I see." [16]Some of the Pharisees said, "This man is not from God, because He does not keep the Sabbath." Others said, "How can anyone who is a sinner do such miracles?" And there was a division among them. [17]They asked the blind man again, "What do you have to say about Him, since He opened your eyes?" He said, "He is a prophet."

[18]The Jews did not believe that the man had been blind and had recovered his sight until they called his parents. [19]They asked them, "Is this your son? You say he was born blind? How then can he now see?" [20]His parents answered, "We know that this is our son and that he was born blind, [21]but how it is that he now sees we don't know. And we don't know who opened his eyes. He is of age; he should speak for himself." [22]His parents said this because they were afraid of the Jews, for the Jews had agreed that anyone who acknowledged that Jesus was the Messiah would be put out of the synagogue. [23]That is why his parents said, "He is of age; ask him."

[24]Again they called the man who had been blind. They said, "Give glory to God! We know that this man is a sinner." [25]The man said, "Whether He is a sinner or not, I do not know. The one thing I know is that I was blind and now I see." [26]Then they asked him again, "What did He do to you? How did He open your eyes?" [27]He answered them, "I told you already, but you don't listen. Why would you want to hear it again? Do you want to be His disciples too?" [28]Then they swore at him and said, "You are His disciple! We are the disciples of Moses. [29]We know that God spoke to Moses. As for this man, we don't know where He comes from." [30]The man answered them and said, "Now, that is a strange thing. You don't know where He comes from, and yet He opened my eyes. [31]Now we know that God doesn't listen to sinners, but if anyone is a worshiper of God and does God's will, God listens. [32]Not since the beginning of the world has anyone heard of the eyes of one who was born blind being opened. [33]If this man were not from God, He could do nothing." [34]They said to him, "You have been a sinner since you were born, and you would teach us?" And they threw him out.

[35]Jesus heard that they had thrown him out. When He found him, He said to him, "Do you believe in the Son of Humanity?" [36]He answered, "Who is He, Rabbi, that I may believe in Him?" [37]Jesus said, "You have seen Him. He is the One talking with you." [38]He said, "O God, I believe." And he bowed down before Him. [39]Jesus said, "For judgment I came into this world, so that those who do not see may see, and that those who see may become blind." [40]The Pharisees who were with Him heard this and said to Him, "Are we blind also?" [41]Jesus said to them, "If you were blind, you would not be so wrong; but now that you say you can see, your error remains.

JESUS THE GOOD SHEPHERD

[10:1]"Truly I say to you, anyone who does not enter the sheepfold by the door, but climbs up some other way, is a thief and a robber. [2]But He who comes in through the door is the shepherd of the sheep. [3]To Him the gatekeeper opens the gate. The sheep listen to His voice. He calls His own sheep by name and leads them out. [4]When He has brought out His own sheep, He goes before them. And the sheep follow Him, for they know His voice. [5]They will not follow a stranger but will run away, for they do not know the voice of the stranger."

[6]Jesus told them this parable, but they did not understand what He was saying to them. [7]Then Jesus said to them again, "Truly I say to you, I am the gate for the sheep. [8]All who preceded Me are thieves and robbers, but the sheep did not listen to them. [9]I am the gate. Anyone who comes in through Me will be saved and will go in and out and find pasture. [10]The thief comes only to steal, to kill and to destroy. I came that they might have life and have it abundantly. [11]I am the good shepherd. The good shepherd lays down His life for the sheep. [12]The hired worker is not the shepherd who owns the sheep. The hired worker sees the wolf coming, leaves the sheep and runs away. Then the wolf catches the sheep and scatters them. [13]The hired worker runs away, because the hired worker does not care for the sheep. [14]I am the good shepherd. I know My own and My own know Me, [15]just as My heavenly Parent knows Me and I know My heavenly Parent. I lay down My life for the sheep. [16]I have other sheep who are not of this fold. I must bring them also. They will listen to My voice and become one flock with one shepherd. [17]Therefore My heavenly Parent loves Me, because I lay down My life in order to take it up again. [18]No one takes it from Me; I lay it down voluntarily. I have the authority to lay it down, and I have the authority to take it up again. I have received this authorization from My heavenly Parent." [19]Again there was a division among the Jews over the things He said. [20]Many of them said, "He has a demon and is raving. Why listen to Him?" [21]Others said, "These are not the words of one who has a demon. Can a demon open the eyes of the blind?"

THE LEADERS REFUSE TO BELIEVE JESUS

[22]It was winter, and the Feast of Dedication was at Jerusalem. [23]Jesus was walking in the temple in Solomon's Walkway. [24]The Jews gathered around Him and said, "How long are You going to keep us in suspense? If You are the Messiah, tell us plainly." [25]Jesus answered them, "I told you, but you do not believe. The works that I do in My heavenly Parent's name witness for Me. [26]But you don't believe because you are not My sheep. [27]My sheep hear My voice. I know them, and they follow Me. [28]I give them eternal life, and they will never, never perish. Nor can anyone snatch them out of My hand. [29]My heavenly Parent who gave them to Me is greater than all, and no one is able to take them out of My heavenly Parent's hand. [30]I and My heavenly Parent are one."

[31]Again the Jews picked up stones to stone Him. [32]Jesus said to them, "I have shown you many good works from My heavenly Parent. For which of these do you stone Me?" [33]The Jews answered, "We are not stoning You for a good work, but for blasphemy, because You, a human, make Yourself God." [34]Jesus answered them, "Is it not written in your law, 'I said, you are gods'? [35]If the Scripture called them gods to whom the word of God came - and the Scripture cannot be set aside - [36]then why do you accuse the One whom My heavenly Parent consecrated and sent into the world of blasphemy because I said, 'I am the Son of God'? [37]If I am not doing the works of My heavenly Parent, do not believe Me. [38]But if I do, though you do not believe Me, believe the works. Then you will know and believe that My heavenly Parent is in Me

and that I am in My heavenly Parent." ^{39}Again they tried to arrest Him, but He escaped from their hands ^{40}and went away again beyond the Jordan to the place where John first baptized. He stayed there ^{41}and many came to Him. They said, "John did no miracles, but everything that John spoke about this man was true." ^{42}And many believed in Him there.

JESUS' FRIEND LAZARUS DIES

$^{11:1}$Now in Bethany, the town of Mary and her sister Martha, a man named Lazarus was sick. ^{2}This was the Mary who anointed Jesus with ointment and wiped His feet with her hair. Her brother Lazarus was sick. ^{3}Therefore his sisters sent word to Jesus, saying, "Rabbi, the one You love is sick." ^{4}When Jesus heard this, He said, "This sickness is not for the purpose of death, but for the glory of God, so that God's Son may be glorified through it." ^{5}Now Jesus loved Martha and her sister and Lazarus. ^{6}Yet when He heard that Lazarus was sick, He remained two days in the place where He was. ^{7}After this, He said to His disciples, "Let us go back to Judea." ^{8}His disciples said to Him, "Rabbi, the Jews just recently tried to stone You! Are You going there again?" ^{9}Jesus answered, "Are there not twelve hours in the day? Those who walk in the daylight do not stumble, because they see by this world's light. ^{10}But those who walk in the night stumble, because the light is not in them."

^{11}After that, He said to them, "Our friend Lazarus has fallen asleep, but I am going to waken him from sleep." ^{12}Then His disciples said, "If he is asleep, he will get well." ^{13}Jesus had been speaking of his death, but they thought that He was talking about sleep. ^{14}Then Jesus said to them plainly, "Lazarus is dead. ^{15}And I am glad for your sake that I was not there, so you may believe. Now let us go to him." ^{16}Then Thomas, who was called the Twin, said to his fellow disciples, "Let us go also, so we may die with Him."

JESUS GOES TO THE HOME OF LAZARUS, MARTHA AND MARY

^{17}When Jesus arrived, He found that Lazarus had already been in the tomb four days. ^{18}Now Bethany was less than two miles from Jerusalem, ^{19}and many of the Jews had come to comfort Martha and Mary concerning their brother. ^{20}When Martha heard that Jesus was coming, she went to meet Him, but Mary remained in the house. ^{21}Martha said to Jesus, "Rabbi, if You had been here, my brother would not have died. ^{22}Yet I know that even now God will give You whatever You ask." ^{23}Jesus said to her, "Your brother will arise." ^{24}Martha said to Him, "I know that he will arise in the resurrection on the last day." ^{25}Jesus said to her, "I am the resurrection and the life. Those who believe in Me will live, even though they die. ^{26}And those who live and believe in Me will never, never die. Do you believe this?" ^{27}She said to Him, "Yes, Rabbi, I believe that You are the Messiah, the Son of God who is coming into the world."

^{28}After she said this, she went and called her sister Mary and said to her privately, "The Teacher has come and is asking for you." ^{29}When Mary heard this, she got up quickly and went to Him. ^{30}Jesus had not come into town, but was still at the place where Martha had met Him. ^{31}The Jews who were in the house with Mary comforting her saw her rise hastily and go out. They followed her, thinking that she was going to the tomb to weep there. [32]When Mary came to where Jesus was and saw Him, she fell at His feet. She said to Him, "Rabbi, if You had been here, my brother would not have died." [33]When Jesus saw her weeping, and the Jews who came with her also weeping, He sighed and was deeply moved. [34]He asked, "Where have you laid him?" They said to Him, "Rabbi, come and see." [35]Jesus wept. [36]The Jews said, "See how He loved him!" [37]But some of them said, "Could not He who opened the eyes of the blind do something to keep this man from dying?"

JESUS GOES TO LAZARUS' TOMB

[38]Again sighing deeply, Jesus went to the tomb. It was a cave, and a stone was laid against it. [39]Jesus said, "Take away the stone." Martha, the sister of the dead man, said to Him, "Rabbi! By this time there will be a bad smell! He has been in there four days!" [40]Jesus said to her, "Did I not tell you that if you believed you would see the glory of God?" [41]They took away the stone. Jesus looked upward and said, "My heavenly Parent, I thank You that You have heard Me. [42]I know that You always do hear Me, but I said this for the sake of the people who stand by so that they will believe that You sent Me."

LAZARUS COMES OUT OF THE TOMB

[43]After He said this, He called out with a loud voice, "Lazarus! Come out!" [44]He who was dead came out, bound hand and foot with strips of cloth, and his face was wrapped with a cloth. Jesus said to them, "Unwrap him and let him go." [45]Then many of the Jews who had come to visit Mary and had seen what Jesus did believed in Him, [46]but some of them went to the Pharisees and told them what Jesus had done.

THE LEADERS RESOLVE TO PUT JESUS TO DEATH

[47]The chief priests and the Pharisees gathered the council and said, "What should we do? This man is performing many signs. [48]If we let Him go on this way, everyone will believe in Him. Then the Romans will come and take both our place and our nation." [49]But one of them, named Caiaphas, who was high priest that year, said to them, "You know nothing at all. [50]Keep in mind that it is better for us that one man die for the people than for the whole nation to perish." [51]He did not speak this on his own, but as high priest that year he prophesied that Jesus would die for the nation. [52]And not only for the nation; but also that He would bring together as one the people of God scattered abroad. [53]So from that day on they planned to put Jesus to death.

[54]Therefore Jesus no longer walked openly among the Jews, but went to a town called Ephraim in a region near the wilderness. He remained there with His disciples. [55]The Jewish Passover was near, and many went from the country up to Jerusalem before the Passover to purify themselves. [56]They looked for Jesus and said among themselves as they stood in the temple, "What do you think? Will He come to the Feast?" [57]Now the chief priests and the Pharisees had given orders that anyone who knew where He was should tell them so they might arrest Him.

MARY ANOINTS JESUS WITH AN EXPENSIVE PERFUME

[12:1]Six days before the Passover, Jesus went to Bethany where He had raised Lazarus from the dead. [2]They made Him a supper there and Martha served. Lazarus was one of those at the table with Jesus. [3]Mary took a pound of very costly ointment made of pure nard, anointed Jesus' feet and wiped His feet with her hair. The house was filled with fragrance from the ointment. [4]Then one of His disciples, Judas Iscariot, who was going to betray Him, said, [5]"Why was this ointment not sold for a large sum and the money given to the poor?" [6]He said this, not because he cared for the poor, but because he was a thief and had the money bag and helped himself to what was put into it. [7]Jesus said, "Let her alone. She has kept this for the week of My burial. [8]The poor you have with you always, but you will not always have Me."

THE LEADERS MAKE PLANS TO KILL JESUS AND LAZARUS

[9]A large crowd of Jews found out that Jesus was there. They came, not only to see Him, but also to see Lazarus whom He had raised from the dead. [10]Therefore the chief priests planned to put Lazarus to death also, [11]for on account of Lazarus many Jews were leaving them and believing in Jesus.

JESUS BORROWS A DONKEY AND FULFILLS PROPHECY

[12]The next day, the crowd who had come to the Feast heard that Jesus was coming to Jerusalem. [13]They took palm branches and went out to meet Him, shouting, "Hosanna! Blessed is He who comes in the name of Yahweh! The King of Israel!" [14]Jesus found a young donkey and sat on it, for it is written: [15]"Do not be afraid, O people of Zion. Look! Your king is coming, sitting on a donkey's colt." [16]These things His disciples did not understand at first, but when Jesus was glorified, they remembered that these things were written about Him and that the people had done these things to Him. [17]The people who were with Him when He called Lazarus out of the tomb and raised him from the dead told everyone. [18]That was the reason the crowd met Him, for they heard that He had done this miracle. [19]The Pharisees said among themselves, "You see? Our efforts are failing! Look! The whole world has gone after Him!"

GENTILES COME TO SEE JESUS

[20]There were some Greeks among those who came up to worship at the Feast. [21]They came to Philip, who was from Bethsaida in Galilee, and asked him, "Sir, may we see Jesus?" [22]Philip went to tell Andrew, and Andrew and Philip went to tell Jesus. [23]Jesus said to them, "The hour has come for the Son of Humanity to be glorified. [24]Truly I say to you, unless a grain of wheat falls to the ground and dies, it remains alone. But if it dies, it brings forth much fruit. [25]If you love your life, you will lose it; but if you hate your life in this world, you will keep it for life eternal. [26]Anyone who serves Me must follow Me. Where I am, there will My servant be also. If you serve Me, My heavenly Parent will honor you.

JESUS PRAYS FOR GOD'S WILL TO BE DONE

[27]"Now My Soul is in turmoil. What can I say? 'O God, save Me from this hour'? But for this purpose I came to this hour! [28]O God, glorify Your name!"

A voice came from heaven saying, "I have glorified it! And I will glorify it again." [29]The people who were standing there said, "It thundered!" Others said, "An angel spoke to Him!" [30]Jesus said, "This voice did not come for My sake, but for yours.

[31]"Now is the judgment of this world; now the prince of this world will be thrown out. [32]And I, if I am lifted up from the earth, will draw all people to Myself." [33]He said

this to foretell the way He would be put to death.

THE PEOPLE WONDER WHY JESUS DOES NOT STAY AND REIGN

[34]The people said, "We have heard from the law that the Messiah remains forever. How then can You say, 'The Son of Humanity must be lifted up'? Who is this Son of Humanity?" [35]Jesus said to them, "For yet a little while the light will be with you. Walk while you have the light, lest darkness come upon you. For those who walk in darkness do not know where they are going. [36]Believe in the light while you have the light, so that you may become children of the light." After Jesus spoke these words, He departed and hid Himself from them.

ISAIAH'S PROPHECIES FULFILLED

[37]Though He had performed many miraculous signs before them, they did not believe in Him. [38]Thus the saying of Isaiah the prophet was fulfilled: "Who has believed our report, and to whom was the arm of Yahweh revealed?" [39]Therefore they could not believe, because Isaiah also said, [40]"God blinded their eyes and hardened their hearts, so that they would not see with their eyes or understand with their hearts and turn for Me to heal them." [41]Isaiah said these things because he saw and spoke of God's glory.

THE SECRET BELIEVERS

[42]Nevertheless many among the authorities believed in Him. But because of the Pharisees they did not acknowledge it, lest they be put out of the synagogue. [43]They loved the praise of humans more than the praise of God.

UNBELIEVERS WILL BE JUDGED BY JESUS' WORDS

[44]Jesus said in a loud voice, "Anyone who believes in Me, believes not only in Me, but also in the One who sent Me. [45]When you look at Me, you also see the One who sent Me. [46]I have come as light into the world, so that no one who believes in Me remains in darkness. [47]I do not judge those who hear My words and do not obey them. I did not come to judge the world, but to save the world. [48]Those who reject Me and do not accept My words have a judge. The word that I have spoken will judge them on the last day. [49]I have not spoken on My own authority, but My heavenly Parent who sent Me has commanded Me what to say and what to speak. [50]And I know that My heavenly Parent's command brings life everlasting. Whatever I say, then, is exactly what My heavenly Parent has told Me to say."

JESUS WASHES THE DISCIPLES' FEET

[13:1]Now before the Feast of the Passover, Jesus knew that His time had come when He would leave this world and go to His heavenly Parent. Having loved His own who were in the world, He loved them completely. [2]When supper was being served, the devil put into the heart of Judas Iscariot the desire to betray Jesus. [3]Jesus knew that His heavenly Parent had given all things into His hands and that He had come from God and was going back to God. [4]So during the meal Jesus got up, laid aside His robe, took a towel and tied it around His waist. [5]Then He poured water into a basin and began to wash the disciples' feet and wipe them with the towel that was around His waist. [6]When He came to Simon Peter, Peter said to Him, "Rabbi! You are going to wash my feet?" [7]Jesus said to him, "You don't understand what I am doing now, but later you will understand." [8]Peter said to Him, "You must never, never wash my feet!" Jesus answered, "If I do not wash you, you have no part in Me." [9]Simon Peter said to Him, "Rabbi! Not only my feet, but also my hands and head!" [10]Jesus said to him, "A person who has bathed does not need to wash, except for the feet, but is completely clean. And you are clean, but not all of you." [11]Jesus knew who would betray Him. That is why He said, "You are not all clean."

THE LAST SUPPER

[12]After He had washed their feet and put on His robe, He sat down again and said to them, "Do you know what I have done for you? [13]You call Me Teacher and Rabbi, and you are right, for so I am. [14]If I, then, your Rabbi and Teacher, have washed your feet, you also ought to wash one another's feet. [15]I have given you an example, so that you may do as I have done for you. [16]Truly I say to you, the slave is not greater than the owner, nor is the messenger greater than the one who sent. [17]If you know these things, happy are you if you do them.

THE BETRAYER

[18]"I am not talking about all of you; I know whom I have chosen. But the Scripture must be fulfilled that says, 'He who eats bread with Me has lifted up his heel against Me.' [19]I tell you now before it happens, so that when it happens you will believe that I Am. [20]Truly I say to you, anyone who receives the one I send, receives Me. And anyone who receives Me, receives the One who sent Me.

[21]After Jesus said this, His Spirit became troubled. He said, "Truly I say to you, one of you will betray Me." [22]The disciples looked at one another, wondering which one He meant. [23]Reclining at Jesus' side was the disciple whom Jesus loved. [24]Simon Peter beckoned to him and said, "Ask Him which one it is." [25]John then leaned back on Jesus' chest and asked Him, "Rabbi, who is it?" [26]Jesus answered, "It is the one to whom I will give this piece of bread I moisten." When He had moistened the piece of bread, He gave it to Judas Iscariot. [27]After Judas took the piece of bread, Satan entered him. Jesus said to him, "What you do, do quickly." [28]No one else at the table knew why He said this to Judas. [29]Some thought that because Judas had the money bag, Jesus had told him to buy what was needed for the Feast or that he should give something to the poor. [30]Judas accepted the piece of bread and immediately went out. And it was night.

A NEW COMMANDMENT

[31]After he had gone out, Jesus said, "Now the glory of the Son of Humanity will be revealed; now God's glory will be revealed through Me. [32]God will be given glory because of Me. I, God's Son, will also be given glory. God will do this very soon. [33]Little children, I am with you only a little longer. You will seek Me, but as I said to the Jews, so now I say to you: Where I am going, you cannot come. [34]A new commandment I give you: Love one another! Love one another as I have loved you. [35]Everyone will know that you are My disciples if you love one another."

PETER IS TOLD THAT HE WILL DENY JESUS THREE TIMES

[36]Simon Peter said to Jesus, "Rabbi, where are You going?" Jesus answered him, "You cannot follow Me now to where I am going, but you will follow Me later." [37]Peter

said to Him, "Why can't I follow You now? I would lay down my life for You." [38]Jesus answered him, "You would lay down your life for Me? Truly I say to you, before the rooster crows you will deny Me three times.

HOMES IN HEAVEN

[14:1]"Let not your hearts be troubled. You believe in God; believe also in Me. [2]In My heavenly Parent's house are many dwellings. If it were not so, I would have told you. I go to prepare a place for you. [3]And if I go and prepare a place for you, I will come again and take you to Myself, so that where I am you may be also. [4]You know where I am going, and you know the way." [5]Thomas said to Him, "Rabbi! We don't know where You are going, so how can we know the way?" [6]Jesus said to him, "I am the way, the truth and the life. No one comes to My Parent but by Me. [7]If you know Me, you know My heavenly Parent also. From now on you know and have seen My heavenly Parent."

PHILIP ASKS TO SEE GOD

[8]Philip said to Him, "Rabbi, show us Your heavenly Parent and we will be satisfied." [9]Jesus said to him, "Have I been with you all this time and you don't know Me, Philip? Anyone who has seen Me has seen My heavenly Parent. How then can you say, 'Show us Your heavenly Parent'? [10]Don't you believe that I am in My heavenly Parent and My heavenly Parent is in Me? The words that I speak to you are not My own; My heavenly Parent who lives in Me is doing these things. [11]Believe Me that I am in My heavenly Parent and My heavenly Parent is in Me, or else believe Me because of the works. [12]Truly I say to you, if you believe in Me, the works that I do, you will do also. Greater works than these will you do, because I go to My heavenly Parent. [13]Whatever you ask in My name, I will do, so that My heavenly Parent may be glorified through Me. [14]If you ask Me anything in My name, I will do it.

THE PROMISED HOLY SPIRIT WILL BE WITH YOU

[15]"If you love Me, you will remember My commandments. [16]I will ask My heavenly Parent, and My heavenly Parent will give you another Encourager, so the Encourager may live with you forever: [17]the Spirit of truth, whom the world cannot receive, because it does not see or know the Encourager. But you know the Encourager, for the Encourager lives with you and will be in you. [18]I will not leave you alone; I will come to you. [19]In a little while the world will see Me no more. But you will see Me. Because I live, you will live also. [20]On that day you will know that I am in My heavenly Parent, and you in Me and I in you. [21]The one who has My commandments and keeps them is the one who loves Me. If you love Me, you will be loved by My heavenly Parent, and I will love you and show Myself to you."

[22]Judas (not Iscariot) said to Him, "Rabbi, why are You going to show Yourself to us and not to the world?" [23]Jesus replied, "If you love Me, you will remember My words. My heavenly Parent will love you, and We will come to you and make Our home with you. [24]The person who does not love Me will not remember My words. These words you hear are not Mine but are the words of My heavenly Parent who sent Me. [25]I have spoken these things to you while I am yet with you, [26]but the Encourager, the Holy Spirit whom our heavenly Parent will send in My name, will teach you all things and remind you of everything I have said to you.

[27]"Peace I leave with you; My peace I give you. I do not give to you as the world does. Do not let your heart be troubled or afraid. [28]You heard Me say to you, 'I am going away and I will come to you.' If you love Me, you will rejoice because I go to My heavenly Parent, for My heavenly Parent is greater than I. [29]And now I have told you before it happens, so that when it happens, you will believe. [30]I cannot talk with you much longer, for the ruler of this world is coming. The devil has no claim on Me, [31]but the world must be made aware that I love My heavenly Parent, and as My heavenly Parent commands Me, so I do. Come, let us go.

THE VINE AND THE BRANCHES

[15:1]"I am the true vine and My heavenly Parent is the gardener. [2]My heavenly Parent takes away every branch in Me that does not bear fruit. And My heavenly Parent prunes clean every branch that bears fruit, so that it bears more fruit. [3]Now you are clean because of the word I have spoken to you. [4]Remain in Me, and I will remain in you. As the branch cannot bear fruit by itself unless it remains on the vine, neither can you unless you remain in Me. [5]I am the vine; you are the branches. If you remain in Me, and I in you, you will bear much fruit. Without Me you can do nothing. [6]The one who does not remain in Me is thrown away like a branch and withers. Then it is gathered and thrown into the fire and burned. [7]If you remain in Me and My words remain in you, ask for what you want and it will be done for you. [8]By this is My heavenly Parent glorified: that you bear much fruit and show that you are My disciples. [9]As My heavenly Parent loves Me, so I love you. Remain in My love. [10]If you remember My commandments, you will remain in My love, even as I remember My heavenly Parent's commandments and remain in My heavenly Parent's love. [11]I have spoken these things to you so that My joy may be in you and so that your joy may be full.

[12]"This is My commandment: Love one another as I have loved you. [13]You can have no greater love than to lay down your life for your friends. [14]You are My friends if you do what I command you. [15]I no longer call you servants, for the servant does not know the owner's business. But I call you friends, for I have made known to you all that I heard from My heavenly Parent. [16]You have not chosen Me, but I have chosen you to go and bear fruit, fruit that will remain. Then our heavenly Parent will give you whatever you ask in My name. [17]This is My command to you: Love one another.

WORLDLY PEOPLE HATE JESUS

[18]"If the world hates you, remember, it hated Me first. [19]If you belonged to the world, the world would love you as its own. But because you do not belong to the world, and I have chosen you out of the world, the world hates you. [20]Remember what I said to you, 'The servant is not greater than the owner of the house.' If they persecuted Me, they will also persecute you. If they obeyed My word, they will also obey yours. [21]They will do all these things to you because of My name and because they do not know the One who sent Me. [22]If I had not come and spoken to them, they would not be guilty of sin, but now they have no excuse for their sin. [23]Anyone who hates Me hates My heavenly Parent also. [24]If I had not done the works among them that no one else has ever done, they would not be guilty of sin, but now they have seen

and hated both Me and My heavenly Parent. [25]This fulfills the word that is written in their law: 'They hated Me without cause.' [26]But when the Encourager comes, whom I will send to you from our heavenly Parent, the Spirit of truth who goes out from our heavenly Parent, the Encourager will testify about Me. [27]You also will testify, because you have been with Me from the beginning.

[16:1]"I have told you these things so that you will not fall away. [2]They will put you out of the synagogue, and indeed, the time is coming when those who kill you will think they are serving God. [3]They will do these things because they have not known My heavenly Parent or Me. [4]I have told you this, so that when the time comes you will remember that I told you about them. I did not tell you this at the beginning, because I was with you. [5]But now I am going to the One who sent Me, and none of you asks Me, 'Where are You going?' [6]Sorrow has filled your hearts because I have said this to you. [7]Nevertheless I tell you the truth: It is to your advantage that I go away; for if I do not go away, the Encourager will not come to you. But if I depart, I will send the Encourager to you. [8]The Encourager will come and will admonish the world about sin and righteousness and judgment: [9]about sin, because they do not believe in Me; [10]about righteousness, because I am going to My heavenly Parent and you will see Me no more; [11]about judgment, because the prince of this world is judged.

[12]"I still have many things to say to you, but you cannot bear them now. [13]The Spirit of truth will come and guide you into all truth. The Spirit of truth will not speak alone, but will speak what has been spoken above and show you things to come. [14]The Spirit of truth will glorify Me and will take what is Mine and show it to you. [15]Everything My heavenly Parent has is Mine; therefore I said that the Spirit of truth will take what is Mine and show it to you.

[16]"In a little while you will not see Me. Then in a little while you will see Me again."

[17]His disciples said among themselves, "What is this that He says to us: 'A little while you will not see Me. Then in a little while you will see Me again' and 'I go to our heavenly Parent'?" [18]And they said, "What does He mean when He says, 'A little while'? We don't know what He means."

[19]Jesus knew that they wanted to question Him, and He said to them, "Are you inquiring among yourselves what I meant when I said, 'A little while and you will not see Me. Then in a little while you will see Me again'? [20]Truly I say to you, you will weep and mourn, but the world will rejoice. You will be sorrowful, but your sorrow will be turned into joy. [21]A woman in labor has anguish because her time has come. But as soon as the child is born, she no longer thinks about the anguish, but is joyful that a baby is born into the world. [22]Now you are distressed, but I will see you again, and your hearts will rejoice. And no one will take your joy away from you.

ASK IN JESUS' NAME

[23]"In that day you will not ask Me anything. Truly I say to you, whatever you ask our heavenly Parent in My name, our heavenly Parent will give you. [24]Until now you have not asked for anything in My name. Ask and you will receive and your joy will be full. [25]"I have spoken certain things to you in proverbs. The time is coming when I will no longer speak to you in proverbs, but will tell you plainly about our heavenly Parent.

[26]In that day you will ask in My name. I am not saying that I will ask our heavenly Parent for you, [27]for our heavenly Parent loves you because you love Me and believe that I came from God. [28]I came from My heavenly Parent and have come into the world. Now I am leaving the world and going back to My heavenly Parent."

[29]His disciples said to Him, "Now You are speaking plainly and not in proverbs. [30]Now we know that You know all things and that no more questioning of You is necessary. Because of this we believe that You came from God."

[31]Jesus answered them, "Do you now believe? [32]Beware! The hour is coming, yes, and has now come, when each of you will be scattered to your own place. You will send Me away alone. Yet I will not be alone, because My heavenly Parent is with Me. [33]I have spoken these things to you, so that in Me you may have peace. In the world you will have distress, but be of good cheer; I have overcome the world."

JESUS PRAYS FOR THOSE WHO WILL FOLLOW

[17:1]After speaking these words, Jesus looked up to heaven and said, "My dear Parent, the hour has come. Glorify Your Son, so that Your Son may glorify You. [2]You have given Me authority over all flesh, so that I may give eternal life to all You have given Me. [3]And this is eternal life: that they may know You, the only true God, and Jesus the Messiah whom You have sent. [4]I glorified You on earth; I finished the work You gave Me to do. [5]Now glorify Me alongside Yourself with the glory I had with You before the world was.

[6]"I declared Your name to those You gave Me from the world. They were Yours, You gave them to Me and they have kept Your word. [7]Now they know that all You have given Me comes from You, [8]for I have given them the words You gave Me and they accepted them. They truly know that I came from You and believe that You sent Me. [9]I pray for them. I am not praying for the world, but for those You have given Me, for they are Yours. [10]All Mine are Yours and Yours are Mine, and I am glorified through them. [11]Now I am coming to You! I am no longer in the world, but they are in the world. Holy Parent, keep through Your name those whom You have given Me so they may be one, just as We are One. [12]While I was with them I kept them safe by the power of that name You gave Me. Not one of them has been lost but the one who was destined to be lost, so that the Scripture might be fulfilled.

[13]"Now I am coming to You! These things I speak in the world, so that they may have My joy fulfilled in themselves. [14]I have given them Your word, but the world has hated them because they are not of the world, even as I am not of the world. [15]I do not ask that You take them out of the world, but that You keep them from evil. [16]They are not of the world, even as I am not of the world. [17]Make them holy through Your truth; Your word is truth. [18]As You sent Me into the world, I have sent them into the world. [19]For their sakes I sanctify Myself, so that they too may be made holy.

[20]"Nor do I pray for these alone, but also for other followers who will believe in Me through their words. [21]I pray that they may all be one, as You, My heavenly Parent, are in Me, and I am in You, and that they also may be one in Us, so that the world believes that You sent Me. [22]I have given them the glory that You have given Me so that they may be one, even as We are one; [23]I in them, and You in Me, that they may

be made complete in oneness, and so the world knows that You sent Me and have loved them as You love Me. [24]Dear Parent, I want those You have given Me to be with Me where I am, so that they may enjoy the glory You have given Me because You loved Me before the creation of the world. [25]O righteous Parent, the world does not know You. But I know You, and these know that You sent Me. [26]I have made Your name known to them, and still make it known, so that the love with which You love Me may be in them, and I in them."

THE GARDEN OF GETHSEMANE
[18:1]After Jesus prayed, He and His disciples went over the brook Kidron to a place where there was a garden, and they went into it. His disciples, [2]and Judas who betrayed Him, knew the place, for Jesus often met there with His disciples.

JUDAS BETRAYS JESUS
[3]Judas took a squad of soldiers and officers from the chief priests and Pharisees and went there with lanterns and torches and weapons. [4]Knowing all that would happen to Him, Jesus went out and said to them, "Whom do you seek?" [5]They answered Him, "Jesus of Nazareth." Jesus said to them, "I Am." Judas, the one who betrayed Him, was standing with them. [6]As Jesus said to them, "I Am," they went backward and fell to the ground.

[7]He asked them again, "Whom do you seek?" and they said, "Jesus of Nazareth." [8]Jesus answered, "I told you that I Am. If you are seeking Me, let these others go." [9]This was so the word might be fulfilled that He had spoken: "Of those whom You gave Me, I lost none." [10]Then Simon Peter, who had a sword, drew it and struck the high priest's servant, cutting off his right ear. The servant's name was Malchus. [11]Jesus said to Peter, "Put your sword back in its sheath. The cup that My heavenly Parent has given Me - should I not drink it?"

JESUS IS TIED AND TAKEN TO THE OLD HIGH PRIEST
[12]Then the soldiers and their commander and the officers of the Jews arrested Jesus and bound Him. [13]They led Him away to Annas first. He was the father-in-law of Caiaphas, the high priest that year. [14]Caiaphas was the one who had counseled the Jews that it was better that one man die for the people.

PETER DENIES KNOWING JESUS
[15]Simon Peter and another disciple followed Jesus. That disciple was known to the high priest and went in with Jesus into the courtyard of the high priest, [16]but Peter stood outside by the gate. Then that other disciple, who was known to the high priest, went out and spoke to the girl who stood at the gate and brought Peter in. [17]The girl said to Peter, "Aren't you one of that man's disciples?" Peter said, "I am not." [18]The servants and officers had made a fire of coals and were standing around it, for it was cold. They warmed themselves, and Peter stood with them and warmed himself.

JESUS IS SENT TO THE HIGH PRIEST
[19]The high priest questioned Jesus about His disciples and His teaching. [20]Jesus answered him, "I spoke openly to the world. I always taught in the synagogue and in the temple where all the Jews gather. I said nothing in secret. [21]Why do you question Me? Ask those who heard Me. They know what I said." [22]When He said this,

one of the officers standing there struck Jesus with his hand and said, "Is that any way to answer the high priest?" [23]Jesus answered him, "If I have spoken wrongly, say so; but if what I said was true, why do you hit Me?" [24]Then Annas sent Him bound to Caiaphas the high priest.

PETER DENIES JESUS THE THIRD TIME

[25]As Simon Peter stood warming himself, they said to him, "Aren't you one of His disciples?" He denied it and said, "I am not." [26]One of the servants of the high priest, a relative of the man whose ear Peter cut off, said, "Didn't I see you in the garden with Him?" [27]Peter denied it again, and immediately a rooster crowed.

JESUS IS TAKEN TO THE ROMAN GOVERNOR

[28]They led Jesus from the house of Caiaphas to the Governor's palace. It was dawn. They did not go into the palace, lest they be defiled and could not eat the Passover. [29]Therefore Pilate came out to them and said, "What accusation do you bring against this man?" [30]They answered him, "If He were not a criminal, we would not have brought Him to you." [31]Pilate said, "Take Him and judge Him according to your law." The Jews said, "It is not lawful for us to put anyone to death." [32]Thus was fulfilled what Jesus had foretold regarding the way He would die.

[33]Pilate went back into the palace and summoned Jesus. He said to Him, "Are You the King of the Jews?" [34]Jesus answered, "Do you ask this on your own, or have others told you about Me?" [35]Pilate answered, "Am I a Jew? Your own nation and the chief priests brought You to me. What have You done?" [36]Jesus answered, "My realm is not of this world. If My realm were of this world, My servants would fight so that I would not be surrendered to the Jews; but now My realm is elsewhere." [37]Then Pilate said to Him, "Then You are a king!" Jesus answered, "You say that I am a king. To this was I born and for this I came into the world, to witness to the truth. Everyone who is of the truth hears My voice." [38]Pilate said, "What is truth?"

After Pilate said this, he went out to the Jews and said to them, "I find no fault in Him. [39]But you have a custom whereby I release to you someone at Passover. Do you want me to release to you the King of the Jews?" [40]Then they all clamored anew, "Not this man, but Barabbas." Barabbas was a revolutionary.

THE SOLDIERS MOCK JESUS

[19:1]Pilate took Jesus and had Him whipped. [2]The soldiers plaited a crown of thorns and put it on His head. They put a purple robe on Him [3]and said, "Hail! The King of the Jews!" and struck Him repeatedly in the face. [4]Pilate went out again and said to the Jews, "Look! I am bringing Him out to you to let you know that I find no reason to condemn Him." [5]When Jesus came out wearing the crown of thorns and the purple robe, Pilate said to them, "Look at the man!" [6]When the chief priests and the officers saw Him, they cried out, "Crucify! Crucify!" Pilate said to them, "Take Him and crucify Him yourselves; I find no reason to condemn Him."

[7]The Jews said, "We have a law. By our law He ought to die because He made Himself the Child of God." [8]When Pilate heard this, he was even more afraid. [9]He went back into the palace and said to Jesus, "Where are You from?" Jesus did not answer him. [10]Pilate said, "You won't speak to me? Don't You know that I have the authority

to release You, as well as the authority to crucify You?" [11]Jesus answered, "You have no authority over Me except what is given to you from above. Therefore the one who handed Me over to you has the greater sin."

PILATE WANTS TO FREE JESUS

[12]From then on Pilate sought to release Him, but the Jews cried out, "If you let this man go, you are not Caesar's friend. Anyone who makes himself a king opposes Caesar." [13]When Pilate heard this, he brought Jesus out and sat down on the judgment seat in a place called The Pavement. [14]It was Preparation Day for the Passover. The hour was about noon. Pilate said to the Jews, "Look at your king!" [15]But they cried out, "Away with Him! Away with Him! Crucify Him!" Pilate said to them, "Shall I crucify your king?" The chief priests answered, "We have no king but Caesar!" [16]Then Pilate handed Him over to them to be crucified.

JESUS IS CRUCIFIED AT CALVARY

They took Jesus, [17]and He carried His cross to a place called Calvary, which in Hebrew is called Golgotha. [18]There they crucified Him and two others, one on each side, with Jesus between them.

[19]Pilate wrote a title and put it on the cross. It read, JESUS OF NAZARETH - THE KING OF THE JEWS. [20]Many of the Jews read this title, for the place where Jesus was crucified was near the city. It was written in Hebrew, Greek and Latin. [21]The chief priests of the Jews said to Pilate, "Don't write, 'THE KING OF THE JEWS,' but write, 'HE SAID, I AM KING OF THE JEWS.' [22]Pilate answered, "What I have written, I have written."

THE SOLDIERS CAST LOTS FOR JESUS' GARMENTS

[23]When the soldiers had crucified Jesus, they took His garments and divided them into four parts, one for each soldier. They also took His robe. The robe was seamless, woven from top to bottom. [24]Therefore they said among themselves, "Let's not tear it, but let's cast lots for it to see whose it shall be." This happened so that the Scripture would be fulfilled which said, "They divided My garments among them, and for My clothing they cast lots." The soldiers did these things.

JESUS GIVES HIS MOTHER INTO THE CARE OF THE BELOVED DISCIPLE

[25]Near the cross of Jesus stood His mother, His mother's sister, Mary the wife of Clopas and Mary Magdalene. [26]Jesus saw His mother and the disciple He loved standing there, and He said to His mother, "Mother, here is your son!" [27]Then He said to the disciple, "Here is your mother!" And from that hour that disciple took her into his home.

JESUS YIELDS UP HIS SPIRIT

[28]After this, knowing that all was now finished and that Scripture was about to be fulfilled, Jesus said, "I am thirsty." [29]A jar full of vinegar stood there. They filled a sponge with vinegar, put it on a stalk of hyssop and put it to His mouth. [30]When He had taken the vinegar, Jesus said, "It is finished," and He bowed His head and yielded up His Spirit.

GOD'S PASSOVER LAMB

[31]Because it was Preparation Day, and so that the bodies would not remain on the cross on the Sabbath, for that Sabbath was the great one, the Jews asked Pilate to have the men's legs broken and their bodies taken down. [32]Therefore the soldiers came and broke the legs of the first man, and then of the other one crucified with Him. [33]When they came to Jesus and saw that He was dead already, they did not break His legs. [34]But one of the soldiers pierced His side with a spear, and immediately blood and water came out. [35]The man who saw all this has testified so that you also may believe. His witness is authentic, and he knows that he tells the truth. [36]These things happened so the Scriptures would be fulfilled: "Not a bone of His will be broken." [37]And another Scripture says: "They will look upon Him whom they pierced."

JOSEPH AND NICODEMUS BURY JESUS IN THE GARDEN TOMB

[38]After this, Joseph of Arimathea asked Pilate if he could take the body of Jesus. Joseph was a disciple of Jesus, but had kept it secret because he was afraid of the Jewish leaders. Pilate gave him permission, and Joseph came and took the body of Jesus away. [39]Nicodemus, who had at first gone to see Jesus at night, came also, bringing a mixture of about seventy-five pounds of myrrh and aloes. [40]They took the body of Jesus and bound it in linen cloth with the spices in the manner of Jewish burials. [41]In the place where He was crucified there was a garden, and in the garden was a new tomb in which no one had ever been laid. [42]They laid Jesus there because it was the Jewish Preparation Day and the tomb was nearby.

MARY MAGDALENE DISCOVERS THE EMPTY TOMB

[20:1]In the dimness of dawn on the first day of the week, Mary Magdalene came to the tomb and saw the stone moved away. [2]She ran to Simon Peter and to the other disciple whom Jesus loved and said to them, "They have taken our Rabbi out of the tomb, and we don't know where they have put Him!" [3]Peter and the other disciple jumped up and went to the tomb. [4]They both ran, but the other disciple ran faster than Peter and got to the tomb first. [5]Stooping down, he saw the linen cloth lying there, but he did not go in. [6]When Simon Peter got there, he went into the tomb and saw the linen cloths lying there. [7]The cloth that had been around His head was not lying with the linen cloths, but was rolled up in a place by itself. [8]Then that other disciple who had come to the tomb first went in. He saw and believed, [9]for as yet they did not understand the Scripture that said that Jesus must rise from the dead. [10]Then the disciples went back to their homes.

MARY MAGDALENE TALKS TO TWO ANGELS

[11]Mary stood outside the tomb weeping. As she wept, she stooped down and looked into the tomb. [12]She saw two angels in white sitting where the body of Jesus had been lying, one at the head and the other at the feet. [13]They said to her, "Why are you weeping?" She replied, "They have taken Him away, and I don't know where they have laid Him."

MARY MAGDALENE TALKS TO A DIFFERENT-LOOKING JESUS

[14]After she said this, she turned around and saw Jesus standing there, but she did not recognize that it was Jesus. [15]"Why are you weeping?" Jesus asked. "Who are you looking for?" Supposing Jesus to be the gardener, she said, "Sir, if You have removed Him, tell me where You have laid Him and I will take Him." [16]Jesus said to her, "Mary." She turned to Jesus and said, "Rabboni!" (which means Teacher). [17]Jesus said to her, "Do not hold on to Me, for I have not yet ascended to My heavenly Parent. Go to My disciples and say to them, 'I am ascending to My Parent and your Parent, to My God and your God.'" [18]Then Mary Magdalene went and told the disciples that she had seen Jesus and that Jesus had spoken these things to her.

JESUS APPEARS TO THE DISCIPLES AND THEY RECEIVE THE SPIRIT

[19]In the evening of that first day of the week, the disciples were together, with the doors locked for fear of the Jews. Jesus came and stood among them and said, "Peace to you!" [20]Jesus' hands and side bore wound marks, and Jesus showed these to the disciples. The disciples were overjoyed to see Jesus. [21]Then Jesus said to them, "Peace to you! As My heavenly Parent has sent Me, even so I send you." [22]After saying this, Jesus breathed on them and said, "Receive the Holy Spirit. [23]If you forgive the sins of anyone, they are forgiven. If you do not forgive them, they are not forgiven."

THOMAS BECOMES CONVINCED THAT JESUS IS GOD

[24]One of the twelve, Thomas the Twin, was not with them when Jesus came. [25]The other disciples said to him, "We have seen Jesus." But he said to them, "Unless I see in His hands the print of the nails and put my hand into His side, I will not believe." [26]Eight days later the disciples were again inside with the doors locked, and Thomas was with them. Jesus came and stood among them and said, "Peace to you!" [27]Then Jesus said to Thomas, "Put your finger here, and look at My hands. Reach out your hand and put it into My side. Do not doubt, but believe." [28]Thomas said to Jesus, "My Sovereign and my God!" [29]Jesus said to him, "You believe because you see Me. Blessed are those who have not seen and yet believe."

[30]Jesus did many other signs in the presence of the disciples which are not written in this book. [31]But these are written so that you may believe that Jesus is the Messiah, the Child of God, and that by believing you may have life through Jesus' name.

JESUS APPEARS TO SEVEN DISCIPLES FISHING IN GALILEE

[21:1]Later on Jesus again appeared to the disciples at the Sea of Tiberias. This is how it happened: [2]Simon Peter, Thomas the Twin, Nathanael from Cana in Galilee, the sons of Zebedee and two other disciples were together. [3]Simon Peter said to them, "I'm going fishing." They said to him, "We'll go with you." They went out and got into a boat, but that night they caught nothing. [4]When daybreak came, Jesus was standing on the shore, but the disciples did not know it was Jesus.

JESUS TELLS WHERE THE FISH ARE

[5]Jesus called to them, "Little ones, have you any fish?" They answered, "No." [6]Jesus said to them, "Cast the net on the right side of the boat and you will find some." They cast it therefore, and now they were unable to drag it in because there were so many fish. [7]The disciple whom Jesus loved said to Peter, "It's Jesus!"

When Simon Peter heard that it was Jesus, he pulled on his fisher's coat that he had taken off and jumped into the water. [8]The other disciples came in the boat dragging the net full of fish, for they were only about one hundred yards from shore.

THE DISCIPLES EAT A MEAL WITH JESUS

[9]When they came ashore, they saw a fire of coals with fish on it and some bread. [10]Jesus said to them, "Bring some of the fish you just caught." [11]Simon Peter went aboard and dragged the net to shore. It was full with one hundred and fifty-three big fish; but though there were so many, the net was not torn. [12]Jesus said to them, "Come and have some breakfast." None of the disciples dared ask who Jesus was; they knew who Jesus was. [13]Jesus took the bread and gave it to them and then offered them some fish in the same way. [14]This was now the third time that Jesus appeared to the disciples after being raised from the dead.

PETER IS INSTRUCTED TO CARE FOR JESUS' SHEEP

[15]When they had finished breakfast, Jesus said to Simon Peter, "Simon son of John, do you love Me more than these?" He answered, "Yes Rabbi, You know I love You." Jesus said, "Feed My lambs." [16]Jesus said to him again a second time, "Simon son of John, do you love Me?" He said to Jesus, "Yes, Rabbi, You know I love You." Jesus said, "Take care of My sheep." [17]Jesus said to him the third time, "Simon son of John, do you love Me?" Peter was grieved because Jesus said to him the third time, "Do you love Me?" Peter said to Him, "Rabbi, You know all things! You know that I love You." Jesus said to him, "Feed My sheep. [18]Truly I say to you, when you were young, you dressed yourself and walked wherever you wished; but when you become old, you will stretch out your hands and another will dress you and carry you where you do not wish to go." [19]Jesus said this to foretell by what death Peter would glorify God. Then Jesus said to Peter, "Follow Me."

THE BELOVED DISCIPLE

[20]Peter turned and saw the disciple whom Jesus loved following them. He was the one who had leaned on Jesus' chest at supper and asked, "Rabbi, who is the one who will betray You?" [21]Seeing him, Peter said to Jesus, "Rabbi, what about him?" [22]Jesus said to Peter, "If I desire for him to remain till I come, what is that to you? You must follow Me." [23]Then this saying spread abroad among the believers that this disciple would not die. Yet Jesus did not say to him that he would not die. He just said, "If I desire for him to remain till I come, what is that to you?"

[24]This is that disciple who testifies about these things and wrote them down, and we know that his testimony is true. [25]There are also many other things that Jesus did, and I suppose that if every one of them were to be written down, even the world itself could not contain the books that would be written.

ℐcts

LUKE CONTINUES THE LETTER TO THEOPHILUS

1:1In my first book, O Theophilus, I wrote of all that Jesus began to do and teach 2until the day He was taken up. Before He was taken up, He gave instructions through the Holy Spirit to the apostles He had chosen. 3He appeared and proved Himself alive to them in many ways after His suffering. They saw Him for forty days and He spoke to them about the realm of God. 4One time while He was with them He commanded, "Do not depart from Jerusalem, but wait for the promise of God which you heard Me speak about. 5For John baptized with water, but you will be baptized with the Holy Spirit in a few days."

JESUS DEPARTS FROM EARTH

6While they were all together, they asked Him, "Rabbi, are You going to restore the realm of God to Israel at this time?" 7He said to them, "It is not for you to know the times or seasons that My heavenly Parent has set. 8But you will receive power when the Holy Spirit comes upon you, and you will be witnesses for Me in Jerusalem, in all Judea and Samaria, and to the ends of the earth." 9After He said this, He was lifted up while they watched, and they saw a cloud carry Him upward out of their sight. 10As they stared at Him going up into the sky, suddenly two people in white clothing stood by them 11and said, "Men of Galilee, why are you standing here gazing into the sky? This same Jesus, who has been taken up from you into the sky, will come back in the same way you have seen Him go into the sky."

THE DISCIPLES PRAY IN THE UPPER ROOM

12Then they returned to Jerusalem from the Mount of Olives, which is a Sabbath day's walk from Jerusalem. 13When they got there, they went up to the upper room where Peter, John, James, Andrew, Philip, Thomas, Bartholomew, Matthew, James the son of Alphaeus, Simon the Zealot and Judas the son of James were staying. 14All these, together with the women and Mary the mother of Jesus and His brothers, were constantly devoting themselves to prayer.

THE ELEVEN PICK ANOTHER DISCIPLE TO REPLACE JUDAS

15In those days Peter stood up among the disciples (about one hundred and twenty were there) and said, 16"Brothers and sisters, the Scripture had to be fulfilled which the Holy Spirit spoke through the mouth of David long ago concerning Judas, who guided those who arrested Jesus, 17though he was one of our number and was chosen as part of this ministry. 18Judas bought a field with the money he got for his unjust act. There he fell headlong, burst open in the middle and all his bowels poured out. [19]Everyone living in Jerusalem heard about this, and they called the place the Field of Blood. [20]It is written in the book of Psalms, 'May his house be desolate and may no one live in it,' and 'May another take his place.' [21]Therefore of these who accompanied us all the time that Jesus went in and out among us, [22]beginning from the time when John was baptizing until the day Jesus was taken up from us, one of these must be a witness with us of His resurrection."

[23]They appointed two: Joseph called Barsabbas (whose other name was Justus) and Matthias. [24]They prayed, "God, You know everyone's heart. Show which of these two You choose [25]to take the part of this ministry and apostleship which Judas left to go to his own place," [26]and they threw out their lots. The lot fell to Matthias and he was numbered with the eleven apostles.

THE HOLY SPIRIT COMES AND FILLS THEM ALL

[2:1]When the day of Pentecost came, they were all together in one place. [2]Suddenly a sound came from heaven like a rushing mighty wind. It filled the whole house where they were sitting [3]and they saw tongues like fire separate and hover upon each of them. [4]They were all filled with the Holy Spirit and began to speak in other tongues as the Spirit enabled them.

JEWS OF THE DISPERSION HEAR THE NOISE

[5]Devout Jews were sojourning at Jerusalem from every nation under heaven. [6]When they heard the noise, a crowd gathered in confusion, because they all heard the others speaking in their own language. [7]They were all amazed and marveled one to another, "Look! Are not these who speak Galileans? [8]How do we each hear our own native language? [9]Parthians, Medes, Elamites, residents of Mesopotamia, Judea, Cappadocia, Pontus, Asia, [10]Phrygia, Pamphylia, Egypt, the parts of Lybia around Cyrene, visitors from Rome, both Jews and Jewish converts, [11]Cretans and Arabs - we hear them speaking in our own language the wonders of God." [12]Amazed and baffled, they said to one another, "What does this mean?" [13]Others said mockingly, "They are full of wine."

PETER REMINDS THE CROWD WHAT THE PROPHET SAID

[14]But Peter stood up with the eleven, raised his voice, and said, "You people of Judah and all who live in Jerusalem, try to understand this; hear my words. [15]These are not drunk as you suppose; it is only the middle of the morning! [16]This is that which was spoken by the prophet Joel: [17]'It will come to pass in the last days, says God; I will pour out My Spirit upon all flesh. Your sons and your daughters will prophesy, your youths will see visions and your elders will dream dreams. [18]On My men and women servants I will pour out My Spirit in those days and they will prophesy. [19]I will show wonders in heaven above and signs on the earth below: blood and fire and smoke like mist. [20]The sun will be turned to darkness and the moon to blood before that great and memorable day of Yahweh comes. [21]And it will come to pass that whoever calls on the name of Yahweh will be saved.'

[22]"People of Israel, hear these words: Jesus of Nazareth was a man approved by God among you by miracles, wonders and signs which God did through Him in your midst, as you yourselves know. [23]He was handed over by the prearranged plan and

foreknowledge of God, and you had wicked men crucify and kill Him. [24]But God raised Him up and released Him from the pains of death, because it was not possible for Him to be held by it. [25]David said concerning God, 'I am mindful of You 'always before me; because You are at my right hand, I will not waver. [26]Therefore my heart is glad and my tongue rejoices; my body also will rest in expectation. [27]For You will not leave my soul in hell, nor let Your Holy One see decay. [28]You make known to me the paths of life, and in Your presence is fullness of joy.'

[29]"Believers, let me speak freely to you about your ancestor David. He died and was buried, and his tomb is with us to this day. [30]Since he was a prophet, and knowing that God had promised with an oath to him to raise up one of his descendants to sit on his throne, [31]he foresaw and spoke of the resurrection of the Messiah - that His soul would not be left forgotten in hell, nor His flesh undergo decay. [32]God raised up this Jesus, and we all witnessed it. [33]Exalted therefore to the right hand of God, He received from God the promised Holy Spirit. He is the One who pours out what you now see and hear. [34]For David did not ascend into the heavens, but he himself said, 'God said to the Messiah: Sit at My right hand [35]till I make Your enemies Your footstool.' [36]Therefore let all Israel clearly know that God made this same Jesus whom you crucified to be both Sovereign and Messiah."

PETER EXPLAINS HOW TO RECEIVE THE PROMISE

[37]When they heard this, they were pierced to the heart. They said to Peter and the rest of the apostles, "Friends, what shall we do?" [38]Peter said, "Repent and be baptized, every one of you, in the name of Jesus the Messiah for the forgiveness of your sins and you will receive the gift of the Holy Spirit. [39]For the promise is to you and your children and to all who are far off - to as many as our God will call." [40]And with many other words he testified and pleaded, "Save yourselves from this warped generation."

THREE THOUSAND REPENT AND ARE BAPTIZED

[41]Those who gladly welcomed his words were baptized, and that day there were added about three thousand souls. [42]They devoted themselves to the apostles' teaching, fellowship, the breaking of bread and prayers. [43]Fear came upon every soul, and many wonders and signs were done by the apostles. [44]All who believed were together and had everything in common. [45]They sold their possessions and goods and gave the money to whoever had a need. [46]They devotedly met daily with one accord in the temple court, breaking bread from house to house, eating their food with gladness and simplicity of heart, [47]praising God and having favor with all the people. And God added daily to the congregation those who were being saved.

A CRIPPLE IS HEALED IN THE NAME OF JESUS

3:[1]Peter and John went up together to the temple about mid-afternoon for prayer. [2]A certain man who had been lame from birth was being carried to the temple entrance called the Beautiful Gate. He was laid there every day. He asked alms of those who entered the temple there. [3]When he saw Peter and John about to go into the temple, he asked for alms. [4]Peter looked intently at him, as did John, and said, "Look at us." [5]The man looked at them, expecting to get something from them. [6]Then

Peter said, "Silver and gold have I none, but what I have I give you. In the name of Jesus Christ of Nazareth, walk!" [7]He took him by the right hand and lifted him up, and immediately his feet and ankle bones received strength. [8]Leaping up, he stood and walked. He went with them into the temple, walking and leaping and praising God. [9]All the people saw him walking and praising God. [10]They knew he was the one who sat for alms at the Beautiful Gate of the temple, and they were filled with amazement and wondered what had happened to him.

PETER GIVES GOD THE CREDIT FOR THE HEALING

[11]As the healed cripple clung to Peter and John, all the people were astonished and ran headlong toward them in what is called Solomon's Walkway. [12]Seeing this, Peter said to the people, "People of Israel, why do you marvel at this? Why do you stare at us, as if by our own power or holiness we made this man walk? [13]The God of Abraham, Isaac and Jacob - the God of our ancestors - has honored Jesus, God's servant, whom you denied and handed over in the presence of Pilate, though Pilate had decided to let Him go. [14]You denied the holy and righteous One and asked that a murderer be pardoned. [15]You killed the Creator of Life, whom God then raised from the dead. We saw it with our own eyes. [16]This man whom you see and recognize was made strong through faith in the name of Jesus. Yes, faith in Jesus has given this man wholeness in the presence of you all.

[17]"Now I know that you and your leaders did not completely understand, [18]but this is that which God foretold through all the prophets and which God's suffering Messiah fulfilled. [19]Therefore repent and return to God so that your sins may be blotted out. Then times of refreshing will come from the presence of God [20]and God will send Jesus, the Messiah who was proclaimed to you. [21]But Jesus must stay in heaven until the time of the total restoration that God has spoken of through the prophets since ancient times. [22]Moses said, 'God will raise up a prophet for you like me from among your people. You must listen to everything God says to you. [23]Every soul who does not listen to that prophet will be destroyed from among the people.' [24]Moreover, all the prophets from Samuel and those who followed after have foretold these days. [25]You are the children of the prophets and of the covenant which God made with our ancestors. For God said to Abraham, 'Through your descendants will all the people of the earth be blessed.' [26]Having raised up Jesus as a servant, God sent Jesus to you first to bless you by turning each of you away from your wicked ways."

THE LEADERS ARREST PETER AND JOHN

[4:1]As they spoke to the people, the priests, the captain of the temple guard and the Sadducees came up to them, [2]pained that they were teaching the people and proclaiming in Jesus the resurrection from the dead. [3]They arrested them and put them in jail until the next day, for it was evening. [4]But many of those who heard the message believed. The number was now about five thousand.

[5]The next day the Jewish elders and leaders and scribes [6]met with Annas the high priest, Caiphas, John, Alexander and all who belonged to the priest's family in Jerusalem. [7]The leaders brought Peter and John in and asked, "By what power or by what name have you done this?" [8]Then Peter, filled with the Holy Spirit, said to them,

"You leaders and elders of the people, [9]if we are being examined this day for the good deed done to a crippled man and are being asked how he was made whole, [10]let it be known to you and to all the people of Israel that by the name of Jesus the Messiah from Nazareth, whom you crucified, but whom God raised from the dead - by Him this man stands here before you whole. [11]He is 'the stone the builders rejected, which has become the headstone of the corner.' [12]Salvation is found in no one else, for no other name under heaven is given among humans by which they may be saved."

[13]When they saw the assurance of Peter and John and perceived that they were unlettered and uneducated, they were amazed and apprehensive, for Peter and John had been with Jesus. [14]And, seeing the man who was healed standing with them, they could say nothing against them. [15]So they ordered them to leave the council. Conferring among themselves, [16]they said, "What can we do to these men? That a remarkable miracle has been done by them is evident to all those who live in Jerusalem, and we cannot deny it. [17]But to keep this from spreading any further among the people, we should warn them not to speak anymore to anyone in this name." [18]They called them and commanded them not to speak at all or teach in the name of Jesus. [19]But Peter and John answered them, "Whether it be right in the sight of God to listen to you more than to God, you be the judge. [20]But we cannot stop speaking of the things that we have seen and heard." [21]So when they had further threatened them, they let them go. They could find no way to punish them because of the people, for everyone glorified God because of what had been done. [22]The man in whom this miracle of healing took place was over forty years old.

THE DISCIPLES JOYFULLY PRAISE GOD

[23]Free to go, they went to the other believers and reported all that the chief priests and elders had said to them. [24]When the others heard, they lifted up their voices to God with one accord and said, "O Sovereign God who made heaven and earth and sea and all that is in them, [25]by the mouth of Your servant David You said, 'Why do the nations rage and the people imagine vain things? [26]The kings of the earth take a stand and the rulers gather together against God and against God's Messiah.' [27]For Herod and Pontius Pilate met together with the unbelievers and the people of Israel against Your holy servant Jesus, whom You anointed [28]to do whatever Your hand and Your purpose had determined beforehand be done. [29]And now, God, take note of their threats and give Your servants courage to speak Your message [30]by stretching forth Your hand to heal and do signs and wonders in the name of Your holy servant Jesus." [31]When they had prayed, the place where they were gathered was shaken; and they were all filled with the Holy Spirit and spoke the message of God boldly.

[32]The many who believed were of one heart and one soul. None of the believers claimed that anything they possessed was their own, but they had all things in common. [33]With great power the apostles gave witness to the resurrection of Jesus, and great grace was upon them all. [34]There was no one among them who lacked, for as many as possessed lands or houses sold them and brought the money from what was sold. [35]They laid it at the apostles' feet, and distribution was made to each according to any need. [36]And Joseph, a Levite from Cyprus who was given the name

Barnabas by the apostles (which can be interpreted, Son of Encouragement), [37]sold his land and brought the money and laid it at the apostles' feet.

ANANIAS AND SAPPHIRA LIE TO THE OTHER BELIEVERS

[5:1]But a certain man named Ananias and his wife Sapphira sold a property. [2]With his wife's knowledge, he kept back part of the price. He brought the rest and laid it at the apostles' feet, [3]but Peter said, "Ananias, how has Satan so filled your mind that you could lie to the Holy Spirit and keep back part of the price of the land? [4]Before it was sold, was it not yours? And after it was sold, was it not yours to do with as you pleased? Why have you conceived this thing in your mind? You have not lied to humans but to God." [5]When Ananias heard these words, he fell down and gave up his spirit. Great fear came upon all those who heard these things. [6]The youths came and wrapped him up, carried him out and buried him.

[7]About three hours later his wife came in, not knowing what had happened. [8]Peter said to her, "Tell me, did you sell the land for this much?" She said, "Yes, that is how much we got." [9]Then Peter said, "Why did you agree together to test the Spirit of God? Listen! The feet of those who buried your husband are at the door, and they will carry you out too." [10]At this she fell at his feet and yielded up her spirit. The youths came in, and, finding her dead, carried her out and buried her by her husband. [11]Great fear came upon the whole congregation and everyone who heard about it.

MIRACLES AND HEALINGS

[12]Many miracles and wonders were done among the people by the hands of the apostles. They were all together in Solomon's Walkway. [13]None of the rest dared join them, even though they were well thought of by the people. [14]More and more believers were increasingly added to God, multitudes of men and women. [15]In addition, they brought the sick out into the streets and laid them on beds and mats, so that even the shadow of Peter going by might fall on some of them. [16]Crowds came also from the towns around Jerusalem, bringing the sick and those who were vexed by unclean spirits. They were all healed.

AN ANGEL RESCUES THE APOSTLES

[17]Then the high priest and all those who were with him of the sect of the Sadducees were filled with indignation and took a stand. [18]They arrested the apostles and put them in the public jail. [19]But during the night an angel of God opened the doors of the jail, brought them out, and said, [20]"Go and stand in the temple and tell the people the full meaning of this new life." [21]After they heard this, they went into the temple early in the morning and started teaching.

Meanwhile, the high priest and those who were with him called the council and the full senate of the people of Israel together and sent to the jail to have the prisoners brought. [22]But the officers went to the jail and did not find them. They returned and reported, [23]"We found the jail securely locked and the guards standing outside in front of the doors, but we opened the doors and found no one inside." [24]When the high priest and the captain of the temple guard and the chief priests heard these things, they wondered what this would lead to. [25]Then someone came and told them, "The men that you put in jail are standing in the temple teaching the people." [26]Then the captain of the guard went with his officers and brought them. They did not use force, for they were afraid the people would stone them. [27]They brought them and made them stand before the council. The high priest asked them, [28]"Didn't we command you not to teach in that name? Look! You have filled Jerusalem with your teachings and intend to blame us for this man's death." [29]Then Peter and the apostles said, "We must obey God rather than humans. [30]The God of our ancestors raised up Jesus, the One you killed by hanging Him on a cross. [31]God exalted Him with power as Prince and Savior to bring repentance and forgiveness of sins to Israel. [32]We are witnesses of these things, and so is the Holy Spirit, whom God has given to those who obey God."

[33]When they heard this, they were exasperated. They were determined to kill them, [34]but a Pharisee named Gamaliel, a teacher of the law who was respected by all the people, stood up in the council and gave orders that the apostles be taken out for a while. [35]He said to the council, "Men of Israel, be cautious in regard to what you intend to do with these men. [36]Some time ago Theudas rose up and claimed to be somebody, and about four hundred joined him. But he was killed, all his followers were scattered and it came to nothing. [37]After this, Judas the Galilean rose up at the time of the census and drew away many people after him. He also perished, and all his followers were scattered. [38]And now I say to you, have nothing to do with these men. Leave them alone. For if their purpose and this undertaking is of human origin, it will fail. [39]But if it is from God, it cannot fail, and you may even find yourselves fighting against God." [40]They were convinced by him, and they called the apostles and had them whipped. Then they commanded them not to speak in the name of Jesus and let them go. [41]The apostles departed from the presence of the council, rejoicing that they had been counted worthy of suffering shame for Jesus' name, [42]and daily in the temple and in every house they continued to teach and announce the good news that Jesus is the Messiah.

SEVEN ARE CHOSEN TO SERVE THE PEOPLE

[6:1]In those days, as the number of disciples was increasing, the Greek-speaking Jews complained to the Aramaic-speaking Jews that their widows were being neglected in the daily distribution. [2]Then the twelve called the community of disciples and said, "It is not reasonable for us to neglect the message of God to serve tables. [3]Therefore, believers, select seven men from among you of good standing who are spiritually-minded and wise whom we may appoint over this business. [4]Then we will give ourselves continually to prayer and the ministry of the word." [5]This logic was unanimously approved. They chose Stephen, a man full of faith and the Holy Spirit, Philip, Prochorus, Nicanor, Timon, Parmenas and Nicolas of Antioch, a convert to Judaism. [6]These they brought before the apostles, and the apostles prayed and laid hands on them. [7]So the message of God spread. The number of disciples in Jerusalem greatly increased, and a large number of priests were obedient to the faith.

STEPHEN IS FALSELY ACCUSED

[8]Stephen, full of faith and power, did great wonders and signs among the people. [9]But some Jews from Cyrene and Alexandria from the Synagogue of the Libertines (as

it was called), and some from Cilicia and Asia, disputed with Stephen. [10]But they were not able to resist the wisdom and the Spirit by which he spoke. [11]So they persuaded some men to say, "We have heard Stephen blaspheme Moses and God," [12]and they stirred up the people and the elders and the scribes. They seized him and brought him before the council. [13]There they presented false witnesses who said, "This man never stops speaking blasphemous words against this holy place and the law. [14]We heard him say that this Jesus of Nazareth will destroy this place and change the customs Moses gave us." [15]All those who sat in the council looked at Stephen, and they saw that his face was like the face of an angel.

STEPHEN ANSWERS BY TELLING ISRAEL'S HISTORY

[7:1]The high priest asked, "Are these things so?" [2]Stephen answered, "Sisters and brothers, mothers and fathers, listen. The God of glory appeared to our ancestor Abraham in Mesopotamia before he lived in Haran. [3]God said to Abraham, 'Leave your country and your people and come to a land that I will show you.' [4]Abraham left the land of the Chaldeans and lived in Haran. From there, when his father died, God moved him to this land where you now live. [5]God gave him no inheritance here, not even enough to set his foot on, yet God promised to give it to him and to his descendants after him as a possession. Though he had no child, [6]God assured him that his descendants would sojourn in a strange land where they would be slaves and be abused for four hundred years. [7]'I will judge the nation that makes them slaves,' God said, 'and after that they will come out and serve Me in this place.' [8]Then God gave Abraham the covenant of circumcision. Abraham became the father of Isaac and circumcised him the eighth day. Isaac became the father of Jacob, and Jacob became the father of our twelve ancestors. [9]Our ancestors were jealous of Joseph and sold him into Egypt. But God was with him [10]and released him from all his afflictions. God gave him favor and wisdom in the presence of Pharaoh the king of Egypt and put him in command of Egypt and all the people in Pharaoh's palace. [11]Then a famine and great suffering came over all the land of Egypt and Canaan, and our ancestors could find no food. [12]When Jacob heard that there was grain in Egypt, he sent out our ancestors the first time. [13]On the second visit Joseph made himself known to his brothers, and Joseph's family became known to Pharaoh. [14]Then Joseph sent and called for his father Jacob and all his family, seventy-five in all. [15]So Jacob went down to Egypt, and he and our ancestors died there. [16]Their bodies were carried over to Shechem and laid in the tomb that Abraham bought for a sum of money from the sons of Hamor of Shechem. [17]As the time approached for God to fulfill the promise to Abraham, the people greatly multiplied in Egypt. [18]Then another king arose who knew nothing of Joseph. [19]He dealt deceitfully with our people and abused our ancestors by making them abandon their young infants outside so they would not live. [20]At that time Moses was born, a child favored by God. Moses was cared for in his parents' home for three months. [21]When he was abandoned, Pharaoh's daughter took him and cared for him as if he were her own. [22]Moses was trained in all the wisdom of the Egyptians and was mighty in words and deeds. [23]When he was forty years old, it came into his heart to visit his people, the descendants of Israel. [24]Seeing one of them wronged, he went to his defense and avenged him by striking the Egyptian. [25]Moses supposed that his people would understand that God was using him to rescue them, but they did not. [26]The next day he saw two Israelites fighting, and he tried to make peace between them. 'Men,' he said, 'you are brothers! Why do you wrong one another?' [27]But the one who was hurting the other one shoved Moses away and said, 'Who made you a ruler and judge over us? [28]Are you going to kill me like you killed that Egyptian yesterday?' [29]When Moses heard that, he fled to the land of Midian. There he made his home and had two sons. [30]Forty years went by, and an Angel appeared to him in the wilderness of Mount Sinai in a flame of fire in a bush. [31]Moses looked and was amazed by what he saw. As he came near to look closely, God's voice came, saying, [32]'I am the God of your ancestors, the God of Abraham, Isaac and Jacob.' Then Moses trembled and was afraid to look. [33]God said to him, 'Take your sandals off, for the place where you are standing is holy ground. [34]I have surely seen the affliction of My people in Egypt. I have heard their groaning and have come down to tear them away. Now come, I will send you to Egypt.' [35]This is the Moses they rejected by saying, 'Who made you a ruler and a judge?' God sent him as ruler and redeemer by the power of the Angel who appeared to him in the bush. [36]He led them out and did wonders and miracles in the land of Egypt and at the Red Sea and for forty years in the wilderness. [37]This is that Moses who said to the people of Israel, 'God will raise up a prophet for you like me from among your people.' [38]Moses is the one who was in the congregation in the wilderness with our ancestors and with the Angel who spoke to him on Mount Sinai. He received living words to give to us [39]which our ancestors would not obey, but rejected. In their hearts they turned back to Egypt, [40]saying to Aaron, 'Make us gods to go before us, for we don't know what has become of this Moses who brought us out of the land of Egypt.' [41]In those days they made a calf, offered sacrifices to the idol and rejoiced in the works of their hands. [42]God turned away and left them to worship the host of heaven, as it is written in the book of the prophets: 'O house of Israel, it was not to Me you brought sacrifices and offerings for forty years in the wilderness. [43]Indeed, you took along the tent of Moloch and the star of your god Rephan, the idols you made to worship. And so I will send you away beyond Babylon.' [44]Our ancestors had the tabernacle of testimony in the wilderness, and it was made as God had directed according to the pattern Moses had seen. [45]Later, Joshua and our other ancestors brought it into the land of the nations who were driven out by God before them. There it stayed until the days of David. [46]David found favor before God and desired to build a temple for the God of Jacob. [47]But it was Solomon who built God a temple. [48]Nevertheless, the Most High does not live in temples made by humans. As the prophet says: [49]'Heaven is My throne and earth is My footstool. God asks: what temple could you build for Me? What is the place of My rest? [50]Has not My hand made all this?'

[51]"You stiffnecked people have uncircumcised hearts and ears! You always resist the Holy Spirit! As your ancestors were, so are you. [52]Which of the prophets did your ancestors not persecute? They killed those who announced beforehand the coming of the Holy One, whom you now have betrayed and murdered. [53]You have received the

law by means of angels and have not obeyed!"

STEPHEN IS STONED TO DEATH

[54]When they heard all this, they were cut to the heart and gnashed their teeth at him. [55]But Stephen, full of the Holy Spirit, looked into heaven and saw the glory of God and Jesus standing at the right hand of God. [56]He said, "Look! I see the heavens opened and the Son of Humanity standing at the right hand of God!" [57]Then they cried out with a loud voice and covered their ears. All together they rushed at him, [58]drove him out of the city and began to stone him. The witnesses laid their coats at the feet of a young man named Saul. [59]While they were stoning him, Stephen was praying, "O Jesus, receive my spirit!" [60]He sank to his knees and cried out with a loud voice, "O God! Do not put this sin in their books!" After he said this, he fell asleep.

[8:1] And Saul was there, consenting to his death.

THE CHURCH IS PERSECUTED

At that time there was a great persecution against the congregation at Jerusalem, and all except the apostles were scattered throughout the countryside of Judea and Samaria. [2]Some godly men carried away Stephen, mourning deeply for him. [3]But Saul ravaged the church, entering house after house and dragging men and women off to prison. [4]Those who had been scattered went everywhere telling what had happened.

PHILIP SPREADS THE GOOD NEWS

[5]Philip went down to a city in Samaria and told them about the Messiah. [6]The people all paid close attention to what Philip said when they saw and heard the miracles he did, [7]for unclean spirits that were holding on to many came shrieking out with a loud cry. Many paralytics and cripples were healed, [8]and there was great joy in that city.

[9]Now a certain man named Simon had been practicing magic for some time in the city and astounding the people of Samaria, claiming to be someone great. [10]Everyone from the least to the greatest paid him close attention and said, "He has a great divine power." [11]They regarded him highly, because for a long time he had astounded them with magic. [12]But when they believed Philip's good news concerning the realm of God and the name of Jesus Christ, they were baptized, both men and women. [13]Then Simon himself believed and was baptized. He stayed close to Philip and was astounded as he saw the miracles taking place.

THE SAMARITANS RECEIVE THE HOLY SPIRIT

[14]Now the apostles who were at Jerusalem heard that Samaria had accepted the plan of God. They sent Peter and John to them, [15]and they came down and prayed for them that they might receive the Holy Spirit. [16]As yet the Holy Spirit had not fallen upon any of them; they were only baptized in the name of Jesus. [17]So they laid hands on them, and they received the Holy Spirit.

SIMON THE MAGICIAN IS REBUKED

[18]Simon saw that the Holy Spirit was given through the laying on of the apostles' hands. He offered them money, [19]saying, "Give me this ability too, so that whoever I lay hands on will receive the Holy Spirit." [20]But Peter said to him, "May your money perish with you because you thought that the gift of God could be purchased with

money. [21]You have neither share nor inheritance in this matter, for your heart is not right in the sight of God. [22]Therefore repent of this wickedness of yours and pray to God. Perhaps God will forgive you for the thoughts of your heart. [23]For I perceive that you are poisoned by bitterness and controlled by wickedness." [24]Simon said, "Pray to God for me, so that none of what you spoke comes upon me."

[25]When Peter and John had attested to and proclaimed the message of God, they started back for Jerusalem and told the good news in many Samaritan villages.

AN ANGEL GIVES PHILIP INSTRUCTIONS

[26]The angel of God spoke to Philip and said, "Get up and go south along the road that goes down from Jerusalem to Gaza through the wilderness." [27]Philip set out and came upon an Ethiopian eunuch. He was the minister in charge of all the treasure of Candace, the queen of the Ethiopians. He had been to Jerusalem to worship [28]and was now going home. He was seated in his chariot reading Isaiah the prophet. [29]The Spirit said to Philip, "Go over and stay close to that chariot." [30]Philip ran over and heard him reading the prophet Isaiah. Philip asked, "Do you understand what you are reading?" [31]"How can I," he answered, "unless someone guides me?" And he invited Philip to come and sit with him. [32]The place in the Scripture he was reading was this: "He was led like a sheep to the slaughter, and as a lamb before its shearer is silent, so he did not open his mouth. [33]In his humiliation his rights were denied. As for his contemporaries, who could understand? For his life was taken from the earth." [34]The eunuch asked Philip, "Tell me, I pray, is the prophet speaking of himself or someone else?" [35]Then Philip began at that very Scripture and explained to him about Jesus.

PHILIP BAPTIZES THE QUEEN'S TREASURER

[36]As they were going along the road, they came to some water. "Look," the eunuch said, "there is some water. What is to prevent me from being baptized?" [37]Philip said, "If you believe with all your heart, you may." He answered, "I believe that Jesus Christ is the Child of God," [38]and he ordered the chariot stopped. They both went down into the water and Philip baptized him.

PHILIP IS TRANSLATED TO AZOTUS

[39]When they came up out of the water, the Spirit of God caught up Philip. The eunuch saw him no more, and he went on his way rejoicing. [40]Philip appeared at Azotus and traveled through all the towns, telling the good news as far as Caesarea.

JESUS SPEAKS TO SAUL ON THE DAMASCUS ROAD

[9:1]But Saul, still breathing murderous threats against the disciples of God, went to the high priest [2]and requested letters from him to the synagogues in Damascus, so that if he found any followers of the Way, whether men or women, he could bring them bound to Jerusalem. [3]As he came near Damascus on his journey, suddenly a light from heaven shone around him. [4]He fell to the ground and heard a voice say, "Saul, Saul, why do you persecute Me?" [5]Saul asked, "Who are You, Rabbi?" The voice said, "I am Jesus whom you are persecuting. [6]Get up and go into the city and you will be told what you must do." [7]The men who were traveling with Saul stood there speechless. They heard a voice but did not see anyone. [8]When Saul got up from the ground, his eyes were open but he could not see anything. They led him by the hand

and brought him into Damascus. [9]He was three days without sight, and he did not eat or drink.

GOD SENDS A DISCIPLE TO LAY HANDS ON SAUL

[10]There was a disciple in Damascus named Ananias. God said to him in a vision, "Ananias?" and he answered, "Here I am, O God." [11]God said to him, "Go to the street that is called Straight and inquire at the house of Judas for Saul of Tarsus. Right now he is praying. [12]In a vision he sees a man named Ananias coming in and laying hands on him to recover his sight." [13]Ananias answered, "O God! I have heard from many about this man and the harm he has done to Your saints at Jerusalem. [14]And here he has authority from the chief priests to arrest all who call on Your name." [15]But God said to him, "Go! He is a chosen instrument of Mine to carry My name to nations and to rulers and to the people of Israel. [16]I will show him how much he must suffer for My name." [17]Ananias went. He went to that house, laid his hands on Saul and said, "Brother Saul, the Sovereign Jesus who appeared to you on the road as you were coming here sent me so that you might recover your sight and be filled with the Holy Spirit." [18]Immediately something like scales fell from Saul's eyes. He recovered his eyesight, got up and was baptized. [19]Then he ate some food and was strengthened.

SAUL'S CONVERSION ANGERS THE JEWS

Saul stayed several days with the disciples at Damascus, [20]and he immediately began to tell in the synagogues that Jesus is the Messiah, the Child of God. [21]All who heard were amazed and said, "Isn't this the man who attacked those who called on this name in Jerusalem and who came here to arrest people and bring them to the chief priests?" [22]Saul grew increasingly strong and perplexed the Jews living at Damascus by showing that Jesus is the Messiah. [23]After many days went by, the Jews made plans to kill him, [24]but Saul found out about their plans. They watched the gates day and night to kill him, [25]but one night the disciples took him and let him down the wall in a basket.

BARNABAS BEFRIENDS SAUL

[26]Saul returned to Jerusalem and attempted to join the disciples, but they were all afraid of him and did not believe that he was a disciple. [27]But Barnabas took him and brought him to the apostles. He told them how Saul had seen Jesus on the road, how Jesus had spoken to him and how Saul had spoken openly at Damascus in the name of Jesus. [28]So Saul moved freely among them at Jerusalem, [29]and he spoke boldly in the name of Jesus. He talked and argued with the Greek-speaking Jews, but they made plans to kill him. [30]When the believers heard about this, they took him down to Caesarea and sent him off to Tarsus. [31]Then the congregations throughout all Judea and Galilee and Samaria were united and edified, and walking in the fear of God and the encouragement of the Holy Spirit, they increased.

PETER HEALS A PARALYZED MAN AT LYDDA

[32]As Peter traveled about from place to place, he visited the saints who lived at Lydda. [33]There he found a man named Aeneas, who was paralyzed and had been bedridden for eight years. [34]Peter said to him, "Aeneas, Jesus the Messiah makes you whole! Get up and make your bed." Immediately he got up, [35]and all those who lived

at Lydda and Sharon saw him and turned to God.

PETER BRINGS A WOMAN BACK FROM THE DEAD AT JOPPA

[36]Now at Joppa there was a certain disciple named Tabitha (which may be translated Gazelle) who was always doing good works and compassionate deeds. [37]Now it came to pass in those days that she became sick and died. They bathed her and laid her in an upper room. [38]The disciples heard that Peter was in Lydda, and since Joppa was near there, they sent two men to urge him to come at once. [39]Peter went with them, and when he arrived, they took him to the upper room. All the widows stood around him weeping and showing the coats and cloaks that Dorcas had made while she was with them. [40]But Peter sent them all out, kneeled down and prayed. Turning to the body, he said, "Tabitha, stand up." She became aware of Peter, opened her eyes and sat up. [41]He gave her his hand and helped her up. Then he called the saints and widows and presented her alive. [42]This became known throughout Joppa and many believed in God. [43]And so it came about that he stayed many days in Joppa with a tanner named Simon.

AN ANGEL TELLS CORNELIUS TO SEND FOR PETER

[10:1]At Caesarea there was a man named Cornelius, a centurion in what was called the Italian regiment. [2]He and all his family were reverent and feared God, often giving to the poor and always praying to God. [3]One day in mid-afternoon he had a vision. He clearly saw an angel of God come to him and say, "Cornelius." [4]He looked at the angel and was afraid, but said, "What is it, O mighty one?" The angel said to him, "Your prayers and your gifts to the poor have gone up and are remembered by God. [5]Now send men to Joppa and ask for Simon who is called Peter. [6]He is the guest of Simon the tanner, whose house is by the sea." [7]When the angel who had spoken departed, Cornelius called two of his servants and a godly soldier who was his attendant. [8]He told them everything and sent them to Joppa.

PETER SEES A VISION OF FORBIDDEN FOOD

[9]The next day, as they were on their journey and nearing the city, Peter went up on the housetop about noon to pray. [10]He became very hungry and wanted to eat, but while they were making it ready, he fell into a trance. [11]He saw heaven opened and something like a large sheet being let down to earth by its four corners. [12]In it were all kinds of four-footed animals of the earth and venomous reptiles and birds of the air. [13]A voice came to him, "Stand up, Peter. Kill and eat!" [14]But Peter said, "O God, I cannot! I have never eaten anything common or unclean." [15]Then the voice came to him again. "You must not call common what God has cleansed!" [16]This happened three times, and then the sheet was taken back up to heaven.

[17]Now while Peter was wondering to himself what this vision meant, the man who had been sent by Cornelius had made inquiry for Simon's house and stood before the gate. [18]They called out and asked if Simon who was called Peter was staying there. [19]As Peter was thinking about the vision, the Spirit said to him, "Some men are looking for you. [20]Get up and go downstairs. Go with them without any misgivings, for it was I who sent them." [21]Peter went down to the men and said, "I am the one you are looking for. What is the reason for your coming?" [22]They said, "Cornelius the

centurion, a good man who fears God and who is well-spoken of among all the Jewish people, was directed by a holy angel to send for you. He was told to invite you to his house so he could hear what you have to say." 23Peter invited them in to spend the night. The next day Peter left with them, and some of the congregation from Joppa went along.

24The following day they entered Caesarea. Cornelius had been waiting for them and called together his family and close friends. 25As Peter was coming in, Cornelius met him and fell at his feet in worship. 26But Peter said to him, "Stand up; I am just a man." 27As they talked together, they went in and found many people gathered. 28Peter said to them, "You know that it is unlawful for a Jew to associate with or visit someone from another nation. But God has shown me that I should not call anyone common or unclean. 29Therefore I came without objecting as soon as I was sent for. Now may I ask why you sent for me?" 30Cornelius said, "Four days ago as I was praying at this hour, a person with shining clothes stood before me 31and said, 'Cornelius, your prayer has been heard and your gifts to the poor are remembered in the sight of God. 32Therefore send to Joppa for Simon who is called Peter. He is a guest in the house of Simon the tanner by the sea.' 33Therefore I sent for you immediately, and it was good of you to come. Now we are all here present before God to hear everything that God has commanded you to say."

PETER TELLS CORNELIUS ABOUT JESUS

34Peter said, "I now realize the truth - God does not show favoritism, 35but accepts those from every nation who fear God and do what is right. 36God sent a message to the people of Israel announcing peace through Jesus Christ, who is Sovereign of all. 37That message, as you know, has spread throughout all Judea. It began in Galilee after the baptism that John preached, 38when God anointed Jesus of Nazareth with the Holy Spirit and power. He went about doing good and healing all who were oppressed by the devil, for God was with Him. 39We are witnesses of everything He did in the land of the Jews and in Jerusalem. They murdered Him by hanging Him on a cross. 40But God raised Him up on the third day and allowed Him to appear, 41not to all the people, but to us witnesses who were chosen beforehand who ate and drank with Him after He rose from the dead. 42He commanded us to tell the people and to testify that it is He who was ordained by God to judge the living and the dead. 43All the prophets have given evidence regarding Him, that through His name everyone who believes in Him receives forgiveness of sins."

GENTILES RECEIVE THE HOLY SPIRIT

44While Peter was still speaking these words, the Holy Spirit affectionately embraced all those who heard what was said. 45All the circumcised believers who had come with Peter were astonished that the gift of the Holy Spirit had been poured out on Gentiles also, 46for they heard them speaking in tongues and extolling God. Then Peter said, 47"Could anyone refuse to let these people be baptized with water? They have received the Holy Spirit just as we have." 48So he commanded them to be baptized in the name of Jesus the Messiah. Then they asked Peter to stay with them for a few days.

PETER IS ACCUSED OF EATING WITH GENTILES

^{11:1}The apostles and the congregation in Judea heard that the Gentiles had also accepted the plan of God. ²So when Peter returned to Jerusalem, the Jews contended with him ³and said, "You went in and ate with Gentiles!" ⁴Then Peter began from the beginning and explained to them, ⁵"I was in the city of Joppa praying, and in a trance I saw a vision. I saw something like a large sheet come down toward me, let down from heaven by its four corners. ⁶When I looked in it, I saw four-footed animals of the earth and venomous reptiles and birds of the air. ⁷I heard a voice say to me, 'Stand up, Peter! Kill and eat!' ⁸But I said, 'O God! I cannot, for I have never eaten anything common or unclean.' ⁹But the voice came to me again from heaven, 'You must not call common what God has cleansed!' ¹⁰This happened three times, and then everything was taken back up into heaven. ¹¹At that very moment, three men who had been sent to me from Caesarea came to the house where I was. ¹²The Spirit told me to go with them and have no misgivings. I went, along with six of the congregation, and we entered the man's house. ¹³He told us how he had seen an angel standing in his house and saying, 'Send men to Joppa and ask for Simon who is called Peter. ¹⁴He will tell you things by which you and all your family will be saved.' ¹⁵As I began to speak, the Holy Spirit embraced them just as happened to us at the beginning. ¹⁶Then I remembered what Jesus had said, 'John baptized with water, but you will be baptized with the Holy Spirit.' ¹⁷If then God gave them the same gift that was given to us when we believed in Jesus the Messiah, who was I, that I could forbid God?" ¹⁸When they heard this, they stopped objecting and praised God, saying, "Then God has granted the repentance that leads to life to the Gentiles also!"

BARNABAS IS SENT TO ANTIOCH

¹⁹Now those who had been scattered by the persecution that arose because of Stephen traveled as far as Phoenicia, Cyprus and Antioch, telling the message to the Jews. ²⁰Some of them from Cyprus and Cyrene went to Antioch and told the good news about Jesus to the Greeks. ²¹The hand of God was with them, and a great number believed and turned to God. ²²Criticism of this was heard in the congregation in Jerusalem, and they sent Barnabas to Antioch. ²³When he arrived and saw the influence of God, he was happy. He encouraged them to stay close to God with open hearts. ²⁴He was a good man, full of the Holy Spirit and faith, and many people were brought to God. ²⁵Then Barnabas went to Tarsus to look for Saul. ²⁶When he found him, he went with him to Antioch. Then for a whole year they met with the congregation and taught many people. The disciples were first called Christians at Antioch.

²⁷In those days, prophets from Jerusalem came to Antioch. ²⁸One of them named Agabus stood up and made known by the Spirit that there would be a great famine throughout the empire. This came to pass in the days of Claudius. ²⁹The disciples decided, each according to their individual resources, to send help to the congregation living in Judea. ³⁰This they did, sending it to the elders by the hands of Barnabas and Saul.

HEROD KILLS JAMES AND ARRESTS PETER

12:1It was about that time that Herod the king arrested and persecuted some of the congregation. 2He had James the brother of John killed with the sword. 3And when he saw that this pleased the Jews, he arrested Peter also. This was during the days of Unleavened Bread. 4He seized Peter and put him in prison. He put four squads of soldiers in charge of him, intending to bring him out for a public trial after the Passover. 5Peter was kept in prison, but the congregation prayed fervently to God for him.

AN ANGEL FREES PETER

6The night before Herod was going to bring him out for trial, Peter was asleep between two soldiers, bound with two chains. The guards by the entrance kept an eye on the prison. 7Suddenly an angel from God appeared and a brilliant light illuminated the prison. The angel tapped Peter on his side to waken him, saying, "Stand up quickly!" The chains fell off his hands, 8and the angel said to him, "Get dressed and put on your sandals!" He did. Then the angel said to him, "Put your coat on and follow me." 9Peter followed the angel out, unaware that what the angel had done was real. He thought he was seeing a vision. 10They passed the first and the second guards and came to the iron gate that leads into the city (which opened to them of its own accord). When they had gone out and passed one street, suddenly the angel disappeared.

11When Peter was himself again, he thought, "Now I know this is real! God sent an angel and released me from the hand of Herod and all that the Jewish people were expecting." 12Realizing this, he went to the house of Mary the mother of John Mark, where many people were gathered together praying. 13When Peter knocked at the door of the porch, a girl named Rhoda came to answer. 14She recognized Peter's voice and was so overjoyed that, instead of opening the door, she ran inside and told them that Peter was standing at the door. 15They said to her, "You're crazy!" But she kept insisting that it was so. Then they said, "It must be his guardian angel." 16Meanwhile Peter continued knocking. When they opened the door and saw him, they were astonished. 17But he signaled to them with his hand to be quiet and told them how God had brought him out of the prison. He said, "Tell this to James and to the congregation." Then he departed and went to another place.

18When morning came, there was panic among the soldiers. What had become of Peter? 19Herod questioned the guards and had a search made for him, but they did not find him, so Herod commanded that the guards be put to death. Then he went down from Judea to Caesarea and stayed there.

HEROD'S DEATH IS CAUSED BY AN ANGEL

20Herod and the people of Tyre and Sidon did not like each other, but they came to him, after making friends with Blastus, the king's consultant. They asked for peace, because their country was dependent on the king for food. 21On a set day Herod sat on his throne arrayed in royal robes and made a speech to them. 22The people shouted, "It is the voice of a god, not a human!" 23Immediately the angel of God struck him because he did not give God the glory, and he was eaten by worms and died.

[24]The word of God continued to grow like the sunrise. [25]Barnabas and Saul finished their mission and returned from Jerusalem, taking with them John Mark.

BARNABAS AND SAUL SENT OUT

[13:1]In the congregation at Antioch there were certain prophets and teachers: Barnabas, Simeon called Niger, Lucius of Cyrene, Manaen who had been brought up with Herod the tetrarch, and Saul. [2]As they ministered to God and fasted, the Holy Spirit said, "Separate Barnabas and Saul for Me for the work to which I have called them." [3]So they fasted and prayed, laid hands on them and sent them off.

A MAGICIAN AT THE GOVERNOR'S COURT OPPOSES PAUL

[4]Sent out by the Holy Spirit, they went down to Seleucia. From there they sailed to Cyprus. [5]When they reached Salamis, they proclaimed the word of God in the Jewish synagogues. John Mark was with them as their assistant. [6]They walked across the island. At Paphos they found a certain Jewish magician named Bar-Jesus [7]who was a friend of the governor, Sergius Paulus, a prudent man. He called for Barnabas and Saul and asked to hear the word of God. [8]But Elymas the magician opposed them, seeking to turn the governor from the faith. [9]Then Saul (who was also called Paul), filled with the Holy Spirit, looked intently at him [10]and said, "You child of the devil! You are full of tricks and every easy way. You enemy of everything that is right, when will you stop perverting the right ways of God? [11]And now the hand of God is upon you. You will be blind and not see the sun for awhile." Immediately dimness like a shadow alighted on him, and he groped about, seeking a hand to lead him. [12]The governor saw what had happened and he believed, astonished at the teaching of God.

PAUL ARGUES FOR CHRISTIANITY

[13]Paul and his companions set sail from Paphos. They came to Perga in Pamphylia and John Mark left them and returned to Jerusalem. [14]They left Perga and arrived at Antioch in Pisidia. On the Sabbath they went into the synagogue and sat down. [15]After the reading of the law and the prophets, the leaders of the synagogue sent a man to say to them, "Brothers, if you have any word of encouragement for the people, say it." [16]Paul stood up, signaled with his hand and said, "Fellow Israelites and others who fear God, listen closely. [17]The God of the people of Israel chose our ancestors and exalted the people when they lived as strangers in the land of Egypt. With uplifted arm God brought them out, [18]and for forty years endured them in the wilderness. [19]God destroyed seven nations in the land of Canaan, and divided their land to our ancestors by lot [20]over about four hundred and fifty years. After that, God gave them judges until Samuel the prophet. [21]Then they asked for a king, and for forty years God gave them Saul the son of Kish, a man of the tribe of Benjamin. [22]After removing Saul, God raised up David to be their king, of whom God testified, 'I have found David the son of Jesse to be a man after My own heart, one who will do everything I desire.' [23]From David's descendants God brought to Israel Jesus the savior, as promised. [24]Before His coming, John proclaimed the baptism of repentance to all the people of Israel. [25]As John was completing his work, he said, 'Who do you think I am? I am not the Messiah. But watch, there is one coming after me whose sandals I am not worthy to untie.' [26]Fellow Jews, and any among you who fear God, to you is this message of

salvation sent. [27]The residents of Jerusalem and their leaders did not recognize Jesus, nor the words of the prophets which are read every Sabbath, and which they fulfilled by condemning Him. [28]Though they found no crime worthy of death, they asked Pilate that He be killed. [29]When they fulfilled all that was written about Him, they took Him down from the cross and laid Him in a tomb. [30]But God raised Him from the dead, [31]and for many days He was seen by those who came with Him from Galilee to Jerusalem. They are His witnesses to the people. [32]The promise that was made to our ancestors is the good news that we bring to you [33]which God has fulfilled for us their children. God raised up Jesus as it is written in the second Psalm: 'You are My Child. This day I have begotten You.' [34]God raised Jesus up from the dead, never again to decay, and God said, 'I will give you the holy and sure blessings promised to David.' [35]Another psalm says, 'You will not allow Your Holy One to see decay.' [36]After David had served God's purposes in his own generation, he died and was laid with his ancestors and knew decay. [37]But the One whom God raised did not know decay. [38]Be it known to you, therefore, that through Jesus you are set free from your sins. [39]All of you who believe in Jesus are considered innocent of everything from which you could not be considered innocent through the law of Moses. [40]Beware therefore, lest there come upon you what is spoken of by the prophets: [41]'Watch, you scoffers, and wonder and perish. For I am doing something in your days that you would not believe, even if someone were to tell you.'"

[42]As Paul and Barnabas went out of the synagogue, the people begged them to speak to them on the next Sabbath. [43]After the congregation dispersed, many of the Jews and Gentile believers followed them. Paul and Barnabas talked with them and convinced them to continue in the favor of God.

[44]On the next Sabbath almost the whole city gathered to hear them tell about God. [45]But certain Jews were jealous when they saw the crowds and spoke against what was said by Paul, contradicting and blaspheming. [46]Then Paul and Barnabas boldly said, "It was necessary that the explanation from God be spoken to you first. Since you reject it and judge yourselves unworthy of everlasting life, we will turn to those who are not Jews. [47]For God commanded us: 'I have set you as a light for the nations, that you may bring salvation to the ends of the earth.'"

[48]The people heard this and were glad. They cherished the message of God, and as many as were appointed to everlasting life believed. [49]And the message of God was published throughout all the region. [50]But the Jews stirred up the elegant religious women and the foremost men of the city. These stirred up persecution against Paul and Barnabas and expelled them from their region. [51]But Paul and Barnabas shook the dust of their feet off against them and went to Iconium. [52]And the disciples were filled with joy and with the Holy Spirit.

[14:1]At Iconium, Paul and Barnabas went into the Jewish synagogue and spoke in such a way that a great many Jews and Greeks believed. [2]But the unbelieving Jews stirred up the Gentiles and turned them against the disciples. [3]Nevertheless Paul and Barnabas remained there a long time and spoke confidently about God. The Almighty gave evidence that the message of God's favor was true by giving them the power to do miracles and wonders. [4]But the people of the city were divided; some sided with the Jews and some with the apostles. [5]When an impulse arose among the Gentiles and the Jews, along with their leaders, to abuse them and stone them, [6]Paul and Barnabas became aware of it. They fled to Lystra and Derbe, cities in Lycaonia, and to the surrounding region. [7]There they told the good news.

PAUL AND BARNABAS ARE THOUGHT TO BE GODS

[8]At Lystra there was a man who was unable to walk. He had been crippled from the time he was born and had never walked. [9]As he sat and listened to Paul speak, Paul looked at him. Seeing that he had faith to be healed, [10]Paul said with a loud voice, "Stand up on your feet!" and he jumped up and walked. [11]The people saw what Paul had done, and they loudly said, "The gods have come down to us and have become like humans!"

[12]They called Barnabas Jupiter, and because Paul was the main speaker, they called him Mercury. [13]Then the priest of the temple of Jupiter which was outside the city brought oxen and garlands to the gates. He and the people would have offered sacrifices to the apostles, [14]but when Barnabas and Paul heard about this, they tore their clothes and ran in among the throng, crying out, [15]"Friends! Why are you doing this? We are humans just like you! We are here to tell you good news! Turn from this emptiness to the living God who made heaven and earth and sea and everything in them! [16]In times past God allowed all the nations to walk in their own ways. [17]Nevertheless, God did good and gave us rain from heaven and fruitful seasons, filling our hearts with food and gladness so that we might know there is a God." [18]Yet even with these words, they scarcely restrained the people from sacrificing to them.

PAUL IS STONED AND DRAGGED OUT OF THE CITY

[19]Then some Jews from Antioch and Iconium came and convinced the people to stone Paul. Supposing him dead, they dragged his body out of the city. [20]But as the disciples stood around him, he got up and went into the city.

BARNABAS AND PAUL VISIT OTHER TOWNS IN GALATIA

The next day Paul left with Barnabas for Derbe. [21]They told the good news in that city and made many disciples. Then they returned to Lystra, Iconium and Antioch, [22]strengthening the souls of the disciples, encouraging them to continue in the faith, and saying, "Through many tribulations we must enter the realm of God." [23]They chose elders for them in every congregation, and with prayer and fasting they commended them to the Holy One in whom they believed. [24]They went through Pisidia and came to Pamphylia. [25]When they had told the news in Perga, they went down to Attalia. [26]From there they sailed to Antioch, the place where they had been put into God's care for the work they had now fulfilled. [27]When they arrived, they gathered the congregation together and told all that God had done with them, even opening the door of faith to the Gentiles. [28]And they stayed there a long time with the disciples.

PAUL AND BARNABAS ARE SENT TO JERUSALEM

[15:1]Certain people came down from Judea and taught the believers, "Unless you are circumcised in the way that Moses taught, you cannot be saved." [2]Because of this,

Paul and Barnabas argued and disputed with them, and they determined that Paul and Barnabas and certain others should go up to Jerusalem to the apostles and elders about this question. [3]After being sent on their way by the congregation, they passed through Phoenicia and Samaria and told about the conversion of the Gentiles. They caused great joy there among all the believers.

[4]When they arrived at Jerusalem, they were welcomed by the congregation and the apostles and elders, and they told all the things that God had done with them. [5]Then certain believers of the party of the Pharisees stood up and said that it was necessary to circumcise Gentile converts and command them to keep the law of Moses. [6]The apostles and elders met together to consider this matter, [7]and after much discussion, Peter got up and said to them, "Believers, you know that in the early days God chose me from among you to tell the good news to the Gentiles so that they would believe. [8]And God, who knows the heart, showed approval by giving them the Holy Spirit, just as was done to us. [9]God made no distinction between us, but purified their hearts by faith. [10]Now then, why do you test God by putting a yoke on the neck of the disciples that neither our ancestors nor we were able to bear? [11]For we believe that through the favor bestowed by Jesus Christ we are saved, just as they are."

[12]The whole assembly became silent and listened as Barnabas and Paul told about the miracles and wonders God had worked among the Gentiles through them. [13]After they finished speaking, James said, "My friends, listen to me. [14]Simon has told us how God first came to the Gentiles to take out of them a people for the Name. [15]The words of the prophets agree with this, for it is written: [16]'After this I will return and rebuild the fallen house of David. I will rebuild it from the ruins and restore it. [17]Then the rest of humanity will seek God - all the nations who are called by My name - says the Almighty who does all these things [18]and made them known long ago.' [19]Therefore it is my conclusion that we should not make it harder for the Gentiles who are turning to God. [20]Instead we should write to them to abstain from anything polluted by idols, from immorality and from blood. [21]For Moses from of old has been published in every city and is read in the synagogues every Sabbath."

THE LETTER TO THE GENTILE CHRISTIANS

[22]Then the apostles and elders and the whole congregation decided to choose Judas Barsabbas and Silas, esteemed men of the congregation, to send to Antioch with Paul and Barnabas. [23]They sent this letter with them:

"Greetings to the congregations in Antioch, Syria and Silicia from the apostles and elders. [24]We have heard that certain ones who went out from us, and to whom we gave no commandment, have troubled you with words and subverted your souls by saying, 'You must be circumcised and keep the law.' [25]With one accord we have agreed to choose some men to send to you with our beloved Barnabas and Paul, [26]men who have imperiled their lives for the name of Jesus the Messiah. [27]Therefore we are sending Judas and Silas to tell you these same things. [28]For it seemed good to the Holy Spirit and to us to lay upon you no greater burden than these necessities: [29]that you abstain from food offered to idols, from blood and from immorality. Keep yourselves from these and you will do well. Farewell."

THE LETTER IS JOYFULLY RECEIVED

[30]The four were sent off to Antioch, where they gathered the congregation together and delivered the letter. [31]When the congregation read it, they rejoiced because of the encouragement. [32]Judas and Silas, who were themselves prophets, said much to encourage and strengthen the congregation. [33]After a while, the congregation sent them off in peace to those who sent them. [34]But Silas decided to stay there. [35]Paul and Barnabas remained in Antioch with many others, teaching and telling the good news about God.

BARNABAS AND PAUL SEPARATE

[36]After some days, Paul said to Barnabas, "Let's go back and visit the congregations in every city where we told the message of God and see how they are." [37]Barnabas wanted to take John Mark with them, [38]but Paul was not in favor of taking him because he had deserted them in Pamphylia and had not gone on with them in the work. [39]The contention was so sharp that they parted, and Barnabas took John Mark and sailed to Cyprus. [40]Paul chose Silas and departed, commended by the congregation to the care of God, [41]and he went through Syria and Cilicia strengthening the congregations.

TIMOTHY JOINS PAUL AND SILAS

[16:1]Paul went to Derbe and Lystra. A disciple named Timothy was there, whose mother was a Jewish believer and whose father was a Greek. [2]The congregations in Lystra and Iconium spoke well of Timothy, [3]and Paul wanted to take Timothy along with him. Paul circumcised Timothy because of the Jews that lived in the area, for they all knew that his father was Greek. [4]As they went from city to city, they delivered the laws that had been decided upon by the apostles and elders in Jerusalem for them to obey. [5]So the congregations were strengthened in the faith and increased in number daily.

PAUL IS DIRECTED BY A VISION

[6]Paul and his co-workers traveled through the region of Phrygia and Galatia, but the Holy Spirit did not let them tell the good news in Asia. [7]They went as far as Mysia and attempted to enter Bithynia, but the Spirit of Jesus would not let them go on. [8]So they passed by Mysia and went down to Troas.

[9]A vision appeared to Paul one night. There stood a man from Macedonia who pleaded with him, "Come over into Macedonia and help us!" [10]After Paul had seen the vision, we were agreed that God had called for us to tell the good news to them, and we immediately got ready to go into Macedonia.

LYDIA

[11]We sailed away from Troas and made a straight run to Samothrace. The next day we arrived at Neapolis. [12]From there we went to Philippi, a Roman colony and the foremost city in that part of Macedonia. We stayed there in that city several days. [13]On the Sabbath we went out the city gate to the riverside, where prayer was usually offered. We sat down and spoke to the women who had gathered. [14]One of those listening was a woman named Lydia from the city of Thyatira. She was a seller of

purple cloth and a worshiper of God, and God opened her heart to respond to what Paul said. [15]After she and her family were baptized, she gave an invitation, "If you judge me to be faithful to God, come and stay in my house." She urged us until we accepted.

PAUL AND SILAS ARE THROWN INTO PRISON

[16]One day as we were going to the place of prayer, we met a slave girl who had a spirit of divination. [17]She followed Paul and the rest of us, shouting, "These people are servants of the Most High God, and they are showing you the way of salvation." [18]She did this for many days, until Paul tired of it. He turned and said to the spirit, "I command you in the name of Jesus Christ to come out of her!" Immediately it came out. [19]When her owners saw that their chance of making money was gone, they seized Paul and Silas and dragged them into the marketplace to the authorities. [20]They brought them before the magistrates and said, "These men are Jews, and they are causing trouble in our city [21]by teaching customs that are not lawful for us Romans to accept or follow." [22]The crowd was aroused to attack them, and the magistrates tore the clothes off Paul and Silas and ordered them beaten with rods. [23]After they had inflicted many blows on them, they threw them into prison and ordered the jailer to guard them carefully. [24]Having received such orders, he threw them into the inner prison and fastened their feet in the stocks.

THE JAILER AND HIS FAMILY BECOME BELIEVERS

[25]About midnight Paul and Silas were praying and singing praises to God, and the other prisoners were listening to them. [26]Suddenly there was a great earthquake, and the foundations of the prison were shaken. Immediately all the doors flew open and everyone's chains came loose. [27]When the jailer woke up and saw the prison doors open, he thought the prisoners had escaped. He drew out his sword, intending to kill himself, [28]but Paul shouted, "Don't harm yourself! We are all here!" [29]The jailer called for a light, rushed in, and kneeled down before Paul and Silas. [30]Then he brought them out and said, "What must I do to be saved?" [31]They answered, "Believe in Jesus Christ and you will be saved, you and your family." [32]Then they told the message of God to him and to all the others in his house. [33]The jailer took them that very hour and washed their wounds. He and all his family were baptized at once. [34]He brought them into his house, set food before them and the whole family rejoiced to have found faith in God.

[35]When morning came, the magistrates sent the officers to say, "Let those men go." [36]The jailer told Paul, "The magistrates sent word to let you go, so come out now and go in peace." [37]But Paul said to the officers, "They beat us publicly without a trial and threw us into prison, though we are Roman citizens. Now they want to send us away quietly? No, let them come themselves and bring us out." [38]The officers told these words to the magistrates. The magistrates were afraid when they heard that they were Roman citizens, [39]and they came and apologized to them. Then they brought them out and begged them to leave the city. [40]They left the prison and went to Lydia's house. After they met with the believers, they encouraged them and departed.

THE THESSALONIANS

17:1They traveled through Amphipolis and Appolonia and went on to Thessalonica where there was a Jewish synagogue. 2Paul went in to them as usual. For three Sabbaths he reasoned with them out of the Scriptures, 3explaining the Scriptures and proving that Christ had to suffer and then rise from the dead. "This Jesus I am telling you about is the Messiah!" he said. 4Some of them believed and joined Paul and Silas. A great many devout Greeks and a good number of influential women also believed. 5But the unbelieving Jews zealously gathered some worthless fellows from the marketplace, formed a mob and set the city in an uproar. They mobbed Jason's house and sought to bring Paul and Silas out to the people. 6They did not find them, so they dragged Jason and some others to the city authorities, shouting, "The ones who have turned the world upside down have come here also 7and Jason has taken them into his home! They are acting contrary to the laws of Caesar by saying there is another king - this Jesus." 8The crowd and the city authorities were alarmed when they heard this, 9and they made Jason and the others pay a fine before letting them go.

UNBELIEVING JEWS THREATEN PAUL

10The congregation immediately sent Paul and Silas away by night to Berea. On arriving they went into the Jewish synagogue. 11The people of Berea were more agreeable than those in Thessalonica. They accepted the teaching willingly and searched the Scriptures daily to see if these things were so. 12Many of the Jews believed, as did a number of prominent Greek women, and many men also. 13But when the Jews of Thessalonica heard that the story of God was being taught by Paul at Berea, they came there and stirred up the people. 14The congregation immediately sent Paul to the seacoast, but Silas and Timothy stayed there.

PAUL GOES ON TO ATHENS

15Those who escorted Paul brought him to Athens. They then went back with instructions for Silas and Timothy to join Paul as soon as possible. 16While Paul waited for them in Athens, his spirit within him was vexed when he saw that the city was so full of idols. 17In the synagogue he argued with the Jews and the Gentile worshipers. Day after day he also argued with everyone he met in the marketplace. 18Then certain Epicurean and Stoic philosophers disputed with him. As Paul was telling them the good news about Jesus and the resurrection, someone asked, "What is this seed-picker trying to say?" Another said, "He seems to be promoting some foreign god." 19They got him and brought him to the court at Mars Hill and asked, "May we know what this new teaching is that you are presenting? 20You are bringing certain strange things to our ears, and we want to know what they mean." 21All the Athenians and foreigners visiting there spent their time doing nothing but telling about or listening to something new. 22So Paul stood up in front of the council and said, "People of Athens, I see that in every way you are very religious, 23for as I walked around and looked at your gods, I found an altar with this inscription: TO AN UNKNOWN GOD. I am here to tell you about the God you worship but do not know. 24"The God who made the world and everything in it is the God of heaven and earth and does not live in temples made by people. [25]God is not served by human hands, as though God needed anything, for it is God who gives everyone life and breath and everything else. [26]From one breath God made every nation of people to inhabit the whole earth, and God decided when and where every nation would live. [27]God did this so that they might seek and perhaps reach out and find God, though God is not far from any one of us. [28]For in God we live and move and have our being. As some of your own poets have said, 'We are God's offspring.' [29]Since we are the offspring of God, we must not think that God is like a statue of gold or silver or stone inspired by human skill. [30]In the past God overlooked this lack of knowledge. But now God commands all humans everywhere to repent, [31]for God has appointed a day to justly judge the world through an ordained man. God has proven this to everyone by raising Him from the dead." [32]When they heard about the resurrection of the dead, some yawned. But others said, "We want to listen to you again about this." [33]After that, Paul departed from the council. [34]But certain ones stuck with him and believed. Among them was Dionysius, a member of the city council, a woman named Damaris and others with them.

THE CORINTHIANS

[18:1]After this Paul left Athens and went to Corinth, [2]where he met a certain Jew named Aquila, a native of Pontus. Aquila had recently come from Italy with his wife Priscilla because Claudius had commanded all Jews to depart from Rome. Paul went to see them, [3]and because he was also a tentmaker, he stayed and worked with them. [4]Every Sabbath he reasoned in the synagogue, trying to persuade the Jews and the Greeks. [5]When Silas and Timothy came from Macedonia, Paul devoted all his time to testifying to the Jews that Jesus is the Messiah. [6]When they opposed him and were abusive, he shook his garment at them and said, "Now you have been warned and I am innocent. From now on I will go to the Gentiles." [7]Paul left and moved into the house of Justus, a worshiper of God who lived next door to the synagogue. [8]Crispus, the leader of the synagogue, and all his family believed in God. And many of the Corinthians who heard him believed and were baptized. [9]One night God spoke to Paul in a vision, "Do not be afraid! Keep on speaking! Let no one silence you, [10]for I am with you. No one will attack you to harm you, for I have many people in this city." [11]So he continued teaching the message of God among them for a year and a half.

[12]While Gallio was governor of Greece, the Jews joined together against Paul. They brought him into court [13]and said, "This man is persuading people to worship God contrary to the law." [14]As Paul was about to open his mouth, Gallio said to the Jews, "If this were some wrong or wicked crime, I might reasonably bear with you Jews. [15]But if it is a question of words and names and your law, look to it yourselves. I will not judge such matters," [16]and he dismissed them from the court. [17]When they all seized Sosthenes, the leader of the synagogue, and beat him in the courtroom, Gallio remained unconcerned.

THE EPHESIANS

[18]Paul stayed a good while in Corinth. He then took his leave of the congregation and sailed for Syria. Priscilla and Aquila went with him. He had his hair cut off in

Cenchrea, for he had made a vow. [19]When they got to Ephesus, they parted. Paul entered the synagogue and reasoned with the Jews. [20]They wanted him to stay a longer time with them, but he did not consent. [21]Bidding them farewell, he said, "I will come back to you if it is God's will."

Paul set sail from Ephesus [22]and landed at Caesarea. He went up, greeted the congregation and then went down to Antioch. [23]After spending some time there, he departed and went from place to place through the region of Galatia and Phrygia, strengthening all the disciples.

APOLLOS, AQUILLA AND PRISCILLA ENCOURAGE THE EPHESIANS
[24]A certain Jew named Apollos, who was born in Alexandria, came to Ephesus. He was an eloquent man and capable with the Scriptures. [25]He had been instructed in the Way and with fervent spirit spoke and taught accurately about Jesus, though he only knew the baptism of John. [26]He began boldly in the synagogue, and when Aquila and Priscilla heard him, they took him and explained the way of God more exactly. [27]When he wanted to go to Greece, the congregation encouraged him and wrote to the disciples to welcome him. When he got there, he was a great help to those who had become believers through God's favor, [28]for he powerfully refuted the Jews publicly, showing by the Scriptures that Jesus is the Messiah.

PAUL RETURNS TO THE EPHESIANS
[19:1]While Apollos was at Corinth, Paul took the inland road to Ephesus. Finding some disciples, [2]he asked them, "Did you receive the Holy Spirit when you believed?" They answered, "No, we have not even heard that there is a Holy Spirit." [3]Paul asked, "Then what baptism did you receive?" They answered, "John's baptism." [4]Then Paul said, "John's baptism was a baptism of repentance. He told the people to believe in the One who was coming after him, that is, in Jesus." [5]When they heard this, they were baptized in the name of Jesus. [6]Then Paul laid his hands upon them, the Holy Spirit came upon them and they spoke in tongues and prophesied. [7]There were about twelve of them in all. [8]Paul went into the synagogue and spoke boldly for three months, reasoning persuasively about the realm of God. [9]But some became hard and refused to believe; they criticized the Way before the people. So Paul left them, separated the disciples and reasoned with them in the lecture hall of Tyrannus. [10]This continued for two years, so that all the Jews and Greeks who lived in and around Ephesus heard the story of Jesus.

MIRACLES THROUGH HANDKERCHIEFS
[11]God delighted to do extraordinary miracles through the hands of Paul. [12]Handkerchiefs and aprons that had touched his body were brought to the sick, and their diseases left them and the evil spirits went out of them.

THE SEVEN SONS OF SCEVA
[13]Then some Jews who went around exorcising those who had evil spirits with an oath attempted to use the name of Jesus. "We order you under oath in the name of Jesus whom Paul preaches," they said. [14]Seven sons of a Jewish high priest named Sceva were doing this. [15]The evil spirit answered, "Jesus I know and Paul I know, but who are you?" [16]Then the man who had the evil spirit in him leaped on them,

overpowered them and tore their clothes off. They fled out of that house naked and bleeding. [17]This became known to all the Jews and Greeks living around Ephesus, and fear seized them all.

THE NEW BELIEVERS RENOUNCE THEIR OLD WAYS

The name of Jesus was esteemed, [18]and many believers came and confessed and admitted their deeds. [19]Many of those who had practiced magic brought their books and publicly burned them. When they calculated the value of these, they found it to be fifty thousand pieces of silver. [20]Thus the message of God went out with intense vigor and prevailed.

THE ARTISANS OF EPHESUS

[21]After all this was over, Paul was led by the Spirit to go through Macedonia and Greece and on to Jerusalem. "After I have been there," he said, "I must also go to Rome." [22]He sent Timothy and Erastus, two of his helpers, to Macedonia while he stayed on in Asia for a while. [23]About that time there arose a great uproar about the Way. [24]A silversmith named Demetrius who made silver shrines of Diana which brought much prosperity to the artisans [25]called them together with the workers in related occupations and said, "Friends, you know that with this craft we make our living. [26]You also have seen and heard how this Paul has persuaded and turned away many people. In Ephesus and practically all of Asia he is saying that there are no gods made with hands. [27]There is danger that not only this our craft will be proven false, but also that the temple of the great goddess Diana, whom all Asia and the world worships, will be despised and her magnificence destroyed." [28]They agreed. They were full of wrath and cried out, "Great is Diana of the Ephesians!" [29]Then the whole city was filled with confusion. They seized Gaius and Aristarchus, Paul's traveling companions from Macedonia, and rushed with one accord into the theater. [30]Paul wanted to go in to the people, but the disciples would not let him. [31]Some of the officials of Asia who were his friends sent a warning to him not to venture into the theater. [32]The assembly was in confusion. Some were shouting one thing and some another. Most of them did not know why they were there. [33]The Jews pushed Alexander forward, and some of the crowd thought that he might be the instigator. Alexander made a gesture with his hand and wanted to make a defense to the people; [34]but when they realized he was a Jew, they all shouted together for two hours, "Great is Diana of the Ephesians!" [35]Finally the town clerk quieted the people and said, "Citizens of Ephesus, what person does not know that the city of the Ephesians is the guardian of the temple of the great goddess Diana and of her stone that fell from the sky? [36]Since these things cannot be denied, you ought to be quiet and not do anything rash. [37]You have brought these men here who are neither temple robbers nor blasphemers of our god. [38]If Demetrius and the artisans with him have a complaint against anyone, the courts are open and there are judges. Let them bring charges. [39]If you require anything else, it must be decided in a lawful assembly. [40]We are in danger of being called into question regarding this day's uproar, and there is no excuse we may give to account for this mob." [41]Having said this, he dismissed the assembly.

$^{20:1}$After the uproar had ceased, Paul called together the disciples, embraced them and departed for Macedonia. ^{2}After traveling through that region and giving them much encouragement, he went to Greece ^{3}and sojourned there for three months. The Jews plotted against him as he was about to sail for Syria, so he decided to return through Macedonia. ^{4}He was accompanied by Sopater the son of Pyrrhus from Berea, Aristarchus and Secundus from Thessalonica, Gaius from Derbe, Timothy, and Tychicus and Trophimus from Asia. ^{5}These went on ahead and waited for us at Troas. ^{6}We sailed away from Philippi after the days of Unleavened Bread. Five days later we joined them at Troas and remained there seven days.

THE YOUNG MAN WHO FELL FROM A WINDOW

^{7}On the first day of the week the disciples met together for communion. Paul spoke to them, and since he was ready to depart the next day, he talked until midnight. ^{8}There were many lamps in the upper room where we were meeting. ^{9}A young man named Eutychus was sitting in a window, and as Paul continued to speak, the young man was overcome with sleep. He fell from the third story and was picked up dead. ^{10}Paul went down and put his arms around him and said, "Don't be alarmed, for his life is in him." ^{11}Then he went back up and ate the communion meal. He talked a long while and then departed at daybreak. ^{12}They brought the young man in alive, and they were greatly comforted.

PAUL CONTINUES TOWARD JERUSALEM

^{13}We went aboard a ship and sailed to Assos, where we intended to take Paul aboard, for he had arranged to go on foot. ^{14}When he met us at Assos, we took him aboard and went on to Mitylene. ^{15}We sailed from there and were opposite Chios the next day. The next day we crossed to Samos and the following day we came to Miletus. ^{16}Paul decided to sail past Ephesus so that he would not lose time in Asia. He was in a hurry to be in Jerusalem, if possible, on the day of Pentecost.

^{17}From Miletus, Paul sent to Ephesus and called the elders of the congregation. ^{18}When they came, he said to them, "You know that from the first day I came to Asia in what manner I have lived among you in all seasons, ^{19}serving God with all humility and with many tears, and the testing that befell me because of the plots of the Jews. ^{20}I kept back nothing that might have helped you, but have publicly taught you from house to house, ^{21}testifying to both the Jews and the Greeks repentance toward God and faith toward Jesus. ^{22}And now, I go bound in the Spirit to Jerusalem, not knowing what will befall me there. ^{23}But the Holy Spirit tells me in every city that prison and affliction await me. ^{24}I do not count my life dear to myself; I only desire to cheerfully finish my race and the work I have received from Jesus and testify to the good news of the favor of God. ^{25}And now, listen! I know that none of you among whom I have proclaimed the realm of God will see my face again. ^{26}Therefore I tell you this day that I am not responsible for anyone's life. ^{27}For I have not hesitated to declare to you the whole purpose of God. ^{28}Watch yourselves and the flock which the Holy Spirit has put in your care. Tend the congregation of God which Jesus purchased with His own blood. ^{29}I know that after my departure, unrelenting wolves will come in among you and will not spare the flock. ^{30}People from your own congregation will arise and speak twisted things to draw disciples away after them. ^{31}Therefore, watch! Remember that for three years I never ceased warning everyone night and day, with tears. ^{32}And now, believers, I commend you to God and to the good news of God's favor which is able to build you up and give you an inheritance among all those who have been made holy. ^{33}I have coveted no one's silver or gold or clothing. ^{34}You yourselves know that these hands have provided the necessities for myself and for those who were with me. ^{35}I have shown you that by working hard you ought to help the weak. Remember the words of our Rabbi Jesus, who said, 'It is more blessed to give than to receive.'" ^{36}After Paul said this, he kneeled and prayed with them all. ^{37}They all wept loudly and put their arms around Paul's neck and kissed him, ^{38}sorrowing most of all because he had said that they would never see his face again. Then they went with him to the ship.

$^{21:1}$After we departed from them, we sailed a straight course to Cos. The next day we went to Rhodes, and from there to Patara. ^{2}Finding a ship sailing over to Phoenicia, we went aboard and set out. ^{3}Cyprus appeared on our left as we sailed for Syria. We landed at Tyre, for there the ship was to unload its cargo. ^{4}We found disciples and stayed with them seven days. They said to Paul by the Spirit not to go up to Jerusalem. ^{5}When it was time to go, we departed and went our way. All of the disciples and their wives and children escorted us out of the city. We kneeled on the shore and prayed ^{6}and said goodbye to one another. We boarded the ship, and they returned home again. ^{7}When we finished our voyage from Tyre, we landed at Ptolemais. We greeted the congregation and stayed with them one day.

^{8}The next day we left and went to Caesarea. We stayed at the home of Philip the evangelist, one of the seven. ^{9}He had four unmarried daughters who had the gift of prophecy. ^{10}After we had been there many days, a prophet named Agabus came down from Judea. ^{11}He came to us, took Paul's belt, bound his own hands and feet and said, "Thus says the Holy Spirit: This is the way the Jews at Jerusalem will bind the man who owns this belt and hand him over to the Gentiles." ^{12}When we heard this, we and the people of that place begged him not to go up to Jerusalem. ^{13}But Paul answered, "Why are you weeping and breaking my heart? I am ready, not only to be bound, but also to die at Jerusalem for the name of Jesus." ^{14}He could not be made to change his mind, so we kept still and said, "May God's will be done."

^{15}After those days, we packed up our baggage and went to Jerusalem. ^{16}Some of the disciples from Caesarea went with us and brought with them Mnason of Cyprus, a venerable disciple with whom we could lodge. ^{17}When we arrived at Jerusalem, the congregation warmly welcomed us. ^{18}The next day we went with Paul to see James. All the elders were present. ^{19}Paul greeted them and described in detail what God had done among the Gentiles through his work. ^{20}They listened to this and praised God. They said to Paul, "Yes, brother, but consider how many thousands of Jews here are also believers. And they all have very strong feelings about the law of Moses. ^{21}They have heard that you teach those Jews who live among the Gentiles to forsake Moses, telling them not to circumcise their children or observe our customs. ^{22}Therefore what should we do? They will certainly hear that you have come, ^{23}so do what we tell you. These four men have taken a vow. ^{24}Go with them to the temple and be purified with them by having your heads shaved. Pay their expenses, and everyone will know that they were wrongly informed about you and that you obediently conform to the law of Moses. [25]As for the Gentile believers, we have written and decreed that they abstain from food offered to idols, from blood and from immorality."

[26]The next day Paul took the men and was purified with them. Then he went into the temple to declare when the days of purification would be completed and when an offering would be made for each of them.

PAUL IS BEATEN AND ARRESTED

[27]When the seven days were almost over, the Jews from Asia saw Paul at the temple. They stirred up all the people and laid hands on him, [28]shouting, "People of Israel! Help! This is the one who teaches everyone everywhere against our people and the law and this temple! He has also brought Greeks in here and polluted this holy place!" [29]They had previously seen Trophimus the Ephesian with Paul in the city and assumed that Paul had brought him into the temple. [30]The whole city was stirred up and the people came running. They took Paul and dragged him out of the temple. Immediately the doors were shut. [31]As they attempted to kill him, a report came to the Roman commander that all Jerusalem was in an uproar. [32]He immediately took soldiers and centurions and ran down to them. When the people saw the commander and the soldiers, they stopped beating Paul. [33]The commander came over and arrested him and ordered him bound with two chains. Then he demanded to know who he was and what he had done. [34]Some shouted one thing and some another among the crowd, and he could not find out the facts because of the uproar. So he commanded Paul be taken to the barracks. [35]When Paul came to the steps, he had to be carried by the soldiers because of the violence of the mob, [36]for the huge crowd of people all around shouted, "Away with him!"

PAUL TELLS HIS STORY

[37]As Paul was being taken into the barracks, he said to the commander, "May I speak to you?" He answered, "Do you know Greek? [38]Aren't you that Egyptian who made a disturbance a while back and led four thousand fanatics out into the wilderness?" [39]Paul said, "I am a Jew and a citizen of the noble city of Tarsus in Cilicia. I ask you to let me speak to the people." [40]He gave him permission. Paul stood on the steps, held up his hand to the people and there was a great hush. He spoke in Hebrew, saying, [22:1]"Brothers and sisters, mothers and fathers, hear now my plea before you." [2]When they heard him speak to them in Hebrew, they became very quiet. Paul said, [3]"I am a Jew born in Tarsus in Cilicia, brought up in this city at the feet of Gamaliel, taught according to the most exact law of our ancestors and was just as zealous for God as all of you are this day. [4]I persecuted the men and women of the Way to the death, binding and putting them in prison, [5]as also the high priest and the elders can verify. I obtained letters from them to the Jews in Damascus and went there to bring these people bound to Jerusalem to be punished. [6]As I made my journey and was coming near Damascus about noon, suddenly a great light from heaven shone around me. [7]I fell to the ground and heard a voice say to me, 'Saul, Saul, why do you persecute Me?' [8]I answered, 'Who are You, Rabbi?' and Jesus said to me, 'I am Jesus

ofNazareth whom you persecute.' [9]Those who were with me saw the light, but did not hear the voice of the One who spoke to me. [10]I said, 'What shall I do?' and Jesus said to me, 'Get up and go into Damascus. There you will be told everything that is appointed for you to do.' [11]Although I could not see because of the glory of that light, I was led by the hand by those who were with me and I came into Damascus. [12]A man named Ananias, a devout observer of the law and well thought of by all the Jews who lived there, [13]came to me and said, 'Brother Saul, recover your sight!' and at once I could see him. [14]He said, 'The God of our ancestors has chosen you to know God's will and to see the Righteous One and to hear the voice from the mouth of Jesus. [15]You will be His witness to all people of what you have seen and heard. [16]And now, why do you hesitate? Stand up, be baptized and wash away your sins, calling on His name.' [17]And it came to pass that when I returned to Jerusalem and was praying in the temple, I fell into a trance [18]and saw Jesus saying to me, 'Hurry and quickly get out of Jerusalem, for they will not accept your testimony about Me.' [19]I said, 'Rabbi, they know that I went from synagogue to synagogue to imprison and beat those who believed in You. [20]When the blood of Your servant Stephen was shed, I was standing there consenting to his death and guarding the clothes of those who killed him.' [21]Jesus said to me, 'Go, for I will send you far away to the Gentiles.'"

[22]They listened to Paul up to this word. Then their voices became loud and they shouted, "Away with such from the earth! He is not fit to live!" [23]As they shouted and flung off their coats and threw dust into the air, [24]the commander ordered that Paul be brought into the barracks. He told them to examine Paul by whipping so that he might know why they were shouting at Paul. [25]As they tied him with thongs, Paul said to the centurion standing there, "Is it lawful for you to whip a Roman citizen without a trial?" [26]When the centurion heard that, he went and told the commander, "Watch what you do, for this man is a Roman." [27]The commander came and said to him, "Tell me, are you a Roman?" Paul said, "Yes." [28]Then the commander said, "I paid a lot of money to get my citizenship." Paul replied, "But I was born a citizen." [29]Then those who were going to examine him quickly withdrew. The commander himself was afraid when he realized that he had bound a Roman citizen.

[30]The commander wanted to know for sure why Paul was accused by the Jews. The next day he released him from the chains and commanded the chief priests and all their council to appear. Then he brought Paul and stood him before them.

[23:1]Paul looked at the council and said, "My fellow Jews, I have lived before God with a clear conscience to this day." [2]At this the high priest Ananias commanded those who stood by Paul to strike him on the mouth. [3]Paul said to him, "God will strike you, you whitewashed wall! For you sit there to judge me according to the law, but you command me to be struck in violation of the law." [4]Those standing there said, "Would you insult God's high priest?" [5]Then Paul said, "Brothers, I did not know that he was the high priest; for it is written, 'You shall not speak evil of a leader of your people.'"

[6]Paul was aware that some in the council were Sadducees and some were Pharisees, so he called out, "My fellow Jews, I am a Pharisee and the son of a Pharisee. I am on trial because of my hope in the resurrection of the dead!" [7]When he

said this, a controversy arose between the Pharisees and the Sadducees and the assembly was divided, [8]for the Sadducees say there is no resurrection or angels or spirits, but the Pharisees acknowledge them all. [9]A great outcry arose, and the scribes who were Pharisees stood up and fiercely insisted, "We find no fault in this man. If a spirit or an angel spoke to him, who are we to fight God?" [10]Then the controversy became so violent that the commander feared that Paul would be pulled to pieces by them. He commanded the soldiers to go down and take him by force from among them and bring him to the barracks. [11]That night God stood by Paul and said, "Have courage, for as you testified about Me in Jerusalem, so you must witness at Rome."

[12]The next day certain Jews conspired together and bound themselves with an oath to neither eat nor drink until they had killed Paul. [13]More than forty joined this conspiracy. [14]They went to the chief priests and elders and said, "We have bound ourselves by an oath not to eat anything until we have killed Paul. [15]Now then, you and the council must ask the commander to bring him down to you as though you wanted to know more information concerning him. We are ready to kill him before he even comes near." [16]But the son of Paul's sister heard of the plot and went to the barracks and told Paul. [17]Paul called one of the centurions and said, "Bring this young man in to the commander, for he has something to tell him." [18]The centurion took him in to the commander and said, "Paul the prisoner called me and asked me to bring this young man to you; he has something to tell you." [19]The commander took him by the hand and went aside in private and asked, "What is it you have to tell me?" [20]The youth said, "The Jews have agreed to ask that you bring Paul down to the council tomorrow as though they wanted to know more information about him. [21]But do not yield to them, for more than forty men are waiting who have bound themselves with an oath to neither eat nor drink till they have killed him. Now they are ready and waiting for a word from you." [22]At this the commander let the young man go, saying, "Do not tell anyone that you told this to me." [23]Then he called two centurions and said, "Get ready two hundred soldiers, seventy cavalry and two hundred guards to go to Caesarea three hours after sunset tonight. [24]Provide horses for Paul to ride on and bring him safely to Felix the governor." [25]And he wrote the following letter:

[26]Claudius Lysias to:

The Most Excellent Governor Felix.

Greetings!

[27]This man was seized by the Jews and they would have killed him, but I came with troops and rescued him when I learned that he is a Roman citizen. [28]Wanting to know the crime they were accusing him of, I brought him to their council. [29]I found he was being accused over questions regarding their law, but there were no charges against him that deserved death or imprisonment. [30]When I was told that the Jews were plotting against the man, I immediately sent him to you. I also ordered his accusers to state their charges against him before you. Farewell.

PAUL IS TAKEN TO CAESAREA

[31]The soldiers did as they were ordered. They took Paul by night and brought him as far as Antipatris. [32]The next day they returned to the barracks, letting the cavalry

go on with him. [33]These went on to Caesarea, delivered the letter to the governor and presented Paul to him. [34]When the governor read the letter, he asked what province Paul was from. When he learned that he was from Cilicia, [35]he said, "I will hear your case when your accusers come," and he commanded that Paul be kept in Herod's palace.

PAUL IS TRIED BEFORE GOVERNOR FELIX

[24:1]After five days, Ananias the high priest came down with the elders and Tertullus the lawyer. They disclosed the charges against Paul before the governor. [2]The lawyer began his accusations by saying to the governor, "Of a truth, it is by you that we enjoy great peace, and it is by your providence that very worthy deeds are done for this nation, [3]and we accept it always and in all places, most noble Felix, with all thankfulness. [4]Notwithstanding that I be not further tedious to you, I pray that you in your clemency hear a few words. [5]For we have found this man to be a pestilent fellow, a stirrer of sedition among all the Jews throughout the world and a ringleader of the sect of the Nazarenes. [6]He also went about to profane the temple, but we seized him and would have judged him according to our law. [7]Then the commander Lysias came. With great violence he took him away out of our hands [8]and commanded his accusers to come to you, of whom yourself will acknowledge whereof we accuse him." [9]The Jews agreed and said this was so.

[10]Then the governor nodded to Paul to speak. Paul replied, "I know that for many years you have administered justice to this nation, so I cheerfully make my defense. [11]As you may know, twelve days ago I went up to Jerusalem to worship. [12]They never found me disputing with anyone in the temple or stirring up the people in the synagogues or in the city. [13]Neither can they prove the things they now accuse me of. [14]But this I acknowledge to you: I worship the God of my ancestors as a follower of the Way, which they call a sect, believing all that is written in the law and the prophets. [15]I have the same hope in God which they themselves await, that there will be a resurrection of the dead, both of the just and the unjust. [16]Therefore I always do my best to not offend God or humans. [17]Now, after being gone many years, I returned to bring my people gifts for the poor and to offer sacrifices. [18]While I was doing this, they found me as I completed my purification in the temple. There was no crowd with me, nor any disturbance. But certain Jews from Asia [19]ought to be here before you with their complaints, if they have anything against me. [20]Or let these who are here tell if they found any crime in me when I stood before the council, [21]unless it was that one thing I said as I stood among them: It is because of the resurrection of the dead that I am being judged by you today." [22]Felix was well informed about the Way, and after he heard these things, he put the Jews off, saying, "When Lysias the commander comes down, I will inquire further into your dispute." [23]He commanded a centurion to keep Paul in custody. He was to have some liberties, and his friends were allowed to take care of his needs.

[24]Some days later Felix arrived with his Jewish wife Drusilla. He sent for Paul and listened to him concerning faith in Jesus the Messiah. [25]But when Paul talked of justice and self-control and the judgment to come, Felix trembled and said, "You may

go now. When I have a convenient time I will call you." [26]At the same time he hoped that Paul would give him money, so he sent for him frequently to talk with him. [27]But after two years, Porcius Festus took the place of Felix. Wanting to gratify the Jews, Felix left Paul in chains.

PAUL APPEARS BEFORE GOVERNOR FESTUS

[25:1]Three days after coming to the province, Festus went up from Caesarea to Jerusalem. [2]Then the high priest and the Jewish leaders warned him about Paul and urgently [3]requested that he favor them by sending him to Jerusalem. They were plotting to kill him along the way. [4]But Festus replied that Paul would be kept at Caesarea and that he himself would be going there shortly. [5]"Therefore," he said, "let the capable among you go down with me and accuse this man if he has done anything wrong." [6]Festus stayed among them ten more days and then went down to Caesarea. The next day he sat on the judgment seat and commanded that Paul be brought. [7]When he came, the Jews who had come down from Jerusalem stood around him and brought many weighty complaints against Paul which they could not prove. [8]Paul answered, "I have committed no offense against the law of the Jews or against the temple or against Caesar." [9]But Festus, preferring to do the Jews a favor, answered Paul and said, "Are you willing to go up to Jerusalem and be judged there on these charges before me?" [10]Paul answered, "I am now standing in Caesar's court where I ought to be judged. I have done no wrong to the Jews, as you very well know. [11]If I have done wrong or committed any crime worthy of death, I do not refuse death. But if there is no truth in the things they accuse me of, no one can freely hand me over to them. I appeal to Caesar!" [12]Festus conferred with his advisers. Then he said, "You appeal to Caesar? Then to Caesar you shall go!"

PAUL PRESENTS HIS CASE BEFORE THE KING AND QUEEN

[13]A few days later, King Agrippa and Bernice came to Caesarea to officially welcome Festus. [14]Since they were staying several days, Festus put Paul's case before the king, saying, "There is a man here who was left in custody by Felix. [15]When I was at Jerusalem, the chief priests and the elders of the Jews warned me about him. They desire judgment against him, [16]but I told them that it was not the custom of the Romans to freely hand over anyone to die before the accused had met the accusers face to face and had an opportunity to make a defense against the accusations. [17]Therefore when they came here, the very next day I sat on the judgment seat and commanded the man brought in. [18]The accusers stood up against him, but they did not accuse him of any of the things I expected. [19]Instead, they had certain questions against him about their own religion and about a dead man named Jesus whom Paul claims is alive. [20]I did not know how to investigate such matters, so I asked if he would go to Jerusalem and be judged there regarding these things. [21]But Paul appealed to be held for a hearing before the emperor, so I commanded him to be held until I could send him to Caesar." [22]Then Agrippa said to Festus, "I have been wanting to hear the man myself." Festus replied, "Tomorrow you shall hear him."

[23]The next day Agrippa and Bernice came with great pomp to the hearing, preceded by the military officers and prominent people of the city. Festus commanded

Paul brought in, ²⁴and Festus said, "King Agrippa, and all who are present here with us, here is the man about whom all the Jewish people, both here and in Jerusalem, have appealed to me. They are determined that he not live any longer, ²⁵but I have found that he has done nothing worthy of death. And when he himself appealed to the emperor, I decided to send him. ²⁶But I have nothing certain to write about him to the emperor. Therefore I have brought him before all of you, and especially you, King Agrippa, so that after examination I may have something to write. ²⁷For it seems unreasonable to me to send a prisoner without indicating the charges against him."

26:1Agrippa said to Paul, "You are permitted to speak for yourself." Then Paul lifted up his hand and began his defense. ²"I consider myself fortunate to defend myself before you today, King Agrippa, regarding all the things I am accused of by the Jews, ³especially since you are familiar with all the customs and controversies among the Jews. Therefore I ask you to listen to me patiently. ⁴My manner of life from my youth, which was spent among my own people and in Jerusalem, is known to all the Jews. ⁵They have known from the beginning, if they would testify, that according to the strictest sect of our religion I lived as a Pharisee. ⁶And now I am standing trial because I hope in the promise made by God to our ancestors. ⁷This is the same promise our twelve tribes hope to attain as they fervently serve God day and night. And it is this hope, King Agrippa, that the Jews are accusing me of. ⁸Why does it seem incredible to you that God raises the dead? ⁹I myself once thought that I ought to do everything possible to oppose the name of Jesus Christ. ¹⁰And that is what I did in Jerusalem. I received authority from the chief priests and put many of the saints in prison. And when they were put to death, I cast my vote against them. ¹¹I punished them often in all the synagogues and tried to make them blaspheme. In increasing rage against them, I even pursued them to foreign cities. ¹²One time I was going to Damascus with the authority and permission of the chief priests. ¹³At midday, O king, I and those who journeyed with me saw a light from the sky shining brighter than the sun around me. ¹⁴We all fell to the ground, and I heard a voice speaking to me in the Hebrew language, 'Saul! Saul! Why do you persecute Me? It is hard for you to kick against the pricks.' ¹⁵Then I asked, 'Who are You?' and He answered, 'I am Jesus, whom you are persecuting. ¹⁶Now get up and stand on your feet, for I have appeared to you for the purpose of making you a servant and a witness of what you have seen and what I will show you. ¹⁷I will rescue you from your people and from the Gentiles. I am sending you ¹⁸to open their eyes, to turn them from darkness to light and from the power of Satan to God, so that they may receive forgiveness of their sins and an inheritance among those who are made holy by faith in Me.' ¹⁹After that, King Agrippa, I was not disobedient to the heavenly vision. ²⁰I first declared to those in Damascus, then to Jerusalem and throughout all Judea and to the Gentiles, that they should repent and turn to God and live praiseworthy lives to show they had repented. ²¹For this the Jews caught me in the temple and tried to kill me. ²²But I have been helped by God to this very day, giving evidence to both small and great, and I say nothing other than what the prophets and Moses said would happen, ²³that the Messiah would suffer, and that He, the first to rise from the dead, would proclaim the light to our people and to the Gentiles."

[24]As Paul made his plea, Festus said with a loud voice, "Paul, you are raving! All your learning is making you crazy!" [25]Paul replied, "I am not crazy, most noble Festus, but I am speaking reasonable words of truth. [26]You, O king, know about these things and I speak frankly before you, for I cannot believe that these things are unknown to you. All this was not done in a corner. [27]King Agrippa, do you believe the prophets? But I know that you do." [28]Then Agrippa said to Paul, "You almost persuade me to become a Christian." [29]Paul said, "I wish to God that not only you, but also all who hear me this day would sooner or later become as I am, except for these chains."

[30]After Paul finished speaking, the king stood up, and then the governor and Bernice and those who sat with them. [31]They withdrew and said to one another, "This man has done nothing deserving death or imprisonment." [32]Then Agrippa said to Festus, "This man could have been set free if he had not appealed to Caesar."

PAUL SAILS FOR ROME

[27:1]When it was decided that we should sail to Italy, they entrusted Paul and certain other prisoners to a Roman army officer named Julius. [2]Embarking on a ship from Adramyttium which was ready to sail for ports along the coast of Asia, we put out to sea. Aristarchus, a Macedonian from Thessalonica, was with us. [3]The next day we moored at Sidon, and Julius courteously allowed Paul to visit his friends and be refreshed. [4]From there we put out to sea and sailed on the lee side of Cyprus because the winds were contrary. [5]When we had crossed the open sea off Cilicia and Pamphylia, we came to Myra in Lycia. [6]There the centurion found a ship from Alexandria sailing for Italy and he put us aboard. [7]We sailed slowly for many days, and the wind would scarcely allow us to come opposite Cnidus. The wind would not permit us to go on, so we sailed the lee side of Crete opposite Salmone. [8]Passing it with difficulty, we came to a place called Fair Havens near the city of Lasea. [9]Since much time had been lost, sailing had become dangerous, for the Fast was over. Paul advised, [10]"Gentlemen, I can see that this voyage will bring damage and much loss, not only to the cargo and ship, but also to our lives." [11]But the centurion was more convinced by the captain and owner of the ship than by what Paul said. [12]Since the harbor was unsuitable to winter in, the majority wanted to sail away from there in hope of reaching Phoenix, a harbor in Crete facing southwest and northwest.

A WINTER STORM WRECKS THE SHIP

[13]The south wind blew softly. Thinking that they had what they wanted, they weighed anchor and sailed close to the shore of Crete. [14]But before long a stormy wind called a Noreaster arose and intensified. [15]The ship was caught and could not head up into the wind, so we ran before it. [16]As we sailed in the lee of an island called Cauda, we brought aboard the lifeboat after much work. [17]After the lifeboat was hoisted up, they tied ropes around the ship to hold the ship together. Then, fearing lest they be driven onto the shoals of Africa, they struck sail and were driven along. [18]We were so violently tossed by the storm that the next day they began to throw the cargo overboard. [19]The third day we threw the ship's tackle overboard with our own hands. [20]For many days neither sun nor stars appeared. The storm raged on, so that all hope of being saved was abandoned. [21]After the men had gone many days without eating,

Paul stood up and said, "Gentlemen, you should have listened to me and not sailed from Crete to incur this damage and loss. ^{22}But now I urge you to cheer up, for there will be no loss of life among you, just the ship. ^{23}Last night an angel of the God to whom I belong and whom I serve stood by me ^{24}and said, 'Do not be afraid, Paul! You must stand before Caesar, and even now God has given you all those who sail with you.' ^{25}Therefore gentlemen, cheer up, for I believe God. It will be just as it was told to me, ^{26}and we will be driven up on a certain island."

^{27}The fourteenth night came. At about midnight as we were being tossed about in the sea, the sailors sensed that they were approaching land. ^{28}They sounded and found twenty fathoms. They went a little farther and sounded again and found fifteen fathoms. ^{29}Then, fearing lest we be driven up on the rocks, they threw four anchors from the stern and prayed for the dawn. ^{30}The sailors wanted to flee from the ship, so they let the lifeboat down into the sea, pretending that they were going to stretch out ropes from the bow. ^{31}Paul said to the centurion and the soldiers, "Unless these stay with the ship, you cannot be saved." ^{32}Then the soldiers cut the ropes to the lifeboat and let it go.

^{33}As the day dawned, Paul urged them all to eat some food, saying, "This day is the fourteenth day you have been on watch, continually fasting and eating nothing. ^{34}Therefore I urge you to eat some food for the sake of your health, for not a hair of your heads will be lost." ^{35}After he said this, he took bread and thanked God in the presence of them all. Then he broke it and began to eat. ^{36}They were all cheered and took some food themselves. ^{37}All together there were two hundred and seventy six souls on the ship. ^{38}When they had eaten enough, they lightened the ship by throwing the wheat into the sea.

AGROUND ON THE ISLAND OF MALTA

^{39}When daylight came, they did not recognize the land. but they saw a bay and a beach. They were determined, if possible, to get the ship to shore there. ^{40}They cut loose the anchors and left them in the sea, while loosening the ropes that held the rudders. Then hoisting the foresail to the wind, they made for the beach. ^{41}The ship ran aground at a place where two currents met. The bow stuck and remained immovable, and the stern was broken by the violence of the waves. ^{42}The soldiers' plan was to kill the prisoners, lest any of them swim away and escape, ^{43}but the centurion, wanting to save Paul, kept them from their plan. He commanded those who could swim to jump first and get to land. ^{44}The rest followed on boards and pieces of the ship. And so it came about that all escaped safely to land.

$^{28:1}$After we had escaped, we recognized the island called Malta. ^{2}The islanders treated us with exceptional kindness. They welcomed us all and kindled a fire, for it was raining and cold. ^{3}Paul gathered a bundle of sticks and put them on the fire. A viper came out because of the heat and fastened on his hand. ^{4}When the islanders saw the snake hanging on his hand, they said among themselves, "No doubt this man is a murderer. He escaped from the sea, but justice will not allow him to live." ^{5}But Paul shook the snake off into the fire and was unharmed. ^{6}They watched for him to swell up or suddenly fall down dead, but after watching a long time and seeing no harm come to him, they changed their minds and said he was a god.

^{7}In that part of the island were estates of the governor of the island, whose name was Publius. He welcomed us and entertained us courteously for three days. ^{8}The father of Publius happened to be sick with fever and dysentery. Paul went in to see him, prayed, laid his hands on him and healed him. ^{9}After this happened, others on the island who had diseases came and were healed also. ^{10}They honored us with many honors, and when we departed they gave us whatever we needed.

PAUL ARRIVES IN ROME

^{11}After three months we departed on a ship that had wintered on the island, the Castor and Pollux of Alexandria. ^{12}Landing at Syracuse, we stayed three days, ^{13}and from there we tacked around and came to Rhegium. After one day the south wind blew, and the next day we came to Puteoli. ^{14}There we found friends and were invited to stay with them seven days. And so we came to Rome. ^{15}When the congregation there heard about us, they came as far as the Forum of Appius and the Three Taverns to meet us. When Paul saw them, he thanked God and was encouraged. ^{16}When we came into Rome, Paul was allowed to stay by himself, with a soldier to guard him.

PAUL TELLS THE ROMAN JEWS ABOUT JESUS

^{17}After three days, Paul called the Jewish leaders together. When they came, he said to them, "My fellow Jews, though I committed nothing against our people or the customs of our ancestors, I was arrested in Jerusalem and handed over to the Romans. ^{18}They examined me and would have let me go, because there was no reason to put me to death. ^{19}But the Jews objected and I was forced to appeal to Caesar, not that I had any accusation to make against my nation. ^{20}That is why I asked to see you and speak with you, for it is because of the hope of Israel that I am bound with this chain." ^{21}They said to him, "We have not received any letters from Judea concerning you, nor have any Jews said anything harmful about you. ^{22}But we want to hear what you think, for we know that in regard to this sect, it is everywhere spoken against."

^{23}They arranged a day, and many came to him where he was staying. From morning till night he explained and gave evidence for the realm of God, trying to convince them about Jesus from both the law of Moses and the prophets. ^{24}Some believed what was said, and some did not. ^{25}They did not agree among themselves. They began to leave after Paul made one statement: "The Holy Spirit spoke well by Isaiah the prophet to our ancestors, ^{26}saying,'Go tell this people: You listen, but do not understand; you see, but do not comprehend. ^{27}Deaden the hearts of this people and make their ears heavy, lest they see with their eyes and hear with their ears and understand with their hearts and turn and be healed.' ^{28}Therefore let it be known to you that the salvation of God has been sent to the Gentiles. They will listen." ^{29}After he said this, the Jews departed and had much argument among themselves.

^{30}Paul stayed two whole years in his own rented house and welcomed all who came to see him. ^{31}He boldly told about the realm of God and taught about our Sovereign Jesus Christ unhindered.

Romans

$^{1:1}$From Paul, a servant of Christ Jesus, called to be an apostle, set apart to tell the good news of God ^{2}which God promised long ago through the prophets in the holy Scriptures. ^{3}This good news concerns God's Child Jesus Christ. Christ was descended from the seed of David according to the flesh, ^{4}but through the Spirit of Holiness Christ was declared the Child of God in power by the resurrection from the dead. ^{5}Through Christ, and for the sake of Christ's name, we received grace and apostleship to bring about among all nations the obedience that comes from faith. ^{6}You also are among those called to belong to Jesus the Christ.

^{7}To all who are in Rome, beloved of God, called to be saints: Goodwill and peace to you from God our heavenly Parent and from our Sovereign Jesus Christ.

^{8}First, I thank my God through Jesus Christ for all of you. Your faith is spoken of throughout the whole world. ^{9}God is my witness that I constantly mention you in my prayers as I serve with all my might telling others the good news about God's Child. ^{10}I pray that somehow now at last I might succeed by God's will to come to you. ^{11}I long to see you, so that I may share with you a spiritual gift to strengthen you. ^{12}That is, I'll be encouraged by your faith when I'm with you, and you by mine. ^{13}Now I want you to know, believers, that I often made plans to come to you, but was prevented till now. I desire to reap a harvest among you as well, just as among the other Gentiles. ^{14}For I have an obligation to the educated and the ignorant, to both the wise and the foolish. ^{15}Therefore I am eager to preach the gospel to all of you at Rome as well. ^{16}I am not ashamed of the gospel, for it is the power of God to rescue everyone who believes; to the Jew first, but also to the Gentile. ^{17}Through the gospel the righteousness of God is being revealed from faith to faith. As it is written, "The just shall live by faith."

GOD'S RESPONSE TO UNRIGHTEOUS HUMANS

^{18}The wrath of God is being revealed from heaven against all the ungodliness and wickedness of those who restrain the truth by their wickedness. ^{19}What can be known about God is plain to them, for God has shown it to them. ^{20}God's invisible characteristics, eternal power and divine nature have been clearly seen and understood in the things that have been made since the creation of the world, so that they are without excuse. ^{21}Though they knew of God, they did not honor or thank God. They debated pointlessly and their senseless thoughts were obscure. ^{22}Professing to be wise, they became fools ^{23}and exchanged the glory of the immortal God for images made to look like mortal humans, birds, animals and reptiles.

[24]Because of their lustful thoughts, God gave them over to dishonoring their bodies among themselves. [25]They exchanged the truth of God for a lie and worshiped and served the creature rather than the Creator, who is blessed forever. Amen.

SOME RESULTS OF NOT HONORING GOD

[26]For this reason God gave them over to disgraceful passions. Even the females changed natural sexual intercourse into what is against nature. [27]In the same way the males gave up natural sexual intercourse with the female and burned with lust for one another, the male with the male doing what is shameful, and taking back into themselves the appropriate binding penalty for their error. [28]Since they did not want to retain any knowledge of the Almighty, God gave them over to a perverted mind and things that should not be done. [29]They are filled with every kind of unrighteousness, wickedness, covetousness, maliciousness, envy, murder, wrangling, deceit, malice, gossip, [30]slander, profanity, insolence, pride and boasting. They are contrivers of evil, disobedient to parents, [31]senseless, faithless, unloving and ruthless. [32]They know God's decree that those who practice such things deserve death, but they continue to do these things and think well of others who do the same.

ONLY GOD MAY JUDGE

[2:1]You people who judge others are inexcusable. When you judge another, you condemn yourself, for you, the judge, do the same things. [2]We know that God rightly judges those who do these things. [3]You people who judge others but do these same things, do you think that you will escape the judgment of God? [4]Or do you despise the riches of God's goodness and tolerant patience, not knowing that the kindness of God is meant to lead you to repentance? [5]Because of your hard and unrepentant hearts, you are storing up wrath against yourself on the day of wrath when the righteous judgment of God will be revealed.

[6]God will render to all people according to their deeds. [7]For those who seek glory, honor and immortality by patiently continuing to do good, there will be everlasting life. [8]But for those who are contentious and refuse the truth and yield to evil, there will be indignation and wrath. [9]There will be tribulation and anguish for everyone who does evil, the Jew first and the Gentile also, [10]but glory, honor and peace for everyone who does good, the Jew first and the Gentile also. [11]There is no favoritism with God.

[12]All who sin without having God's law will perish without the law. And all who sin within the law will be judged by the law. [13]It is not the hearers of the law who are righteous in God's sight. It is those who obey the law who will be justified. [14]When the Gentiles who do not have the law do by nature what the law requires, then they are a law to themselves, even though they don't have the law. [15]This shows that the effect of the law is written on their hearts, while their conscience also verifies their thoughts, meanwhile accusing or else excusing them [16]on that day when God will judge the secrets of everyone through Jesus Christ in accordance with my gospel.

[17]Now if you call yourself a Jew and rely on the law and boast about God [18]and know God's will and approve what is best, being instructed from the law, [19]and are confident that you are a guide for the blind, a light for those in darkness, [20]an instructor of the ignorant, a teacher of the simple, having in the law the formula for

knowledge and truth - [21]you then who teach others, do you teach yourself? You who preach, "Do not steal," do you steal? [22]You who say, "Do not commit adultery," do you commit adultery? You who abhor idols, do you take things from idol shrines? [23]You who boast about the law, do you dishonor God by breaking the law? [24]As it is written, "The name of God is blasphemed among the Gentiles because of you."

[25]Circumcision is truly beneficial if you obey the law. But if you break the law, your circumcision has become uncircumcision. [26]If the uncircumcised obey the requirements of the law, will not their uncircumcision be regarded as circumcision? [27]And will not the one who is not circumcised and yet fulfills the law judge you who break the law, though you have the Scriptures and circumcision? [28]For the real Jew is not only the one who is circumcised in the flesh. [29]The real Jew is the inward one. Circumcision is of the heart and the spirit and not in the writings. Therefore one's praise comes, not from humans but from God.

[3:1]What advantage then in being a Jew? Or what benefit in circumcision? [2]There are many benefits! First of all, the Jews were entrusted with the utterances of God. [3]What if some were unbelieving? Does their unbelief mean that God is unfaithful? [4]Of course not. God is true, though every human be a liar. As it is written, "You are justified when You speak and right when You judge." [5]But if our unrighteousness invites comparison with the righteousness of God, what can we say? That God is unjust to punish us? Now I'm using human logic. [6]No! For then how could God judge the world? [7]But what if by lying, I bring honor to the truth of God? Why would I yet be judged a sinner? [8]You might as well say, "Why not do evil so that good may come?" Some people are slanderously reporting that we teach this. Their condemnation is deserved.

ALL ARE GUILTY

[9]What then? Do we excel? No, by no means. For we have already charged that both Jew and Gentile are under sin. [10]As it is written, "None are righteous; no, not one. [11]There is no one who understands, none who seek God. [12]They have all turned away, they are altogether useless. There is not one who does good; no, not one. [13]Their throat is an open grave. They use their tongues to deceive. The poison of asps is under their lips. [14]Their mouths are full of curses and bitterness. [15]Their feet are swift to shed blood. [16]Destruction and misery are in their ways. [17]They do not know the way of peace, [18]nor is the fear of God before their eyes." [19]Now we know that whatever the law says, it says to those under the law, in order that every mouth might be silenced and all the world shown guilty before God. [20]Therefore by keeping the law, no flesh will be justified in God's sight, for through the law comes recognition of sin.

ALL HAVE SINNED

[21]But now we see a way to be righteous before God quite separate from the law, as told to us by the law and the prophets. [22]God makes us righteous through our faith and belief in Jesus Christ. No matter who we are, [23]all have sinned and come short of the glory of God. [24]We are justified freely by God's grace through the ransom offered by Christ Jesus, [25]whom God presented as an atonement through faith in Christ's

blood. This shows God's righteousness, because God patiently overlooked the sins of the past [26]in order to show at the present time the justice of justifying those who believe in Jesus.

ALL MAY BE SAVED BY FAITH

[27]What about boasting? It is excluded. By what law? The law of works? No, by the law of faith. [28]For we conclude that humans are justified by faith separate from keeping the law. [29]Is God the God of the Jews only? Is God not also the God of the Gentiles? Yes, of the Gentiles also, [30]since there is one God. God will justify both the circumcised and the uncircumcised through faith. [31]Do we invalidate the law through faith? Of course not. On the contrary, we support the law.

ABRAHAM'S EXAMPLE OF FAITH

[4:1]What then are we to say that our ancestor Abraham found? [2]If Abraham was justified by works, he could boast - but not before God. [3]What does Scripture say? "Abraham believed God, and it was credited to him as righteousness." [4]Now, a worker's pay is not credited to the worker as a gift, but as wages. [5]But to one who does not work but believes in the One who justifies the ungodly, faith is credited as righteousness. [6]In the same way, David describes the blessedness of the one to whom God credits righteousness without works: [7]"Blessed are those whose offenses have been forgiven and whose sins have been covered. [8]Blessed are those whose sins Yahweh will not keep an account of." [9]Was this blessedness on the circumcised, or also on the uncircumcised? For we have been saying that faith was credited to Abraham as righteousness. [10]How then was it credited? Was he circumcised or uncircumcised? It was when he was uncircumcised! [11]Later he was circumcised, and it was a sign of the faith he had when he was uncircumcised. Thus he became the ancestor of all those who believe, though they are uncircumcised, so that righteousness may be credited to them also. [12]He is also the ancestor of the circumcised, who are not only circumcised, but who also walk in the steps of that faith our ancestor Abraham had when he was uncircumcised.

[13]The promise made to Abraham and his descendants that he would possess the world did not come through the law, but through the righteousness of faith. [14]If Abraham and his descendants could receive the things that God promised by following the law, then faith is meaningless and the promise is worthless. [15]For the law brings wrath. But where there is no law, there is no law-breaking. [16]Therefore the promise depends on faith, is given by grace and is firmly guaranteed to all Abraham's descendants who believe. The promise is not only to those of the law but is to all those who share Abraham's faith, for Abraham is the ancestor of us all. [17]As it is written: "I have made you an ancestor of many nations." This promise was made by the God in whom Abraham believed, the God who brings the dead to life and calls those things which are not as though they existed.

[18]When Abraham's situation was hopeless, he had hope and believed God, who said, "So shall your descendants be." Thus Abraham became the ancestor of many nations. [19]He was about a hundred years old, yet he did not consider the deadness of Sarah's womb or his almost-dead body. Abraham was not weak in faith. [20]He did not

stagger in unbelief before the promise of God, but was strong in faith, which honored God. [21]Abraham was fully persuaded that what God promised, God was able to do. [22]Therefore this was credited to him as righteousness. [23]Now, what was credited to him was not written for him alone, [24]but for us also. It will be credited to us also, for we believe in the One who raised Jesus from the dead. [25]Jesus was handed over for our offenses and raised for our acquittal.

FAITH BRINGS PEACE WITH GOD

[5:1]Therefore, having been justified by faith, we have peace with God through Jesus Christ. [2]Through faith in Christ we have access into this grace in which we stand, and we expectantly boast about the glory of God. [3]And not only that, but we boast of tribulation also, knowing that tribulation leads to perseverance, [4]perseverance leads to character and character leads to hope. [5]And hope does not disappoint, for the love of God is poured into our hearts by the Holy Spirit who is given to us. [6]At the time when we were yet without strength, Christ died for the ungodly. [7]Now, rarely will someone die for someone else; yet perhaps for a good friend someone might dare to die. [8]But God shows love for us, in that while we were yet sinners, Christ died for us. [9]So now, justified by Christ's blood, how much more will we be saved from wrath through Christ! [10]For if when we were enemies we were reconciled to God by the death of God's Child, now that we are reconciled, how much more will we be saved by that Child's life? [11]Not only that, but we also boast in God because our Sovereign Jesus Christ has now restored us to favor.

ADAM AND JESUS CHRIST

[12]Sin entered the world through one human. Death came as a consequence of sin, and so death passed on to all humans, for all sinned. [13]Now, until the law was given, sin was in the world. But no account was kept of sin when there was no law. [14]Nevertheless, death reigned from Adam to Moses, even over those who did not sin in the same way as Adam did. Adam was a type of the One to come. [15]But the offense and the love gift are not the same. For if through the offense of Adam many died, how much more does the grace of God through the gift of grace from Jesus Christ overflow to many! [16]God's love gift is not like Adam's offense, in that Adam's one judgment resulted in the death verdict, while God's love gift justifies many offenses. [17]If death became the rule because of Adam's offense, then those who take hold of God's abundant grace and the gift of righteousness will rule in life through Jesus Christ that much more! [18]Therefore, just as all humans are condemned by Adam's one offense, so also by the righteousness of Christ are all humans justified and live. [19]For just as by one human's disobedience many were made sinners, so also by the obedience of One many will be made righteous.

[20]Then the law came and offenses increased. But where sin increased, grace increased more, [21]so that just as sin ruled and brought death, so also grace can now rule through righteousness to bring everlasting life through Jesus Christ.

BAPTIZED INTO NEWNESS OF LIFE

[6:1]What shall we say then? Should we continue to sin so that God will favor us more? [2]Of course not. How can we who are dead to sin live any longer in it? [3]Don't you know that all of us who were baptized into Christ Jesus were baptized into Christ's death? [4]Through baptism we are buried with Christ in death so that, just as Christ was raised from the dead by the glorious power of God, we also may walk in newness of life. [5]For if we are united with Christ in death, then we also will be resurrected. [6]We know that our old self was crucified with Christ so that the sinful body might be made powerless and so that we would no longer be slaves to sin. [7]For anyone who is dead is freed from sin. [8]Now if we are dead with Christ, we believe that we will also live with Christ. [9]For we know that Christ was raised from the dead and cannot die again. Death no longer has dominion over Christ. [10]Christ died to sin, once for all. But the life Christ lives is to God. [11]So also you must reckon yourselves dead to sin but alive to God through Christ Jesus.

[12]Therefore do not let sin reign in your mortal body so that you obey its lusts. [13]Do not yield your bodies to sin as instruments of unrighteousness, but yield yourselves to God as people who are alive from the dead. Yield your bodies as instruments of righteousness to God! [14]Sin must not have dominion over you, for you are not under the law but under God's grace.

SLAVES OF SIN OR SLAVES OF GOD

[15]What then? Shall we sin because we are not under the law, but under God's grace? Of course not. [16]You know well enough that when you yield yourselves as slaves you must be obedient, whether you are obedient to sin, which brings death, or to obedience, which brings godliness. [17]Thank God that, though you were the slaves of sin, you obeyed from the heart that form of instruction that was given to you. [18]Then, made free from sin, you became the slaves of godliness.

[19]I use ordinary examples because of the weakness of your flesh. You used to yield your bodies as slaves to uncleanness and wrong after wrong, but now you must yield your bodies as slaves to purity and godliness. [20]For when you were the slaves of sin, you were not restrained by godliness. [21]What fruit do you have from the past, of which you are now ashamed? The consequence of those actions is death. [22]But now, set free from sin and enslaved to God, you have the fruit of holiness. The result is eternal life. [23]For the wages of sin is death, but the gift of God is eternal life through Jesus Christ.

OUR NEW LIFE IN CHRIST COMPARED TO MARRIAGE

[7:1]Believers, surely you know, for I speak to those who know the law, that the law has dominion over a person only as long as that person lives. [2]For example, if a woman is married, she is bound by the law to her husband as long as he lives. But if the husband dies, she is released from that law. [3]If, however, she marries another man while her husband is still living, she will be considered unfaithful. But if her husband is dead, she is exempt from that law and she will not be considered unfaithful if she marries another man. [4]So too, believers, you also have become dead to the law because of the body of Christ in order to become another's; the One who was raised from the dead. In this way you may be productive for God. [5]For while we were influenced by the flesh, the sinful passions stirred up by the law worked in our bodies and made our bodies bear fruit for death. [6]But now we are released from the law, having died to what once restrained us so that we can serve in newness of Spirit, and not in the old way of the written law.

THE TRUE NATURE OF SIN

[7]What shall we say then? That the law is sin? Of course not. Yet it was the law that made me know what sin was. I would not have known I was coveting if the law had not said, "You shall not covet." [8]But sin, finding an opportunity in the commandment, produced all kinds of covetousness in me. For apart from the law, sin is dead. [9]I was once alive apart from the law; but the commandment came, sin became alive and I died. [10]So the commandment, which is to bring life, brought death instead. [11]For sin, finding an opportunity in the commandment, deceived me and killed me. [12]We know that the law is holy. The commandment is also holy, just and good. [13]Did that which is good bring death to me? Of course not. It was sin. Sin was forced to show its true nature; and sin produced death in me through what is good. And so, through the commandment, sin is exposed as utterly sinful.

[14]We know that the law is spiritual; but my body is unspiritual and sold as a slave to sin. [15]The things that I do seem out of my control. I do not do what I want to do; but what I hate, that I do. [16]If I do what I don't want to do, then I agree that the law is good. [17]Therefore it is not I doing it, but sin living within me. [18]For I know that nothing good lives in me, that is, in my flesh. The desire is here within me, but I do not find the way to accomplish good. [19]The good that I want to do, I do not do. But the evil that I do not want to do, that I do. [20]Now, if I do what I don't want to do, then it is not I who do it, but it is sin living in me. [21]I find then this principle: When I want to do good, evil is right here with me. [22]I delight in God's law in my inner self; [23]but I see another law in my body warring against the law of my mind and making me a prisoner of the law of sin that is in my body. [24]O wretched human that I am! Who will rescue me from this body of death? [25]I thank God that Jesus Christ is the way. So then, with my mind I serve God's law, but with my body the law of sin.

FOLLOW THE SPIRIT

[8:1]There is therefore now no condemnation for those who belong to Christ Jesus. [2]For the law of the Spirit of life in Christ Jesus has set me free from the law of sin and death. [3]For what the law could not do because the flesh was weak, God did by sending Christ in the likeness of sinful flesh. God condemned sin in the flesh [4]so that the requirements might be fulfilled in us who do not follow the urges of the flesh but follow the urges of the Spirit. [5]Those who follow the urges of the flesh are interested in the flesh, but those who follow the urges of the Spirit are interested in the Spirit. [6]To be fleshly minded is death, but to be spiritually minded is life and peace. [7]The purposes of the flesh are hostile toward God. The flesh does not obey the law of God, nor indeed can it. [8]Therefore those who are in the flesh cannot please God. [9]But you are not in the flesh but in the Spirit - if the Spirit of God lives in you. If you do not have the Spirit of Christ, you are not Christ's. [10]If Christ is in you, the body is dead because of sin, but the Spirit gives life because of righteousness. [11]If the Spirit of the One who raised Jesus from the dead lives in you, then that same One will also give life to your mortal bodies through the Spirit who lives within you. [12]Therefore, believers, we are not obligated to the flesh to live according to the urges of the flesh. [13]If you live according to the urges of the flesh, you will die. But if through the Spirit you put to death the deeds of the flesh, you will live.

[14]All those who are led by the Spirit of God are the children of God. [15]For you have not received a spirit of slavery to make you afraid again, but you have received a Spirit of adoption. With the help of the Spirit we cry, "My heavenly Parent!" [16]The Spirit verifies to our spirit that we are the children of God, [17]and if children, then heirs - heirs and joint heirs with Christ - so that we may also be glorified with Christ.

FUTURE GLORY

[18]I do not consider the sufferings of this present time comparable to the glory that will be revealed to us. [19]With intense anticipation the creation waits for God's children to be revealed. [20]For the creation did not choose to lack purpose, but was subjected by God in hope, [21]for creation itself will also be freed from slavery to destruction and share in the glorious freedom of the children of God. [22]We know that the whole creation has been groaning in the pains of childbirth until now. [23]And not only creation, but we who have the firstfruits of the Spirit groan within ourselves as we wait for our adoption and the redemption of our bodies. [24]We are saved by this hope. But hope that is seen is not hope, for who hopes for what they can see? [25]But if we hope for what we can't see, we patiently wait for it. [26]In the same way, the Spirit also helps us in our weakness, for we don't know how to pray as we should. But the Spirit intercedes on our behalf with groans that are not expressed in words. [27]And the One who searches our hearts knows the Spirit's intent as God intercedes for the saints according to the divine will.

[28]We know that all things work together for good for those who love God, for those who are called according to God's purpose. [29]Those whom God knew beforehand were predestined to be conformed to the image of God's Child so that Christ might be the firstborn of a large family. [30]Those God predestined were also called; and those God called were also justified; and those who were justified were also glorified.

WHO WILL CONDEMN US WHOM GOD HAS JUSTIFIED?

[31]What then shall we say about this? If God is for us, who can be against us? [32]The Holy One who did not spare Christ, but gave Christ up for us all, will also, in addition to Christ, give us all things! [33]Who will make a charge against God's chosen? It is God who justifies. [34]Who is there to condemn? Christ who died and was raised is even now at the right hand of God. And furthermore, Christ is interceding for us. [35]Who can separate us from the love of Christ? Can tribulation or distress or persecution or hunger or nakedness or danger or war? [36]As it is written: "For Your sake we are killed all the day long; we are considered as sheep for slaughter." [37]But in all these things we are more than conquerors through the One who loves us. [38]For I am persuaded that neither death, nor life, nor angels, nor principalities, nor powers, nor things present, nor things to come, [39]nor height, nor depth, nor anything created will be able to separate us from the love of God that is in Christ Jesus.

GOD'S PEOPLE IN HISTORY

9:1I am telling the truth in Christ. My conscience, in union with the Holy Spirit, also assures me that I am not lying. 2I have great heaviness and continual grief in my heart 3and would willingly pray to be excommunicated from Christ for the sake of my people, my kin according to the flesh, 4who are Israelites. Theirs is the adoption, the glory, the covenants, the giving of the law, the worship and the promises. 5Theirs are the ancestors from whom descended, according to the flesh, Christ, who is over all. May God be blessed forever. Amen.

6It is not as though the word of God failed. But not all those who are descended from Israel are the chosen people. 7Not all of Abraham's descendants are considered his children, for, "Through Isaac shall your descendants come." 8This means that the children of the flesh are not the children of God, but the children of the promise are considered the true descendants. 9These are the words of the promise: "At this time I will come and Sarah shall have a son."

10Another example: Rebecca conceived two children by our forefather Isaac. 11When the twins were not yet born and had done nothing good or bad, God showed that the elect were not chosen on the basis of works, but were those God wanted. 12Rebecca was told, "The older shall serve the younger." 13As it is written, "Jacob I loved, but Esau I hated." 14What shall we say then? Is God unjust? Of course not. 15For God said to Moses, "I will have compassion on whom I have compassion, and I will have pity on whom I have pity." 16Therefore it does not depend on human will or effort, but on God's compassion. 17For the Scripture says to Pharaoh, "For this purpose I raised you up, that I might show My power through you, and that My name might be declared throughout all the earth." 18Therefore God has compassion on whomever God wishes and God hardens whomever God wishes.

19You might say to me, "Why does God still find fault, for who can resist God's will?" 20But who are you, O human, to talk back to God? Shall the thing formed say to the One who formed it, "Why have You made me like this?" 21Does not the potter have the right to make from a lump of clay one vessel honored and another less honored? 22But what if God, willing to demonstrate wrath and power, patiently endured those people worthy of wrath and destruction? 23God waited patiently to make the riches of divine glory known to the people who were prepared beforehand for glory. 24We whom God called are those people, both Jews and Gentiles.

25As God says in Hosea, "I will call those not My people 'My people' and those not loved 'loved'." 26And it shall come to pass: In the place where it was said to them, "You are not My people," there they will be called the children of the living God. 27Isaiah proclaimed concerning Israel, "Though the number of the children of Israel be as the sand of the sea, only a remnant will be saved. 28Yahweh will finish the work and cut it short in righteousness, for Yahweh will make a short work of the earth." 29As Isaiah said beforehand, "If the mighty Yahweh had not left us a remnant, we would be like Sodom, we would resemble Gomorrah."

30What shall we say then? That the Gentiles who did not pursue righteousness attained righteousness, even the righteousness that is of faith, 31but Israel who pursued the law of righteousness did not attain it? [32]Why is that? Because it was not by faith, but by works of the law. They stumbled at that stumbling stone. [33]As it is written, "Look! I lay in Zion a stumbling stone and rock of offense. The one who trusts in that rock will not be put to shame."

IT IS JESUS THE CHRIST WHO WILL SAVE YOU

[10:1]Believers, my heart's desire and prayer to God for Israel is that they may be saved. [2]I testify that they have a zeal for God, but it is not based on knowledge. [3]For they, ignorant of God's righteousness and going about to establish their own righteousness, have not submitted to the righteousness of God. [4]For Christ is the end result of the law, bringing righteousness to everyone who believes. [5]Moses describes the righteousness that is of the law in this way: "The person who does these things will live by them." [6]But the righteousness that is of faith speaks this way: Do not say in your heart, "Who will ascend up to heaven?" (that is, to bring Christ down), [7]or, "Who will descend into the deep?" (that is, to bring Christ up from the dead). [8]But what does it say? "The word is near you - in your mouth and in your heart." This is the word of faith we preach: [9]If you acknowledge with your mouth that Jesus is Sovereign and believe in your heart that God raised Christ from the dead, you will be saved. [10]For with the heart you believe and are justified, and with the mouth you acknowledge and are saved. [11]The Scripture says, "The one who has faith will not be disappointed." [12]There is no difference between Jew and non-Jew, for the same God is Sovereign of all and is able to richly bless all who ask for help. [13]For "everyone who calls on the name of Yahweh will be saved."

THE IMPORTANCE OF THE MESSAGE

[14]How can they call on the One in whom they do not believe? And how can they believe in the One of whom they have not heard? And how can they hear without a preacher? [15]And how can they preach unless they are sent? As it is written, "How beautiful are the feet of those who announce the good news of peace and bring glad tidings of good things." [16]But all have not obeyed the good news. For Isaiah says, "Who has believed our report?" [17]So then, faith comes by hearing, and hearing by the word of God. [18]But, I ask, didn't they hear? Indeed they did. "The sound went out to all the earth, and their words to the ends of the world." [19]But I ask, didn't Israel understand? First Moses says, "I will offend you with a non-people; with a foolish nation I will anger you." [20]Isaiah is very bold and says of God, "I was found by those who did not seek Me; I appeared to those who did not ask for Me." [21]But to Israel God says, "I spread out My hands all day to a rebellious and contrary people."

A FAITHFUL FEW FIND GOD

[11:1]I ask then, has God rejected Israel? Of course not. I myself am an Israelite of the seed of Abraham of the tribe of Benjamin. [2]God has not rejected Israel. God chose them from of old. Surely you know what the Scripture says about Elijah - how he interceded with God concerning Israel, saying, [3]"O God, they have killed Your prophets and destroyed Your altars. I alone am left, and they seek my life!" [4]What did God answer him? "I have reserved for Myself seven thousand who have not bent their knee to Baal." [5]At the present time there is also a remnant chosen by grace. [6]And if by grace, then not by works. Otherwise, grace would not be grace. [7]What then? Israel did not find what it looked for. But the chosen found it. The rest were hardened. [8]As it is written, "God gave them a spirit of stupor, eyes so they could not see and ears so they could not hear, as it is to this day." [9]David said, "Let their table become a snare, a trap, a scandal and a retribution to them. [10]Let their eyes be darkened so they do not see and their backs bent down forever."

ISRAEL'S FALL HAS BECOME THE WORLD'S OPPORTUNITY

[11]I ask then: Have they stumbled, never to rise? Of course not. But their offense has brought salvation to the Gentiles in order to make Israel jealous. [12]Now if the offense of Israel brings riches to the world, and Israel's failure brings riches to the Gentiles, how much more will Israel's completion be!

[13]I am speaking to you Gentiles, inasmuch as I am the apostle to the Gentiles. I value my service [14]in the hope that I may provoke my people to be jealous and so be saved. [15]For if the rejection of Israel means the world restored to favor - what will their renewal be, but life from the dead? [16]For if the first piece of bread [Israel] is holy, then the whole loaf [the rest of the world] is holy. And if the root is holy, so are the branches. [17]Some of the branches have been broken off, and you Gentiles, being a wild olive, have been grafted in among the native branches. And now you partake with the olive branches of the richness of the roots. [18]Don't think that you are better than the broken-off branches! You do not give life to the root, but the root gives life to you. [19]You may say, "The branches were broken off so that I could be grafted in." [20]Its true that they were broken off because of unbelief, but you stand through faith. Do not have proud thoughts, but be afraid. [21]For if God did not spare the natural branches, neither will you be spared. [22]Consider the goodness and severity of God: severe toward those who fell, but good toward you - if you continue to trust in God's goodness. Otherwise, you also will be cut off. [23]And if Israel does not continue in unbelief, they also will be grafted in, for God is able to graft them in again. [24]If you were cut out of the olive tree which is wild by nature and grafted into a good olive tree, how much easier will these natural branches be grafted onto their own olive tree?

[25]Believers, lest you be conceited, I do not want you to be unaware of this mystery: A hardening has happened to part of Israel until the full number of Gentiles come in. [26]Then all Israel will be saved. As it is written, "The Redeemer will come out of Zion and turn ungodliness away from Jacob. [27]This is what I promised to do for them when I take away their sins." [28]In regard to the good news, they are enemies on account of you. But as the chosen people, they are beloved for the sake of their ancestors. [29]The gifts and call of God are irrevocable. [30]Just as you who once did not believe God have now received compassion through Israel's unbelief, [31]so also Israel who does not believe will receive compassion just as you received compassion. [32]For God has confined all in unbelief in order to have compassion upon all. [33]O the depth of the riches, wisdom and knowledge of God! How unsearchable are God's judgments; God's ways are past finding out! [34]Who has known the mind of God? Who has been God's counselor? [35]Who has given anything to God, that God should repay them? [36]From God and through God and to God are all things. To God be the glory forever!

PRESENT YOURSELVES HUMBLY TO GOD FOR SERVICE

$^{12:1}$I beseech you therefore, believers, because of the compassion of God, to present your bodies as living sacrifices, holy and acceptable to God. This is the logical way for you to worship. ^{2}Do not be conformed to this world, but be transformed by the renewing of your mind. Then you will be able to discern what God's good and agreeable and perfect will is. ^{3}I know how kind God has been to me. Therefore I say to all who are among you: do not think of yourselves more highly than you ought to, but think modestly according to the measure of faith that God has given each of you. ^{4}Just as we have many parts in our one body, and all parts do not have the same function, ^{5}so we are all one body in Christ and all part of one another. ^{6}We have different gifts to use in response to the grace that is offered to us. If our gift is prophecy, we should prophesy in proportion to our faith. ^{7}If it is serving, we should serve. If it is teaching, we should teach. ^{8}If it is encouraging, we should encourage. If it is giving, we should do it generously. The one who rules should be diligent, and the one who shows compassion should do it cheerfully.

^{9}Love must be genuine. Detest what is evil. Cling to what is good. ^{10}Cherish one another with love. Respectfully honor one another. ^{11}Never lack diligence, but be aglow in the spirit, serving the Lord. ^{12}Rejoice in hope, persevere under pressure, continue to pray, ^{13}share in the needs of the saints, practice hospitality, ^{14}bless those who persecute you (bless and do not curse), ^{15}rejoice with those who rejoice, weep with those who weep, ^{16}live in harmony with one another, don't be haughty, associate with humble people, don't be conceited, ^{17}don't repay injury with injury, try to behave in a worthy manner ^{18}and do your best within your power to live at peace with everyone.

^{19}Dearly beloved, do not retaliate yourselves, but allow God to take revenge. For it is written, "Vengeance is Mine; I will repay, says Yahweh." ^{20}Therefore, "If your enemy is hungry, feed your enemy. If your enemy is thirsty, give your enemy a drink. By doing this you will heap coals of fire upon your enemy's head." ^{21}Do not be overcome by evil, but overcome evil with good.

SUBMIT TO AUTHORITY

$^{13:1}$All must submit themselves to the governing authorities. There is no authority but from God, and the authorities that are there have been assigned their places by God. ^{2}Therefore anyone who opposes the authorities is standing against the arrangement of God, and those who do so will be punished. ^{3}Government is not a terror to those who do good, but to those who do evil. If you don't want to be afraid of the authorities, do what is good and they will praise you, ^{4}for they are the servants of God for your good. But if you do what is wrong, be afraid, for they do not carry the sword for nothing. For they are the servants of God and the avengers of wrath upon the evildoer. ^{5}Therefore you need to be obedient, not only to avoid wrath, but also for the sake of conscience. ^{6}That is the reason you pay taxes. For they are God's servants, continually attending to your needs. ^{7}Therefore render to all their due: taxes to whom taxes, tolls to whom tolls, respect to whom respect, honor to whom honor.

^{8}Owe nothing to anyone except what you owe in love to one another. If you love others, you have fulfilled the law. [9]For the commandments, "You shall not commit adultery," "You shall not kill," "You shall not steal," "You shall not covet" and any other commandment are summed up in the commandment, "You shall love others as yourself." [10]Love does no wrong to others, therefore love is the fulfillment of the law. [11]Knowing the times we live in, we know that it is time to wake from sleep, for our salvation is now nearer than when we first believed. [12]The night is nearly spent; the day is fast approaching. Therefore let us put away the deeds of darkness and put on the armor of light. [13]Let us conduct ourselves with dignity as in the day, not in revelry and drunkenness, not in promiscuity and shameless conduct, not in quarreling and envy. [14]Instead, clothe yourselves with our Sovereign Jesus Christ and make no provision for the lusts of the flesh.

BE CONSIDERATE OF OTHER PEOPLE'S OPINIONS

[14:1]Welcome those who are weak in the faith. Do not offer your opinion of their opinions. [2]For some have faith to eat everything, while others who are weak in faith eat vegetables. [3]Those who eat everything must not despise those who do not; and those who do not eat everything must not judge those who do. God has accepted them also. [4]Who are you to judge someone else's servants? Before God they stand or fall. And they will stand, for God is able to make them stand. [5]Some people esteem one day as special, others esteem every day the same. Let all be fully persuaded in their own minds. [6]Those who consider certain days important do it to honor God. Those who eat everything eat to honor God and give thanks to God. Those who do not eat everything also do it to honor and give thanks to God. [7]None of us live or die for ourselves. [8]If we live, we live for God; and if we die, we die for God. Whether we live or die, we are Christ's. [9]Christ died and returned to life in order to be Sovereign over both the dead and the living. [10]So why do you judge others? And why do you despise some? We will all stand before the judgment seat of God. [11]For it is written, "As I live, says Yahweh, every knee shall bend to Me and every tongue shall acknowledge God." [12]So then, each of us must give an account of ourselves to God.

CHRISTIAN CONDUCT

[13]Therefore let us not judge one another anymore. Rather, make up your mind not to do anything that will cause another believer to sin. [14]I know and am persuaded in Christ Jesus that no food is unclean in itself. But to the one who thinks anything is unclean, to that person it is unclean. [15]If another person is grieved by what you eat, you are not behaving with love. Do not by your eating destroy someone for whom Christ died. [16]Do not let your right to eat be spoken of as evil. [17]For God's realm is not food and drink, but righteousness, peace and joy in the Holy Spirit. [18]The one who serves Christ in these things is pleasing to God and approved by humans. [19]Therefore let us pursue the things that make for peace and build one another up. [20]Do not destroy the work of God over food. All of it is indeed clean, but it is wrong to eat anything that causes someone to sin. [21]Neither eating meat nor drinking wine is good if it causes someone to stumble. [22]Keep your convictions between yourself and God. Blessed are those who do not feel condemned when doing what they approve. [23]Those who doubt are condemned by eating when they do not eat with faith. For

whatever is not done in faith is sin.

$^{15:1}$We who are strong ought to bear with the weaknesses of the weak. Instead of pleasing ourselves, ^{2}let us please others for their good and build them up. ^{3}Christ certainly did not live selfishly. As it is written, "The insults of those who insult You have fallen upon Me." ^{4}All those things that were written in the past were written for our instruction, so that through patience and the encouragement of the Scriptures we might have hope. ^{5}Now may the God who gives endurance and encouragement grant that you live at peace with one another as you follow Christ Jesus, ^{6}so that with one mind and one mouth you may glorify the God and heavenly Parent of our Sovereign Jesus Christ.

^{7}Therefore welcome one another, even as Christ welcomed you, to the glory of God. ^{8}For I tell you that Christ became a servant of the circumcised for the sake of God's truth in order to confirm the promises to the ancestors ^{9}so that the Gentiles might glorify God because of God's compassion. As it is written, "For this cause I acknowledge You among the Gentiles and sing to Your name." ^{10}And again it says, "Rejoice, O Gentiles, with God's people." ^{11}And again, "Praise God, all you Gentiles; praise God, all you people." ^{12}Isaiah says, "A root of Jesse will be raised up to reign over the nations. The Gentiles will have hope because of that One." ^{13}Now may the God of hope fill you with joy and peace in your faith so that you abound in hope through the Holy Spirit.

PAUL, THE PUBLIC SERVANT OF THE GENTILES

^{14}Believers, I am persuaded that you are full of goodness, filled with all knowledge and able to instruct one another. ^{15}Nevertheless, believers, I have written to you more boldly on some points as a way of reminding you. Because of the kindness of God, ^{16}I am a public servant to the Gentiles. I serve the gospel of God as a priest, so that the Gentiles may be an acceptable offering, sanctified by the Holy Spirit. ^{17}I have reason to boast through Christ Jesus regarding my service to God. ^{18}I will not dare to speak of anything except what Christ has done through me in making the Gentiles obedient by word and deed ^{19}through mighty signs and wonders by the power of the Spirit of God. From Jerusalem around to Illyricum I have made replete the gospel of Christ. ^{20}In fact, it has been my desire to preach the gospel where Christ was not known, lest I build upon another's foundation. ^{21}But as it is written, "Those who were never told about Christ will see, and those who have never heard will ponder." ^{22}For this reason I have often been impeded from coming to you. ^{23}But now, having no more work in these parts, and since for many years I have had a great desire to see you, ^{24}when I journey to Spain I will come to you to be helped on my way there, after I have had the satisfaction of being with you for a while. ^{25}But now I go to Jerusalem to minister to the saints, ^{26}for it pleased Macedonia and Achaia to make a contribution to the poor among the saints at Jerusalem. ^{27}It pleased the Gentile Christians to do it, though they do have an obligation to the Jewish Christians. For if the Gentiles were made partakers of the spiritual blessings of the Jewish Christians, their duty is to minister to those Jews in material blessings. ^{28}Therefore when I have finished this task and have delivered this money to them, I will visit you on the way to Spain. ^{29}I am sure that when I come to you, I will come in the fullness of the blessing of Christ. [30]Now I beseech you, believers, through our Sovereign Jesus Christ and through the love of the Spirit, to strive together with me by praying to God for me [31]so that I may be kept safe from the unbelievers in Judea and so that my errand to Jerusalem may be accepted by the saints. [32]Then God will let me come to you and be joyfully refreshed. [33]Now may the God of peace be with you all. Amen.

GREETINGS TO THE SAINTS

[16:1]I commend to you our sister Phoebe, who is a minister of the church at Cenchrea. [2]Welcome her in a way that is appropriate for saints and give her any assistance she may need from you. She has been an encourager to many people, and myself too. [3]Greet Priscilla and Aquila, my helpers in Christ Jesus. [4]They risked their lives for my life. Not only I, but also all the churches of the Gentiles give them thanks. [5]Greet also the church that is in their home. Greet my dear Epaenetus, who is the first convert to Christ in Asia. [6]Greet Mary, who worked very hard for you. [7]Greet Andronicus and Junias, my kin and fellow prisoners. They are eminent among the apostles and were followers of Christ before me. [8]Greet Ampliatus, my dear friend, whose faith is in God. [9]Greet Urbanus, our helper in Christ, and my beloved Stachys. [10]Greet Apelles, approved in Christ. Greet those from the household of Aristobulus. [11]Greet Herodion, my kin. Greet those from the household of Narcissus, who are believers. [12]Greet Tryphaena and Tryphosa, who work hard for Christ. Greet beloved Persis, who also works hard for Christ. [13]Greet Rufus, chosen by Christ. Greet his mother, who has been a mother to me also. [14]Greet Asyncritus, Phlegon, Hermes, Patrobas, Hermas and the believers with them. [15]Greet Philologus and Julia, Nereus and his sister, and Olympas and all the saints with them. [16]Greet one another with a holy kiss. All the churches of Christ greet you.

[17]Now I beseech you, believers, to watch out for those who cause divisions and snares contrary to the teaching you have learned; avoid them. [18]For those who are like that do not serve our Sovereign Jesus Christ, but only themselves. By fine words and flattering speeches they deceive the minds of the simple. [19]Your loyalty to the gospel has become known to everyone; therefore I am glad on your behalf. Yet I desire you to be wise concerning good and innocent concerning evil. [20]The God of peace will bruise Satan under your feet shortly. The grace of our Sovereign Jesus Christ be with you.

[21]My fellow worker Timothy greets you, as do Lucius, Jason and Sosipater, my kin. [22]I, Tertius, who wrote this letter, greet you in Christ's name. [23]My host Gaius and the whole church greet you. The city treasurer Erastus and our brother Quartus greet you. [24]The grace of our Sovereign Jesus Christ be with you all. Amen.

[25]Now to the One who is able to establish you according to my gospel and the preaching of Jesus Christ according to the revelation of the mystery that was silent for ages [26]but now revealed by the prophetic Scriptures of the Eternal God and made known to all nations through the obedience of faith, [27]to the only wise God be glory through Jesus Christ forever! Amen.

First Corinthians

GREETINGS

1:1Paul, called to be an apostle of Jesus Christ by the will of God, and Sosthenes our brother, 2to the church of God at Corinth, to those set apart for God by Christ Jesus and called to be saints, including those in every place who call on the name of Jesus Christ: 3Goodwill and peace to you from God our heavenly Parent and from our Sovereign Jesus Christ.

4I always thank my God for you because of the grace of God which is given to you in Christ Jesus, 5for in everything you say and comprehend you are enriched by Christ. 6Everything that you heard about Christ became part of your lives, 7and you do not lack any spiritual gift as you wait for Christ to appear. 8Christ will be part of your lives until the return, so that you will be blameless on the day of Christ. 9God can be trusted, the One who called you into fellowship with God's Child, Jesus Christ our Sovereign.

DISAGREEMENTS AMONG BELIEVERS

10I appeal to you, believers, in the name of Jesus Christ, that you all speak agreeably and that there be no divisions among you. Be perfectly united and of the same mind and judgment. 11I have been told by some in Chloe's family that there are arguments among you. 12What I mean is this: Each of you says, "I am with Paul," or "I am with Apollos," or "I am with Peter," or "I am with Christ." 13Is Christ divided? Was Paul crucified for you? Were you baptized in the name of Paul? 14I am thankful that I baptized none of you except Crispus and Gaius, 15lest anyone say that I baptized in my name. 16I did baptize the family of Stephanas, but I do not remember whether I baptized anyone else. 17Christ did not send me to baptize, but to announce the good news - and not with proverbial wisdom, lest the cross of Christ be meaningless.

WORLDLY WISDOM IS NOT THE WAY TO GOD

18The message of the cross is foolishness to those who are perishing, but to those of us who are being saved it is the power of God. 19For it is written, "I will destroy the wisdom of the wise and bring to nothing the cleverness of the clever." 20Where are the wise? Where are the scholars? Where are this world's philosophers? Has not God made the wisdom of this world foolishness? 21The world through its wisdom did not know God, but it pleased the all-wise God to save those who would believe through the "foolishness" of preaching. 22The Jews require a sign and Greeks seek wisdom, 23but we preach Christ crucified, a stumbling block to Jews and foolishness to

Greeks. [24]But to those who are called, both Jews and Greeks, Christ is the power of God and the wisdom of God. [25]For the foolishness of God is wiser than human wisdom, and the weakness of God is stronger than human strength.

[26]Believers! Consider who you were when you were called! Not many of you were wise according to the world, not many influential, not many from noble families. [27]But God chose what the world considers foolish to confound the wise; God chose what the world considers weak to confound the mighty; [28]God chose the common and the despised and those who are nothing to bring to nothing those who are of the world [29]so that no one could boast in God's presence. [30]Because of God, you are united with Christ Jesus; and Christ makes us wise, righteous, holy and redeemed in God. [31]Therefore, as it is written, "Let those who boast, boast in Christ."

[2:1]Believers, I did not come to you declaring the testimony of God with excellent words of wisdom, [2]for I determined to speak only about Jesus Christ and His death on the cross. [3]I was with you in weakness and fear and much trembling. [4]My speech and my preaching were not with enticing words of human wisdom, but were a demonstration of Spirit and power, [5]so that your faith would not stand on human wisdom, but on God's power. [6]Yet we do speak wisdom among those who are spiritually mature, although not the wisdom of this world or of the rulers of this world (who are becoming powerless). [7]We speak the hidden, secret wisdom of God, which God ordained before the world for our glory, [8]and which none of the rulers of this world understood. If they had understood, they would not have crucified the glorious Son. [9]But as it is written, "Eye has not seen, nor ear heard, nor has anyone even imagined what God has prepared for those who love God." [10]But God reveals it to us by the Spirit.

The Spirit searches everything, even the deep things of God. [11]Who knows the thoughts of a person except the spirit inside that person? In the same way, no one knows the thoughts of God except the Spirit of God. [12]Now we have not received the spirit of the world, but the Spirit who is from God, so that we may understand what God has given us. [13]This is what we speak, not in words that human wisdom teaches, but what the Holy Spirit teaches, comparing spiritual things with spiritual. [14]The unspiritual do not receive the things from the Spirit of God, for these things are foolishness to them. Nor can the unspiritual know these things that are spiritually discerned. [15]Those who are spiritual question everything, but they themselves are questioned by no one. [16]"For who has known the mind of the Almighty, that one might instruct God?" But we have the mind of Christ.

THE WAY TO WISDOM

[3:1]Believers, I cannot speak to you as spiritual but as worldly, even as babes in Christ. [2]I have fed you with milk, not solid food. You were not ready, nor are you now ready. [3]You are still worldly. Where there is envy, strife and division among you, are you not worldly and walking as humans? [4]While one says, "I am with Paul," and another, "I am with Apollos," are you not worldly? [5]Who is Paul? Who is Apollos? They are servants by whom you believed, even as God gave to each. [6]I planted, Apollos watered, but God caused the growth. [7]So neither the one who plants nor the one who waters is anything; it is God who causes the growth. [8]The one who plants and the one who waters are equally important. Each will receive a reward according to their effort. [9]Apollos and I are laborers together for God. You are God's field and God's building. [10]According to the grace of God that has been given to me as an experienced builder, I laid the foundation and another is building upon it. But you must be careful how you build. [11]For no one can lay any other foundation than that which is already laid, which is Jesus Christ. [12]If you build upon this foundation with gold, silver, precious stones, wood, hay or straw, [13]your work will be apparent. On the day of Christ your work will be tested by fire and your work will be revealed for what it is. [14]If the work that you built on the foundation remains, you will receive a reward. [15]If your work is burned, you will suffer loss; but you yourselves will be saved, yet only as through the fire. [16]Don't you know that you are the temple of God and that the Spirit of God lives in you? [17]If anyone defiles the temple of God, God will destroy that person. For the temple of God is holy, and you are that temple.

[18]Do not deceive yourselves. If any of you think you are wise in this world, you should become a fool so that you may become truly wise. [19]For the wisdom of this world is foolishness with God. As it is written, "God catches the wise in their craftiness," [20]and again, "God knows that the thoughts of the wise are vain." [21]So do not boast about what mere humans have done. For all things are yours, [22]whether Paul or Apollos or Peter or the world or life or death or the present or the future, all are yours. [23]And you are Christ's; and Christ is God's.

BE CAREFUL WHAT YOU SAY

[4:1]You should think of us as servants of Christ who have been trusted with the mysteries of God. [2]God requires servants to be worthy of that trust. [3]In this regard it matters little to me whether I am judged by you or by a human court. I do not even judge myself. [4]I do not know of any wrong I have done, but that does not make me innocent, for the One who judges me is God. [5]Therefore judge nothing before the time; wait until Christ comes. Christ will bring the hidden things of darkness into the light and reveal the secrets of human hearts. Then each person will receive praise from God. [6]And now, believers, I have applied all this to myself and Apollos so that you may learn through us not to go beyond what is written. None of you should become puffed up or consider one teacher more important than another. [7]What makes you different? What do you have that was not given to you? If it was given to you as a gift, why do you boast? [8]Now you have everything! Now you are rich! You reign as royalty without us. I wish that you truly reigned, so that we could reign with you.

[9]It seems that God has put us apostles at the end of the line, like those condemned to die in the arena. We are made a spectacle before the world, before angels as well as humans. [10]We are fools for Christ, but you are wise in Christ. We are weak, but you are strong. We are despised, but you are honored. [11]To this present hour we are hungry, thirsty, poorly clad, beaten and homeless. [12]We work hard with our hands. When we are reviled, we bless. When we are persecuted, we endure. [13]When we are

slandered, we pray. We are treated like the filth of the world and the scum of the earth to this day.

[14]My beloved children in Christ, I am not writing this to shame you, but to warn you. [15]Though you have ten thousand to instruct you about Christ, remember that you have only me as your parent. For in Christ Jesus I became your spiritual parent through the gospel. [16]Therefore I urge you to imitate me. [17]That is the reason I sent you Timothy. He is my beloved and faithful son in Christ. He will help you remember my ways in Christ that I teach everywhere in every congregation. [18]Now some of you are puffed up, as though I were not coming to you. [19]But I will come to you shortly, if God wills, and then I will know if these puffed up ones just talk, or if they have power. [20]For God's realm is not only words, it is power. [21]What will you have? Should I come to you with a rod, or with love and a spirit of gentleness?

STAY AWAY FROM BELIEVERS WHO SIN

[5:1]It is actually reported that there is sexual sin among you, and of a kind that is unheard of even among the Gentiles: a man is living with his father's wife. [2]And you are puffed up! Rather, you ought to mourn. The one who did this deed should no longer be allowed among you. [3]For I, though absent in body, am present in spirit and have already judged the one who has done this. [4]When you are gathered together in the name of Jesus Christ and I am there in spirit and the power of our Sovereign Jesus is present, [5]hand this man over to Satan for the destruction of the flesh so that his spirit may be saved on the day Christ returns.

[6]Your boasting is not good. Don't you know that a little yeast will ferment the whole batch of dough? [7]Therefore purge out the old yeast so that you may be like fresh bread made without yeast, as you really are. For Christ, our Passover lamb, has been sacrificed. [8]Therefore let us keep the Feast, not with the old bread made of malice and wickedness, but with the new bread made of purity and truth.

[9]I wrote to you in my letter not to keep company with those who live in sexual sin. [10]I did not mean to include all the worldly sinners who are covetous or greedy or who worship idols, for then you would have to leave the world. [11]But I am now writing to tell you that you must not keep company with people who consider themselves believers if they are immoral or greedy or idolaters or abusive or drunkards or thieves. Do not even eat with people like that. [12]What have I to do with judging those who are not part of the church? But should you not judge those who are in the church? [13]God judges those who are outsiders. Therefore drive that wicked person away from among you.

CHRISTIANS MUST NOT TAKE THEIR COMPLAINTS TO UNBELIEVERS

[6:1]Dare any of you who have a complaint against another take it to court before the ungodly and not before the saints? [2]Don't you know that the saints will judge the world? And if the world is to be judged by you, are you unfit to judge the smallest complaint? [3]Don't you know that you will judge the angels? How much more what pertains to this life! [4]If you have disagreements pertaining to things of this life, have them judged by those who are least esteemed in the congregation. [5]I say this to shame you. Is it true that there is no one wise enough among you able to settle a disagreement between believers? [6]But believers go to court against other believers! And their cases are tried before unbelievers! [7]You have utterly failed one another because you have legal disputes among yourselves. Wouldn't it be better to be wronged? Wouldn't it be better to be defrauded? [8]But you even wrong and defraud other believers!

FLEE FROM SIN

[9]Don't you know that the unrighteous will not inherit God's realm? Do not be deceived. No libertines or idolaters or adulterers or catamites or sodomites [10]or thieves or greedy persons or drunkards or abusers or extortioners will inherit God's realm. [11]And such were some of you. But you are washed, you are made holy, you are regarded as innocent in the name of our Sovereign Jesus Christ and by the Spirit of our God.

[12]All things are lawful for me, but all things are not advantageous. All things are lawful for me, but I will not be made a slave of anything. [13]Food is for the stomach and the stomach for food, but God will destroy them both. The body is not for sexual sin, but for God. God will provide for the needs of the body. [14]God raised up Jesus and will also raise us up with power. [15]Don't you know that your bodies are part of the body of Christ? Should I then take a part of the body of Christ and make it part of the body of a prostitute? Of course not. [16]Don't you know that the one who is united with a prostitute is one body with the prostitute? For Scripture says, "The two will be one flesh." [17]But the one who is united to Christ is one in spirit with Christ. [18]Flee from sexual sin. Every other sin that a human commits is outside the body, but those who commit sexual sins are committing sin against their own bodies. [19]Don't you know that your body is the temple of the Holy Spirit, who is in you, whom you have from God? You are not your own; [20]you were bought for a price. Therefore honor God with your body.

RELATIONSHIPS

[7:1]Now concerning the things you wrote about: Those who do not marry do well. [2]Nevertheless, because of sexual sins, every man should have his own wife and every woman should have her own husband. [3]The husband should render every kindness to his wife, and likewise the wife to her husband. [4]The wife does not have authority over her own body, but the husband does. Likewise the husband does not have authority over his own body, but the wife does. [5]Do not deprive one another except for a while by mutual consent while you take a holiday for prayer and worship. But come together again, lest Satan tempt you because of your lack of self-restraint. [6]I say this as a concession and not as a command.

[7]I wish that all were as I am, but everyone has a unique gift from God, one this and one that. [8]Therefore I say to the unmarried and the widows: It is good for you to remain as I am. [9]But if you cannot exercise self-restraint, then marry. It is better to marry than to burn. [10]And to the married I command (not I, but God): A wife must not leave her husband. [11]But if she does leave, she must remain unmarried or be

reconciled to her husband. A husband must not divorce his wife. [12]But to the rest I say (not God, but I): If a brother in Christ has a wife who is not a believer and she agrees to live with him, he must not divorce her. [13]And if a sister in Christ has a husband who is not a believer and he agrees to live with her, she must not divorce him. [14]For the unbelieving husband is made holy through his believing wife, and the unbelieving wife is made holy through her believing husband. If this were not true, your children would be unclean; but since this is true, they are holy. [15]If the unbeliever leaves, let the unbeliever leave. A brother or sister is not bound in such cases. God has called us to peace. [16]For how do you know, O wife, whether you will save your husband? And how do you know, O husband, whether you will save your wife?

[17]Everyone should continue to live as Christ called you to live. This is what I ordain in all the churches. [18]Were you already circumcised when you accepted God's call? Do not become uncircumcised. Were you uncircumcised when you were called? Do not be circumcised. [19]Circumcision is nothing and uncircumcision is nothing; but keeping the commandments of God, that is something. [20]Each of you should remain in the situation you were in when you were called. [21]Were you a slave when you were called? Do not worry about it. But if you can be made free, do it. [22]The one who is called to Christ and is a slave is free before Christ. Likewise, the one who is called and is free is Christ's slave. [23]You were bought for a price; do not become the slaves of humans. [24]Believers, each one of you should remain with God in the situation in which you were called.

[25]Now concerning the unmarried, I have no command from God. Yet I give my judgment as one who is faithful by the mercy of God. [26]I think that because of the present difficult times it is good for believers to remain as they are. [27]Are you married? Do not seek a divorce. Are you unmarried? Do not seek marriage. [28]But it is not a sin to marry. Nevertheless, those who marry will have troubles, and I would like to spare you that. [29]But this I say, believers: the time is short. Those remaining who have spouses should live as though they had none, [30]those who are sad should live as though they were not, those who are happy should live as though they were not, those who buy should live as though they owned nothing, [31]those who use worldly things should live as though they did not care for them. For the world as we know it is passing away. [32]But I do not want you to worry. The unmarried man cares for the things of God and how to please God. [33]But the married man cares for the things of the world and how to please his wife. [34]There is also a difference between a married and an unmarried woman. The unmarried woman cares about the things of God because she wants to be holy in both body and spirit. But the married woman cares for the things of the world because she wants to please her husband. [35]I am saying these things to be helpful to you, not to throw a noose around you. I would rather have you live appropriately and untiringly serve God without distraction. [36]But if a man thinks that he is behaving improperly toward an unmarried woman because she has passed the flower of youth and needs to marry, let him do what he must; it is no sin, let them marry. [37]Nevertheless, the man who is convinced in his mind and is able to bear the

strain, having power over his own will and making up his mind not to marry, does well. [38]So then, those who marry do well, but those who do not marry do better.

[39]A wife is bound by the law as long as her husband lives. But if her husband dies, she is at liberty to marry anyone who is a believer. [40]But my opinion is that she will be happier if she remains unmarried - and I think I have the Spirit of God.

BE DISCRIMINATING

[8:1]Now regarding food offered to idols. We know that we all have knowledge. Knowledge puffs up, but love builds up. [2]If you think that you know anything, you do not yet know what you ought to know. [3]But if you love God, you are known by God. [4]Therefore regarding the eating of food offered to idols: we know that an idol is nothing in the world and that there is no God but one. [5]For though there are those that are called gods, whether in the sky or on earth (as indeed there are many gods and many authorities), [6]yet for us there is but one God, the Source, from whom everything comes and for whom we live; and one Creator, Jesus Christ, through whom everything comes and through whom we live. [7]Nevertheless, not everyone has this knowledge. Some are so used to idols that to this day when they eat they think of the food as having been offered to an idol. Their conscience is bothered because it is weak. [8]Food does not affect our relationship with God, for we are neither better if we eat nor worse if we do not eat. [9]But be careful that your freedom does not become a stumbling block to those who are weak. [10]For if one who is weak sees you who have knowledge eating in an idol's temple, will not that person's conscience be encouraged to eat what is offered to idols? [11]Through your knowledge, the weak believer for whom Christ died will perish! [12]When you sin this way against other believers and wound their consciences, you sin against Christ. [13]Therefore, if what I eat offends another believer, I will never eat that food again, lest I cause another believer to stumble.

THE RIGHTS OF AN APOSTLE

[9:1]Am I not an apostle? Am I not free? Have I not seen Jesus? Are not you my work in Christ? [2]Even if I am not an apostle to others, at least I am to you. You are the seal of my apostleship in Christ. [3]My answer to those who examine me is this: [4]Don't we have the right to eat and drink? [5]Don't we have the right to take a believing wife with us, as do the brothers of Jesus, and Peter and the other apostles? [6]Is it only Barnabas and I who do not have the right to quit working?

[7]Who is ever drafted into war and provides their own rations? Who plants a vineyard and does not eat some of the grapes? Who tends the cows and does not drink some of the milk? [8]Am I using mere human logic? Does not the law say the same thing? [9]For it is written in the law of Moses, "You shall not muzzle the ox that treads out the grain." Is it oxen that God is concerned about? [10]No, God said this for our sake. No doubt it was written for our sake, because when the plower plows and the thresher threshes, they hope for a share in the harvest. [11]If we have sown spiritual seeds among you, is it asking too much if we reap a temporal harvest? [12]If others have this right among you, should we not even more? Nevertheless, we have not used this right. Instead we endure everything in silence, lest we hinder the good news of Christ.

[13]Don't you know that those who serve in the temple get their food from the temple, and those who attend the altar get a share of what is offered on the altar? [14]In the same way, God commanded that those who preach the gospel should receive their living from the gospel. [15]But I have used none of these rights, nor do I write this to claim these rights. It would be better for me to die than to be unable to boast about this. [16]But when I preach the gospel, I cannot boast. I am compelled to preach the gospel, and woe to me if I don't! [17]If I were preaching willingly, I could claim a reward, but if I preach against my will, then I am only fulfilling the responsibility that is put upon me.

[18]What is my reward then? Just that when I preach the gospel, I offer the gospel without charge, and thus do not misuse my rights from the gospel. [19]For though I am not a slave to anyone, I have made myself a servant to all in order to win more people to Christ. [20]To the Jews I became like a Jew in order to win the Jews. To those who are under the law of Moses I became like one under the law in order to win those who are under the law. [21]To those without the law I became like one without the law (not without the law of God, for I am under the law of Christ) in order to win those without the law. [22]To the weak I became like the weak in order to win the weak. I have become all things to all people in order to save some by any possible means. [23]This I do for the gospel in order to share it with you.

[24]Don't you know that in a race everyone runs, but only one runner wins the prize? So run in order to win! [25]Anyone who endeavors to accomplish something exercises self-control. In this world they obtain a crown that lasts only a short time, but we will win one that lasts forever. [26]Therefore I do not run aimlessly or compete like one beating the air. [27]I keep my body under control, lest somehow, after I have preached to others, I am disqualified.

ADMONITIONS

[10:1]Believers, I do not want you to be ignorant. All our ancestors were under the cloud, all passed through the sea, [2]all were baptized into Moses in the cloud and in the sea, [3]all ate the same spiritual food [4]and all drank the same spiritual drink; for they drank from that spiritual Rock that followed them, and that Rock was Christ. [5]But God was not pleased with most of them, and they were slain in the wilderness. [6]These things were our examples so that we would not long for what is worthless as they longed for it. [7]Do not worship the things of this world as some of them did. As it is written, "The people sat down to eat and drink and rose up to play." [8]Do not commit sexual sins as some of them did. In one day twenty-three thousand died. [9]Do not test God as some of them did. They were destroyed by serpents. [10]Do not grumble as some of them did. They were destroyed by the destroyer. [11]All these things happened to them as examples and are written for our admonition, for we live in the last days. [12]Therefore, if you think you are upright, be careful lest you fall.

[13]No temptation has come upon you that is not common to humans. God is faithful and will not allow you to be tempted beyond what you can bear. When you are tempted, God will make a way to escape so that you are able to bear it. [14]Therefore,

dearly beloved, flee from the things of the world. [15]I speak as to the wise, so judge what I say.

[16]The cup of blessing we bless, is it not participation in the blood of Christ? The bread we break, is it not participation in the body of Christ? [17]Because there is one loaf, we are all one body; for we are all partakers of that one loaf. [18]Look at the people of Israel. Don't those who eat the sacrifices partake from the altar? [19]What am I saying then? That an idol is anything, or that what is offered in sacrifice to idols is anything? [20]No, but the Gentiles sacrifice to demons, not to God. I do not want you to associate with demons. [21]You cannot drink the cup of Christ and the cup of demons. You cannot partake from Christ's table and from the table of demons. [22]Are we trying to provoke God to jealousy? Are we stronger than God?

[23]Some of you say, "Everything is lawful." But not everything is beneficial. Everything is lawful, but not everything edifies. [24]You should not seek your own good, but rather the good of others. [25]Eat whatever is sold in the meat market, asking nothing of your conscience. [26]For "The earth is God's, and the fullness thereof." [27]If an unbeliever invites you to a meal and you are inclined to go, eat whatever is set before you and ask nothing of your conscience. [28]But if anyone says to you, "This was offered to idols," do not eat it out of consideration of the one who told you and because of conscience [29](not your own conscience, but the other person's). Why should my freedom be based upon someone else's conscience? [30]If I am grateful for the food, why am I criticized for eating what I thank God for? [31]Whatever you eat or drink or whatever you do, do it all to the glory of God. [32]Give no offense to the Jews, to the Greeks or to the church of God, [33]even as I try to please everyone in everything. I do not seek my own blessing, but that of many, so that they may be saved.

[11:1]Follow me, even as I follow Christ. [2]I praise you for always remembering me and holding to the teachings as I gave them to you. [3]I want you to know that husbands are essential to Christ, wives are essential to their husbands and Christ is essential to God.

PAUL'S GUIDELINES FOR WORSHIP

[4]Every husband who prays or prophesies with his head covered dishonors his head. [5]And every woman who prays or prophesies with her head uncovered dishonors her head, for it is the same as if her head were shaved. [6]If a woman does not cover her head, she should have her hair cut off. But if it is unbecoming for a woman to have her hair cut off or shaved, then she should cover her head. [7]A man should not cover his head, for he is the image and reflection of God. But woman is the reflection of man. [8]For man was not made from woman, but woman from man; [9]nor was man created for woman, but woman was created for man. [10]A woman should have a symbol of authority on her head for this reason and because of the angels. [11]Nevertheless, as created beings, woman is essential to man and man is essential to woman. [12]For woman came from man and man comes from woman. But all come from God. [13]Judge for yourselves; is it appropriate for a woman to pray to God with her head

uncovered? [14]And does not nature teach you that if a man has long hair it is unnatural? [15]But if a woman has long hair, it is glorious, for her hair is given to her for a covering. [16]If anyone wants to quarrel about this, I can only say that neither we nor the churches of God have any other custom.

[17]In the following instructions I do not praise you, for your meetings result in harm and not in good. [18]First of all, I hear that when you meet together there are divisions in the congregation, and I partly believe it. [19]Of course there must be differences among you to show which ones are approved! [20]When you come and meet together, it is not the communion supper you eat, [21]for each of you eats before the others have an opportunity. And while one is still hungry, another has had too much to drink! [22]What is this? Don't you have homes to eat and drink in? Or do you despise the church of God and belittle those who have nothing? What shall I say to you? Shall I praise you for this? No, I do not praise you. [23]For I have received from God that which I entrusted to you: On the night when Jesus was betrayed He took bread; [24]and when He had given thanks, He broke it and said, "Take and eat; this is My body which is broken for you. Do this in remembrance of Me." [25]In the same way, after supper He took the cup and said, "This cup is the new covenant in My blood. Do this, as often as you drink it, in remembrance of Me." [26]For as often as you eat this bread and drink this cup you make known Christ's death until Christ returns.

[27]Therefore, whoever eats the bread or drinks the cup in an unworthy way sins against the body and blood of Christ. [28]Everyone must examine themselves before eating the bread and drinking the cup. [29]If you eat and drink without fear, you eat and drink judgment upon yourself for not discerning the body of Christ. [30]For this reason many are weak and sickly among you and many have died. [31]If we judged ourselves, we would not be judged. [32]When we are judged, we are chastened by God so that we will not be condemned along with the world. [33]Therefore, believers, when you come together to eat, be courteous to one another. [34]If you are hungry, you should eat at home, lest you come together and be judged. The rest I will set in order when I come.

SPIRITUAL GIFTS

[12:1]Now concerning spiritual gifts, believers, I do not want you to be ignorant. [2]You know that when you were unbelievers you went astray and relied upon dumb idols. [3]Therefore I want you to understand that no one speaking by the Spirit of God says, "Jesus be cursed." And no one can say, "Jesus is God," except by the Holy Spirit.

[4]Now there are a variety of gifts, but they are all from the same Spirit. [5]And there are a variety of ways to serve, but they are all from the same God. [6]And there are a variety of works, but it is the same God who works all in all. [7]A manifestation of the Spirit is given to each person for the good of all. [8]To one the word of wisdom is given by the Spirit, to another the word of knowledge by the same Spirit, [9]to another faith by the same Spirit, to another gifts of healing by the same Spirit, [10]to another the working of miracles, to another prophecy, to another discerning of spirits, to another different kinds of tongues, to another the interpretation of tongues. [11]All these are the work of one and the same Spirit, who gives them to each individual as the Spirit wishes.

[12]As the body is one and has many parts, and all the parts of that body, though many, are one body, so it is with Christ. [13]By one Spirit we were all baptized into one body - whether Jew or Gentile, slave or free - and have all been given the one Spirit to drink. [14]For the body is not one part, but many. [15]If the foot should say, "Because I am not a hand, I do not belong to the body," does it then not belong to the body? [16]If the ear should say, "Because I am not an eye, I do not belong to the body," does it then not belong to the body? [17]If the whole body were an eye, how could it hear? If the whole body were an ear, how could it smell anything? [18]But God has arranged the parts of the body in the way that God wanted them to be. [19]If they were all one part, where would the body be? [20]As it is, there are many parts, but one body. [21]The eye cannot say to the hand, "I have no need of you," nor can the head say to the feet, "I have no need of you." [22]On the contrary, those parts of the body that seem to be weak are absolutely necessary; [23]and those parts of the body that we think are less dignified we treat with greater dignity. Our unattractive parts have a utility [24]that our attractive parts don't need. But God has put the body together and given the highest dignity to the parts that lacked [25]so that there would be no division in the body and so that the parts would have equal regard for one another. [26]When one part suffers, all the parts suffer with it. If one part is honored, all the parts rejoice with it.

[27]You are the body of Christ and the parts that share in it. [28]God has set in the church first apostles, second prophets, third teachers, after that miracle-workers, healers, helpers, administrators and tongues-speakers. [29]Are all apostles? Are all prophets? Are all teachers? Do all work miracles? [30]Do all have the gift of healing? Do all speak in tongues? Do all interpret? [31]But earnestly desire the best gifts. And now I will show you a more excellent way.

LOVE

[13:1]Though I speak with the tongues of humans and of angels, but have not love, I am only blaring brass or a clanging cymbal. [2]And though I have the gift of prophecy and understand all mysteries and all knowledge, and though I have enough faith to move mountains, but do not have love, I am nothing. [3]Though I give all my goods to feed the poor, and though I give my body to be burned, but do not have love, it profits me nothing. [4]Love suffers long and is kind. Love does not envy, love does not brag, love is not puffed up. [5]Love is courteous, does not insist on its own way, is not irritable, makes no list of wrongs, [6]is not happy with wickedness, sympathizes with the truth, [7]bears all things, believes all things, hopes all things, endures all things. [8]Love never fails. But where there are prophecies, they will fail. Where there are tongues, they will cease. Where there is knowledge, it will pass away. [9]For we know only a portion and we prophesy only a part. [10]But when that which is perfect comes, that which is partial will pass away. [11]When I was a child, I spoke like a child, I understood like a child, I thought like a child. But when I became an adult, I put away childish things. [12]Now we see through a glass darkly, but when that which is perfect comes, we will see face to face. Now I know in part, but then I will know completely, as completely as God knows me. [13]What then remains? Faith, hope and love, these three. But the greatest of these is love.

THE IMPORTANCE OF SPIRITUAL GIFTS

14:1Pursue love and desire spiritual gifts, especially the gift of prophecy. 2Those who speak in a tongue do not speak to humans, but to God, for no one understands them. They speak mysteries through the Spirit. 3But those who prophesy speak to humans to edify, build up and encourage. 4Those who speak in a tongue edify themselves, but those who prophesy edify the congregation. 5I wish that all of you spoke in tongues, but I would rather have you prophesy. For those who prophesy are greater than those who speak in tongues, unless they interpret, so that the church may be edified. 6Believers, if I come to you and speak in tongues, what benefit will I be to you unless I speak to you either by revelation or by knowledge or by prophesying or by teaching? 7Even lifeless instruments like the flute and harp make sounds, but unless they make distinct notes, how will anyone recognize the tune? 8And if the trumpet sounds an uncertain blast, who will prepare for battle? 9It is the same with you. Unless you utter with the tongue words that are easy to understand, how will people know what is said? You will just be speaking into the air. 10Without doubt there are many languages in the world, and none are without significance. 11But if I do not know the meaning of the language, I will be like a foreigner to the one who speaks, and that person will be a foreigner to me. 12It is the same with you. Since you are zealous for spiritual gifts, seek to excel in the gifts that build up the congregation. 13Therefore those who speak in a tongue should pray for the ability to interpret. 14For if I pray in a tongue, my spirit prays, but my mind is unfruitful. 15What then? I will pray with the Spirit, and I will pray with my mind also. I will sing with the Spirit, and I will sing with my mind also. 16When you bless with the Spirit, how will those in the room who are unlearned say "Amen" to your thanksgiving, since they do not understand what you are saying? 17Even though you give thanks well, the others will not be helped.

18I thank God that I speak in tongues more than all of you. 19Yet in the church I would rather speak five words with my mind that can be understood than ten thousand words in a tongue. 20Believers, stop thinking like children. Be infants in regard to evil, but in your thinking be mature. 21In the law it is written, "With other tongues and the lips of strangers I will speak to this people, yet even then they will not listen to Me, says Yahweh." 22Therefore tongues are a sign, not for those who believe, but for those who do not believe. And prophesying is not for those who do not believe, but for those who believe. 23If the whole congregation comes together and everyone is speaking in tongues and some who are unlearned or unbelievers come in, will they not say you are lunatics? 24But if all prophesy, and some who do not understand or who do not believe come in, they will be convicted by all and be judged by all. 25Thus the secrets of their hearts will become known, and, falling on their faces, they will worship God and report that God is truly among you.

26Well, believers, what then? When you come together, everyone has a psalm, a teaching, a revelation, a tongue or an interpretation. Let all things be done for edification. 27If anyone speaks in a tongue, two or three at the most should take their turn; and someone should interpret. 28If there is no interpreter, the one who speaks in tongues should keep silent in the church and speak inwardly to God. 29Two or three prophets may speak, and the others should listen carefully. [30]If someone sitting there receives a revelation, the one speaking should stop. [31]You may all prophesy, one at a time, so that all may learn and be encouraged. [32]The spirits of the prophets are subject to the prophets. [33]God does not delight in confusion, but in peace.

DECORUM

As in all the congregations of the saints, [34]women should be quiet in the churches. They are not permitted to make small talk, but must be responsive to the needs of others, as the law says. [35]If they are determined to learn about something, let them ask their husbands at home, for it is improper for women to chitchat in church. [36]What? Did the thoughts of God originate with you? Are you the only ones they came to? [37]If you think you are a prophet or spiritual, then acknowledge that the things I write to you are the commandments of God. [38]If some ignore this, let them be ignored. [39]Believers, zealously desire to prophesy and do not forbid speaking in tongues. [40]Let everything be done decently and in order.

THE GOOD NEWS ABOUT THE RESURRECTION

[15:1]Believers, I remind you of the good news that I preached to you, which you received and on which you stand. [2]You are saved by this good news if you continue believing what I preached to you. If not, then your faith was of no use. [3]For I gave you first of all what I was given: that Christ died for our sins in accordance with the Scriptures, [4]was buried, was raised the third day in accordance with the Scriptures [5]and was seen by Peter and then by the twelve. [6]After that Christ was seen by over five hundred believers at one time. Most of them are still alive, though some have died. [7]After that Christ was seen by James, and then by all the apostles. [8]And last of all Christ was seen by me, as if to a person born at the wrong time. [9]For I am the least of the apostles. I am not even fit to be called an apostle, because I persecuted the church of God. [10]But by the grace of God I am what I am. And God's grace was not wasted on me, for I worked harder than all the rest - yet not I, but the grace of God that was with me. [11]Therefore, whether I or they, this is what we preach and what you believed. [12]Now if it is proclaimed that Christ rose from the dead, how can some among you say that there is no resurrection of the dead? [13]If there is no resurrection of the dead, then Christ is not risen. [14]And if Christ is not risen, then our preaching is in vain and your faith is in vain. [15]Not only that, but we would be false witnesses of God, for we have testified that God raised Christ from the dead. If God did not raise Christ from the dead, then the dead are not raised.

[16]If the dead do not rise, then Christ has not been raised. [17]And if Christ has not been raised, your faith is meaningless and you are still in your sins. [18]Then those who died believing in Christ are also lost. [19]If it is only in this life that we have hope in Christ, then we are the most pitiful of humans. [20]But Christ has been raised from the dead and has become proof that those who sleep in death will also be raised.

[21]Since it was a human who initiated death, it is also a human who initiated the resurrection of the dead. [22]For as in Adam all die, even so in Christ will all be made alive. [23]But everyone in their proper order: Christ the firstfruits, and then, at Christ's

coming, those who belong to Christ. ^{24}Then will come the end, when Christ hands the realm over to Almighty God after overcoming every ruler, authority and power. ^{25}For Christ must reign until God has put every enemy under Christ's feet. ^{26}The last enemy to be destroyed will be death. ^{27}For "God has put all things under Christ's feet." But when God said, "all things are put under," it is clear that God is not included under Christ. ^{28}When all are subordinate to Christ, then Christ will also be subordinate to God, who made all obedient to Christ. Then God will be all in all.

^{29}What about those who are baptized on behalf of the dead? If the dead do not rise at all, why are they baptized on behalf of the dead? ^{30}And why do we face danger every hour? ^{31}As sure as I boast about you in Christ Jesus, I die every day. ^{32}If I fought wild beasts at Ephesus for mere human reasons, what was the advantage to me? If the dead do not rise, "Let us eat and drink, for tomorrow we die!" ^{33}Do not be deceived. "Bad friends are the ruin of good character." ^{34}Wake up to godliness and sin no more. There are some who do not have a knowledge of God. I say this to your shame.

^{35}Some ask, "How are the dead raised? What kind of body will they have?" ^{36}Froth! That which you sow does not come to life unless it dies. ^{37}And when you sow it, you do not sow the body that will be - you sow a seed such as wheat or some other grain. ^{38}God gives it the body that God is pleased with; each seed is given its own body. ^{39}All flesh is not the same. One is the flesh of humans, another of animals, another of fish and another of birds. ^{40}There are celestial bodies and terrestrial bodies. But the glory of the celestial is one, and that of the terrestrial is another. ^{41}There is one glory of the sun, another glory of the moon and another glory of the stars. And star differs from star in glory. ^{42}So also the resurrection of the dead. What is sown perishable will be raised imperishable. ^{43}What is sown in disgrace will be raised in glory. What is sown in weakness will be raised in power. ^{44}What is sown a natural body will be raised a spiritual body. As sure as there are natural bodies, there are spiritual bodies. ^{45}As it is written, "Adam, the first human, was made a living soul," but the last Adam was made a life-giving spirit. ^{46}The spiritual was not first. The natural was first, and after that came the spiritual. ^{47}The first Adam was from the dust of the earth. The second Adam was from heaven. ^{48}Those who are on the earth are like the one from the earth. Those who are in heaven are like the One from heaven. ^{49}And just as we have borne the likeness of the earthly one, so shall we bear the likeness of the heavenly One.

^{50}This I say, believers: Flesh and blood cannot inherit God's realm! The perishable does not inherit the imperishable. ^{51}Listen closely, I will tell you a mystery: we will not all sleep! But we will all be changed, ^{52}in a moment, in the twinkling of an eye, at the last trumpet. For the trumpet will sound, the dead will be raised imperishable and we will be changed. ^{53}The perishable will put on the imperishable, and the mortal will put on immortality. ^{54}When the perishable has put on the imperishable, and the mortal has put on immortality, then the saying that is written will be brought to pass: "Death is swallowed up in victory." ^{55}"O death, where is your sting? O grave, where is your victory?" [56]The sting of death is sin, and the strength of sin is the law. [57]But thanks be to God, who gives us the victory through Jesus Christ. [58]Therefore, my beloved friends, be steadfast and immovable, always excelling in God's work. For you know that the work you do for God is never wasted.

PAUL'S TRAVEL PLANS

[16:1]Now, concerning the collection for the saints: You must do what I told the churches of Galatia to do. [2]On the first day of every week each of you should set aside part of your income, as God prospers you, so that you will not need to take a collection when I come. [3]Then when I come, I will give a written recommendation to whomever you approve and send them with your love gift to Jerusalem. [4]If it seems worthwhile for me to go also, then we can travel together. [5]I am coming to you after I pass through Macedonia. [6]Perhaps I will stay with you, even for the winter, and then you can send me on to wherever I go. [7]I do not want to see you now only in passing, but I hope to stay a while with you, if God permits.

[8]I will remain at Ephesus until Pentecost, [9]for a great door has opened to me for effective ministry and there are many adversaries. [10]If Timothy comes, see that he has nothing to fear when he is with you; for he is doing God's work, as I am. [11]Let no one despise him, but send him on his way in peace so that he can come back to me. I will look for him with the other believers. [12]Now regarding Apollos, I greatly desired for him to come to you with the others, but he chose not to come at this time. Nevertheless, he will come when he has an opportunity.

FINAL GREETINGS AND REMINDERS

[13]Be alert! Stand firm in the faith. Be courageous and strong. [14]Do everything with love. [15]You know that the members of the household of Stephanas were the first converts in Greece and that they devoted themselves to the ministry of the saints. I urge you, believers, [16]to submit to these people and everyone else who helps and labors. [17]I am happy at the coming of Stephanas, Fortunatus and Achaicus, for they supplied what I missed by being away from you. [18]They have refreshed my spirit and yours, therefore they should be recognized. [19]The churches of Asia greet you. Aquila and Priscilla greet you heartily in Christ. [20]All the believers greet you. Greet one another with a holy kiss. [21]I, Paul, write this greeting with my own hand!

[22]May those who do not love God be separated from God forever! [23]May the grace of our Sovereign Jesus be with you! [24]My love be with you all in Christ Jesus. Amen.

Second Corinthians

GREETINGS

1:1From Paul, an apostle of Jesus Christ by the will of God, and brother Timothy, to the church of God at Corinth, and to all the saints in all of Greece: 2Goodwill and peace to you from God our heavenly Parent and from our Sovereign Jesus Christ.

3Bless the God and heavenly Parent of our Sovereign Jesus Christ, the God of compassion and every consolation 4who consoles us in all our troubles. We are able to console those who are in any trouble with the consolation we ourselves have received from God. 5Just as we share in the sufferings of Christ, so also we share in the consolation Christ gives. 6If we are afflicted, it is for your consolation and salvation. If we are encouraged, it is for your consolation. This will help you endure the same sufferings we suffer. 7Our hope for you is steadfast, for we know that as you partake of the suffering, you will also partake of the consolation.

8We do not want you to be unaware, believers, of the troubles that came upon us in Asia. We were burdened so much beyond our strength that we despaired even of life. 9Yes, within ourselves we felt a death sentence. This was so that we would not trust in ourselves but in God who raises the dead. 10It was God who rescued us from so perilous a death, and God does rescue us. It is God in whom we trust, and God will continue to rescue us. 11You can help by praying for us. Then many people will give thanks for us and the blessings we have received in answer to all your prayers.

THE REASON FOR PAUL'S CHANGE OF PLANS

12We boast because of the testimony of our conscience. We have behaved in the world, and especially toward you, with single-minded and godly purity. We have not done this with worldly wisdom but by the grace of God. 13For we will not write anything to you that you cannot read and understand. I trust that you will understand until the end, 14as you have already understood us in part, that you can be as proud of us as we are of you on the day Christ Jesus returns.

15I was planning to come to you before, so that you might have two visits from me 16as I passed through Corinth to Macedonia and returned to you. Then you could have helped send me on my way to Judea. 17When I thought about these things, did I do it lightly? Do I make plans in a worldly way, saying, "Yes, yes," and "No, no" in the same breath? 18But as God is trustworthy, our word to you was not "Yes" and "No." 19For God's Child Jesus Christ, whom Sylvanus, Timothy and I preached to you, was not "Yes" and "No," but has always been "Yes." 20For all the promises of God are in

Christ "Yes" and in Christ "Amen" to the glory of God through us. [21]Now the One who establishes us with you in Christ and anoints us is God. [22]God also sealed us and gave us the down-payment of the Spirit in our hearts.

[23]God is my witness that it was to spare you that I did not come as yet to Corinth. [24]Not that we rule over your faith. We help you for your joy, for it is by faith you stand.

[2:1]Since another visit to you would cause distress, I decided not to visit; [2]for if I make you sad, who is there to make me glad? Only you whom I made sad! [3]I wrote this to you so that when I come I will not have distress from those who ought to make me rejoice. For I have confidence in you that when I have joy, all of you will too. [4]I wrote to you out of much affliction, with anguish of heart and many tears; not to grieve you, but that you might know the abundant love I have for you.

FORGIVENESS

[5]I do not want to be too hard on you. If anyone has caused grief, they have not caused it to me, but in some measure - I mustn't be too hard on you - to all of you. [6]The punishment that many of you have inflicted on that man is sufficient. [7]Now you ought to forgive and comfort him so that he will not be swallowed up by too much sorrow. [8]Therefore I urge you to confirm your love for him. [9]I wrote to you so that I might find out whether you would be obedient in everything. [10]Anyone you forgive, I forgive also. For if I forgive anything - if there was anything to forgive - I forgive for your sake in the presence of Christ, [11]lest Satan get an advantage over us; for we are not ignorant of Satan's purposes.

THE APOSTOLIC MINISTRY

[12]When I came to Troas to preach Christ's gospel, a door was opened to me by Christ. [13]But I had no rest in my spirit, because I did not find my brother Titus there. So I left them and went to Macedonia.

[14]Now thanks be to God, who always causes us to triumph in Christ and reveals the fragrance of divine knowledge through us wherever we go, [15]we are to God the sweet scent of Christ among those who are saved and among those who are perishing. [16]To those who are perishing, we are the smell of death leading to death. To those who are saved, we are the fragrance of life leading to life. Who is adequate for these things? [17]We are not like the many others who cheapen the word of God. We speak sincerely because God sent us, and in the sight of God we speak in Christ.

[3:1]Do we begin to commend ourselves again? Or do we need, as some do, letters of recommendation to you and from you? [2]You are our letter, written on our hearts, and known and read by all. [3]You are revealed as the letter from Christ sent by us, written not with ink, but by the Spirit of the living God. And not on tablets of stone, but on the tablets of the heart.

[4]We have this confidence in Christ in God's presence. [5]Not that we are competent of ourselves to analyze anything. Our competence comes from God, [6]who made us able ministers of the new covenant, which is not of the letter but of the Spirit. The letter kills, but the Spirit gives life.

[7]The law that created a teaching that leads to death was engraved on tablets of

stone. It was so glorious that the people of Israel could not gaze at the face of Moses because of the glory on his face, though it was already fading. [8]Will not the teaching of the Spirit be more glorious? [9]If the teaching of condemnation was glorious, how much more will the teaching of righteousness exceed it in glory? [10]The old law had no glory in comparison to the glory that surpassed it. [11]For if that which was done away with was glorious, how much more glorious is that which remains? [12]Since we have such a hope, we speak with great boldness; [13]not like Moses who put a veil over his face to keep the people of Israel from gazing at it as the radiance faded. [14]Their minds were hardened, and to this day the same veil remains during the reading of the old covenant. The veil is removed only in Christ. [15]Even to this day when Moses is read, the veil is on their hearts. [16]Nevertheless, when anyone turns to God, the veil is taken away. [17]God is the Spirit, and where the Spirit of God is, there is freedom. [18]And all believers, who with unveiled faces look as if in a mirror at the glory of God, are being changed into the same image from glory to glory by the Spirit of God.

[4:1]Therefore since we have this ministry and have received mercy, we do not weaken. [2]We have renounced secret shameful practices. We do not use trickery or handle the word of God deceitfully, but by telling the truth we commend ourselves to everyone's conscience in the sight of God. [3]If our good news is veiled, it is veiled to those who are perishing. [4]The god of this world has blinded the minds of unbelievers, lest the light of the glorious good news of Christ, who is the image of God, shine upon them. [5]We do not proclaim ourselves, but Jesus Christ the Omnipotent. We ourselves are your servants for Jesus' sake. [6]For the God who told the light to shine out of darkness has shone in our hearts to let us know that the glory of God may be seen in the face of Jesus Christ.

[7]We have this treasure in earthen vessels to show that this superior power is from God and not from us. [8]We are troubled on every side, but not distressed; perplexed, but not in despair; [9]persecuted, but not forsaken; thrown down, but not destroyed. [10]We are always carrying in our bodies the death of Jesus, so that the life of Jesus may be seen in our bodies. [11]For we who are alive are always in danger of death for Jesus' sake, so that Jesus may be revealed through our mortal flesh. [12]Thus the death of Jesus is working in us, but the life of Jesus is working in you.

[13]We have the same spirit of faith that is written of: "I believed, therefore I spoke." We also believe and therefore speak. [14]We know that the One who raised Jesus up from the dead will also raise us up with Jesus and will lead us with you into God's presence. [15]All this is for you, so that as grace is shown to more and more people, thankfulness may overflow to honor God. [16]Therefore we do not weaken. Though our bodies are deteriorating, our inner spirit is renewed day by day. [17]For our light and momentary affliction works in us a far greater and eternal weight of glory. [18]We do not look at the things that are seen, but at the things that are not seen. The things that are seen are temporal, but the things that are not seen are eternal.

[5:1]We know that if our earthly house [our body] is destroyed, we have a building from God, a house not made with human hands, eternal in the heavens. [2]For this we groan, earnestly desiring to be clothed with our heavenly house. [3]For if we are clothed, we will not be found naked. [4]While we are in this earthly house we groan, burdened with our nakedness and wanting our mortality to be swallowed up by life. [5]The One who made us has given us the Spirit as a guarantee of this.

[6]We always have courage, although we know that while we are at home in the body we are absent from Christ. [7]We walk by faith and not by sight. [8]Though we have courage, we would rather be absent from the body and present with Christ. [9]And so we labor, whether present or absent, to please Christ. [10]For we must all appear before the judgment seat of Christ, so that everyone may receive back what they have done in the body, whether good or bad.

[11]Therefore, knowing the fear of God, we attempt to persuade others. As we are open before God, I trust that we are open to you as well. [12]We are not commending ourselves again to you, but are giving you an occasion to boast on our behalf. In this way you will have an answer for those who boast about mere appearances and not about what is in the heart. [13]If we are insane, it is for God. If we are of sound mind, it is for you. [14]The love of Christ compels us. We believe that, if one died for all, then all died. [15]Christ died for all so that those who are living would no longer live for themselves but for the One who died for them and rose again.

[16]Therefore from now on we do not judge anyone according to what they seem to be. In the past we may have judged Christ in that way, but we no longer do so. [17]Anyone who is in Christ is a new creature! Old things have passed away. Look! All things have become new! [18]Everything is from God, who reconciled us to holiness through Christ and has given us the ministry of reconciliation. [19]This means that God was reconciling the world to holiness through Christ, not charging the errors of humans against them, and committing to us the message of reconciliation. [20]We are now Christ's ambassadors, and God is appealing to you through us. We pray that on Christ's behalf you will become reconciled to God. [21]For God made the One who knew no sin to be a sin-offering for us, so that through Christ we might become the righteousness of God.

[6:1]As Christ's co-workers, we beg you not to receive the grace of God lightly. [2]God says, "I heard you in an acceptable time; in the day of salvation I helped you." Be alert! Now is the acceptable time. Look! Today is the day of salvation.

[3]We try not to give offense in anything, so that the ministry will not be blamed. [4]But in all things we commend ourselves as the ministers of God: in cheerful endurance, in moments of affliction, in difficulties, in calamities, [5]in beatings, in imprisonments, in riots, in labors, in sleeplessness, in fasting, [6]in purity, in knowledge, in longsuffering, in kindness, in the Holy Spirit, in unfeigned love, [7]in speaking the truth, in the power of God, through the weapons of righteousness in the right hand and in the left, [8]through honor and dishonor, through slander and praise; as deceivers, yet true; [9]as unknown, yet well-known; as dying, yet alive; as chastened, yet not killed; [10]as sorrowful, yet always rejoicing; as poor, yet making many rich; having nothing, yet possessing everything. [11]O Corinthians, we have spoken freely to you; we have opened our

hearts to you. [12]We have not stopped caring for you, but you have stopped caring for us. [13]In repayment (I speak as to my children), make room in your hearts for us.

[14]Do not be unequally yoked with unbelievers, for what fellowship has righteousness with unrighteousness? What communion has light with darkness? [15]What accord has Christ with the unreliable one? What part the believer with the unbeliever? [16]What agreement the temple of God with idols? For we are the temple of the living God. As God said, "I will live with them and walk among them. I will be their God and they will be My people. [17]Therefore come out from among them and be separate, says God. Touch no unclean thing and I will receive you. [18]I will be a Parent to you and you will be My sons and daughters, says God Almighty."

[7:1]Since we have these promises, beloved, let us cleanse ourselves from any stain of the flesh or spirit, perfecting holiness through the fear of God.

[2]Make room for us! We have wronged no one; we have ruined no one; we have defrauded no one. [3]I do not say this to condemn you, for I have said before that you are in our hearts and that we die or live with you. [4]I have confidence in you, yes, I boast proudly about you. I am filled with comfort; in all our troubles, I am overjoyed.

[5]When we came into Macedonia, our flesh had no rest. We were troubled on every side - fighting on the outside and fears within. [6]But God, the One who comforts those who are downcast, comforted us by the arrival of Titus. [7]And not only by his coming, but also by the encouragement you gave him. He told us of your longing and your mourning and your favorable thoughts toward me. When I heard this, I rejoiced even more.

[8]Even if I caused you sorrow with that letter, I don't regret it. I did feel badly at first, for I perceive that the letter made you sad for a time. [9]But now I rejoice, not that you were made sad, but that your sadness led to repentance. For you felt godly sadness, and therefore received no injury from us. [10]For godly sadness leads to repentance, and repentance leads to salvation that is lasting. But worldly sadness leads to death. [11]Look at what this godly sadness accomplished in you: it produced earnestness, accountability, indignation, fear, longing, zeal and vindication. In every way you have shown yourselves to be innocent in this matter. [12]So, although I wrote to you, it was not because of the one who had done the wrong or because of the one who was wronged. It was to show you in the sight of God how devoted you are to us. [13]Therefore we were encouraged. And we were even more encouraged by the joy of Titus, for his spirit was refreshed by all of you. [14]I had boasted to him about you, and you did not embarrass me. We have always spoken the truth to you, and even our boasting before Titus is found to be the truth. [15]His affection toward you is even greater as he remembers your obedience and how you received him with fear and trembling. [16]I rejoice that I can have complete confidence in you.

REASONS FOR GENEROSITY

[8:1]Moreover, believers, we want you to know of the grace that God has bestowed on the churches of Macedonia. [2]In the great trial of their affliction and deep poverty, they have overflowed with rich generosity. [3]I can testify that they gave willingly of themselves as much as they could, and beyond what they could. [4]They urgently begged us to receive their gift so that they could share in the ministry to the saints. [5]This was more than we expected. They first gave themselves to Christ, and then to us, doing the will of God. [6]When this happened, we urged Titus, who had already begun, to finish this act of goodwill with you. [7]Since you excel in everything - faith and its expression, knowledge in all diligence and goodwill toward us - see that you excel in this act of goodwill also. [8]I do not say this as a command. I am seeking to prove the sincerity of your love by comparing it to the eagerness of others. [9]For you know that our Sovereign Jesus Christ was kind enough to give up the wealth of heaven and become poor so that you might become rich. [10]And here is my advice regarding what is expedient for you: A year ago you were the first to give and the first to have an interest in giving. [11]Now you should give so that your readiness to give may equal what you actually give, as your ability allows. [12]If there is willingness, it is accepted according to what one has, not according to what one does not have. [13]I do not mean that others should be at ease and that you should be burdened, [14]but that in all fairness your abundance at this time would supply their need. Then their abundance will sometime supply your need. [15]As it is written, "Those who gathered much had nothing left over, and those who gathered little had no lack."

[16]Thanks be to God who put into the heart of Titus the same eagerness that I have for you. [17]For he not only accepted our appeal, but, being earnest of his own accord, he went to you. [18]We sent with him the brother who is praised in all the churches for his work with the gospel. [19]This brother was chosen by the churches to travel with us as we carry the offering which we willingly bring to Jerusalem for the glory of God. [20]We are trying to avoid having anyone blame us for the way we administer this generosity. [21]We intend to do the honest thing, not only in the sight of God, but also in the sight of humans.

[22]We are also sending another brother who has always proven diligent. He is eager to be even more diligent after I told him of the confidence I have in you. [23]Regarding Titus, he is my partner and helper concerning you. As for the others going with him, they are delegates of the churches and an honor to Christ. [24]Show them the proof of your love and the reason for our boasting about you to all the churches.

[9:1]In regard to helping the saints, there is no necessity for me to write to you, [2]for I know your willingness to help. I boast about it to the Macedonians, telling how you were ready a year ago. Your zeal has inspired many of them. [3]Nevertheless I have sent these friends so that you may be prepared, lest our boasting about you in this matter be in vain. [4]Otherwise some Macedonians may come with me and find you unprepared. Then we, and indeed you, would be ashamed because of this confidence. [5]Therefore I thought it necessary to encourage these friends to come to you beforehand and prepare in advance your gift, so that it might be ready as a gracious gift, and not as a gift you are obligated to give. [6]Remember, whoever sows sparingly will also reap sparingly, and whoever sows bountifully will also reap bountifully. [7]Each of you should give as you decide in your heart, not grudgingly or of necessity. For God loves a cheerful giver. [8]And God is able to abundantly favor you so that you always have all you need and abound in every good work. ^{9}As it is written, "They dispersed their gifts to the poor. Their righteousness remains forever." ^{10}Now the One who provides seed for the sower and bread for food will both multiply your seed and increase the fruits of your righteousness. ^{11}Thus you will be enriched in every way so that you are able to be generous to everyone and bring glory to God through us. ^{12}For this service that you do not only provides for the needs of the saints, but also overflows into much thankfulness to God. ^{13}Those who receive your gifts will praise God when they see your submission to the gospel of Christ and your generous sharing with them and everyone. ^{14}They pray for you and long to be with you because of the great favor that God has shown to you. ^{15}Thanks be to God for the indescribable gift of Christ.

FURTHER ADMONISHMENTS

$^{10:1}$I, Paul, beg you with the humility and gentleness of Christ. You say that in your presence I am timid, but when absent I am bold toward you. ^{2}I pray that when I am present I may not have to show that confidence which I boldly use against those who judge us according to worldly standards. ^{3}Though we live in this world, we do not fight our battles as the world does. ^{4}The weapons of our warfare are not of this world, but as God empowers us, we are able to pull down strongholds. We demolish ^{5}arguments and every lofty idea that exalts itself against the knowledge of God, taking captive every thought to make it obedient to Christ. ^{6}When your obedience is complete, we are ready to punish anyone who does not obey.

^{7}Do not look at outward appearances. If you are sure you are Christ's, then think again; for just as you belong to Christ, so we also belong to Christ. ^{8}Even if I boast too much about the authority that Christ has given us for your edification and not for your destruction, I will not be ashamed. ^{9}I am not trying to frighten you with my letters. ^{10}Some say my letters are weighty and powerful but my bodily presence is weak and my speeches are nothing. ^{11}Let these people consider that what we say in our letters when we are absent will be done in deed when we are present.

^{12}We do not dare count ourselves among the number who commend themselves. When they measure themselves by themselves and compare themselves to themselves, they are not wise. ^{13}We do not boast beyond measure, but only within the limits of the sphere of service God has given us, a sphere that reaches even to you. ^{14}We are not stretching ourselves too far when we reach out to you, for we were the first to reach Corinth with the good news of Christ. ^{15}We do not boast of things that cannot be measured, such as the labor done by others. Instead, having hope that your faith is increasing, our work will be enlarged by you abundantly within the sphere we have. ^{16}Then we can tell the good news in places beyond you, and not boast in a sphere which has already been prepared by someone else. ^{17}Scripture says, "Let those who boast, boast in Christ." ^{18}It is not the one who is self-approved who is approved, but the one Christ approves.

$^{11:1}$I wish that you would bear with me a little in my foolishness. And indeed, you do bear with me. ^{2}I am jealous over you with a godly jealousy, for I have promised you as a pure virgin to one husband - to Christ. ^{3}I am afraid that your minds will be led away from a sincere commitment to Christ, just as the snake used subtle means to beguile Eve. [4]For if anyone comes preaching another Jesus whom we have not preached, or you receive another spirit which you have not received, or you hear another gospel from the one you accepted, you accept it readily enough.

[5]I do not consider myself in any way inferior to the highest-ranked apostles. [6]Though I am a poor speaker, I do know what I'm talking about. We have made this thoroughly known to you in every way.

[7]Was it wrong for me to humble myself in order to lift you up by preaching the good news of God free of charge? [8]I robbed other churches, accepting wages from them to serve you. [9]When I was present with you and wanted something, I was a burden to no one. What I lacked, the believers from Macedonia supplied. In everything I kept myself from being a burden to you, and I will continue to do so. [10]As sure as the truth of Christ is in me, no one in all of Greece shall stop me from boasting. [11]Why? Because I don't love you? God knows I do. [12]But I do what I do in order to stop those who would like to boast of being just like us. [13]They are false apostles and deceitful workers masquerading as apostles of Christ. [14]And no wonder, for Satan also masquerades as an angel of light. [15]Therefore it is not surprising if Satan's servants masquerade as servants of righteousness. Their end will be according to their works.

PAUL BOASTS

[16]I say again, let no one think I am a fool. But if you do, then accept me as a fool so that I may boast a little. [17]That which I now say I speak, not from Christ, but as if in a fit of folly and in the very essence of boasting. [18]Seeing that many boast in a worldly way, I will boast also. [19]For you gladly put up with fools, since you are so wise. [20]You put up with those who enslave you, those who devour you, those who take advantage of you, those who bully you and those who hit you in the face. [21]I am ashamed to say that we were too weak for that. Yet in whatever way they are bold (I speak foolishly), I am bold also. [22]Are they Hebrews? So am I. Are they Israelites? So am I. Are they descendants of Abraham? So am I. [23]Are they servants of Christ? (Again I speak like a fool.) I am more. Labors? Far greater. Whipped? More severely. Imprisoned? More frequently. Exposed to death? More often. [24]Five times the Jews gave me thirty-nine lashes. [25]Three times I was beaten with rods, once I was stoned, three times I was shipwrecked, I drifted a night and a day on the open sea, [26]journeying often, endangered by floods, endangered by robbers, endangered by my own people, endangered by Gentiles, endangered in the city, endangered in the country, endangered on the sea, endangered by false associates, [27]in weariness and pain, in sleeplessness often, in hunger and thirst, in fastings often, in cold and nakedness [28]and besides all these other things there comes upon me daily the concerns of all the congregations. [29]Who is weak and I am not weak? Who is offended and I do not burn? [30]If I must boast, I will boast concerning my weakness. [31]The God and heavenly Parent of our Sovereign Jesus Christ, who is blessed forever, knows I am not lying. [32]In Damascus the governor under King Aretas guarded the city with a garrison and desired to apprehend me, [33]but I was let down through a window in the wall and escaped from his clutches.

PAUL'S JOURNEY TO PARADISE

12:1No doubt it is not expedient for me to boast, yet I want to tell you about visions and revelations from God. 2I know a man in Christ who fourteen years ago (whether in the body or out of the body I do not know - God knows) was caught up to the third heaven. 3And I know that this man (whether in the body or out of the body I do not know - God knows) 4was caught up into Paradise and heard unspoken words that a human is not permitted to utter. 5Of such I will boast; yet of myself I will not boast, except of my weaknesses. 6Even if I desired to boast, I would not be a fool, for I tell the truth. But I forebear, lest anyone think more of me than what they see or hear of me 7and cause me to become conceited.

PAUL'S THORN IN THE FLESH

Lest I become too conceited because of these surpassing revelations, I was given a thorn in the flesh, a messenger of Satan to buffet me. 8Three times I begged God to take it away from me 9but was told, "My grace is sufficient for you, for strength is made perfect through weakness." Most gladly therefore I boast of my weaknesses, so that the power of Christ may rest on me. 10Therefore I take pleasure in weaknesses, in insults, in constraints, in persecutions and in distress for the sake of Christ. For when I am weak, then I am strong.

PAUL JUSTIFIES HIMSELF

11I have made a fool of myself, but it is all your fault. I ought to be commended by you, for in nothing am I less than the highest-ranked apostles, though I am nothing. 12Signs, wonders and mighty deeds are the mark of a true apostle, and these things were done consistently in your presence. 13In what way were you ever inferior to other congregations, except that I was not a burden to you? Forgive me for this. 14I am ready to come to you for the third time, and I will not be a burden to you. I do not seek what is yours, but you. The children ought not to save up for the parents, but the parents for the children. 15I will very gladly spend and be spent for you, though the more abundantly I love you, the less I am loved.

16Although I was not a burden to you, yet, shrewd fellow that I am, I caught you with guile. 17Did I make a gain from you through any of those whom I sent to you? 18I urged Titus to go, and I sent another believer with him. Did Titus make a gain from you? Did we not walk in the same Spirit and follow the same steps? 19Do you think we are excusing ourselves to you? We speak as Christians in the presence of God. Dearly beloved, we do all things for your good. 20I fear that when I come you will not be what I would like you to be and that I will not be what you would like me to be. Will there be disputes, envy, wrath, strife, backbiting, whispering, haughtiness and disorder? 21When I come again, will my God make me ashamed when I visit you? Will I mourn the many who have sinned already and not repented of the impure sexual lust and shameful things they have committed?

FINAL ADMONITIONS AND GREETINGS

13:1This is the third time I am coming to you. As Scripture says, "In the mouth of two or three witnesses will every word be established." 2I told you before when I was with you the second time, and now I write to those who sinned previously and all you others: If I come again, I will not spare, [3]since you seek proof that Christ is speaking through me. Christ is not weak toward you, but powerful among you. [4]Though He was crucified in weakness, yet Christ now lives by the power of God. We are weak like Christ was, but we also will live by the power of God, just as Christ does.

[5]Examine yourselves to see if you are in the faith. Test yourselves. Surely you know that Christ is in you - unless you fail the test! [6]I hope you know that we have not failed the test. [7]Now I pray to God that you do nothing wrong. Not so we will appear to have passed the test, but so that you might do what is right, even though we appear to have failed. [8]For we can do nothing against the truth, but only for the truth. [9]We are glad when we are weak and you are strong. Our prayer is for your perfection. [10]I write these things while absent, so that when I am with you I will not need to speak to you sharply according to the authority that God has given me - for building you up, not for tearing you down.

[11]Finally, believers, be joyful. Be perfect, be encouraged, be of one mind, live in peace. The God of love and peace will be with you. [12]Greet one another with a holy kiss. [13]All the saints salute you. [14]The grace of our Sovereign Jesus Christ and the love of God and the communion of the Holy Spirit be with you all. Amen.

Galatians

1:1 Paul, an apostle - not sent from humans or by humans, but by Jesus Christ and God His heavenly Parent who raised Him from the dead - **2**and all the believers with us, to the congregations in Galatia: **3**Goodwill and peace to you from God our heavenly Parent and from our Sovereign Jesus Christ. **4**Christ gave Himself for our sins so as to release us from this present evil world according to the will of God our heavenly Parent. **5**To God be the glory forever and ever. Amen.

6I am astonished that you are so soon removed from the One who called you into the favor of Christ and are turning to another gospel. **7**Not that there is another, but some are troubling you and are determined to pervert the gospel of Christ. **8**Therefore if we or an angel from heaven preach any other gospel to you than the one we preached to you, may that one be cursed. **9**As we said before and now I say again: If anyone preaches any other gospel to you than the one you received, may that one be cursed. **10**Am I seeking the approval of humans, or of God? I do not seek to please humans, for if I pleased humans, I would not be the servant of Christ.

11Believers, I certify to you that the gospel that was preached by me is not of human origin. **12**I neither received it nor was taught it by humans, but rather by revelation from Jesus Christ. **13**For you have heard of my behavior in Judaism, how I persecuted the church of God and ravaged it. **14**I advanced in the Jewish religion faster than the rest of my generation, being far more zealous of the traditions of my ancestors. **15**But when God, who chose me before I was born and through grace called me, was pleased **16**to reveal the Son to me so that I could preach Christ among the nations, I did not immediately confer with flesh and blood. **17**Nor did I go up to Jerusalem to those who were apostles before me. Instead, I went to Arabia. Later I returned to Damascus. **18**After three years I went up to Jerusalem to see Peter and stayed with him fifteen days. **19**I saw none of the other apostles except James, the brother of Jesus. **20**You know that what I am writing to you is the truth; before God I am not lying. **21**Afterward I went into the regions of Syria and Cilicia. **22**I was personally unknown to the congregations of Judea who were in Christ. **23**They had only heard that the one who formerly persecuted them was now preaching the faith he once destroyed, **24**and they glorified God because of me.

2:1 Fourteen years later I went up again to Jerusalem with Barnabas. I also took Titus with me. **2**I went up by revelation and communicated to them the gospel that I preach among the Gentiles, but privately to those who seemed to be in agreement, lest by any means I should run or had run in vain. **3**Titus was in Jerusalem with me. He lest by any means I should run or had run in vain. [3]Titus was in Jerusalem with me. He was not compelled to be circumcised, even though he was a Greek. [4]But certain false believers who were smuggled in stealthily to spy out the liberty we have in Christ Jesus wanted to keep us in bondage. [5]In order that the gospel might continue with you, we did not give in to them for one moment. [6]But of those who seemed to be something (whatever they were, it makes no difference to me - God has no favorites), their aspirations added nothing to me. [7]On the contrary, they saw that the gospel to the uncircumcised was committed to me, just as the gospel to the circumcised was to Peter. [8]For the One who worked effectively through Peter in the apostleship to the circumcised also worked through me to the Gentiles. [9]When James, Peter and John, who seemed to be pillars, perceived the grace that was given to me, they gave Barnabas and me the right hand of fellowship, so that we might go to the Gentiles and they to the circumcised. [10]They asked only that we remember the poor, the very thing I was diligent to do.

[11]When Peter came to Antioch, I withstood him to his face, because he was in the wrong. [12]For before certain ones arrived with James, he used to eat with Gentiles. But when they came, he withdrew and separated himself because he feared those of the circumcision. [13]Other Jews acted hypocritically in the same way. Barnabas was also involved in their hypocrisy. [14]When I saw that they did not walk uprightly according to the truth of the gospel, I said to Peter before them all, "If you, a Jew, live like a Gentile, why do you compel the Gentiles to live like Jews?"

[15]We who are Jews by birth and not Gentile sinners [16]know that a person is not justified by obeying the law, but by faith in Jesus Christ. We believe that in Jesus Christ we will be justified. Justification is by faith in Christ and not by the deeds of the law, for no flesh will be justified by obeying the law. [17]But if we seek to be justified by Christ and then are found to be sinners, is Christ then the promoter of sin? Of course not. [18]But we are sinners if we try to go back to relying on the law to save us. [19]I am dead to the law so that I may now live for God. [20]I am crucified with Christ, nevertheless I live. Yet not I, but Christ lives in me. And the life that I now live in the flesh, I live by faith in God's child, who loved me and gave Himself for me. [21]I do not ignore the grace of God, but if righteousness comes by the law, then Christ died in vain.

JUSTIFICATION IS BY FAITH, NOT BY WORKS

3:1O foolish Galatians, who bewitched you? Before your eyes it was shown how Jesus Christ was crucified. [2]This one thing I would like to learn from you: Did you receive the Spirit by the deeds of the law or by hearing with faith? [3]Are you so foolish? Having begun in the Spirit, are you now made perfect by the flesh? [4]Have you suffered so many things in vain? Was it in vain? [5]The One who gives you the Spirit and works miracles among you, is it by the deeds of the law or by hearing with faith?

[6]Remember, Abraham believed God and it was credited to him as righteousness. [7]You should know then that those who have faith are the children of Abraham. [8]The Scripture, foreseeing that God would justify the nations through faith, announced the good news to Abraham in advance by saying, "Through you will all nations be blessed." [9]So those with faith are blessed along with faithful Abraham.

[10]As many as rely on obeying the law are under the curse. For it is written, "Cursed is everyone who does not continue to do everything that is written in the book of the law." [11]Yet that no one is justified by the law in the sight of God is evident, for, "The just shall live by faith." [12]The law is not based on faith, for, "The one who does these things will live by them." [13]Christ redeemed us from the curse of the law by becoming a curse for us. For it is written, "Cursed is everyone who hangs on a tree," [14]so that the blessing of Abraham might come on the Gentiles through Jesus Christ, and so that we might receive the promise of the Spirit through faith.

[15]Believers, humanly speaking, when a covenant is confirmed, no one can take anything from it or add to it. [16]Now the promises were made to Abraham and his Seed. God does not say, "And to seeds," as to many, but to one: "And to your Seed," which is Christ. [17]And this I say: The law that came four hundred and thirty years later cannot annul the covenant that was confirmed by God and make the promise of no effect. [18]For if the inheritance depends on the law, it no longer depends on a promise. But God gave it to Abraham as a promise.

[19]Why then the law? It was added because of wrongdoing until that one Seed came to whom the promise was made. The law was instituted by angels in the hand of a go-between. [20]Now a go-between is not needed for one, but God is one. [21]Is the law, then, against the promises of God? Of course not. For if a law had been given which could give life, then righteousness would have come by the law. [22]But Scripture included everyone under sin so that what was promised through faith in Jesus Christ might be given to those who have faith. [23]But before faith came, we were hemmed in by the law and confined until faith was revealed. [24]The law was our tutor to bring us to Christ so that we might be justified by faith.

FAITH WILL INHERIT THE PROMISES

[25]After faith comes, we are no longer under a tutor, [26]and you are all children of God through faith in Christ Jesus. [27]For as many of you as have been baptized into Christ have been clothed with Christ. [28]There is neither Jew nor Gentile, slave nor free, male nor female. You are all one in Christ Jesus. [29]And if you belong to Christ, then you are Abraham's seed and heirs according to the promise.

[4:1]The heirs, as long as they are children, are no different from servants, though the children own everything. [2]They are under tutors and overseers until the time appointed by the parent. [3]In the same way, when we were children, we were slaves to the basic powers of the world. [4]But when the fullness of time had come, God sent the Son, born of a woman, born under the law, [5]to redeem those who were under the law, so that we might receive adoption as God's children. [6]And because you are God's children, God sent the Spirit of the Son into your hearts, crying, "O, My dear Parent." [7]Therefore you are no longer slaves, but God's children; and if God's children, then heirs of God through Christ.

[8]Formerly, when you did not know God, you were slaves to those who by nature are not gods. [9]But now that you have known God, or rather, are known by God, how can you turn back to the weak and cringing elemental spirits to which you desire again to be enslaved? [10]You observe days and months and times and years. [11]I am afraid

for you, lest I have labored over you in vain. [12]I beg you, believers: become like me, for I became like you. You have not wronged me in any way. [13]You know how weak I was when I preached the gospel to you at the first. [14]You didn't despise or reject me, though my body was a trial to you. Instead you received me like an angel of God or even like Christ Jesus. [15]Where is the enthusiasm you had? I testify that, if possible, you would have plucked out your eyes and given them to me. [16]Have I become your enemy now because I tell you the truth? [17]Impostors zealously affect you, but not for good. They would separate you so that you might be zealous for them. [18]It is always good to be zealously affected for good, and not only when I am present with you. [19]My little children, I am again in the pains of childbirth over you until Christ is formed in you. [20]I desire to be present with you now with a different tone in my voice, for I am perplexed about you.

THE ALLEGORY OF HAGAR AND SARAH

[21]Tell me, you who desire to be under the law, don't you listen to the law? [22]It is written that Abraham had two sons, the one by a slave woman and the other by a free woman. [23]The one by the slave woman was born of the flesh, but the one by the free woman was born of the promise. [24]This is an allegory, for these two women represent two covenants. Hagar from Mount Sinai gave birth to children into slavery. [25]This Hagar from Mount Sinai in Arabia represents the present city of Jerusalem, for she and her children are in slavery. [26]But the Jerusalem above, the mother of us all, is free! [27]It is written, "Rejoice, you who do not bear. Break forth and cry, you who do not give birth. For the desolate will have more children than she who had a husband." [28]Now we believers are the children of the promise, just as Isaac was. [29]But back then, the one who was born of the flesh persecuted the one born of the Spirit, even as it is now. [30]Nevertheless, what does Scripture say? "Cast out the slave woman and her son, for the son of the slave woman shall not be heir with the son of the free woman." [31]Therefore, believers, we are not children of the slave woman, but of the free.

THE FREEDOM OF THOSE WHO HAVE FAITH IN CHRIST

[5:1]We are free because Christ has made us free, so do not be entangled again with the yoke of bondage. [2]Beware! I, Paul, say to you that if you allow yourselves to be circumcised, Christ will profit you nothing. [3]For I testify again to every man who is circumcised that he is a debtor to do the whole law. [4]Christ has become of no effect to you who are justified by the law; you are fallen from grace. [5]But with the help of the Spirit we wait and hope to be made right with God through faith. [6]In Christ Jesus, neither circumcision nor uncircumcision accomplishes anything. What matters is faith working through love.

[7]You ran well. Who hindered you, that you did not obey the truth? [8]That persuasion did not come from the One who called you. [9]A little yeast changes the whole loaf. [10]I have confidence in you (through the Almighty) that you agree. But those who trouble you will bear their judgment, whoever they are. [11]Believers, if I still preach circumcision, why do I still suffer persecution? If I still preached circumcision, then the stumbling block of the cross would cause no trouble. [12]I wish that those who trouble you would cut themselves off.

THE DEEDS OF THE FLESH

[13]Believers, you have been called to freedom, only do not use freedom as an occasion for the flesh, but by love serve one another. [14]For all the law is fulfilled in this one saying, "Love others as much as you love yourself." [15]But if you bite and devour one another, take heed that you do not consume one another. [16]I say then: Walk in the Spirit and you will not fulfill the lusts of the flesh. [17]For the lusts of the flesh are against the Spirit; and the Spirit is against the flesh. These are repugnant to one another, and you cannot do what you want. [18]But if you are led by the Spirit, you are not under the law. [19]Now the deeds of the flesh are apparent: sexual sins, dirty thoughts, lack of restraint, [20]worldliness, witchcraft, hostility, quarreling, jealousy, anger, selfishness, disagreements, factions, [21]envy, drunkenness, orgies and the like. I warn you, even as I told you before: those who do such things will not inherit God's realm.

THE FRUITS OF THE SPIRIT

[22]But the fruit of the Spirit is love, joy, peace, patience, kindness, goodness, loyalty, [23]gentleness and self-control. Against such there is no law. [24]Those who belong to Christ Jesus have crucified the flesh with its passions and lusts. [25]If we live in the Spirit, let us also walk in the Spirit. [26]Let us not be self-conceited, for that leads to rivalry and envy of one another.

BE SYMPATHETIC AND HUMBLE

[6:1]Believers, if someone is surprised in a sin, you who are spiritual must restore such a one in a spirit of gentleness, all the while watching out for yourself, lest you also be tempted. [2]Bear one another's burdens and so fulfill the law of Christ. [3]If you think you are something, you are nothing; you deceive yourselves. [4]All must examine their own works; then they can be secure in themselves alone and not in others. [5]All must bear their own burdens. [6]The one who is taught from the word must share every good with the one who teaches.

[7]Do not be deceived; God is not mocked. Whatever you sow, that also will you reap. [8]Those who sow to please their flesh, will from the flesh reap corruption. But those who sow to please the Spirit, will from the Spirit reap life everlasting. [9]Let us not be weary in well-doing, for in due season we will reap if we do not give up. [10]Therefore as we have opportunity, let us do good to everyone, especially to those of the household of faith.

[11]See how heavily I have underlined this letter to you with my own hand. [12]Those who desire to be popular in the flesh would like to compel you to be circumcised, lest they suffer persecution for the cross of Christ. [13]Those who are circumcised do not obey the law but desire to have you circumcised so that they may boast that you are like them. [14]God forbid that I boast of anything but the cross of our Sovereign Jesus Christ. Because of Christ, the world is crucified to me, and I to the world. [15]Neither circumcision nor uncircumcision count for anything. What counts is the new creature. [16]Peace and compassion on all who walk by this rule, and upon the Israel of God. [17]From now on may no one trouble me, for I bear on my body the marks of Christ Jesus. [18]Believers, may the grace of the Sovereign Jesus Christ be with your spirits.

Ephesians

GREETINGS

1:1Paul, an apostle of Jesus Christ by the will of God, to the saints who are at Ephesus and to the faithful in Christ Jesus: 2Grace and peace to you from God our heavenly Parent and from our Sovereign Jesus Christ.

GOD'S GRAND PLAN

3Blessed be the God and heavenly Parent of our Sovereign Jesus Christ, who has blessed us with all the spiritual blessings of heaven through Christ. 4For God chose us in Christ before the creation of the world to be holy and blameless in God's presence. In love 5God predestined us to be adopted as children through Jesus Christ. This was in accord with God's will and pleasure 6in order that we might praise the glorious favor which God honored us with in the Beloved. 7In Christ we have redemption, the forgiveness of sins through His blood according to the riches of God's grace 8which is lavishly given to us in all wisdom and insight. 9God had the pleasure of making known to us the secret purpose set forth in Christ: 10that in the dispensation when time is fulfilled, God will gather everything in heaven and on earth together in Christ.

THE GUARANTEE OF OUR COMING INHERITANCE

11In Christ we have also been given an inheritance, having been predestined according to the purposes of God, who works out all things as planned. 12Therefore let us who were the first to trust in Christ praise God's glory. 13Because you have also heard the word of truth - the good news of your salvation - and have believed in Christ, you have been marked with the seal of the promised Holy Spirit, 14who is the guarantee of our inheritance until we are redeemed and fully praise God's glory.

PAUL'S PRAYER

15Therefore I also, having heard of your faith in our Sovereign Jesus and your love for all the saints, 16do not cease giving thanks for you and mentioning you in my prayers. 17I pray that the glorious heavenly Parent and God of our Sovereign Jesus Christ will give you the spirit of wisdom and revelation and the knowledge of God, 18so that the eyes of your understanding may be enlightened and you may know the hope of God's calling, the riches of the glory of God's inheritance in the saints 19and the working of God's mighty power 20which God showed by raising Christ from the dead and setting Christ on the right hand of God in heaven, 21far above all principalities, authorities, powers, governments and every name that is named, not only in this age, but also in the one to come. 22God put all things under Christ's feet and made Christ the head of all things to the church, 23which is Christ's body, the fullness of the One who completes all things completely.

THE SAINTS ARE SAVED BY FAITH AND CREATED TO DO GOOD WORKS

$^{2:1}$You were dead in misconduct and sin ^{2}when you followed the ways of the world and the prince of the power of the air, the spirit who is now active in those who are disobedient. ^{3}All of us once lived among the disobedient in the lusts of our flesh. We fulfilled the desires of the flesh and our thoughts and were by nature subject to wrath, just like everyone else. ^{4}But God, who is rich in compassion, loved us with a great love and ^{5}made us alive with Christ while we were yet dead in sin. You are saved by God's grace. ^{6}God raised us up to life in the Spirit and gave us a seat in heaven with Christ Jesus, ^{7}so that for all time we might be shown the surpassing riches of God's grace through Christ Jesus. ^{8}For by grace are you saved through faith. It is not of your own doing; it is the gift of God. ^{9}Nor is it because of works, lest anyone should boast. ^{10}For we are made by God and created through Christ Jesus for good works, which God planned from the beginning for us to do.

BOTH GENTILE AND JEW ARE NOW PART OF GOD'S UNIVERSAL CHURCH

^{11}Remember that you were Gentiles in the flesh. Those who were circumcised in the flesh called you "the uncircumcised". ^{12}At that time you were without Christ, non-participants in Israelite citizenship and strangers to the covenants of promise - without hope and without God in the world. ^{13}But now in Christ Jesus you who were once far off have been brought near by the blood of Christ. ^{14}For Christ is our peace. He broke down the dividing wall and made Jew and Gentile one ^{15}by abolishing in His flesh the enmity, which is the law, its commandments and its ordinances so as to bring Jew and Gentile to Himself into one new people and so make peace. ^{16}Thus Jew and Gentile were reconciled to God into one body by way of the cross and our hostility was put to death. ^{17}He came and preached peace to you who were far off and to those who were near, ^{18}for through Christ both Jew and Gentile have access by one Spirit to our heavenly Parent. ^{19}Now, therefore, you are no longer strangers and foreigners but fellow citizens with the saints and the family of God, ^{20}built on the foundation of the apostles and prophets, with Jesus Christ being the chief cornerstone. ^{21}In Christ the whole building is joined together and will grow into a holy temple for God. ^{22}In Christ you also are being built with others by the Spirit into this dwelling place for God.

THE MYSTERY: ALL ARE HEIRS OF SALVATION

$^{3:1}$For this reason, I, Paul, am a prisoner of Jesus Christ for you Gentiles. ^{2}You must have heard of the dispensation of grace that God has given me for your benefit. ^{3}By revelation God made known to me the mystery about which I wrote before in brief. ^{4}When you read it, you will know that I truly understand the mystery of Christ. ^{5}In other ages no one knew this secret, which is now revealed to God's holy apostles and prophets by the Spirit: ^{6}that the Gentiles are fellow heirs with the Jews in the same body. They are partakers of God's promise through the good news of Christ Jesus. ^{7}I was made a minister of this good news by the gift of grace which God has worked in me with great power. ^{8}This grace was given to me, the least of all the saints, so that I might preach among the Gentiles the unsearchable riches of Christ ^{9}and make everyone see their participation in the mystery which from eternity past has been hidden in God, who created all things. ^{10}God's intent was that now, through the church, the principalities and authorities in heaven might have revealed to them the many facets of God's wisdom [11]according to the eternal purpose that God achieved through Christ Jesus our Sovereign. [12]In Christ and through faith in Christ we have the assurance to come before God with confidence. [13]Therefore I beg you not to be discouraged because of my tribulations on your behalf, for they will bring you honor.

[14]For this reason, I bow my knees to the heavenly Parent of our Sovereign Jesus Christ [15]from whom the whole family in heaven and on earth gets its name. [16]I pray that God grant you from the riches of heavenly glory, strength and power by God's Holy Spirit in your inner being, [17]and that Christ dwell in your hearts by faith. Then, rooted and grounded in love, [18]you will be able to comprehend with all the saints how wide and long and high and deep the love of Christ is. [19]I want you to know the love of Christ that surpasses knowledge, so that you may be filled with all the fullness of God. [20]Now to God, who by the power at work in us is able to do much more than anything we ask or think, [21]to God be glory in the church and in Christ Jesus throughout all the ages forever. Amen.

ALL CHRISTIANS ARE ONE IN GOD

[4:1]I, therefore, the prisoner of Christ, encourage you to walk worthy of the calling to which you are called [2]with all humility, gentleness and longsuffering, making allowances for one another with love [3]and endeavoring to keep the unity of the Spirit through the bond of peace. [4]There is one body and one Spirit, just as you are called to one hope through your calling. [5]There is one Christ, one faith, one baptism [6]and one God and heavenly Parent of all, who is above all and through all and in all.

EACH CHRISTIAN HAS A DIVINE GIFT

[7]Each one of us, moreover, has been favored with a gift of grace that Christ has apportioned to us. [8]That is why it says, "Christ ascended on high; Christ led captivity captive and gave gifts to humans." [9]Now, when Christ ascended, what does it mean but that Christ also descended first into the lower parts of the earth? [10]The One who descended is the One who ascended far beyond all heavens to infuse all things. [11]Christ gave some to be apostles, some to be prophets, some to be evangelists and some to be pastors and teachers [12]for the perfecting of the saints, for the work of the ministry and for building up the body of Christ [13]until we all come into the unity of faith, the knowledge of the Child of God and the full measure of the stature of the fullness of Christ. [14]Then we will no longer be children, tossed to and fro and blown about by every wind of doctrine and the crafty deceit of human sinfulness, [15]but, speaking the truth in love, let us grow up to Christ. Christ is the head [16]from whom the whole body is joined together and united by what every joint supplies, so that every part effectively works to make the body grow and build itself up in love.

CHRISTIAN CONDUCT THAT WILL NOT GRIEVE THE HOLY SPIRIT

[17]In Christ's name I order you to no longer live as other Gentiles live. Their thoughts are futile [18]and their understanding is darkened, since they are alienated from the life of God through the ignorance that is in them because of the hardness of their hearts. [19]They have unconcernedly given themselves over to sexual sin and rapaciously pursue their unclean habits. [20]But that is not your understanding of

Christ. [21]Have you not heard God's voice and been taught by Christ about the truth that Christ personifies? [22]Then rid yourself of your selfish former behavior that is corrupt with deceitful lusts [23]and be renewed in the spirit of your mind. [24]Put on the new self that is created in the righteousness and true holiness of God. [25]Put away lying and speak the truth to everyone, for we are all parts of one body. [26]If you become angry, do not sin. Do not let the sun go down upon your wrath. [27]Do not give a foothold to the devil. [28]Those who stole must steal no more. Rather, let them labor with their hands doing good so that they may have something to give to those in need. [29]Let no worthless talk come out of your mouth, but only what is good for building others up and is a blessing to those who hear. [30]Do not grieve the Holy Spirit of God by whom you were marked for that day when you will be redeemed. [31]Let all bitterness, wrath, anger, raised voices, blaming of others and bad feelings be put away from you. [32]Be kind, tenderhearted and forgiving of one another, even as God through Christ's sacrifice has forgiven you.

WAKE UP FROM YOUR DEAD PAST AND LET CHRIST BE YOUR LIGHT

[5:1]Therefore be followers of God like dear children. [2]Walk in love as Christ loved us and gave Himself for us as an offering and fragrant sacrifice to God. [3]Because you are saints, do not let sexual sin, impurity or covetousness be once mentioned among you. [4]Rather, give thanks and do not talk of filthy, foolish or suggestive things that are not fitting. [5]For this you know: no one who is immoral, impure or covetous has any inheritance in the realm of Christ and of God. For the covetous person worships material things. [6]Let no one deceive you with empty words. Because of these things the wrath of God comes upon the disobedient. [7]Therefore do not join in with them. [8]At one time you also were darkness, but now you are full of light from God. Walk as children of light, [9]for from the light comes everything that is good, righteous and true. [10]Try to find out what is pleasing to God. [11]Have no fellowship with the worthless works of darkness, but let light shine on them. [12]It is shameful even to speak of the things they do in secret. [13]But everything revealed by the light becomes visible, for what makes things visible is light. [14]Therefore it is sung, "Awake, O sleeper. Arise from the dead and Christ will be your light."

[15]See then that you live cautiously, not like fools, but like the wise, [16]redeeming the time because the days are evil. [17]Do not be unwise, but understand what God's will is. [18]Do not become drunk with wine, which is reckless and immoral, but be filled with the Spirit. [19]Speak to one another with psalms and hymns and spiritual songs, singing and making melody in your heart to God, [20]always giving thanks for everything to God our heavenly Parent in the name of our Sovereign Jesus Christ.

DEFER TO ONE ANOTHER

[21]Be supportive of one another out of reverence for Christ. [22]Wives, be supportive of your husbands as to God. [23]For the husband is essential to the wife, even as Christ is essential to the church, Christ's body, and is its defender. [24]Just as the church is supportive of Christ, so wives should always be supportive of their husbands. [25]Husbands, love your wives, even as Christ loved the church and gave everything for her [26]in order to sanctify and cleanse her with the washing of water by the word [27]and

present her to Christ as a glorious church without spot or wrinkle, holy and without blemish. [28]In the same way, husbands ought to love their wives as their own bodies. He who loves his wife loves himself. [29]None of us hate our own bodies, but nourish and cherish them. This is what Christ does for the church, [30]for we are part of Christ's flesh and bones. [31]"For this reason a man will leave his father and mother and be united to his wife and the two shall be one flesh." [32]This is a great mystery - but I am speaking of Christ and the church. [33]So all of you should love your spouses as you love yourselves. And respect one another also.

CHRISTIAN CHILDREN

[6:1]Children, obey your parents the way God wants you to, for this is right. [2]"Honor your father and mother" is the first commandment with a promise: [3]"...that it may be well with you and that you may live long upon the earth." [4]Parents, do not provoke your children to anger, but bring them up trained and attentive to God.

[5]Slaves, be obedient to your earthly owners with fear and trembling in singleness of heart as you would obey Christ, [6]not as laborers who need watching, but as the servants of Christ, doing the will of God wholeheartedly. [7]Gladly serve as to God and not to humans, [8]knowing that whatever good you do, you will receive the same from God, whether you are slave or free. [9]Owners, do the same toward them. Refrain from threatening, knowing that your Owner and theirs is in heaven and that there is no favoritism with God.

SPIRITUAL WARFARE

[10]Finally, believers, be strong in the mighty power that is God in you. [11]Put on the whole armor of God, so that you are able to stand against the wiles of the devil. [12]For we do not wrestle against flesh and blood, but against principalities, against powers, against the rulers of the darkness of this world and against spiritual wickedness in high places. [13]Therefore put on the whole armor of God so that you will be able to withstand on the evil day. Then when it is over, you will still be standing. [14]Stand, therefore, with truth fastened around your waist. Have on the breastplate of righteousness, [15]and have your feet shod and ready with the good news about peace. [16]Above all, take the shield of faith, with which you will be able to quench all the fiery darts of the wicked one. [17]Take the helmet of salvation and the sword of the Spirit, which is the word of God, [18]praying always with every prayer and request in the Spirit. Be watchful as you persevere in prayer for all the saints. [19]Pray also for me, so that words may be given to me, and so that I may open my mouth boldly to make known the mystery of the good news [20]for which I am an ambassador in chains. Pray that I speak boldly, as I should.

PERSONAL GREETINGS

[21]Tychicus, a beloved brother and faithful servant of God, will make known to you everything about my affairs and how I am doing. [22]I have sent him to you for this purpose: to bring you news of me and to comfort your hearts. [23]Peace, love and faith to all the believers from God our heavenly Parent and from our Sovereign Jesus Christ. [24]Grace to all those who love our Sovereign Jesus Christ in purity.

Philippians

GREETINGS, ENCOURAGEMENTS AND INSTRUCTIONS

1:1Paul and Timothy, the servants of Christ Jesus, to all the saints in Christ Jesus who are at Philippi, and to the bishops who serve. 2Goodwill and peace to you from God our heavenly Parent and from our Sovereign Jesus Christ. 3I thank my God upon every remembrance of you. 4In every prayer of mine for you, I always pray with joy 5because of your participation in the good news from the first day until now. 6And I am confident of this: that the One who began a good work in you will carry it on to fulfillment until the day of Christ Jesus. 7It is right for me to think this way about you, because I have you in my heart and because both in my chains and in the defense and confirmation of the gospel you partake of God's grace with me. 8For as God is my witness, I greatly long for you with the affection of Christ Jesus. 9I pray that your love may abound more and more in knowledge and perception, 10so that you approve what is excellent and so that you may be sincere and without offense till the day of Christ, 11filled with the fruits of righteousness which come through Jesus Christ for the glory and praise of God.

12I want you to understand, believers, that what happened to me has resulted in the furtherance of the gospel 13and shows everyone in the palace and elsewhere that I am in chains for Christ. 14Many of Christ's followers have become more confident because of my chains and are much more bold about telling what happened without fear.

15Though some preach Christ out of envy to annoy me, others do so with good intentions. 16The latter do it out of love, knowing that I am put here to defend the gospel. 17The former preach Christ underhandedly and insincerely, supposing they can add to my troubles in prison. 18Nevertheless, whether in pretense or in truth, Christ is being preached. In this I rejoice and will rejoice, 19for I know that through your prayers and the help of the Spirit of Jesus Christ that this will result in my release. 20I earnestly expect and hope that I will never be ashamed about anything, but will be outspoken as always, so that Christ is magnified in my body, whether in life or in death. 21For to me, to live is Christ and to die is gain. 22Nevertheless, if I live on in the flesh, this will mean more fruitful labor. Which shall I choose? I don't know. 23I am hard-pressed between the two. I have a desire to depart and be with Christ, which is far better. 24Nevertheless, to remain in the flesh is more needful for you. 25Having this conviction, I know that I will remain and continue with you to help you progress in joy and faith, 26so that your rejoicing may be abundant in Jesus Christ because of me when I come to you again.

[27] Conduct yourselves as if you were worthy of the gospel of Christ, so that whether I come to see you or am absent, I may hear that you stand in one Spirit with one mind, striving together for the faith of the gospel. [28] Do not be alarmed by anything your adversaries do. This will be a sign to them that they will be destroyed and you will be saved. This will be a sign from God [29] that you have been granted on behalf of Christ, not only the privilege of believing in Christ, but also to suffer for Christ. [30] You are now experiencing the same troubles that you saw I had, and now hear that I still have.

[2:1] If you have any encouragement in Christ, any comfort from Christ's love, any fellowship from the Spirit, any inner feeling of compassion, [2] then fulfill my joy and be like-minded, having the same love. And be of one accord and one mind. [3] Let nothing be done out of selfishness or pride, but in lowliness of mind let everyone esteem others better than themselves. [4] Each of you should look after, not only your own needs, but also the needs of others.

[5] Let this way of thinking be in you which was also in Christ Jesus: [6] Being of like nature with God, Christ did not try to be equal with God. [7] Christ gave up everything, took the nature of a servant, was made in the likeness of humans, [8] appeared in human circumstances and became humble and obedient to death, even the death of the cross. [9] Therefore God highly exalted Christ and gave Christ a name that is above every name, [10] that at the name of Jesus every knee shall bow, in heaven and on earth and under the earth, [11] and every tongue acknowledge that Jesus Christ is Sovereign, to the glory of God our heavenly Parent.

BE OBEDIENT TO THE CALL

[12] Therefore, my beloved, as you have always obeyed, not only in my presence, but now much more in my absence, work out your salvation with fear and trembling. [13] For it is God who works in you and who delights to achieve the divine purposes. [14] Do everything without arguing and complaining, [15] so that you may be blameless, innocent and the children of God. Be unstained in the midst of a crooked and perverse generation, among whom you shine like lights in the world, [16] as you hold firmly to the word that gives life. Thus I may boast on the day of Christ that I did not run or labor in vain. [17] And even if my life is sacrificed in service to your faith, I am glad and rejoice with all of you. [18] For this same reason, you should be glad and rejoice with me.

TIMOTHY AND EPAPHRODITUS

[19] If my Sovereign Jesus is willing, I hope to send Timothy to you soon. Then I will be comforted when I know your circumstances. [20] I have no one like-minded who genuinely cares about your circumstances, [21] for all seek their own things and not the things of Christ. [22] You know how Timothy has proven himself by serving with me in the gospel like a son with a father. [23] Therefore I hope to send him presently, as soon as I see how things go with me. [24] And I hope that I also will come shortly, God willing. [25] Yet I deem it necessary to send you Epaphroditus, my brother and companion in my labors, my fellow soldier but your ambassador, and the one who ministers to my needs. [26] He longs for all of you and was distressed because you heard that he was sick. [27] He truly was sick and near death, but God had mercy on him; and not only

him, but also on me, lest I have sorrow upon sorrow. [28]Therefore I am sending him quickly, so that when you see him again you may rejoice and I may be less sorrowful. [29]Receive him gladly and honor him as a believer, [30]for he risked his life and was near death for the work of Christ when you were not able to minister to me.

OUR REAL HOME

[3:1]Finally, believers, rejoice in Christ. I don't mind writing this same thing again and again, because it is good for you. [2]Beware of those who behave like dogs, beware of those who do evil, beware of those who cut. [3]For we are the circumcised, we worship God in the Spirit, we rejoice in Christ Jesus, we put no confidence in the flesh. [4]Though who has more reason to put confidence in the flesh than I? [5]Circumcised on the eighth day, of the stock of Israel, of the tribe of Benjamin, a Hebrew of Hebrews, concerning the law - a Pharisee, [6]concerning zeal - a persecutor of the church, concerning legal righteousness - blameless. [7]But what things were gain to me, those I have counted loss because of Christ. [8]Therefore I count all things as loss compared to the priceless privilege of knowing Christ Jesus my Sovereign. I have suffered the loss of all things because of Christ and count them but dung that I may gain Christ [9]and be found in Christ, not having my own righteousness which is from the law, but that which is through faith in Christ, the righteousness that is from God by faith. [10]I want to know Christ and the power of His resurrection and the fellowship of His sufferings, becoming like Him in His death [11]so that, somehow, I may attain to the resurrection of the dead. [12]Not as though I had already attained it or already been made perfect, but I pursue it to see if I might take hold of Christ Jesus, inasmuch as Christ took hold of me. [13]Believers, I don't think I have fully taken hold of Christ yet. But this one thing I do: forgetting those things that are behind and reaching out to those things that are ahead, [14]I press on toward the goal for the prize to which God calls us upward through Christ Jesus. [15]Let as many as are becoming mature keep this in mind. If anyone thinks otherwise, God will reveal this to you too. [16]Nevertheless, let us live by what we have already learned.

[17]Believers, follow my example and pay attention to those who live according to the pattern we are giving you. [18]For many live, as I have told you often and now tell you in tears, as enemies of the cross of Christ. [19]Their end is destruction, their god is their belly, their lifestyle is their shame. Their minds are on earthly things. [20]But our citizenship is in heaven and we eagerly wait for our Savior from there, our Sovereign Jesus Christ. [21]Christ will change our vile bodies into the likeness of Christ's glorious body by the same energy that enables Christ to subject all things to the divine will.

HOW TO STAND FIRM AS A CHRISTIAN

[4:1]Therefore, my dearly beloved and longed-for fellow believers, my joy and my crown, stand firm! [2]I invite Euodia and Syntyche to quit arguing, since you are believers. [3]Now I ask you, Syzygus, to help those women who labored with me in the gospel, together with Clement and the rest of my co-workers whose names are in the book of life. [4]Rejoice in Christ always - and again I say - rejoice! [5]Let your appropriate behavior be spoken of by everyone. [6]Don't be anxious about anything, but in everything by prayer and supplication with thanksgiving let your requests be made known to God. [7]And the peace of God which passes all understanding will guard your hearts and minds in Christ Jesus. [8]Finally, believers, whatever is true, whatever is honorable, whatever is fair, whatever is pure, whatever calls forth love, whatever is well spoken of, whatever encourages praise, think about these. [9]Those things that you have learned and received and heard and seen in me, do! Then the God of peace will be with you.

THE GENEROSITY OF THE PHILIPPIANS

[10]I greatly rejoice in Christ that now, at the last, your care for me has flourished again. Not that you didn't care, but you lacked opportunity. [11]Not that I am short of money, for I have learned to be content in every circumstance. [12]I know how to act in humble circumstances, and I know how to live with excess. Everywhere and in all things I have been initiated into fullness and hunger, excess and lack. [13]I can do all things through Christ who strengthens me. [14]Nevertheless, it was good of you to share in my affliction. [15]You Philippians know as well as I that in the early days of the gospel, when I departed from Macedonia, no church shared with me in regard to giving and receiving except you. [16]Even in Thessalonica you sent help again and again. [17]Not that I desire a gift, but I desire fruit that may be credited to your account. [18]I have received everything I need and have an abundance. I am full, having received from Epaphroditus what you sent. It is a fragrant offering, an acceptable sacrifice and pleasing to God. [19]And my God will supply all your needs according to the glorious riches that are in Christ Jesus. [20]Now to God our heavenly Parent be the glory forever and ever. Amen.

[21]Greet every saint in Christ Jesus. The believers with me greet you. [22]All the saints greet you, in particular those who are part of Caesar's household. [23]May the grace of our Sovereign Jesus Christ be with you all.

Colossians

1:1Paul, an apostle of Jesus Christ by the will of God, and Timothy our brother, 2to the saints and faithful believers in Christ in Colossae: Goodwill and peace to you from God our heavenly Parent.

PAUL PRAYS FOR HIS FRIENDS

3We always thank God, the heavenly Parent of our Sovereign Jesus Christ, when we pray for you. 4We have heard of your faith in Christ Jesus and your love for all the saints. 5These spring from the hope that is reserved for you in heaven - the hope that you heard about when the good news of the message of truth 6first came to you. This good news is bringing forth fruit and growing in all the world, as it has among you from the day you heard it and understood the truth about the goodwill of God. 7You learned this good news from Epaphras, our dear fellow servant, who is a faithful minister of Christ to you. 8He also declared to us your love in the Spirit. 9For this reason, since the day we heard about you, we do not cease praying for you and asking that you be filled with the knowledge of Christ's will in all wisdom and spiritual understanding, 10so that you may walk in a way pleasing to your Maker. Be fruitful in every good work and increase in the knowledge of God. 11May you be strengthened with all the power that comes from Christ's glorious power so that you may patiently suffer long and joyfully, 12giving thanks to God, who has made us fit to be partakers of the inheritance of the saints in the realm of light. 13God has rescued us from the power of darkness and translated us into the realm of God's Child. 14In God's Child we have redemption, the forgiveness of sins.

CHRIST THE CREATOR

15Jesus Christ is the image of the invisible God, the firstborn of all creation.

16Jesus Christ created everything in heaven and on earth, visible and invisible, whether thrones or governments or principalities or powers. All things were created by Christ and for Christ.

17Christ is before all things, and all things are unified by Christ.

18Christ is the head of the body, the church. Christ is the beginning, the firstborn from the dead, so that in all things Christ is preeminent;

19for in Christ all of God's perfection was pleased to dwell.

20By making peace through sacrificing His blood on the cross, Christ reconciled everything on earth and in heaven back to God.

CHRIST HAS REDEEMED YOU

[21]Once you were enemies and your minds were alienated from God by your wicked works. [22]But now through the physical death of Christ, God has made you holy and unblemished and blameless - [23]if you continue to be grounded and settled in the faith and unmoved from the hope of the gospel that you heard. I, Paul, am a minister of this good news that was preached to every creature under heaven.

CHRIST IN YOU, THE HOPE OF GLORY

[24]I now rejoice in my sufferings for you and complete in my flesh what still remains of Christ's afflictions for the body, which is the church. [25]I am its servant according to God's plan, in order to fully present to you the word of God, [26]which is the mystery of the ages and the generations, and which is now being revealed to the saints. [27]Through the saints, God gladly makes known among the nations the glorious riches of this mystery, which is: Christ in you, the hope of glory. [28]We preach Christ, warning and teaching everyone with all wisdom, so that we may present everyone perfect in Christ Jesus. [29]Therefore I labor with all the strength that Christ works so powerfully in me.

CHRISTIAN CONDUCT

[2:1]I want you to know the great anxiety I have for you and those in Laodicea, as well as the many who do not know me personally. [2]I want their hearts to be encouraged and knit together in love, so that they may be fully assured that they will understand and recognize the mystery of God which is in Christ. [3]In Christ lie hidden all the treasures of wisdom and knowledge. [4]I tell you this, lest anyone beguile you with enticing words. [5]For though I am absent from you in the flesh, yet I am with you in spirit and delight to see how orderly and steadfast your faith in Christ is.

[6]Therefore, as you received Christ Jesus our Sovereign, live in Christ [7]as you were taught, rooted and built up in Christ, established in the faith and abounding with thanksgiving. [8]Be careful that no one spoils you by the delusive selfishness of human tradition that is patterned after the primitive concepts of the world and not after Christ. [9]For in Christ the whole fullness of the Godhead dwells in human form. [10]You are complete in Christ, who is the head of all principalities and powers. [11]In Christ you are circumcised; in Christ you put off the sins of the flesh with the circumcision of Christ that is a circumcision made without hands. [12]Because of your faith in the power of God who raised Christ from the dead, you were buried with Christ in baptism and were then raised with Christ. [13]You were dead in your sins and uncircumcised in your flesh, but God quickened you together with Christ and forgave you all your offenses. [14]Christ blotted out the written ordinances that were against us and which were opposed to us and took them out of the way by nailing them to the cross. [15]Having disarmed the principalities and powers, Christ made an open show of them, triumphing over them by the cross.

[16]Therefore no one should judge you by what you eat or drink, or in regard to a holy day, New Moon or Sabbath. [17]These are a shadow of things to come, but the

reality is in Christ. [18]Let no one who insists on false humility and the worship of angels prevent you from receiving your reward. Their vain minds are puffed up and they intrude with tales of what they have seen. [19]They are no longer part of the Head, from whom all the body, nourished and knit together by ligaments and joints, grows with the growth that is from God.

[20]If you died with Christ to the primitive principles of this world, why are you still living in the world as though you were subject to its ordinances: [21]"Do not touch, do not taste, do not handle," [22]which are all going to perish in use, along with all the other commandments and doctrines of humans? [23]Those ordinances may seem wise which humble and discredit the body, but they have no value as far as the mortification of the flesh.

[3:1]If you have been raised with Christ, then seek those things that are above where Christ is, seated at the right hand of God. [2]Set your affections on the things above, and not on the things that are on the earth. [3]For you are dead and your life is hidden with Christ in God. [4]When Christ who is our life appears, then you also will appear with Christ in glory. [5]Therefore mortify the parts of your earthly body that cause impurity, sensuality, injurious longings and covetousness (which is idolatry). [6]Because of these things, the wrath of God is coming. [7]At one time you also lived that way, [8]but now you must put away all violence, bad-temper, wickedness, verbal abuse and filthy talk. [9]Do not lie to one another, for you have put off the old self with its deeds [10]and have put on the new that is being renewed in knowledge in the image of your Creator. [11]In this new self there is neither Gentile nor Jew, circumcised nor uncircumcised, upper class nor lower class, slave nor free; but Christ is all and is in all.

[12]Therefore, as the holy and beloved chosen of God, put on compassion, kindness, humility, gentleness, [13]tolerance and forgiveness for one another. If one person finds fault with another, forgive that person, even as Christ forgave you. [14]In addition to all these, put on love, which connects all these together into perfection. [15]Let the peace of God rule in your hearts, since to this you were called as one body. And be thankful. [16]Let the word of Christ dwell in you richly as you teach and admonish one another with all wisdom by means of psalms, hymns and spiritual songs, singing with goodwill in your hearts to God. [17]And whatever you do in word or deed, do it all in the name of our Sovereign Jesus, giving thanks to God our heavenly Parent through Jesus.

[18]Wives, be devoted to your husbands, as is fitting for a follower of Christ. [19]Husbands, love your wives, and do not be severe with them. [20]Children, listen attentively to your parents, for this pleases God. [21]Parents, do not provoke your children to resentment, lest they become discouraged. [22]Employees, listen attentively to your employers in this world, not as those courting favor who need watching, but with singleness of heart, fearing God. [23]Whatever you do, do it with all your hearts as to God and not to humans. [24]Know that you will receive an inheritance from the Holy One as a reward, for you serve Christ our Sovereign. [25]Those who do wrong will be repaid for their wrongs, for there is no favoritism.

4:1Owners, give your employees what is fair and equitable, knowing that you also have an Owner in heaven.

2Continue in prayer. Watch for Christ's return with thanksgiving. 3And pray for us, that God will open a door for us to tell the story of the mystery of Christ, for which I am in chains. 4Pray also that I may make the message clear. 5Be wise in your dealings with outsiders, making the most of your opportunities. 6Let your speech be gracious and seasoned with salt, so that you may know how to properly answer everyone.

7Tychicus will tell you all my news. He is a beloved brother, a faithful deacon and a fellow servant of God. 8I have sent him to you for the purpose of letting you know our circumstances and comforting your hearts. 9He is coming with Onesimus, a faithful and beloved brother who is one of you. They will tell you all the things that are happening here. 10My fellow prisoner Aristarchus greets you, and so does Mark, the cousin of Barnabas. You have received instructions concerning him. If Mark comes to you, welcome him. 11Jesus, who is called Justus, also greets you. These Jews are my fellow workers in God's realm and they have been a comfort to me. 12Epaphras, who is one of you and a servant of Christ, greets you. He is always praying fervently for you, so that you may be perfect and filled with everything that is God's will. 13I can tell you that he has a great zeal for you and for those in Laodicea and Hierapolis. 14Luke the beloved physician and Demas greet you. 15Greetings to the believers in Laodicea, and to Nympha and the church in her home. 16When this is read among you, be certain that it is also read in the church at Laodicea. And you likewise are to read the letter to Laodicea. 17Tell Archippus, "Be sure to fulfill the ministry you have received from Christ." 18I, Paul, write this salutation by my own hand. Remember my chains. May God's grace be with you.

First Thessalonians

$^{1:1}$Paul, Silas and Timothy, to the church of the Thessalonians, who belong to God our heavenly Parent and to our Sovereign Jesus Christ. Goodwill and peace to you. ^{2}We give thanks to God continually for all of you, mentioning you in our prayers. ^{3}We always remember your work of faith and labor of love and patient hope in our Sovereign Jesus Christ in the sight of our God and heavenly Parent.

^{4}Believers, we know that God has chosen you, ^{5}for our gospel came to you not only in words, but also in the power and assurance of the Holy Spirit. You know our manner of living when we were among you, and you know that it was for your benefit. ^{6}You became followers of us and of Christ and received the message with joy from the Holy Spirit despite much affliction. ^{7}Thus you were examples to all who believe in Macedonia and Achaia. ^{8}For the word of God rang out from you, not only in Macedonia and Achaia, but also in every other place. Your faith in God has spread abroad so that we need not say anything. ^{9}Those people tell us how we came to you, how you turned to God from idols to serve the living and true God ^{10}and how you are waiting for God's Child from heaven whom God raised from the dead - Jesus, who rescues us from the wrath to come.

$^{2:1}$For you yourselves know, believers, that our coming to you was not in vain. ^{2}Even after we had suffered and were shamefully treated at Philippi, we had courage to tell you the good news of God, despite much opposition. ^{3}For our preaching is not fraudulent or impure or a trick, ^{4}but as we are allowed by God to be entrusted with the good news, so we speak. We do not do this to please humans, for God examines our hearts. ^{5}At no time did we use flattering words, nor did we use pretense to cover up greed, as God is our witness. ^{6}We did not seek praise from humans, either from you or from others, though we might have been quite heavy on you as the apostles of Christ. ^{7}Instead, we were gentle among you, like a mother taking care of her little children. ^{8}We longed for you and were willing to impart to you, not only the good news, but also our very lives. You were dear to us, ^{9}believers. You remember our labor and travail and how we worked night and day so as not to be a burden on any of you as we preached to you the good news of God. ^{10}You are witnesses, and God also, of how holy, just and blameless we behaved among you who believed. ^{11}You know how we encouraged every one of you and begged you to listen, just like a father would do with his children. ^{12}We did this so you would live lives worthy of God, who has called you into the glory of the heavenly realm.

^{13}For this reason we thank God continually, because when you received the word of God which you heard from us, you accepted it. You did not accept it as a message from humans, but as it is in truth, the message from God which actively works in you who believe. [14]You believers became like the churches of God in Judea who are in Christ Jesus, for you were treated by your own people like those churches were treated by their fellow Jews. [15]Those Jews are the ones who killed Christ Jesus and their own prophets and also persecuted us. They do not please God and are opposed to all people. [16]They forbid us to speak salvation to the Gentiles, and so they fill up the cup of their sins. Now the wrath of God has come upon them completely.

[17]Believers, though we were separated from you for a short time, we still think of you constantly. We greatly desire to see you face to face and endeavored very hard to do so. [18]We wanted to come to you. I, Paul, tried again and again, but Satan hindered us. [19]For what is our hope, our joy and our crown of rejoicing? Is it not you in the presence of our Sovereign Jesus Christ at Christ's return? [20]You are indeed our glory and our joy.

[3:1]When we could no longer endure, we decided to remain at Athens alone [2]and send Timothy, our brother and God's servant. He is our fellow laborer in the gospel of Christ and will encourage you and establish you in your faith, [3]so that no one is unsettled by these afflictions. For you yourselves know that we were destined to have troubles. [4]Even while we were with you, we warned you that there would be tribulation. As you know, it has come to pass. [5]For this reason I could no longer endure and I sent to find out about your faith, lest in some way the tempter had tempted you and we had labored in vain. [6]But now Timothy has returned to us from you and brought us good news of your faith and love. He tells us that you fondly remember us always and greatly desire to see us, even as we desire to see you. [7]Therefore, believers, in all our affliction and distress we are encouraged by you because of your faith. [8]For now we live, if you stand firm in Christ. [9]How can we thank God enough for you for all the joy you have brought us in the presence of our God? [10]Night and day we sincerely pray that we may see you again and complete what is lacking in your faith.

[11]Now may God our heavenly Parent and our Sovereign Jesus Christ make it possible for us to come to you. [12]May God make your love increase and abound toward one another and toward everyone, even as ours does toward you. [13]May your lives be established blameless and holy in the presence of our God and heavenly Parent when our Sovereign Jesus Christ comes with all the saints.

[4:1]Furthermore, believers, we beseech you and exhort you by our Sovereign Jesus that, as you have learned from us how to love and please God, you excel more and more. [2]For you know the mandate we gave you from our Sovereign Jesus. [3]The will of God is that you be holy and abstain from sexual immorality. [4]Every one of you should learn how to control your body in a holy and honorable way. [5]Do not give in to lust and longings like the pagans who do not know God.

[6]Do not defraud another believer in business. God is the avenger, as we have warned you previously. [7]God has not called us to uncleanness, but to holiness. [8]The one who would set these instructions aside is disobeying God, not humans. And God

is the One who has given us the Holy Spirit.

[9]Now as for loving one another, I need not write you, for you yourselves are taught by God to love one another. [10]And indeed you do love all the believers in Macedonia. But we beseech you, believers, to do even more. [11]Live a quiet life and mind your own business. Work with your hands as we instructed you [12]and conduct yourselves with dignity toward those who are outside the faith so that you lack nothing.

THE RETURN OF CHRIST WITH THE REDEEMED

[13]Believers, I do not want you to be ignorant concerning those who sleep or to be sad like those who have no hope. [14]If we believe that Jesus died and rose again, then we believe that God will also bring with Jesus those who sleep. [15]Here is a message from Christ through us: We who are alive and remain until the coming of Christ will not precede those who are asleep. [16]For Christ will descend from heaven with a shout and with the voice of the archangel. With a blast from the trumpet of God, the dead in Christ will rise first. [17]Then we who are alive and remain will be caught up together with them in the clouds to meet Christ in the air. And so we will be with Christ forever. [18]Therefore encourage one another with these words.

[5:1]But of the times and the seasons, believers, you have no need for me to write to you, [2]for you know perfectly well that the day of Christ will come like a thief in the night. [3]When people are saying, "Peace and safety," then destruction will come suddenly upon them like labor pains come upon a pregnant woman. They will not escape. [4]But you, believers, are not in the dark. That day will not find you caught like a thief. [5]You are children of light and children of the day. We are not of the night or of darkness. [6]Therefore let us not sleep as others do, but let us watch and be sober. [7]For those who sleep, sleep in the night. And those who get drunk are drunk at night. [8]But we are of the day. So be sober, putting on the breastplate of faith and love and for a helmet the hope of salvation. [9]God has not destined us for wrath, but to receive salvation through our Sovereign Jesus Christ. [10]Christ died for us so that, whether we are awake or asleep, we may live together with Christ. [11]Therefore encourage and strengthen one another, even as you are doing.

[12]Believers, we beseech you to be aware of those who labor among you who are over you in Christ and who admonish you. [13]Esteem them highly and love them for their work. Be at peace among yourselves. [14]We further exhort you, believers, to warn those who are unruly, to encourage the faint of heart, to support the weak and to be patient toward everyone. [15]See that you do not repay injury for injury, but always pursue what is good among yourselves and with everyone else. [16]Rejoice always. [17]Pray without ceasing. [18]In everything give thanks, for this is the will of God in Christ Jesus concerning you. [19]Do not quench the Spirit. [20]Do not despise prophesy. [21]Test everything. Hold fast to that which is good. [22]Avoid even the appearance of evil. [23]May the God of peace completely sanctify you. May your whole spirit, soul and body be kept blameless until the coming of our Sovereign Jesus Christ. [24]Christ who calls you is faithful and will do this. [25]Believers, pray for us. [26]Greet all the believers with a holy kiss. [27]I urge you in the name of Christ to read this letter to all the believers. [28]The goodwill of our Sovereign Jesus Christ be with you!

Second Thessalonians

[1:1]Paul, Silas and Timothy, to the church of the Thessalonians, who belong to God our heavenly Parent and to our Sovereign Jesus Christ. [2]Goodwill and peace to you from God our heavenly Parent and from our Sovereign Jesus Christ.

[3]It is fitting that we owe thanks to God for you always, believers, because your faith keeps growing and the love each of you has for the others increases, [4]so that we ourselves brag about you in the churches of God for your patience and your faith through all the persecutions and tribulations that you endure. [5]This shows, through the righteous judgment of God, that you are to be counted worthy of God's realm, for which you are suffering.

[6]God is righteous and will see that affliction is sent on those who trouble you. [7]God will give rest to you who are troubled, along with us, when Jesus Christ is revealed from heaven with God's mighty angels [8]in flaming fire. God's vengeance will be on those who do not wish to know God and who do not obey the gospel of our Sovereign Jesus Christ. [9]They will be punished with everlasting destruction, forever separated from Christ's presence and from the glory of Christ's power [10]when Christ comes to receive glory from the saints and admiration from all who believe. You will be there also, because our testimony among you was believed.

[11]Therefore we always pray for you, asking that our God would count you worthy of the life you were called to and powerfully fulfill every good purpose of yours and every act of faith, [12]so that the name of Jesus Christ may be glorified in you, and you in Christ, according to the goodwill of our God and of our Sovereign Jesus Christ.

THE COMING OF THE LAWLESS ONE BEFORE THE DAY OF CHRIST

[2:1]Now regarding the coming of our Sovereign Jesus Christ and our being gathered together to be with Christ: We beseech you, believers, [2]not to be disturbed in mind or troubled by a spirit or by a story or by a letter supposedly from us saying that the day of Christ is at hand. [3]Let no one deceive you in any way. That day will not come until the abandonment of loyalty occurs and the man of lawlessness is revealed, the son of destruction [4]who opposes and exalts himself above all that is called God or is worshiped. He will sit in the temple of God and show himself off as God.

[5]Don't you remember that when I was with you I told you these things? [6]And now you know what is holding him back. He will be revealed in his time. [7]For the mystery of iniquity is already at work, only he who now restrains will continue until he is taken out of the way. [8]Then the lawless one will be revealed, but Christ will overthrow him by

breathing on him. He will be rendered powerless by the brightness of Christ's coming. [9]The lawless one will come with the power of Satan and do deceitful miracles, signs and wonders. [10]Those who are perishing will be deceived by every sort of wickedness because they would not accept and love the truth and so be saved. [11]For this reason God sends a strong delusion on them so that they believe the lie. [12]And so all will be judged who have not believed the truth but approve of injustice.

[13]But we owe thanks to God continually for you, believers. You are loved by Christ, because God from the beginning chose you through sanctification by the Spirit and through belief in the truth. [14]God used the good news that we brought, so that you might share in the glory of our Sovereign Jesus Christ. [15]Therefore, believers, stand and hold on to the principles we have taught, whether by word of mouth or by letter. [16]Now may our Sovereign Jesus Christ and God our heavenly Parent who loved us and gave us everlasting encouragement and a sure hope [17]encourage your hearts and establish you in every good thought and work.

[3:1]Finally, believers, pray for us that the message about Christ may march onward and be cherished, even as it is with you. [2]Pray that we may stay out of the flow of unreasonable and hurtful people, for not everyone has faith. [3]But Christ is faithful; Christ will establish you and keep you from calamity. [4]We have confidence in Christ regarding you, that you are doing and will do that which we command. [5]May Christ direct your hearts to the love of God and the cheerful endurance that is Christ.

[6]Now we command you, believers, in the name of our Sovereign Jesus Christ, that you keep away from every believer who lives disorderly and not according to the principles you learned from us. [7]You know that you ought to follow our example. We were not disorderly among you, [8]nor did we eat anyone's food without paying. We worked hard night and day so that we would not be an expense to any of you. [9]Not that we did not have the right, but we wanted to make ourselves an example for you to follow. [10]While we were still with you we commanded you: Anyone who will not work shall not eat. [11]We hear that some live among you who are disorderly, do not work at all and are busybodies. [12]We command and exhort by our Sovereign Jesus Christ that such people quietly get to work so that they may eat their own food.

[13]Believers, do not became weary of doing right. [14]If some do not obey our instructions in this letter, take note of them and do not associate with them. Then they will be ashamed. [15]Yet don't consider them enemies, but caution them as fellow Christians. [16]Now may the God of peace always give you peace in every way, and may Christ be with all of you.

[17]This greeting from Paul is in my own handwriting, which is how I sign every letter. It is the way I write. [18]The goodwill of our Sovereign Jesus Christ be with you all.

First Timothy

1:1 Paul, an apostle of Jesus Christ by the commandment of God our Savior and of Christ Jesus our hope, **2**to Timothy, my genuine son in the faith: Goodwill, mercy and peace from God our heavenly Parent and Christ Jesus our Sovereign.

3I urged you to remain at Ephesus when I went to Macedonia so that you could warn certain people not to teach strange doctrines **4**or give attention to myths and endless genealogies. These only raise more questions, instead of promoting the dispensation of God which is by faith. **5**The goal of the Christian message is love from a pure heart, a good conscience and a sincere faith. **6**Some have swerved and turned aside from these to meaningless babbling. **7**They desire to be teachers of the law, but they don't understand what they are saying or what it is they are offering. **8**We know that the law is good if it is used rightly, **9**and we understand that the law is not made for good people, but for the lawless and disobedient, for the ungodly and for sinners, for the unholy and profane, for those who kill their fathers or mothers, for murderers, **10**for male prostitutes and sodomites, kidnappers, liars, perjurers and any others who do anything contrary to the sound doctrine **11**laid down by the glorious gospel of the blessed God that was entrusted to me.

GRATITUDE FOR GOD'S FORGIVENESS

12I thank Christ Jesus our Sovereign, who enabled me and considered me faithful and put me into the ministry. **13**I was once a slanderous and overbearing persecutor, but I was given mercy because I did it in ignorance and unbelief. **14**Then the goodwill of God overflowed me with the faith and the love that are in Christ Jesus.

15Here is a faithful saying worthy of complete acceptance: Christ Jesus came into the world to save sinners. And I am the worst. **16**But for this reason I was given mercy, so that in me Christ Jesus might show the endless patience that is an example to those who would believe in Christ and live forever. **17**Now to the Sovereign eternal, immortal, invisible, the only wise God, be honor and glory forever and ever. Amen.

18Timothy, my son, I commit this instruction to you according to the prophecies once spoken over you, so that by them you may fight the good fight, **19**holding on to faith and a good conscience. Some have put these away and shipwrecked their faith. **20**Among them are Hymenaeus and Alexander, whom I have turned over to Satan so that they will learn not to blaspheme.

PAUL'S INSTRUCTIONS TO THE PEOPLE OF ANTIQUITY

2:1 Therefore I urge that, first of all, petitions, prayers, intercessions and thanksgiving be made for everyone, **2**and for kings and all those in authority, so that we may lead quiet and peaceable lives in all godliness and honor. [3]This is good and acceptable in the sight of God our Savior, [4]who wants every human to be saved and to come into a knowledge of the truth. [5]For there is one God and one mediator between God and humans - Christ Jesus - the one who came in human form. [6]Christ gave Himself as a ransom for every one, as was attested at the proper time. [7]For this I was appointed a preacher and an apostle (I speak the truth in Christ and do not lie) and a teacher of faith and truth to the Gentiles. [8]I want men everywhere to pray and lift up holy hands without wrath and argument. [9]Women should dress in suitable clothing, modest and reasonable, not with braided hair or gold or pearls or expensive clothes, [10]but with good works, as is becoming for women who profess godliness. [11]They should silently learn in restful quietness. [12]I, Paul, do not allow a woman to teach or to have authority over the man. She must keep quiet. [13]For Adam was formed first, and then Eve. [14]Adam was not deceived, but the woman was deceived and disobedient. [15]She will be saved through childbearing if she continues in faith, love and holiness - with reasonableness.

[3:1]This is a true saying: Those who desire to be bishops desire a good work. [2]Bishops must be blameless, have only one spouse, be vigilant, self-controlled, orderly, hospitable, able to teach; [3]not drinkers or pugnacious, but gentle; not contentious or covetous, [4]but who manage their households well and whose children are obedient and respectful. [5]For if they cannot manage their own households, how can they take care of the church of God? [6]Not novices, lest, lifted up with pride, they incur the same condemnation as the devil. [7]Moreover, they must have a good report from outsiders, lest they be reproached and fall into the snare of the devil.

[8]Likewise, the ministers must be respected, not equivocal or drinkers or greedily sordid, [9]but holding the mystery of the faith with a clean conscience. [10]These must first be tested, and then they may become ministers if they are found blameless. [11]Even so, their spouses must be respectable, not slanderers, but sober and faithful in all things. [12]Ministers must have only one spouse and manage their children and their households well, [13]for those who serve well acquire dignity and great assurance in their faith in Christ Jesus.

FURTHER REVELATIONS AND INSTRUCTIONS

[14]I write you this, hoping to come to you shortly. [15]But if I delay, you will know how you ought to behave in the household of God, which is the church of the living God, the pillar and foundation of truth. [16]Without doubt, the mystery of godliness is great: God appeared in the flesh, was justified by the Spirit, seen by angels, preached among the Gentiles, was believed by the world and was taken up to glory.

[4:1]The Spirit clearly says that in the last days some will depart from the faith and give attention to deceiving spirits and doctrines of demons [2]given through lying hypocrites whose consciences have been seared with a hot iron. [3]They will forbid people to marry or eat certain foods that God created to be received with thanksgiving by those who believe and know the truth. [4]Everything is created by God, and nothing is to be rejected if it is received with thanksgiving, [5]for it is sanctified by the word of God and prayer.

[6]If you remind other believers about these things, you will be a good minister of Christ Jesus, nourished by the words of faith and good doctrine that you have followed. [7]Have nothing to do with silly godless myths, but train yourselves toward godliness. [8]For while bodily training is somewhat profitable, godliness is profitable in every way, having promise for the life that now is and for that which is to come. [9]This is a faithful saying worthy of full acceptance. [10]Therefore we labor and strive, because we trust in the living God who is the Savior of all people, especially those who believe. [11]Command and teach these things.

[12]Let no one despise your youth, but be an example to the believers in speech, in conduct, in love, in faith and in purity. [13]Until I come, attend to reading, preaching and teaching. [14]Do not neglect the gift that is in you which was given you by prophecy when the elders laid hands on you. [15]Take care of these and give yourself wholly to them, so that your progress may be apparent to all. [16]Pay close attention to yourself and the doctrine and continue in these things, for in doing so you will save yourself and those who hear you.

[5:1]Do not rebuke an older man, but appeal to him as you would your father. Treat the younger men as brothers, [2]the older women as mothers and the younger women as sisters, with all purity.

[3]Honor widows who are really widows. [4]But if a widow has children or grandchildren, let them first show respect at home and pay back their parents, for that is acceptable to God. [5]She who is truly a widow and alone trusts in God and continues to petition and pray night and day. [6]But she who lives for pleasure is dead, though she lives. [7]Command the people to do these things so they will be without fault. [8]Those who do not provide for their relatives, and especially for their own family, deny the faith and are worse than infidels.

[9]Any widow enrolled on the list should be at least sixty years old, the wife of one husband, [10]well known for good works, such as: bringing up children, lodging strangers, washing the feet of the saints, relieving the afflicted and volunteering for every good work. [11]But refuse the younger widows, for when their natural desires grow stronger than their devotion to Christ, they want to marry, [12]thus bringing judgment because they cast off their first loyalty. [13]At the same time they learn to be idle and wander from house to house. And not only idle, but tattlers and busybodies also, speaking things they should not. [14]Therefore I want the younger widows to marry, bear children, manage the house and give no occasion to the adversary to reproach them. [15]Some have already turned aside after Satan. [16]If any believers have widows in their families, they must help them, so that the church may help those who are really widows.

[17]Those elders who rule well will be considered worthy of double honor, especially those who labor in the word and doctrine. [18]Scripture says, "You must not muzzle the ox that treads out the grain," and, "The laborer is worthy of a reward." [19]Do not receive an accusation against an elder unless there are two or three witnesses. [20]Rebuke those who sin. Do it in front of everyone so that others will be warned. [21]I charge you before God and our Sovereign Jesus Christ and the chosen angels to observe this

without favoritism or partiality.

²²Do not lay hands on anyone hastily or partake of the sins of others. Keep yourself pure. ²³Do not drink water exclusively, but use a little wine for your stomach and your other frequent infirmities.

²⁴Some people's sins are so obvious that they run ahead of them to judgment. But some appear later. ²⁵Likewise, good works are obvious, and even those that are not cannot be hidden.

^{6:1}Employees who are believers should treat their employers honorably so that the name of God and our teachings won't be slandered. ²Those who have believing employers must not show less respect for them because they are believers. Rather, serve them well for their benefit. They are faithful and beloved by you. Teach and exhort these things. ³Those who teach otherwise and do not consent to the wholesome message of our Sovereign Jesus Christ and the doctrine of godliness ⁴are proud and know nothing. They have a sick need to question every word of the message. This leads to envy, strife, slander, harmful assumptions ⁵and offensive diatribe from people with corrupt minds who have lost the truth and suppose that godliness is a way to make money. ⁶But godliness with contentment is great gain. ⁷For we brought nothing into this world and we can take nothing out. ⁸Having food and clothing, let us be content with that. ⁹Those who desire to be rich fall into temptations and snares and many foolish and harmful lusts that drown humans in destruction and loss. ¹⁰For the love of money is the root of all adversity. Some who have coveted it have been led astray from the faith and have pierced themselves through with many sorrows.

¹¹But you, O man of God, flee from these things! Pursue righteousness, godliness, faith, love, patience and humility. ¹²Fight the good fight of faith. Take hold of the eternal life to which you were called when you professed a good profession before many witnesses. ¹³In the sight of God, who gives life to all, and Jesus Christ, who before Pontius Pilate gave a worthy testimony, I charge you ¹⁴to keep this commandment unblemished and without fault until the appearing of our Sovereign Jesus Christ. ¹⁵In God's time Christ will be shown by the blessed and only Potentate, the Supreme Authority and the Ruler of rulers, ¹⁶who alone has immortality and who lives in unapproachable light, whom no human has seen or can see and to whom honor and power belong forevermore. Amen.

¹⁷Command those who are rich in this world not to have proud thoughts or to trust in uncertain riches but to trust in the living God who richly gives us all things to enjoy. ¹⁸Command that they do good, be rich in good works, be ready to be liberal and willing to share, ¹⁹laying up for themselves a foundation against the time to come when they take hold of eternal life.

²⁰O Timothy, guard that which has been entrusted to you. Avoid the profane philosophical arguments and conflicting theories of what is falsely called knowledge ²¹which some have professed and thereby have deviated from the faith. May God's grace be with you.

Second Timothy

¹:¹Paul, an apostle of Jesus Christ by the will of God according to the promise of life which is in Christ Jesus, ²to Timothy, my beloved son: Goodwill, mercy and peace from God our heavenly Parent and Christ Jesus our Sovereign.

³I serve the God my ancestors did with a pure conscience, as night and day without ceasing I remember you in my prayers and thank God for you. ⁴I remember your tears and greatly desire to see you. Then I will be filled with joy. ⁵I remember the sincere faith of your grandmother Lois and your mother Eunice. And I am sure that you have the same faith. ⁶Therefore I remind you to stir up the flame of the gift of God that is in you through the laying on of my hands. ⁷For God has not given us a spirit of fear, but of power and love and self-control. ⁸Therefore do not be ashamed to tell others about Christ or about me, Christ's prisoner. Suffer hardship for the sake of the gospel by means of the power of God - ⁹who saved us and called us with a holy calling - not because of our works, but because of God's own purpose and goodwill. What was given us in Christ Jesus before the world began ¹⁰has now been revealed by the appearing of our Savior, Jesus Christ. Christ brought life and immortality to light through the good news. ¹¹I was appointed a preacher, an apostle and a teacher of this good news. ¹²That is the reason I am suffering these things. Nevertheless I am not ashamed, for I know whom I have believed and am persuaded that Christ is able to safeguard what I have committed to Christ until that day. ¹³Follow the pattern of the true message you have heard from me as you rest in the faith and love that are in Christ Jesus. ¹⁴Guard the good that was committed to you by the Holy Spirit who lives in us.

¹⁵Did you know that all those in Asia have turned away from me, including Phygelus and Hermogenes? ¹⁶May God show mercy to the family of Onesiphorus. He often refreshed me and was not ashamed of my chains. ¹⁷When he was in Rome, he searched for me diligently and found me. ¹⁸May God grant that he find mercy on judgment day. You know very well all the ways he ministered to me at Ephesus.

²:¹You then, my son, be strong in the grace bestowed by Christ Jesus. ²Commit to faithful Christians what you have heard from me among many witnesses. They must be able to teach others also. ³Endure hardship as a good soldier of Christ Jesus. ⁴No soldier in the military becomes entangled with the affairs of civilian life, lest the commander who chose that soldier be displeased. ⁵If you participate, you will not win a prize unless you participate by the rules. ⁶The farmer who labors must have the first

share of the harvest. [7]Consider what I say, and may God give you understanding in everything. [8]Remember that Jesus Christ, who was descended from David, was raised from the dead. Because of my gospel, [9]I undergo hardship like a criminal in chains. But the message of God is not chained. [10]I endure everything for the sake of the chosen, so that they also may obtain the salvation and eternal glory that is in Christ Jesus. [11]Here is a trustworthy message: If we die with Christ, we will also live with Christ. [12]If we persevere, we will also reign with Christ. If we reject Christ, Christ will also reject us. [13]If we are without faith, Christ remains faithful and will fulfill every promise. [14]Remind the people about this. Warn them before God not to argue and contend. It doesn't do any good, and those who hear may forsake the faith.

[15]Study to show yourself approved by God, a worker who does not need to be ashamed, correctly teaching the truth. [16]Shun the profane philosophical arguments that only lead to more ungodliness. [17]Their words gnaw away like an ulcer. Hymenaeus and Philetus are among those who [18]have erred regarding the truth by saying that the resurrection has already taken place. They destroy the faith of some. [19]Nevertheless, the foundation of God stands sure, having this seal, "Christ knows those who are Christians," and, "Let everyone who names the name of Christ avoid being unjust."

[20]In a great house there are not only vessels of gold and silver, but also of wood and earthenware. Some are for dignified occasions and some for less dignified. [21]Those who become thoroughly cleansed will become vessels of dignity - holy and appropriate for God's use and prepared for every good work. [22]Flee from youthful lusts; pursue righteousness, faith, love and peace along with those who call on God from a pure heart. [23]Avoid foolish and ignorant questions, knowing that they start arguments. [24]The servants of God must not quarrel but be gentle with everyone, communicative and patient, [25]meekly instructing those who are opposed in case God gives them a change of heart leading to a knowledge of the truth. [26]Then they may escape out of the snare of the devil, after being taken captive and kept in slavery.

[3:1]Know this also: Perilous times will come in the last days. [2]People will be lovers of themselves, covetous, boasters, proud, blasphemers, disobedient to parents, unthankful, unholy, [3]hard-hearted toward their families, uncompromising deceivers without self-control, fierce, haters of anything good, [4]treacherous, reckless, puffed up, loving pleasure rather than loving God - [5]having a form of godliness, but denying its power. Turn away from such people. [6]These are the sort who sneak into homes and seduce silly women who are laden with sins and driven by various lusts. [7]These people are ever learning but never able to recognize the truth. [8]Just as Jannes and Jambres withstood Moses, so also these resist the truth. They have corrupt minds and are worthless concerning the faith. [9]But they will not get very far, for their folly will be obvious to everyone, as was the case with those two.

[10]But you fully know my doctrine, manner of life, purpose, faith, long-suffering, love, patience, [11]persecutions, afflictions which came to me at Antioch and Iconium and Lystra and what persecutions I endured. God rescued me from them all. [12]All

those who live godly lives in Christ Jesus will suffer persecution. [13]But degenerate frauds will become worse and worse, deceiving and being deceived. [14]Therefore continue in what you have learned and are assured of, knowing from whom you learned it. [15]For from childhood you have known the holy Scriptures which are able to make you wise enough to want salvation through faith in Christ Jesus. [16]All Scripture is breathed on by God and is profitable for instruction, for reproof, for correction and for training in righteousness, [17]so that a Christian may become perfect and fully equipped for every good work.

[4:1]I urge you before God and our Sovereign Jesus Christ, who will appear to judge the living and the dead in the heavenly realm, [2]preach the message at opportune and inopportune times. Reprove, rebuke and encourage with patient instruction. [3]For the time will come when they will not endure sound doctrine, but with tickling ears they will seek teachers [4]who will turn their ears away from the truth and turn them to myths. [5]Therefore watch yourself in all things, endure affliction, do the work of an evangelist and fully carry out your ministry. [6]I am now ready to be poured out as a sacrifice to God, and the time of my departure is at hand. [7]I fought the good fight, I finished the race, I kept the faith. [8]There remains for me a crown of righteousness that Christ, the righteous judge, will give me on that day. And not to me only, but to all those who long for Christ's appearing.

[9]Make every effort to come to me quickly, [10]for Demas has forsaken me. He loved this present world and departed for Thessalonica. Crescens went to Galatia and Titus to Dalmatia. [11]Only Luke is with me. Get Mark and bring him with you, for he is useful to me in the ministry. [12]I sent Tychicus to Ephesus. [13]When you come, bring the coat I left with Carpus at Troas. And bring the books, especially the parchments. [14]Alexander the coppersmith did me much harm. God will repay him for what he has done. [15]You should be wary of him too, for he greatly opposed our message.

[16]At my first trial no one stood with me. Everyone forsook me; may it not be held against them. [17]Christ stood with me and strengthened me, so that my preaching might be fully known, and so that all the Gentiles would hear. I was rescued out of the mouth of the lion. [18]Christ will rescue me from every harmful act and save me for the heavenly realm. May Christ be glorified forever and ever. Amen.

[19]Greet Prisca and Aquila and the family of Onesiphorus. [20]Erastus remained at Corinth. I left Trophimus sick at Miletum. [21]Make every effort to come before winter. Eubulus, Pudens, Linus, Claudia and all the believers greet you. [22]May our Sovereign Jesus Christ be with your spirit. God's grace be with you.

Titus

¹:¹From Paul, a servant of God and an apostle of Jesus Christ. I was sent to teach God's chosen the faith and knowledge about the truth that leads to godliness ²in anticipation of eternal life. God, who does not lie, promised this eternal life before the world began. ³At the proper time God declared the message through preaching, and it was committed to me by the command of God our Savior.

⁴To Titus, my own son in the faith we share: Goodwill, mercy and peace from God our heavenly Parent and from Christ Jesus our Savior.

⁵The reason I left you in Crete was for you to set in order what was lacking and to ordain elders in every city, as I directed you. ⁶They must be blameless, married to only one spouse, and have trustworthy and well-behaved children who are believers. ⁷A bishop must be blameless as the overseer of God, not self-willed, not irascible, not a drinker, not pugnacious or sordid, ⁸but hospitable, a lover of good, sober, just, holy, temperate, ⁹holding tight the faithful message that was taught, so that bishops may be able by sound doctrine to exhort and convince the opposition.

¹⁰For there are many unruly and vain talkers and deceivers, especially those of the circumcision. ¹¹Their mouths must be stopped. They subvert whole households by teaching things they shouldn't for the sake of money. ¹²One of their own prophets said, "Cretans are always liars, depraved beasts and lazy gluttons." ¹³This report is true. Therefore rebuke them sharply. Then they may become sound in the faith ¹⁴and not pay attention to Jewish myths and the commands of those who turn them from the truth. ¹⁵To the pure all things are pure, but to those who are defiled and unbelieving, nothing is pure. Even their minds and consciences are defiled. ¹⁶They claim to know God, but in what they do they deny God. They are detestable, stubborn and unfit for any good work.

²:¹Speak the things that are suitable as sound doctrine. ²The older men must be circumspect, venerable, temperate and sound in their faith, love and endurance. ³Likewise, the older women must teach what is good and behave reverently. They must not gossip or drink too much wine. ⁴They must teach the young women to be circumspect, to love their husbands and children, ⁵to be discreet, chaste, homemakers and good and obedient to their husbands, so that the message of God is not reviled. ⁶Likewise, exhort the youths to be moderate. ⁷Set them an example of good works in everything: doctrine, purity, respectability ⁸and sound speech that cannot be condemned, so that those who are hostile may be ashamed and have

nothing bad to say about us. [9]Employees, be obedient to your employers and try to please them well in all things, not answering back, [10]not stealing, but showing everyone that you can be fully trusted, so that the doctrine of God our Savior may be appealing.

[11]The favor of God that brings salvation has appeared to everyone, [12]teaching us to deny ungodliness and worldly lusts so we may live in moderation, righteousness and godliness in this present world [13]as we look for the blessed hope and the glorious appearing of our great God and Savior, Jesus Christ. [14]Christ made the sacrifice for us in order to redeem us from all wickedness and to purify for God a people eager to do good. [15]Speak and exhort these things and rebuke with all authority. Let no one despise you.

[3:1]Remind them to be subject to rulers and authorities, to obey, to be ready for every good work, [2]to slander no one, to be peaceable and gentle and to show humility to everyone. [3]For we also were once foolish, disobedient, deceived and enslaved by motley lusts and pleasures, living in malice and envy, hateful and hating one another. [4]But when the kindness and love of God our Savior appeared [5]we were saved, not because of the righteous works we had done, but because of God's mercy and by the washing of rebirth and renewal by the Holy Spirit, [6]whom God poured out on us abundantly through Jesus Christ our Savior, [7]so that justified by God's grace, we could become heirs with the hope of eternal life. [8]This is a trustworthy saying.

I want you to affirm these things constantly, so that those who believe in God may be eager to practice good works. These are good and profitable for everyone. [9]But avoid foolish arguments, genealogies, contentions and controversies about the law, for they are unprofitable and vain. [10]Shun anyone who is a heretic, after the first and second warning, [11]knowing that they are perverted, sinful and self-condemned.

[12]When I send Artemus or Tychicus to you, make every effort to come to me at Nicopolis, for I have decided to winter there. [13]Send Zenas the lawyer and Apollos on their way at once and see that they lack nothing.

[14]Our people must learn to do good works and provide for the necessities so they may be useful.

[15]All those who are with me send you greetings. Greet those who love us in the faith. God's grace be with you all.

Philemon

1:1Paul, a prisoner of Jesus Christ, and Timothy our brother, to Philemon our beloved fellow laborer, 2to our beloved Apphia, to Archippus our fellow soldier and to the church in your home: 3Goodwill and peace to you from God our heavenly Parent and from our Sovereign Jesus Christ.

4I always thank my God as I remember you in my prayers 5because I hear of the love and faith you have for Jesus Christ and all the saints. 6I pray that the sharing of your faith may cause the active acknowledgement of all the good things we have in Christ Jesus. 7I receive great joy and encouragement from your love, because the hearts of the saints have been refreshed by you, my brother.

8Therefore may I be so bold in Christ as to encourage you to do what is proper? 9Rather, in love I urge you. I, Paul, an old man and now also a prisoner for Christ Jesus, 10appeal to you for my son Onesimus, which he has become here in prison. 11In the past he was useless to you, but now he is useful to you and to me. 12I am sending him back to you. Receive him who is my heart. 13I would have liked to have kept him with me, so that in your place he might have ministered to me while I am in chains for the gospel; 14but without your consent I preferred to do nothing, in order that your goodness to me would not be from necessity, but from willingness. 15Perhaps that was why he left you for a while - so you could have him back forever, 16not as a slave this time, but above a slave - a beloved fellow Christian, especially to me, but how much more to you, both as a person and as a believer. 17Therefore if you consider me a friend, welcome him as you would me. 18If he has wronged you or owes you anything, put that on my account. 19I, Paul, writing with my own hand, will repay. I need not even mention the fact that you owe me your very soul. 20Therefore my brother, may I rejoice over you as a follower of Christ? Cheer me up as a fellow Christian, 21for I know you will do more than I ask. I write to you, confident of your obedience.

22And one thing more: Prepare a guest room for me, for I trust that through your prayers I will return to you.

23Epaphras, my fellow prisoner in Christ Jesus, sends you greetings, 24as do Mark, Aristarchus, Demas and Luke, my fellow laborers. 25The grace of our Sovereign Jesus Christ be with your spirit.

Hebrews

THE BRILLIANT SPLENDOR OF JESUS

1:1In many ways and at various times in the past God spoke to our ancestors through the prophets; 2but in these last days God has spoken to us through God's Child, whom God appointed heir of everything and through whom God made the universe. 3God's Child shines with the brightness of God's glory and is the exact likeness of God's person. God's Child Jesus upholds everything by the power of God's word. After washing away our sins, Jesus sat down at the right hand of the Majesty on high.

ANGELS WORSHIP GOD'S CHILD

4Jesus is much greater than the angels, just as the name Jesus inherited surpasses theirs. 5For to which of the angels has God ever said, "You are My Child; today I have begotten You"? Or again, "I will be a Parent to You, and You will be My Child"? 6And again, when God's firstborn is brought into the world, God says, "Let all the angels of God worship My Child."

7About the angels God says, "I make My angels winds and My servants flames of fire." 8But about the Child, God says, "Your throne, O God, is forever and ever. Righteousness is the scepter of Your realm. 9You love righteousness and hate wickedness; therefore God, Your God, has exalted You above Your companions by anointing You with the oil of gladness."

JESUS THE AGELESS CREATOR

10God also says, "In the beginning You laid the foundations of the earth, and the heavens are the work of Your hands. 11They will perish, but You remain. They will all wear out like a garment, 12and, like a garment, You will roll them up. They will be changed, but You remain the same and Your years will never cease." 13To which of the angels has God ever said, "Sit at My right hand till I make Your enemies Your footstool"? 14Are not the angels all serving spirits sent to aid those who will inherit salvation?

THE DANGER OF IGNORING GOD'S MESSAGE

2:1Therefore we must earnestly respond to what we have heard, lest at some time we slip away. 2Since the message spoken by angels was true, and every violation and lack of response received its appropriate punishment, 3how shall we escape if we neglect so great a salvation? This salvation was first spoken of by Christ and was confirmed to us by those who heard it. 4God also testified further with signs, wonders and various miracles and gifts of the Holy Spirit given according to God's will.

ANGELS AND HUMANS

^{5}It is not to angels that God has subjected the world to come, of which we speak. ^{6}There is a place where it is written, "What are humans, that You are mindful of them, or mere mortals, that You visit them? ^{7}You made them a little lower than the angels; You crowned them with glory and honor; ^{8}You put everything in subjection under their feet." By putting everything in subjection to them, You left nothing that is not subject to them. Yet now we do not see everything subject to them. ^{9}But we see Jesus, who for a little while was made a little lower than the angels, crowned with glory and honor through suffering death. Because of the goodwill of God, Jesus died for everyone. ^{10}In the process of bringing many children to glory, it was fitting that God, for whom and by whom all things exist, should make the author of their salvation perfect through suffering. ^{11}For both the One who sanctifies and those who are sanctified all have the same heavenly Parent. That is why Jesus is not ashamed to call them sisters and brothers. ^{12}Jesus says, "I will declare Your name to My people; in the midst of the congregation I will sing praises to You." ^{13}And again, "I will put My trust in God." And again, "Look! Here I am with the children God has given Me!"

JESUS OUR HIGH PRIEST IS LIKE US IN EVERY WAY

^{14}Since the children are flesh and blood, Jesus became like them, so that through death Jesus might destroy the one who holds the power over death (that is, the devil) ^{15}and free those who were kept in slavery all their lives by their fear of death. ^{16}We know that it was not angels that Jesus came to help, but the descendants of Abraham. ^{17}Therefore it was necessary for Jesus to become like us in every way, in order to be a merciful and faithful high priest before God, able to atone for the sins of the people. ^{18}Because Jesus suffered and was tempted, Jesus is able to help those who are tempted.

$^{3:1}$Therefore, holy believers who participate in the heavenly calling, consider the apostle and high priest of our faith ^{2}who was faithful to God, just as Moses was faithful in serving all God's people. ^{3}But Jesus is considered worthy of more glory than Moses, just as one who builds a house is more valuable than the house. ^{4}Every house is built by someone, but God is the builder of all things. ^{5}Moses was a faithful servant to God's people and was a testimony to the things that would be spoken later. ^{6}But Christ is faithful as God's Child to God's people. And we are those people - if we hold on to our confidence and our firm expectation.

DO NOT HARDEN YOUR HEARTS

^{7}Therefore, as the Holy Spirit says, "Today, if you hear God's voice, ^{8}do not harden your hearts as in the rebellion, as in the time of testing in the wilderness ^{9}when your ancestors tempted Me and tested Me and saw My works for forty years. ^{10}I was grieved with that generation and said, 'Their hearts always go astray; they do not know My ways.' ^{11}So I swore in My wrath, 'They will never enter My rest.'" ^{12}Be careful, believers, lest there be in you a wicked, unbelieving heart that forsakes the living God. ^{13}Encourage one another daily while it is called "today," lest any of you become hardened by the deceitfulness of sin. ^{14}For we will be participants with Christ if we firmly hold to the end the confidence we had at the first. ^{15}Scripture says, "If you hear

God's voice today, do not harden your hearts as in the rebellion." [16]Who rebelled after they heard? Was it not those who came out of Egypt with Moses? [17]With whom was God grieved for forty years? Was it not with those who sinned and whose bodies fell in the wilderness? [18]And who was denied with an oath entrance to God's rest? Was it not those who did not believe? [19]So we see that they could not enter because of unbelief.

ENTER INTO GOD'S REST TODAY

[4:1]Though the promise of entering God's rest remains in effect, let us be afraid, lest any among you would even appear to be excluded from it. [2]For the good news was announced to us as well as to them; but the message that they heard did not benefit them, because they did not mix it with faith. [3]We who have believed will enter rest; but as God said, "I swore in My wrath that they will never enter My rest," although God's works have been finished since the world was made. [4]In a certain place God spoke about the seventh day in this way: "And God rested the seventh day from every work," [5]and again, "They will never enter My rest." [6]There remain some who will enter in, but those who first heard the good news did not enter in because they did not believe. [7]Again, God appointed a certain day, and it is "today." God said through David a long time later, "If you hear My voice today, do not harden your hearts." [8]Now if Joshua had given them rest, God would not have spoken later about another day. [9]There remains, therefore, a rest for the people of God. [10]Those who enter God's rest also cease from their work, just as God did. [11]Let us therefore do our best to enter into that rest, lest anyone fall in the same way to unbelief.

[12]The word of God is alive and powerful and sharper than any two-edged sword, piercing through to separate soul and spirit, joints and marrow, and discerning the thoughts and intentions of the heart. [13]Nothing in creation is hidden from God's sight; everything is naked and exposed to the eyes of the One to whom we are accountable.

[14]Since we have a great high priest who has passed through the heavens, Jesus the Child of God, let us hold on to our confession of faith in God's Child. [15]We do not have a high priest who is untouched by sympathy for our frailties. Jesus was tempted in every way that we are, yet Jesus did not sin. [16]Let us therefore come boldly to the throne of grace, so that we may obtain mercy and find grace to help in our time of need.

[5:1]Every high priest chosen from among humans is ordained to act on their behalf before God and to offer gifts and sacrifices for sins. [2]A high priest can have compassion on the ignorant who stray, because high priests are also hampered by frailty. [3]That is the reason the high priest offers personal sacrifices, as well as for the people. [4]High priests do not take this honor upon themselves, but must be called by God as Aaron was. [5]So also, Christ did not become a high priest for personal glory, but God said, "You are My Child, today I have begotten You." [6]God said elsewhere, "You are a priest forever in the succession of Melchizedek." [7]In the days when Christ was in the flesh, He offered up prayers and supplications with strong cries and tears to the One who was able to save Him from death. He was heard because of His reverence. [8]Though He was God's Child, He learned obedience through what He suffered. [9]Having been made perfect, Christ became the source of eternal salvation for all those who obey, [10]because God named Christ a high priest in the succession of Melchizedek.

ACT MATURELY AND GO ON TO PERFECTION

[11]We have many things to say, but it is hard to explain because you are dull of hearing. [12]You need someone to teach you the first principles of God's word again, although by this time you ought to be teachers. You need milk, rather than solid food. [13]Those who drink milk are immature and unskilled in the message of righteousness. [14]But solid food is for those who are mature. By constant practice they have trained their senses to discern between good and evil.

THE WAY TO PERFECTION

[6:1]Let us leave the elementary teachings about Christ and go on to perfection, not laying again the foundation of repentance from dead deeds, faith in God, [2]the doctrine of baptism, the laying on of hands, the resurrection of the dead and eternal judgment. [3]And this we will do, if God permits. [4]It is impossible for those who were once enlightened, who have experienced the heavenly gift, who have received a share in the Holy Spirit [5]and who have experienced the goodness of the word of God and the powers of the world to come [6]to be brought back to repentance if they fall away, for to their loss they are again crucifying and publicly shaming the Child of God.

[7]The ground that drinks in the rain that falls often upon it and produces a suitable crop for the farmer who tills it receives the blessing of God. [8]But the ground that produces thorns and thistles is worthless and ready to be cursed. In the end it will be burned.

[9]Though we speak this way, dear friends, we are sure of better things for you - things that accompany salvation. [10]God is not so unjust as to forget your work and your ministry to the saints and the love you have shown toward the name of God. [11]We desire that every one of you show this same diligence to the end until your hope is fully assured. [12]Do not become lazy, but follow those who through faith and patience inherit the promises.

[13]When God made the promise to Abraham, God said, "I swear by Myself," since there was no one greater to swear by. [14]God said, "With blessing I will bless you and with multiplying I will multiply you." [15]After Abraham patiently waited, he obtained the promise. [16]People swear by someone greater than themselves. An oath is a confirmation that ends all strife. [17]That is why God wanted to show the heirs of the promise that there would never be a change of mind. God confirmed the promise with an oath, [18]so that by these two unchangeables in which it is impossible for God to lie, we who have fled to God for refuge are encouraged to hold on to the hope set before us. [19]This hope is a sure and steadfast anchor for our souls that enters behind the veil, [20]where Jesus, who became a high priest forever in the succession of Melchizedek, has entered as a forerunner on our behalf.

JESUS: OUR GREAT HIGH PRIEST

[7:1]This Melchizedek, the ruler of Salem, priest of the Most High God, met Abraham returning from the slaughter of the kings and blessed him. [2]Abraham gave him a tenth of everything. "Melchizedek" means "righteous ruler." Melchizedek was the ruler of Salem, which also means "peaceful ruler." [3]Without mother, without father, without genealogy, without beginning of days or end of life, like the Child of God, Melchizedek remains a priest forever. [4]Consider how great he was - even our ancestor Abraham gave him a tenth of the spoils! [5]The descendants of Levi who become priests are commanded by the law to take a tithe from their fellow Jews, even though they are descendants of Abraham. [6]Melchizedek was not a descendant of Levi, yet he received tithes from Abraham and blessed him who had the promises. [7]Everyone knows that it is the lesser person who is blessed by the greater. [8]In the case of the priests who receive tithes, they die. In the case of Melchizedek, Scripture says that Melchizedek lives. [9]One might even say that Levi, who received tithes, paid tithes to Melchizedek through Abraham, [10]because Levi was still in the body of his father Abraham when Melchizedek met him.

[11]Through Levi and the priests came the law. If perfection had been attainable through Levi, what further need was there for another priest from the succession of Melchizedek and not from the succession of Aaron? [12]When the priesthood changed, it also necessitated a change in the law. [13]For the One of whom these things are spoken came from a different tribe, and no one from that tribe has ever attended at the altar. [14]It is plain that Christ descended from Judah, and Moses never said that priests could come from that tribe. [15]This becomes more clear when another priest like Melchizedek appears. [16]Christ became a high priest, not because of the laws of this world, but because of the power of an indestructible life. [17]For David prophesied, "You are a priest forever like Melchizedek." [18]Therefore the old commandment is set aside, because it was weak and useless. [19]The law made nothing perfect. But a better hope is introduced by which we may approach God. [20]And not without an oath! Others became priests by swearing an oath, [21]but with an oath God said to Jesus, "I have sworn and will not change My mind, 'You are a priest forever.'" [22]Therefore Jesus has become the guarantee of a better covenant.

[23]Because death did not allow them to continue, there were many priests. [24]But Jesus continues forever with an unchanging priesthood. [25]Therefore those who come to God through Jesus are saved forever, since Jesus always lives to make intercession for them. [26]Jesus is the high priest we need: holy, blameless, undefiled, separated from sinners and raised higher than the heavens. [27]Jesus does not need to offer daily sacrifices for personal sins and for the sins of the people as did the other high priests. Jesus did this once and for all by dying for us. [28]The law makes frail humans high priests, but the oath which came after the law consecrates God's Child, who has been made perfect forever.

JESUS: THE HIGH PRIEST OF A NEW COVENANT

[8:1]The sum of what we are saying is this: We have such a high priest. Jesus sat down at the right hand of the Majesty in heaven [2]and is a minister of the sanctuary. The sanctuary is the true tabernacle that was established by God and not by humans. [3]Every high priest is ordained to offer gifts and sacrifices, and so, it was necessary that Jesus have something to offer. [4]On earth Jesus would not be a priest, for there are priests who offer gifts according to the law [5]and who serve in a sanctuary that is a copy and a shadow of the heavenly one. When Moses was about to set up the tabernacle, he was told, "See that you make everything according to the pattern that was shown to you on the mountain." [6]But now Jesus brings into being a better ministry, because Jesus is the mediator of a nobler covenant established upon nobler promises. [7]If that first covenant had been faultless, there would have been no need for a second. [8]But God found fault with the people and said, "The days are coming when I will make a new covenant with the house if Israel and the house of Judah. [9]It will not be like the covenant I made with their ancestors on the day I took them by the hand to lead them out of the land of Egypt, for they did not continue to live by My covenant and I could not stand to look at them. [10]This is the covenant I will make with the house of Israel in those days: I will put My laws into their minds and write My laws on their hearts. I will be their God, and they will be My people. [11]They will no longer teach their neighbors or each other, saying, 'Know God!' for everyone will know Me, from the least to the greatest. [12]I will be gracious about their wrongdoing and remember their sins no more." [13]By saying, "new," God makes the first covenant obsolete, and what is obsolete and antiquated is ready to disappear.

[9:1]The first covenant had regulations for worship and an earthly sanctuary. [2]A tabernacle was set up. In the first room was the lamp, the table and the showbread in what was called the holy place. [3]Behind the second veil was a tent called the Holy of Holies. [4]In it stood the golden altar of incense and the ark of the covenant overlaid with gold. In the ark was the golden jar of manna, Aaron's rod that budded and the stone tablets of the covenant. [5]The glorious cherubs of God's glory overshadowed the mercy seat above the ark. But we cannot dwell on particulars now. [6]When all this was prepared, then the priests went regularly into the first tabernacle to perform their duties. [7]Once a year the high priest went alone into the second tent with blood to offer for himself and for the shortcomings of the people. [8]By this the Holy Spirit was making plain that the way into the Holy of Holies had not yet been revealed while the first tabernacle was still standing. [9]This can be compared to the present time in which the gifts and sacrifices being offered are not able to perfect the conscience of the worshiper. [10]Various foods, drinks, cleansings and worldly regulations are imposed until the time of restoration.

[11]Then, by way of a greater and more perfect tent not made with hands, that is, not of this creation, Christ came as the high priest of the good things that have now come. [12]Christ did not enter with the blood of goats and calves, but entered the Holy of Holies with blood offered on the cross and obtained eternal redemption once and for all. [13]If the blood of goats and bulls and the ashes of a heifer sprinkled on those who are unclean sanctifies and purifies their flesh, [14]how much more will the blood of Christ? Through the eternal Spirit, Christ offered a perfect sacrifice to God to purge our conscience from deeds that lead to death, so that you might serve the living God. [15]For this reason, Christ is the mediator of the new covenant, so that those who are called may receive the promised eternal inheritance through His death which ransomed them from the wrongs committed under the first covenant.

[16]When there is a will, it must be proven that the one who made it is dead, [17]for a will is only in force after death. It has no force at all while the one who made it is alive. [18]That is why even the first covenant did not take effect without blood. [19]When Moses had spoken every commandment of the law to the people, he took the blood of calves and goats, water, scarlet wool and hyssop. Then he sprinkled the Book and all the people, [20]saying, "This is the blood of the covenant that God has made with you." [21]Moreover, he sprinkled blood on the tabernacle and all the vessels of ministry. [22]By law almost everything is cleansed with blood, and without the shedding of blood there is no forgiveness. [23]Therefore it was necessary for the tabernacle and the vessels, which are copies of those in heaven, to be purified by the blood of animals. But the things in heaven require better sacrifices than these. [24]For Christ did not enter a holy place made by hands that is only a copy of the true one, but Christ entered heaven itself to appear in the presence of God on our behalf. [25]Nor did Christ offer a sacrifice many times, as the high priest does who enters the Holy of Holies every year with blood that is not his own, [26]for then Christ would have had to suffer many times since the creation of the world. But now at the end of the ages Christ has appeared once and for all to annul sin by a final sacrifice. [27]As it is appointed for humans to die only once, and after that the judgment, [28]so also Christ was offered only once to bear the sins of many. And Christ will appear a second time, not to bear sin, but to save those who are eagerly waiting for Christ.

[10:1]The law is but a shadow of the good things to come and not the reality itself. Therefore it can never, by those sacrifices that are repeated year after year, make those who come to worship perfect. [2]Were it otherwise, would they not have stopped being offered? The worshipers, once cleansed, would no longer be conscious of sin. [3]But as it is, those sacrifices are a reminder of sin year after year. [4]It is not possible for the blood of bulls and goats to take away sins. [5]Therefore, when Jesus came into the world, He said, "Sacrifice and offering You did not desire, but a body You prepared for Me. [6]In burnt offerings and sin offerings You took no pleasure. [7]Then I said, 'See, I have come to do Your will, O God, as it is written about Me in the scroll of the Book.'" [8]First He said, "Sacrifices, burnt offerings and sin offerings You did not desire, for they gave You no pleasure" (although they are offered under the law). [9]Then He said, "Look, I have come to do Your will." God does away with the first and establishes the second. [10]By the will of God we are made holy through the offering of the body of Jesus Christ once for all.

[11]Every priest stands day after day performing the same religious functions, offering over and over the sacrifices that can never take away sins. [12]But Jesus offered one sacrifice for sins forever and sat down at the right hand of God, [13]waiting until, "God makes Your enemies Your footstool." [14]By one offering Jesus has perfected forever those who are being made holy. [15]The Holy Spirit also witnesses to us, for the Spirit says, [16]"This is the covenant I will make with them after those days, says God: I will put My laws in their hearts and write them on their minds. [17]Their sins and lawless acts I will remember no more." [18]Where these have been forgiven, an offering for sin is no longer necessary.

[19]Therefore, believers, since we have confidence to enter the Holy of Holies with the blood of Jesus [20]by a way that leads to life which Jesus opened for us through the veil, that is, through His flesh, [21]and since we have a great high priest over the house of God, [22]let us draw near with a receptive heart in full assurance of faith, with our hearts sprinkled and free from a guilty conscience and our bodies washed with clean water. [23]Let us keep on acknowledging our faith without wavering, for the One who promised is faithful. [24]Let us continue to encourage one another and help one another show love and do good works. [25]Let us not stop meeting together, as some have, but let us encourage one another even more as we see the day approaching.

THE CONSEQUENCES OF TURNING AWAY

[26]If we deliberately continue to sin after we have received the knowledge of the truth, no more sacrifice for sins remains, [27]but only the terrifying expectation of judgment and fiery heat that will devour God's adversaries. [28]Anyone who disobeyed the law of Moses died without mercy when confronted by two or three witnesses. [29]How much worse a punishment do you suppose people deserve who trample God's Child underfoot, count as unholy the blood of the covenant that made them holy and insult the Spirit of grace? [30]For we know the One who said, "Vengeance is Mine; I will repay," and again, "God will judge!" [31]It is a fearful thing to fall into the hands of the living God.

PATIENCE WILL BE REWARDED

[32]But remember the former days! After you saw the light, you endured a great and painful fight, [33]sometimes criticized and persecuted, and sometimes siding with those who were treated that way. [34]You had compassion on the prisoners and joyfully accepted the confiscation of your goods, knowing that you yourselves had better and more lasting possessions. [35]Therefore, do not throw away your confidence, for it will be greatly rewarded. [36]You need patience, so that when you have done the will of God, you will receive the promise. [37]In yet a little while, "I will come and will not delay. [38]But My righteous one will live by faith, and if any draw back, My Soul will not be pleased with them." [39]But we are not among those who draw back to loss. Instead, we are among those who believe and are saved.

FAITH

[11:1]Faith is the substance of the things hoped for, the evidence of the things not seen. [2]Because of faith, those of old were approved. [3]By faith we understand that the universe was completed by the word of God, so that what is seen is made from the unseen. [4]By faith Abel offered to God a more excellent sacrifice than Cain, and by faith he was acknowledged as righteous, because God acknowledged his gifts. And by faith Abel yet speaks, though dead. [5]By faith Enoch was translated. He did not see death. He was not found, because God translated him. Before he was translated, it was reported that he pleased God. [6]Without faith it is impossible to please God, for anyone who comes to God must believe that God exists and rewards those who diligently seek God. [7]By faith Noah, warned of things not yet seen, prudently built an ark to save his family. Through that he condemned the world and became an heir of the righteousness that is by faith. [8]By faith Abraham, when he was called to go out to a place that he would later receive as an inheritance, obeyed and set out, not knowing where he was going. [9]By faith he sojourned in the land of promise as a stranger. He lived in tents, as did Isaac and Jacob, heirs with him of the promise. [10]He was looking for the city that has foundations and whose architect and builder is God. [11]By faith Sarah received strength to have a baby when she was old, because she considered faithful the One who promised. [12]Therefore there originated from that one who had become impotent a multitude like the stars of the sky and as numberless as the sands of the seashore. [13]These all died in faith, not receiving the promises. Nevertheless, seeing the promises from afar, they were convinced and welcomed them and acknowledged that they were strangers and pilgrims upon the earth. [14]People who say such things plainly declare that they are seeking a country. [15]If they meant that country from which they came, they certainly had opportunity to return. [16]But their desire was for a better country, that is, a heavenly one. Therefore God has prepared a city for them and is not ashamed to be called their God.

[17]By faith Abraham, when he was tested, offered up Isaac. He who received the promises offered up his only son, [18]although God had said, "Through Isaac will your descendants be named." [19]Abraham believed that God was able to waken even the dead, and in a sense he did receive Isaac back that way. [20]By faith Isaac blessed Jacob and Esau concerning things to come. [21]By faith Jacob, as he was dying, blessed both of the sons of Joseph and worshiped as he leaned on his staff. [22]By faith Joseph, as he died, mentioned the exodus of the people of Israel and gave a command concerning his bones. [23]By faith Moses' parents hid him for three months after his birth, because they saw that he was a beautiful baby. They were not afraid of the king's command. [24]By faith Moses, when he was grown, refused to be called the son of Pharaoh's daughter. [25]He chose to suffer affliction with the people of God, rather than to enjoy the pleasures of sin for a season. [26]He considered reproach for the sake of Christ greater riches than the treasures of Egypt, because he looked forward to the ultimate reward. [27]By faith he left Egypt, not fearing the wrath of the king, for he endured as though he could see the One who is not seen. [28]By faith he kept the Passover and the sprinkling of blood, so that the destroyer of the firstborn would not touch his people. [29]By faith they passed through the Red Sea as if it were dry. When the Egyptians attempted it, they drowned. [30]By faith the walls of Jericho fell, after they were circled seven days. [31]By faith Rahab the harlot, after she welcomed the spies in peace, did not perish with the unbelievers.

[32]What more shall I say? The time is insufficient for me to tell of Gideon, Barak, Samson, Jephthah, David, Samuel and the prophets - [33]who through faith subdued realms, wrought righteousness, obtained promises, shut the mouths of lions, [34]quenched the power of the flames, escaped the edge of the sword, became valiant in battle and turned foreign armies to flight. [35]Women received their dead back to life. Others were tortured and refused to be ransomed. Thus they obtained a better resurrection. [36]Others were tested by mocking and whipping, yes, and chains and imprisonment. [37]They were stoned, they were sawed in two, they were slain with the

sword. They wandered about in sheepskins and goatskins. They were destitute, afflicted and tormented. [38]The world did not deserve to have them. They wandered in deserts and mountains and lived in the dens and caves of the earth. [39]These were all approved through faith, but they did not receive the promise. [40]God provided something better for us, so that they might be made perfect along with us.

[12:1]Therefore, since we are surrounded by so great a cloud of witnesses, let us lay aside every hindrance and the sin that so easily distracts us. Let us run with patience the race that is set before us, [2]looking to Jesus, the author and finisher of our faith, who for the joy that was set before Him endured the cross, despised the shame and sat down at the right side of the throne of God. [3]Consider the One who endured such rejection from sinners, so that you don't become weary and fainthearted. [4]In your struggle against sin, you have not yet resisted to the point of shedding your blood. [5]Have you forgotten the exhortation that speaks to you as children? "My children, do not despise God's chastening, or faint when God rebukes you, [6]for those God loves are corrected, and those God accepts are disciplined." [7]If you can endure correction, God will deal with you as the children of God. What children are not corrected by their parents? [8]If you are not corrected, and we are all corrected, then you are illegitimate and not the real children. [9]We have all had earthly parents who corrected us, and we respected them. Should we not more readily submit to our spiritual Parent and live? [10]Our earthly parents corrected us for a time as seemed best, but God corrects us for our good, so that we may share in God's holiness. [11]Now, no correction seems pleasant at the time, but distressful. But it later yields the peaceable fruit of righteousness to those who have been trained by it. [12]Therefore, strengthen your weak hands, steady your feeble knees [13]and make level paths for your feet. Then the lame will not be turned away, but be healed.

[14]Pursue peace with everyone and strive for holiness, for without holiness no one will see God. [15]Be careful that no one forfeits the goodwill of God and that no source of bitterness springs up to trouble you and defile many. [16]Beware lest anyone be immoral. Beware lest any be like Esau, who sold his birthright for a single meal. [17]You know that later, when he wanted to inherit the blessing, he was rejected. He could find no change of heart, though he sought it zealously with tears.

[18]You have not come to a mountain that can be touched and that is blazing with fire, nor to blackness and darkness and tempest [19]and the blast of a trumpet and a voice speaking words, making the hearers beg that no further word be spoken. [20]They could not endure the command: "If even an animal touches the mountain, it must be stoned." [21]So terrible was the sight, that Moses said, "I am exceedingly afraid and terrified." [22]But you have come to Mount Zion, the city of the living God, the heavenly Jerusalem, to thousands upon thousands of angels, [23]to the general assembly and church of the firstborn whose names are written in heaven, to God the judge of all, to the spirits of the godly made perfect, [24]to Jesus the mediator of the new covenant and to the sprinkled blood that speaks of better things than the blood of Abel. [25]See that you do not refuse the One who speaks, for if those who refused the One who warned them on earth did not escape, how much less will we escape if we turn away from the

One who warns from heaven? [26]God's voice shook the earth then, but now God has promised, "Once more I will shake, not only the earth, but also heaven." [27]This "once more" indicates that the things that cannot be shaken will remain. [28]Since we are receiving a realm that cannot be shaken, let us be grateful and serve God acceptably with reverence and fear, [29]for our God is a consuming fire.

LIVE HOLY LIVES, EXPECT THE UNEXPECTED, BECOME PERFECT

[13:1]Believers, continue to love one another. [2]Do not forget to entertain strangers, for some have unknowingly entertained angels. [3]Remember those in prison as though you were prisoners with them, and those who are suffering as though you also were suffering. [4]Marriage is to be honored by all and the bed pure. God will judge the immoral and the adulterer. [5]Do not be greedy for things, but be content with what you have, for God has said, "I will never leave you nor forsake you. [6]Therefore we should courageously say, "God is my helper, I will not fear. What can humans do to me?"

[7]Remember your leaders who first spoke the message of God to you. Consider their conduct and imitate their faith. [8]Jesus Christ is the same yesterday, today and forever. [9]Do not be carried away by various novel teachings. It is good for the heart to be made strong by God's grace, not by foods which have not benefited those who have become preoccupied with them. [10]We have an altar from which those who serve in the tabernacle have no right to eat. [11]For the bodies of those animals whose blood is brought into the Holy of Holies by the high priest for sin are burned outside the camp. [12]Jesus also suffered outside the gate in order to make people holy with His own blood. [13]Therefore let us go to Jesus outside the camp and share in that humiliation. [14]For here we have no lasting city, rather, we are seeking the city which is to come. [15]Through Jesus, therefore, let us continually offer the sacrifice of praise to God, which is the fruit of our lips acknowledging Jesus' name.

[16]Do not forget to do good and to share with one another, for with such sacrifices God is pleased. [17]Obey those who lead you and submit to their authority, for they watch over your souls as those who must give an accounting. Let them do this with joy and not with grief, for that would be unprofitable for you.

[18]Pray for us. We are sure that we have a good conscience and are willing to live honestly in all things. [19]I implore you to pray frequently, so that I may be restored to you sooner.

[20]Now may the God of peace, who brought that great Shepherd of the sheep, our Sovereign Jesus Christ, back from the dead through the blood of the everlasting covenant, [21]make you perfect in every good work to do the divine will, working in you what is pleasing in God's sight through Jesus Christ, to whom be glory forever and ever. Amen.

[22]Believers, I beg you to accept these words of exhortation, for I have written you a short letter. [23]I want you to know that our brother Timothy has been set free. I will come with him to see you if he comes soon. [24]Greet all your leaders and all the saints. Those from Italy greet you. [25]God's grace be with you all.

James

$^{1:1}$James, a servant of God and of our Sovereign Jesus Christ, to the twelve tribes who are scattered abroad: Greetings.

TROUBLE AND TESTING

^{2}Believers, count it all joy when you have troubles of various kinds, ^{3}knowing that the testing of your faith produces patience. ^{4}Let patience complete its work, so that you may be perfect and complete, lacking nothing.

ASK FOR WISDOM

^{5}If any of you lacks wisdom, you should ask God and it will be given. God gives to everyone generously without finding fault. ^{6}But ask in faith without wavering, for the one who wavers is like a wave of the sea, driven and tossed by the wind. ^{7}That one should not expect to get anything from God. ^{8}Those who are undecided are unstable in every way.

THE UNCERTAINTY OF LIFE

^{9}Believers in humble circumstances should rejoice if they are exalted, ^{10}and the rich when they are made low, for the rich will pass away like the flowers in the grass. ^{11}The sun rises with burning heat, the grass withers and the petals fall. What looked so beautiful will be lost forever. In the same way, the rich will fade away in the midst of their journey.

TEMPTATION

^{12}Blessed are you if you don't give in to temptation. When you have passed the test, you will receive the crown of life that God has promised to those who love God. ^{13}Do not say when you are tempted, "I am tempted by God," for God does not tempt anyone, nor can God be tempted by evil. ^{14}But you are tempted when you are drawn away by your own lust and caught. ^{15}Then lust conceives and brings forth sin, and sin, when it is finished, brings forth death. ^{16}Believers, do not be deceived. ^{17}Every act of generosity and every perfect gift is from above and comes down from our heavenly Parent, who made the lights of heaven and with whom there is neither variation nor shadow of turning. ^{18}Of God's own will we were given birth by the word of truth, so that we might be a kind of firstfruits of God's creation.

RECEIVE GOD'S WORDS WITH HUMILITY

[19]My beloved sisters and brothers, let everyone be swift to listen, slow to speak and slow to wrath. [20]For the wrath of humans does not bring about the righteousness of God. [21]Therefore lay aside all filthiness and every trace of wickedness and receive with humility the implanted word that is able to save your souls.

[22]Be doers of the word and not hearers only, lest you deceive yourselves. [23]For if you are a hearer of the word and not a doer, you are like a person looking at your face in a mirror. [24]You look at yourself and go your way, immediately forgetting what you look like. [25]But if you look into the perfect law that makes free and continue to do so, not being a forgetful hearer but a doer, then you will be blessed in what you do.

TRUE RELIGION

[26]If any among you seem to be religious but do not bridle your tongue, you deceive your own heart and your religion is vain. [27]Pure and undefiled religion before God our heavenly Parent is this: to visit the orphan and the widow in their affliction, and to keep yourself unpolluted by the world.

DO NOT SHOW FAVORITISM

[2:1]Believers, if you have faith in Jesus Christ, you will not show favoritism. [2]If someone wearing a gold ring and fine clothes comes into your congregation, and some poor person in shabby clothes also comes in, [3]if you prefer the one wearing the fine clothes and say, "Sit here, please," but say to the poor one, "Stand there, or if you must, sit on the floor by my feet," [4]have you not shown favoritism among yourselves and become judges with evil thoughts? [5]Listen, my beloved friends, has not God chosen the poor of this world to be rich in faith and heirs of the realm that was promised to those who love God? [6]But you have despised the poor! Don't the rich oppress you and drag you into court? [7]Don't they blaspheme that worthy name by which you are called? [8]If you fulfill the royal law of Scripture that says, "You shall love your neighbor as yourself," you do well. [9]But if you show favoritism, you commit sin and are convicted by the law as lawbreakers. [10]Whoever keeps the whole law but breaks one commandment is guilty of breaking them all. [11]For the One who said, "Do not commit adultery," also said, "Do not kill." So if you do not commit adultery and yet you kill, you become a lawbreaker. [12]Therefore watch what you say and do, for you will be judged by the law that sets us free. [13]Judgment without mercy will be shown to the one who has shown no mercy. Yet mercy triumphs over judgment.

FAITH WITHOUT WORKS IS MEANINGLESS

[14]Believers, what good does it do to say you have faith if you have no works? Can your faith save you? [15]If another believer needs clothes and daily food [16]and one of you says, "Depart in peace! Stay warm and well-fed!" but you do not provide those things that are needed by the body, what good do you do? [17]In the same way, faith alone without works is dead. [18]But someone will say, "You have faith, and I have works." Show me your faith without works, and I will show you my faith by works. [19]You believe that there is one God? You do well. The demons also believe, and tremble. [20]You vain humans, don't you know that faith without works is worthless?

[21]Wasn't Abraham our ancestor justified by works when he offered Isaac his son on the altar? [22]You see, faith cooperated with his works, and by works faith was made perfect. [23]Thus the Scripture was fulfilled that says, "Abraham believed God, and it was counted to him as righteousness." He was called the friend of God. [24]So you see, a person is justified by works and not by faith alone. [25]Furthermore, wasn't Rahab the harlot justified by works when she received the messengers and then sent them out another way? [26]As the body without the spirit is dead, so faith without works is also dead.

CHOOSE CAREFULLY WHAT YOU SAY

[3:1]Believers, not many of you should be teachers, for we know that teachers will receive a stricter evaluation. [2]All of us offend in many ways. If you never offend by what you say, then you are perfect and able to control your whole body. [3]Look at the way we put bits in the mouths of horses so they obey us. We turn their whole body! [4]Look also at the great ships driven by fierce winds, yet they are turned about with a very small rudder wherever the captain wishes. [5]Even so is the tongue a little member that boasts great things. Look at how great a forest fire a little spark kindles.

[6]The tongue is a fire, a world of wickedness set among our body parts that defiles the whole body and sets on fire the surroundings of our life, and is itself set on fire by hell. [7]All kinds of animals, birds, reptiles and sea creatures are being tamed and have been tamed by humans. [8]But no human can tame the tongue. It is an unruly evil, full of deadly poison. [9]With it we bless our God and heavenly Parent, and with it we curse humans who are made in the likeness of God. [10]Out of the same mouth comes blessing and cursing. Believers, this should not be. [11]Does a spring send forth sweet and bitter water in the same place? [12]Can the fig tree bear olives? Or the grapevine figs? Can a spring yield salt water and fresh?

THE GENTLE WISDOM FROM ABOVE

[13]Who is wise and understanding among you? Show by your good conduct that you do everything with gentle wisdom. [14]But if you have bitter envy and strife in your hearts, do not boast and deny the truth. [15]This "wisdom" does not come down from above, but is earthly, sensual, demonic. [16]For where there is envy and strife, there also is confusion and every foul deed. [17]But the wisdom from above is first pure, then peaceable, gentle, easily entreated, full of mercy and good fruit, impartial and sincere. [18]And the fruit of righteousness is sown in peace by those who make peace.

GOD YEARNS FOR US TO LIVE GODLY LIVES

[4:1]What causes the arguments and fights among you? Aren't they from selfish pleasures that war in your body? [2]You long for things, but don't get them. You kill and covet, but can't have them. So you argue and fight. You don't have because you don't ask God. [3]Or you ask and don't receive because you ask wrongly in order to spend what you receive on your selfish desires. [4]You unfaithful people! Don't you know that friendship with the world is enmity toward God? Whoever wants to be a friend of the world becomes an enemy of God. [5]Do you think that Scripture says in vain that the Spirit whom God put within us jealously yearns?

[6]Nevertheless, God gives us more grace. Scripture says, "God resists the proud but gives grace to the humble." [7]Therefore submit to God. Resist the devil and the devil will flee from you. [8]Draw near to God and God will draw near to you. Cleanse your hands, you sinners! Purify your hearts, you indecisive! [9]Endure your trial; mourn and weep; let your laughter be turned to mourning and your joy to heaviness. [10]Humble yourselves in the sight of God and God will lift you up.

[11]Believers, do not speak evil of one another. If you speak evil of one another or judge one another, you speak evil against the law and judge the law. If you judge the law, you are not observing the law, but judging it. [12]There is only one Lawgiver and Judge who is able to save or destroy. Who are you to judge another?

LIVING INDEPENDENTLY FROM GOD IS SIN

[13]Listen, you who say, "Today or tomorrow we will go to such and such a city and stay there a year and buy and sell and make lots of money." [14]How do you know what tomorrow will bring? What is your life? It is just a vapor that appears for a moment and then vanishes. [15]What you ought to say is, "If God is willing, we will live and do this or that." [16]But now you boast in self-confidence. All such boasting is wrong. [17]Anyone who knows what is right and does not do it sins.

TREATMENT OF EMPLOYEES

[5:1]Listen, you rich people, weep and howl over the miseries that will come upon you. [2]Your possessions are rotting and your clothing is moth-eaten. [3]Your gold and silver is corroded, and their corrosion will be a witness against you. It will eat your flesh like fire. You have heaped up riches for the last days, [4]but the laborers who reaped your fields cry out for the wages you kept back by fraud. The cries of the reapers have reached the ears of the Mighty One. [5]You have lived in self-indulgent luxury upon the earth; you have pampered yourselves in the day of slaughter. [6]You condemned and killed the innocent and they did not resist.

BE PATIENT

[7]Believers, be patient until Christ returns. Observe how the farmer waits for the precious fruit from the earth and longs patiently for it while waiting for the early and late rains. [8]Be patient and establish your lives, for the return of Christ is near.

COMPLAINTS

[9]Christians, don't complain against one another, lest you be condemned. Beware! The Judge is standing at the door. [10]As an example of hardship and longsuffering, consider the prophets who spoke in God's name. [11]Remember, we consider those blessed who endured. You have heard of the patience of Job and know what the end was - that God is very compassionate and merciful.

OATHS

[12]Above all, my friends, do not swear either by heaven or by the earth or with any other oath. Let your "Yes" be yes and your "No" be no, lest you fall into condemnation.

PRAY EARNESTLY

[13]Is anyone among you having trouble? You should pray. Is anyone happy? Then sing songs of praise. [14]Are any sick among you? They should call the elders of the church to pray over them, anointing them with oil in God's name. [15]The prayer of faith will save the sick and God will raise them up. If they have committed sins, they will be forgiven. [16]Acknowledge your faults to one another and pray for one another so you may be healed. The fervent prayer of the righteous person avails much. [17]Elijah was a human just like we are. He prayed earnestly that it would not rain, and it did not rain on the land for three years and six months. [18]Then he prayed again and the skies released the rain and the ground brought forth its fruit.

RESTORE THE WANDERERS

[19]Christians, if one of you strays from the truth and someone turns that person back, [20]be assured that the one who turns the sinner from error will save a soul from death and cover over a multitude of sins.

First Peter

1:1Peter, an apostle of Jesus Christ, to the Christians living as strangers in Pontus, Galatia, Cappadocia, Asia and Bithynia. 2You have been chosen according to the foreknowledge of God our heavenly Parent and purified by the Spirit for obedience to Jesus Christ and sprinkling by His blood. Grace to you, and may your peace be multiplied.

THE LIVING HOPE OF THE PEOPLE OF GOD

3Blessed be the God and heavenly Parent of our Sovereign Jesus Christ. Because of God's great mercy we have been born again into a living hope through the resurrection of Jesus Christ from the dead. 4God's people have been born into an inheritance reserved in heaven that will never change or be corrupted or lose its beauty. 5Through faith you are protected by the power of God and your salvation is ready to be revealed at the last day. 6In this you rejoice, though now you may be temporarily afflicted by various troubles. 7These are trials to test your faith, which is more precious than gold (gold is also tested by fire), so that your faith may effectively praise, honor and glorify Jesus Christ when Jesus returns. 8You have not seen Jesus, but you love Jesus! And though you do not see Jesus now, you believe and rejoice with inexpressible and glorious joy, 9for you will receive as the result of your faith the salvation of your souls. 10The prophets who prophesied of the gift that would come to you searched carefully to learn more about this salvation. 11They wanted to know what sort of person or time the Spirit of Christ within them was speaking of, for the Spirit testified beforehand of the sufferings of Christ and the glorious events that would follow. 12It was revealed to these prophets by the power of the Holy Spirit sent from heaven that they were not serving themselves, but you, by telling you the good news. Even the angels would like to know more about these things.

CONDUCT YOURSELVES AS CHRISTIANS - YOU HAVE BEEN BORN AGAIN

13Prepare your thoughts, be sober and confidently expect without wavering the divine grace that will be yours when Jesus Christ is revealed. 14As obedient children, do not conform to the lusts of your former ignorant life. 15The One who called you is holy, so be holy in all you do. 16For it is written, "Be holy, because I am holy." 17If you call the One who judges everyone's work impartially "My heavenly Parent," pass your allotted time away from your home in heaven in reverent fear. [18]You know that it was not with corrupt things like silver and gold that you were rescued from the empty way of life handed down from your ancestors. [19]It was with the precious blood of Christ, a lamb without fault or blemish. [20]Christ was known before the creation of the world, but was revealed in these last times for you. [21]Through Christ you believe in God - who raised Him from the dead and gave Him glory - so that your faith and hope might be in God. [22]Since you have purified yourselves by obeying the truth and have a sincere love for one another, love one another intently with a pure heart. [23]Through the word of the living and unchanging God you have been born again from mortal, not immortal, parents. [24]For, "All flesh is like grass, and all its glory is like a flower in the grass. The grass withers and the flower falls, [25]but the word of God continues forever." And this word is the good news that was announced to you.

REJECT WORLDLY THINGS AND COME TO JESUS

[2:1]Therefore lay aside all malice, deceit, hypocrisy, jealousy and slander. [2]Like newborn babies, crave the pure milk of the word so that you may grow up to be saved, [3]now that you have tasted the goodness of Christ. [4]Come to Jesus, the living stone. Jesus was rejected by humans, but is chosen and precious to God. [5]You also, like living stones, are being built into a holy priesthood in order to offer spiritual sacrifices to God through Jesus Christ. [6]Scripture says, "Watch! I lay in Zion a cornerstone, chosen and precious, and those who have faith in Christ will never be put to shame." [7]Now to you who believe, Christ is precious. But to those who do not believe, "The stone the builders rejected has become the cornerstone," [8]and "a stone that makes them stumble and a rock that makes them fall." They stumble because they disobey the word and fell over that stone, which is what God planned for them. [9]But you are a chosen generation, a royal priesthood, a holy nation, a special people to celebrate the praises of the One who called you out of darkness into God's marvelous light. [10]In times past you were not a people, but now you are the people of God. Once you had not obtained mercy, but now you have obtained mercy.

[11]Beloved, you are only strangers and pilgrims here. Therefore I urge you to abstain from fleshly lusts that war against your souls. [12]Your conduct among unbelievers should be such that, though they speak against you as wrongdoers, they see your good works and glorify God on the day when Christ comes.

SUBMIT TO THE LAW, LOVE ONE ANOTHER, FEAR GOD

[13]Submit to every human authority because of God, whether to the emperor as sovereign, [14]or to magistrates who are sent to punish those who do wrong and praise those who do good. [15]For it is the will of God that by doing good you put to silence the ignorant talk of foolish people. [16]You are the servants of God, so live as though you were born free. But do not use your freedom as an excuse to cause trouble. [17]Honor everyone, love the other believers, fear God, respect the emperor.

FOLLOW CHRIST'S EXAMPLE OF PATIENT SUFFERING

[18]Employees, respectfully obey your employers, not only the good and gentle, but also the cruel. [19]It is gracious of you to endure grief and suffer wrongfully for the sake of God. [20]How are you honored if you are punished for doing wrong and suffer patiently? But if you do well and suffer patiently, that is acceptable to God. [21]To this you were called. Christ suffered for you, leaving you an example, so that you could follow His steps. [22]He committed no wrong, nor was deceit found in His mouth. [23]When He was cursed, He did not curse back. When He suffered, He did not threaten, but committed Himself to the One who judges righteously. [24]He bore our sins in His own body on the cross, so that we might die to sin and live for righteousness. By His wounds you were healed. [25]For you were like sheep going astray, but now you have returned to the Shepherd who guards your souls.

PETER'S ADVICE FOR HUSBANDS AND WIVES

[3:1]In the same way, you wives should respect your husbands. Then if there are some husbands who do not obey the word of God, they may be won over without a word by the conduct of their wives [2]when they see your pure and reverent conduct. [3]Do not limit your attractiveness to plaiting your hair, wearing gold or putting on fine clothes. [4]Instead, let it be the hidden person of the heart, a gentle and calm spirit that is priceless in the sight of God and never grows old. [5]This is the way the holy women of old who trusted in God adorned themselves, by honoring their husbands. [6]Sarah, for example, respected Abraham, calling him husband. You are her daughters as long as you do right and do not fear anything.

[7]Husbands, in the same way, be understanding as you live with your wives. Cherish and esteem them, so that nothing will stand in the way of your prayers. Though physically weaker, they are heirs with you of the gracious gift of life.

CHRISTIAN CONDUCT

[8]Finally, you must all live in harmony and be compassionate. Love the other believers; be sympathetic and humble. [9]Don't pay back injury for injury or insult for insult, but bless, knowing that you yourselves were called to inherit a blessing. [10]If you would love life and see good days, restrain your tongue from evil and your lips from speaking lies. [11]Avoid evil and do good. Seek peace and pursue it. [12]For the eyes of God are upon the righteous and God's ears are open to their prayers. But God opposes those who do evil.

REVELATIONS ABOUT CHRIST

[13]Who will harm you if you stand for what is good? [14]Even if you suffer for what is right, be happy. Don't fear what others fear, [15]but love, honor and fear Christ as Sovereign in your hearts. Always be ready to answer humbly and respectfully anyone who asks you about the confidence that is in you. [16]Have a clear conscience, so that those who slander you as wrongdoers may be ashamed of insulting your good

Christian conduct. [17]It is better to suffer for doing good, if that is the will of God, than for doing evil. [18]For Christ, who was put to death in the flesh but who was raised to life by the Spirit, also once suffered for sins, the just for the unjust, that He might bring us to God. [19]It was in the Spirit that Christ went and preached to the spirits in prison. [20]Those were the ones who were disobedient long ago as God waited patiently while Noah was building the ark. But only eight souls were saved by water. [21]This water is like the water of baptism, also saving us. Not by washing dirt from the body, but by the response of a clear conscience toward God through the resurrection of Jesus Christ. [22]Now Christ has gone into heaven and is at the right hand of God, ruling over angels, authorities and powers.

[4:1]Even as Christ suffered in the flesh, arm yourselves with the same determination. For if you have suffered in the flesh, you stop sinning. [2]Then you do not live the rest of your fleshly life for human lust, but for the will of God. [3]You have spent sufficient time in the past doing what the godless like to do: sex sins, lust, drunkenness, carousing, banqueting and detestable idolatry. [4]They think it strange that you do not join them in the same flood of wasteful behavior, and they call you names. [5]But they will have to give an account to the One who is ready to judge the living and the dead. [6]That is why the good news was told to those who are dead, so that they might be judged as humans in the flesh but live according to God in the spirit.

[7]The end of all things is at hand. Therefore be serious and watch and pray. [8]Above all, remain constant in your love for one another, for love covers a multitude of sins. [9]Be hospitable to one another without grumbling. [10]Everyone has received a gift. Use your gifts to serve one another as good stewards of the varied grace of God. [11]If you speak, speak as one who brings words from God. If you serve, do it with the ability God gives. In this way God will be glorified in everything through Jesus Christ, to whom belongs the glory and power forever and ever. Amen.

BELIEVERS ALSO HAVE TROUBLES

[12]Beloved, do not be surprised at the fiery trial that comes upon you to test you, as though something strange were happening to you. [13]Rather, rejoice that you may take part in Christ's sufferings, so that when Christ's glory is revealed you will be joyful and glad. [14]If you are ridiculed because of the name of Christ, you are blessed, for the glorious Spirit of God rests on you. [15]You must not suffer as a murderer, a thief, a wrongdoer or a meddler. [16]But if you suffer for being a Christian, do not be ashamed; praise God for this. [17]It is time for judgment to begin in the house of God, and if it is first with us, what will be the end of those who do not obey the gospel of God? [18]If the righteous are barely saved, what will happen to the ungodly and the sinner? [19]Therefore let those who suffer according to the will of God commit their souls to their faithful Creator and keep on doing good.

BE WILLING LEADERS AND HUMBLE FOLLOWERS

[5:1]As an elder and a witness of the sufferings of Christ as well as a sharer in the glory that will be revealed, I exhort the elders among you [2]to tend the flock of God among you willingly as God wants you to, and not unwillingly. Don't do it for the sake of money, but with an eager heart. [3]Do not rule over God's heritage, but be an example to the flock. [4]Then when the Chief Shepherd appears, you will receive the unfading crown of glory.

[5]In the same way, you who are younger must defer to the older. Be clothed with humility toward one another, for "God opposes the proud, but favors the humble." [6]Therefore humble yourselves under God's mighty hand, so that you may be exalted in due time. [7]Cast all your cares on God, for God cares about you.

RESIST THE DEVIL IN THE TIME OF TROUBLE

[8]Be sober and vigilant. Your adversary the devil prowls around like a roaring lion looking for someone to devour. [9]Resist the devil! Stand firm in the faith, knowing that other believers around the world are enduring the same afflictions.

[10]After you have suffered a little while, may the God of goodwill who called you to eternal glory through Christ Jesus restore, establish and strengthen you. [11]To God be the power forever and ever. Amen.

FAREWELL

[12]I have written briefly to you with the help of Silas, whom I consider a faithful brother. I exhort you and testify that this is the true grace of God. Stand firm in it. [13]The church at Babylon, chosen with you, greets you. And so does Mark, my son. [14]Greet one another with a kiss of love. Peace to all of you who are in Christ.

Second Peter

1:1Simon Peter, a servant and apostle of Jesus Christ, to those who have obtained a faith as precious as ours through the righteousness of our God and Savior Jesus Christ. 2Goodwill and peace be multiplied to you through the knowledge of God and of our Sovereign Jesus.

YOUR VIRTUOUS CONDUCT WILL INCREASE YOUR KNOWLEDGE OF JESUS

3God's divine power gave us everything we need for life and godliness when Christ called us to share in the divine glory and goodness. 4Through these Christ has given us great and precious promises, so that by them you may participate in the divine nature and escape the corruption that is in the world because of lust. 5Therefore be diligent to add to your faith goodness, and to goodness knowledge, 6and to knowledge self-control, and to self-control endurance, and to endurance godliness, 7and to godliness Christian kindness and to Christian kindness love. 8If you have these and they increase, you will not be inactive or unfruitful in your knowledge of our Sovereign Jesus Christ. 9But if you lack these, you are blind and short-sighted and have forgotten that you have been washed from your former sins. 10Therefore, believers, be diligent to make your calling and election sure. If you do this, you will never fall, 11and you will be given an ample welcome into the eternal realm of our God and Savior Jesus Christ.

12Therefore I will always remind you of these things, although you know them and are established in the truth you have. 13Nevertheless I think it fair, as long as I am in this body, to stir up your memory, 14knowing that I will soon put aside my body, just as our Sovereign Jesus Christ has shown me. 15Moreover, I will endeavor to help you find a way to always remember these things after my death.

PETER: THE WITNESS WHO WAS ON THE MOUNTAIN WITH JESUS

16We did not follow cleverly devised myths when we made known to you the power and coming of our Sovereign Jesus Christ. We were eyewitnesses of His majesty 17as He received honor and glory from God His heavenly Parent. A voice came to Him from the Majestic Glory, saying, "This is My beloved Son with whom I am well-pleased." 18We heard this voice spoken from heaven when we were with Him on the holy mountain.

OLD TESTAMENT PROPHECIES

[19]Therefore the words of the prophets are made more sure. You would do well to heed them, for they are like a light that shines in a dark place until the day dawns and the Morning Star rises in your hearts. [20]Know this first: No prophecy of Scripture comes from the prophet's own interpretation, [21]for prophecy did not come by human will, but humans spoke from God as they were impelled by the Holy Spirit.

FALSE PROPHETS

[2:1]But there were false prophets among the people, even as there will be false teachers among you. They will secretly bring in destructive opinions, even denying Jesus Christ who redeemed them, and so they will bring swift destruction upon themselves. [2]But many will follow their destructive ways. Because of them, the way of truth will be slandered. [3]Because they want your money, these false teachers will greedily exploit you with fictitious stories. Their judgment will not linger, nor will their destruction slumber. [4]For if God did not spare the angels who sinned, but cast them into the deepest part of hell and kept them chained in darkness to be guarded until the judgment; [5]and if God did not spare the ancient world, but brought a flood upon the world of the ungodly, while saving Noah and seven others; [6]and if God condemned Sodom and Gomorrah by turning their cities into ashes, and with their overthrow made them an example of what is going to happen to the ungodly; [7]and if God rescued righteous Lot, who was vexed by the filthy conversation of the wicked, [8]and who lived among them and was tormented in his righteous soul day after day by their lawless deeds; [9]then the Almighty knows how to rescue the godly from adversity and to reserve the unjust for punishment on the day of judgment.

[10]This especially applies to those who contaminate their bodies by living in lust. These false teachers despise authority, are presumptuous and self-willed and are not afraid to slander the shining ones. [11]Yet angels, who are more powerful and mighty, do not slander or accuse these false teachers before God. [12]But these false teachers are instinctive brute beasts, born to be captured and destroyed, speaking evil of that which they do not understand. They will utterly perish in their corruption [13]and will receive the reward of unrighteousness. They consider it pleasure to carouse in the daytime. They are stains and blemishes who revel in delusion as they feast with you. [14]They have eyes full of adultery and cannot refrain from sin. They are accursed children who train themselves in greed and beguile unstable souls.

[15]They have forsaken the right way and have gone astray, following the way of Balaam the son of Beor, who loved the wages of unrighteousness. [16]He was admonished for his transgression when the donkey spoke with a human voice and rebuked the prophet for his foolishness. [17]These people are wells without water and clouds carried by a tempest; the gloom of darkness has been reserved for them. [18]They speak great swelling vanities. Through the incontinent lusts of the flesh they lure people who have just escaped from a life of error. [19]They promise freedom, but they themselves are slaves of corruption, for people are slaves to whatever overcomes

them. [20]For if after they have escaped the foulness of the world through knowledge of our Savior Jesus Christ they are then again entangled in it and overcome, the latter end is worse for them than the beginning. [21]It would have been better for them not to have known the way of righteousness, than to have known it and then turn from the holy commandment they were given. [22]But it happened to them just like in the proverb, "The dog returns to its vomit, and the pig that was washed wallows in the mud."

THE UNGODLY THINK THE WORLD WILL CONTINUE AS IT ALWAYS HAS

[3:1]Beloved, this is the second letter I have written to you. May it help you recollect [2]the predictions that were spoken by the holy prophets and the commandment of the apostles of Christ your savior. [3]Know this first: In the last days scoffers will come, following after their own lusts [4]and saying, "Where is your God? Didn't your God promise to come? Our ancestors went to sleep, yet everything continues as it has been from the first day of creation." [5]They choose to forget that by the word of God the heavens existed from of old and the earth was formed out of water and in the water. [6]The world as it was overflowed with water and perished. [7]By the same word, the heavens and the earth as they are now are reserved for fire. They are being kept for the day of judgment and the destruction of ungodly people. [8]Do not forget, beloved, that one day is as a thousand years with God, and a thousand years are as one day. [9]God's promise is not slow in coming as some suppose. Instead God is patient toward us, not willing that any should perish, but wanting all to come to repentance.

THE DAY OF RECKONING

[10]The day of judgment will come like a thief in the night. On that day the skies will pass away with a crash, the elements will melt from the heat and the earth and all its activities will burn up. [11]Since these will be dissolved, you should conduct yourselves in a holy and godly manner [12]as you look for and hasten the coming day of judgment - the day the skies will be dissolved with fire and the elements will melt with heat. [13]Nevertheless, because of God's promise, we wait for new heavens and a new earth where righteousness will dwell. [14]Therefore, beloved, since you are waiting for these things, be diligent to be found unblemished, blameless and at peace with God.

A RESPECTFUL REFERENCE TO PAUL THE APOSTLE

[15]Remember, the patience of God brings salvation, even as our beloved brother Paul wrote to you with the wisdom that God gave him. [16]He speaks about these things in all his letters. Some are hard to understand, and the ignorant and unstable distort these, as they do other Scripture, to their loss. [17]But you already know these things, beloved. Therefore beware lest you also fall from your steadfastness and are taken off together with the wandering wicked. [18]But grow in the grace and knowledge of our Savior Jesus Christ. To Christ be the glory, both now and forever. Amen.

First John

1:1That which was from the beginning, which we have heard, which we have seen with our eyes, which we have looked at and touched with our hands is our concern - the Word of life. 2That life was clearly revealed. We have seen it and testify to it and declare to you the eternal life that was with God our heavenly Parent and which has been revealed to us. 3That which we have seen and heard we declare to you so that you may have fellowship with us. And our fellowship is with God and with God's Child Jesus Christ. 4We write these things to you so that our joy may be complete.

WALKING IN THE LIGHT

5This is the message that we heard from Christ and announce to you: God is light - in God there is no darkness at all. 6If we say that we have fellowship with God and continue to walk in darkness, we lie and do not practice the truth. 7But if we walk in the light as God is in the light, we have fellowship with one another and the blood of God's Child Jesus cleanses us from all sin.

ALL ARE SINNERS

8If we say that we have no sin, we deceive ourselves and the truth is not in us. 9If we acknowledge our sins, God is faithful and just to forgive us our sins and cleanse us from all unrighteousness. 10If we say we have not sinned, we make God a liar and God's word is not in us.

FORGIVENESS IS AVAILABLE THROUGH JESUS

2:1My little children, I am writing these things to you so you will not sin. But if anyone does sin, we have an advocate with God, Jesus Christ the righteous. 2Jesus is the atonement for our sins, and not ours alone, but also for the sins of the whole world.

WE WALK IN THE LIGHT IF WE OBEY GOD'S COMMANDMENTS

3This is how we are sure that we know God: If we keep God's commandments. 4If you say, "I know God," but don't keep God's commandments, you are a liar and the truth is not in you. 5But in the one who obeys the word is the love of God truly perfected. By this we may know that we are following God: 6The one who claims to be living in God ought to walk as Jesus walked. 7Believers, I am not writing a new commandment to you, but an old commandment which you have had from the beginning. This old commandment is the message you have heard from the beginning. 8Yet I am writing a new commandment! Its truth is in you as it was in Jesus, because the darkness is passing away and the true light is now shining.

THE SECOND COMMANDMENT

[9]If you say that you are in the light, but hate another believer, you are still in the darkness. [10]If you love the other believers, you are living in the light and there is nothing in you to make you stumble. [11]But if you hate another believer, you are in darkness and walking in darkness. You do not know where you are going, for the darkness has blinded your eyes.

DO GOD'S WILL AND LIVE FOREVER

[12]I write to you, little children, because your sins have been forgiven because of Christ's name. [13]I write to you, grown-ups, because you have known the One who is from the beginning. I write to you, youths, because you have overcome the evil one. I write to you, little children, because you have known God. [14]I write to you, grown-ups, because you have known the One who is from the beginning. I write to you, youths, because you are strong. The word of God lives in you and you have overcome the evil one.

[15]Do not love the world or the things in the world. If you love the world, the love of your heavenly Parent is not in you. [16]For everything in the world - the lust of the flesh, the lust of the eyes and the pride in one's present existence - is not from your heavenly Parent, but is from the world. [17]The world and its lusts are passing away, but the one who does the will of God will live forever.

UNGODLY PEOPLE WOULD LEAD YOU ASTRAY

[18]Little children, it is the last hour. And as you have heard that Antichrist is coming, even now many antichrists have come. From this we know that it is the last hour. [19]They went out from us, but they were not of us. If they had been of us, they would have continued with us, but their going showed that they were not of us. [20]But you have an anointing from the Holy One and all understand. [21]I have not written to you because you don't know the truth. You know the truth and know that no lie has a part in the truth.

[22]Who is the liar? Is it not the one who denies that Jesus is the Christ? The one who denies the Parent and God's Child is the antichrist. [23]Whoever denies the Child does not have the Parent, but whoever acknowledges the Child has the Parent also. [24]Let that which you have heard from the beginning stay in you. If that which you have heard from the beginning remains in you, then you also will remain in the Child and in the Parent. [25]And this is the promise that God has promised us: eternal life. [26]I have written these things to you concerning those who would try to lead you astray. [27]The anointing you received from Christ remains in you and you do not need anyone to teach you. Christ's anointing, which is true and no lie, teaches you about all things. And even as Christ taught you, remain in Christ. [28]And now little children, remain in Christ, so that when Christ appears we will have confidence and not be ashamed in front of Christ when Christ comes. [29]If you know that Christ is righteous, you know that everyone who does right is born of Christ.

WHEN WE SEE GOD, WE WILL BE LIKE GOD

3:1Think about how much our heavenly Parent loves us, that we should be called the children of God! The world does not understand us, because it does not understand God. 2Beloved, now we are the children of God, and it does not yet appear what we will be. But we know that when Christ appears, we shall be like Christ, for we shall see Christ as Christ is. 3All who have this hope in Christ purify themselves, even as Christ is pure.

THE TRUE CHILD OF GOD DOES NOT SIN

4Whoever commits sin breaks the law, for sin is a violation of the law. 5You know that Christ appeared to take away our sins, and in Christ is no sin. 6Whoever remains in Christ does not sin, but whoever sins has not seen or known Christ. 7Little children, let no one deceive you - those who do right are righteous, even as Christ is righteous. 8Anyone who commits sin is of the devil, for the devil has been sinning from the beginning. God's Child appeared for this very purpose - to destroy the works of the devil. 9You who are born of God do not sin, because God's seed lives in you. You cannot sin, because you are born of God.

OBEY THE COMMANDMENT TO LOVE ONE ANOTHER

10This is how the children of God and the children of the devil are revealed: Those who do not do right or love the other believers are not of God. 11This is the message that you heard from the beginning: that we should love one another. 12We are not like Cain, who belonged to the evil one and murdered his brother. And why did he murder him? Because his deeds were evil and his brother's were righteous.

13Believers, do not be surprised if the world hates you. 14We know that we have passed from death to life because we love one another. Anyone who does not love continues in death. 15Anyone who hates another is a murderer, and you know that murderers do not have eternal life within them.

16This is how we know what love is: Jesus laid down His life for us. And we ought to lay down our lives for other believers. 17If you have this world's goods and see those in need but do not have compassion on them, how can the love of God be in you? 18My little children, let us not love with words and talk, but with deeds and truth.

CONFIDENCE IN GOD'S PRESENCE

19This is how we will know we belong to the truth and are able to reassure our hearts before God 20if our hearts condemn us, for God is greater than our hearts and knows everything. 21Beloved, if our hearts do not condemn us, we have confidence in God's presence. 22Whatever we ask we receive, because we obey God's commandments and do those things that are pleasing in God's sight. 23And this is God's commandment: that we believe in the name of God's Child Jesus Christ and love one another as God commanded. 24Those who obey Christ's commandments live in God and God in them. And this is how we know that God lives in us: by the Spirit God has given us.

DON'T BE WORLDLY

4:1Beloved, do not believe every spirit, but test the spirits to see if they come from God. Many false prophets have gone out into the world. 2This is how you will know the Spirit of God: Every spirit that acknowledges that Jesus Christ has come in the flesh is from God. 3Every spirit that will not acknowledge that Jesus Christ has come in the flesh is not from God. This is the spirit from the antichrist which you have heard is coming and is even now in the world. 4You are from God, little children. You have overcome them, because greater is the One who is in you than the one who is in the world. 5These false prophets are from the world, therefore they speak as the world speaks. And the world listens to them. 6We are from God. Anyone who knows God listens to us. But those who are not from God will not listen to us. That is how we discern the Spirit of truth and the spirit of error.

GOD LIVES IN YOU AND WILL HELP YOU LOVE OTHERS

7Beloved, let us love one another! For love is from God and everyone who loves is born of God and knows God. 8Those who do not love do not know God, for God is love. 9This is how the love of God was shown to us: God sent the only begotten Child into the world so that we might live through God's Child. 10This is love: not that we loved God, but that God loved us and sent the Child as atonement for our sins. 11Beloved, if God loved us this much, we also ought to love one another. 12No one has ever seen God, but if we love one another, God lives in us and God's love is perfected in us.

13This is how we know that we live in God and God in us: because God has given us of the Spirit. 14We have seen and we testify that God sent the Child to be the Savior of the world. 15If you acknowledge that Jesus is the Child of God, God lives in you and you in God. 16And we are aware of and have faith in the love God has for us.

God is love. Those who live in love, live in God, and God in them. 17This is how love is perfected among us: We have confidence on the day of judgment because, as God is, so are we in this world. 18There is no fear in love. Perfect love drives out fear, for fear has to do with torment. Those who fear have not been perfected in love. 19We love God, because God first loved us. 20If you say, "I love God," but hate another believer, you are a liar. For if you don't love that believer whom you have seen, how can you love God whom you have not seen? 21This is the commandment we have from God: Those who love God must love their fellow believers also.

5:1Whoever believes that Jesus is the Messiah is born of God. And everyone who loves God loves God's children as well. 2By this we know that we love the children of God: when we love God and obey God's commandments. 3For this is the love of God: that we obey God's commandments. And God's commandments are not too hard to obey. 4Whoever is born of God overcomes the world. And this is the victory that has overcome the world: our faith.

THOSE WHO HAVE JESUS HAVE LIFE

[5]Who can overcome the world? Only the one who believes that Jesus is the Child of God. [6]This is the One who came by water and blood: Jesus Christ. Not by water only, but by water and blood. And it is the Spirit who bears witness, because the Spirit is the truth. [7]There are three that bear witness: [8]the Spirit, the water and the blood. And these three agree as one. [9]Do we accept the testimony of humans? God's testimony is greater. And this is the testimony of God: God has testified about the Child. [10]Those who believe in the Child of God have this testimony in their heart. Those who do not believe God are calling God a liar if they do not believe the testimony that God has given about the Child. [11]And this is the testimony: God has given us eternal life, and this life is in God's Child. [12]Those who have the Child have life, and those who do not have the Child of God do not have life.

THE REWARDS OF WALKING IN THE LIGHT

[13]I have written these things to you who believe in the name of the Child of God so that you may know that you have eternal life. [14]And this is the assurance that we have in God: If we ask anything according to God's will, God listens to us. [15]And if we know that God listens to us, then we know we will be granted the requests we ask of God, no matter what we ask.

PRAY FOR EACH OTHER

[16]If you see a believer committing a sin which does not lead to death, you should ask, and God will give that person life. I am referring to those whose sin does not lead to death. There is a sin which leads to death; I do not say that you should pray about that. [17]All injustice is sin. And there is sin which does not lead to death.

GOD'S CHILDREN HAVE THE POWER TO LIVE SINLESS LIVES

[18]We know that those born of God do not keep on sinning. But those who are born of God watch themselves, and the evil one does not become attached to them. [19]We know that we are of God, and the whole world lies prostrate before the evil one. [20]And we know that God's Child has come and given us understanding. And we know the One who is true, God's Child Jesus Christ. Now we know the true God and eternal life. [21]Little children, guard yourselves against false gods.

Second John

A LETTER FROM A SISTER CHURCH

$^{1:1}$The elder, to the select lady and her children, whom I love in the truth. And not I only, but also all those who have known the truth ^{2}because of the truth which lives in us and will be with us forever. ^{3}Goodwill, mercy and peace will be with you from God our heavenly Parent and from God's Child Jesus Christ, in truth and love. ^{4}I rejoice greatly to find some of your children walking in truth, just as we have been commanded by our heavenly Parent. ^{5}And now I ask you, lady, not as though I have written a new commandment to you, but that which we have had from the beginning, that we love one another. ^{6}And this is love, that we follow God's commandments. This is the commandment: Follow that which you have heard from the beginning. ^{7}For many deceivers have gone out into the world who do not acknowledge that Jesus Christ has come in the flesh. Each of these is a deceiver and an antichrist. ^{8}Look to yourselves, so that you do not lose those things we have worked for and so that you may receive a full reward. ^{9}Whoever goes too far and does not stay within the teaching of Christ does not have God. Those who stay within the teaching have both the Parent and the Child. ^{10}If anyone comes to you who does not uphold this teaching, do not welcome them into your house or greet them, ^{11}for those who greet them partake of their evil deeds. ^{12}Having many things to write to you, I would rather not use paper and ink, but I hope to come to you and talk face to face so that our joy may be full. ^{13}The children of your chosen sister greet you.

Third John

^{1:1}The elder, to the beloved Gaius whom I truly love:

²My dear friend, I wish above all that you prosper and be in good health, even as your soul prospers. ³I rejoiced greatly when the brothers came and told of the truth that is in you and how you walk in the truth. ⁴I have no greater joy than to hear that my children walk in truth.

⁵My dear friend, you are loyal in what you do for Christians who are strangers to you. ⁶They have told of your love before the church. You would do well to send them on their way in a manner God would approve, ⁷because it was because of God's name that they went out, taking nothing from the Gentiles. ⁸Therefore we ought to support them and be fellow workers for the truth.

A THREAT TO CHURCH UNITY

⁹I wrote to the church, but Diotrephes, who loves to be preeminent, refuses to admit us. ¹⁰Therefore, if I come, I will remember his deeds and his babbling against us with malicious words. And not content with that, he will not admit other believers. He forbids those who would admit them and puts them out of the congregation.

AN EXAMPLE OF GOOD

¹¹My dear friend, do not imitate what is evil, but rather what is good. Those who do good are of God, but those who do evil have not seen God. ¹²Demetrius has a good testimony of everyone and of the truth itself. We also testify, and you know that our testimony is true.

FAREWELL

¹³I had many things to write, but I will not write to you with pen and ink, ¹⁴for I trust that I will see you shortly and we will speak face to face. ¹⁵Peace to you. Your friends greet you. Greet our friends by name.

Jude

A LETTER TO THE JEWISH CHRISTIAN CHURCHES

^{1:1}Jude, a servant of Jesus Christ and a brother of James, to all who have been called by God. You are loved by God our Parent and kept safe by Jesus Christ. ²May mercy, peace and love be multiplied to you.

THE PURPOSE OF THIS LETTER

³My dear friends, I have been very eager to write to you about our shared salvation. I felt the need to write to you and exhort you to earnestly contend for the faith that was once and for all given to the saints. ⁴Certain people have secretly crept in among you. Their condemnation was written about long ago. These wicked people exchange the goodwill of our God for a lack of restraint and deny our only Sovereign, Jesus Christ.

DESCRIPTION OF THE FALSE TEACHERS

⁵I would like to remind you, though you know this already, that God's people were saved out of the land of Egypt, and afterward God destroyed those who did not believe. ⁶Furthermore, the angels who did not guard their high positions, but left their own home, have been kept in darkness in everlasting chains for judgment on the great day. ⁷In a similar way, Sodom and Gomorrah and the cities around them were utterly unchaste and went after strange flesh. They are set forth as an example of those who suffer the judgment of everlasting fire.

⁸In the same way, these dreamers contaminate their flesh, despise authority and slander the glorious ones. ⁹Yet even Michael the archangel, when contending with the devil and disputing over the body of Moses, did not venture to bring a strong accusation against the devil, but said, "May God rebuke you!" ¹⁰These people slander things they do not understand, and what they do understand instinctively, they spoil. ¹¹Woe to them! They have gone the way of Cain. They run greedily after the error of Balaam for reward. They perish in the rebellion of Korah. ¹²These are rocks in your love feasts, eating without fear, clouds without water carried along by the winds, trees of autumn without fruit, twice dead, plucked up by the roots, ¹³raging waves of the sea foaming out their shame, wandering stars, for whom is reserved the blackness of darkness forever.

14Enoch, the seventh from Adam, prophesied about these, saying, "Be prepared! God is coming with tens of thousands of holy ones 15to execute judgment upon all and to convict all who are ungodly of all their ungodly deeds and all the hard words that ungodly sinners have spoken against God." 16These people are grumblers, complainers and followers of their own lusts. Their mouths speak arrogant words as they pretend to admire others in order to gain advantage over them.

17Beloved, remember the words that were spoken by the apostles of our Sovereign Jesus Christ. 18They told you that there would be mockers in the last times who would follow their own ungodly lusts. 19These are those who separate themselves. They are sensual and do not have the Spirit.

CHRISTIAN CONDUCT IN THE FACE OF ADVERSITY

20But you, beloved, build yourselves up in your most holy faith by praying in the Holy Spirit. 21Keep yourselves in the love of God as you wait for the mercy of our Sovereign Jesus Christ to give you eternal life. 22Have compassion on those who hesitate, 23save others, have mercy with fear. Pull them out of the fire, hating even the garment stained by the flesh.

JUDE'S PRAYER FOR THE BELIEVERS

24Now to the One who is able to keep you from falling, and who is able to present you faultless and with joy before the glorious presence 25of our only God and Savior, be glory and majesty, power and authority, through Jesus Christ our Sovereign, before all time, both now and forever. Amen.

Revelation

A REVELATION IS BROUGHT TO JOHN BY AN ANGEL OF GOD

1:1This is what God revealed to Jesus the Messiah, so that Jesus could tell God's servants what must soon come to pass. God made it known by sending an angel to a servant of God named John. 2John hereby gives evidence regarding the word of God and the testimony of Jesus the Messiah and all that he saw. 3Blessed is the one who reads this book, and blessed are those who hear the words of this prophecy and obey what is written herein. For the time is near.

4John, to the seven churches in Asia: Goodwill and peace to you from the One who is and who was and who is to come and from the seven Spirits who are before God's throne 5and from Jesus the Messiah, the faithful witness, the firstborn from the dead and the ruler of the rulers of the earth. To the One who loves us and freed us from our sins by His blood 6and made us a realm and priests to His God and heavenly Parent - to Jesus be glory and power forever and ever. Amen.

7Be ready! Jesus is coming with the clouds. Every eye will see Jesus, even those who pierced Him; and all the races and clans of the earth will mourn because of Jesus. Yes, these things will happen! Amen.

8"I am the Alpha and the Omega," says the mighty God, "who is, who was and who is to come, the Almighty!"

THE BEGINNING OF THE PROPHETIC VISION

9I, John, your brother and companion in tribulation and in the realm and in the patience given by Jesus, was on the island of Patmos because of the message of God and the evidence given about Jesus the Messiah. 10I was in the Spirit on the seventh day and heard behind me a frightening noise like a trumpet, 11saying, "Write in a book what you see! Send it to the seven churches: Ephesus, Smyrna, Pergamum, Thyatira, Sardis, Philadelphia and Laodicea." 12I turned to see the voice that was speaking to me. I turned and saw seven golden lampstands. 13In the midst of the seven golden lampstands was one like You, O Child of Humanity, clothed with a garment down to Your feet and with a golden belt around Your chest. 14Your head and hair were white like wool, as white as snow, and Your eyes flamed like fire. 15Your feet were like glowing bronze in a furnace, Your voice was like the sound of many waters, 16You held seven stars in Your right hand and out of Your mouth came a sharp two-edged sword. Your face was like the sun shining in its strength, 17and when I saw You, I fell at Your feet as though dead. You laid Your right hand on me and said, "Do not be afraid. I am the First and the Last. 18I am the One who lives and was dead, and look!

I am alive forevermore! I have the keys of hell and death. [19]Write what you have seen and what now is and what will be hereafter. [20]The mystery of the seven stars that you saw in My right hand and the seven golden lampstands is this: The seven stars are the angels of the seven churches, and the seven lampstands are the seven churches.

EPHESUS: YOU HAVE FORSAKEN YOUR FIRST LOVE

[2:1]"To the angel of the church in Ephesus write: I am the One who holds the seven stars in My right hand and who walks in the midst of the seven golden lampstands. [2]I know your works and your labor and your patience. I know that you cannot bear those who are perverted. You have tested those who say they are apostles and are not and have found them to be liars. [3]You have endured and been loyal. You labored for My name and did not tire. [4]Nevertheless I have this against you: You have forsaken your first love. [5]Remember therefore from where you have fallen. Unless you repent and do the things you used to do, I will come to you quickly and remove your lampstand from its place. [6]But this you have: You hate the deeds of the Nicolaitans, which I also hate. [7]If you have ears, then listen to what the Spirit says to the churches. To those who overcome I will give the right to eat from the tree of life that is in the paradise of God.

SMYRNA: YOU WILL BE TESTED AND SUFFER PERSECUTION

[8]"To the angel of the church in Smyrna write: Thus says the First and the Last, who was dead and is alive. [9]I know your tribulation and your poverty - but you are rich! I know the slander of those who say they are Jews and are not but are a synagogue of Satan. [10]Do not fear those things you are about to suffer. The devil will cast some of you into prison so you may be tested, and you will have tribulation for ten days. Be faithful until death and I will give you the crown of life. [11]If you have ears, then listen to what the Spirit says to the churches. Those who overcome will not be hurt by the second death.

PERGAMUM: SOME WILL BE REWARDED

[12]"To the angel of the church in Pergamum write: Thus says the One who has the sharp sword with two edges. [13]I know where you live, where Satan's throne is. You fought for My name and did not deny the faith, even in those days when Antipas, My faithful martyr, was slain in your city where Satan lives. [14]But I have a few things against you: You have some there who hold to the doctrine of Balaam. He taught Balak how to snare the people of Israel into eating food sacrificed to idols and to sin sexually. [15]You also have some who hold to the doctrine of the Nicolaitans. [16]Repent, or I will come to you quickly and fight against you with the sword of My mouth. [17]If you have ears, then listen to what the Spirit says to the churches. To those who overcome I will give some of the hidden manna. And I will give them a white stone with a new name written on it which no one can discern but those who have it.

THYATIRA: THE OVERCOMERS WILL RULE

[18]"To the angel of the church in Thyatira write: Thus says God's Child, whose eyes flame like fire and whose feet shine like bronze. [19]I know your works, your love, your faith, your service, your patience and how your last works are greater than your first. [20]Nevertheless, I have a few things against you because you allowed that woman Jezebel, who calls herself a prophet, to teach and to seduce My servants to commit

sexual sins and to eat food sacrificed to idols. [21]I gave her time to repent of her sexual sins, but she would not. [22]Beware, I will throw her on a bed, and those who commit adultery with her I will throw into great suffering unless they repent of their deeds. [23]I will strike her followers dead. Then all the churches will know that I am the One who searches the minds and the hearts and repays each of you for what you have done. [24]But to the rest of you, and as many as do not follow this teaching and have not known the depths of Satan, I will put on you no other burden. [25]Hold what you have until I come. [26]To those who overcome and do My will until the end I will give power over the nations: [27]'You will rule them with a rod of iron; they will be broken and shattered like pottery,' just as I have received authority from My heavenly Parent. [28]I will also give you the morning star. [29]If you have ears to hear, then listen to what the Spirit says to the churches.

SARDIS: THE OVERCOMERS WILL WALK IN WHITE

[3:1]"To the angel of the church in Sardis write: Thus says the One who holds the seven Spirits of God and the seven stars: I know your works. You have a name that is alive, but you are dead. [2]Be watchful and strengthen what remains that is ready to die, for I have not found your works perfect before God. [3]Therefore remember what you have received and heard. Watch and repent. If you will not watch, I will come like a thief, and you will not know at what hour I come. [4]Yet you have a few there in Sardis who have not soiled their garments. They will walk with Me in white, for they are worthy. [5]Those who overcome will be clothed in white. I will not blot their names out of the book of life, but will acknowledge their names before My heavenly Parent and before the angels. [6]If you have ears, then listen to what the Spirit says to the churches.

PHILADELPHIA: THE DOOR WILL BE OPEN TO YOU

[7]"To the angel of the church in Philadelphia write: Thus says the One who is holy and true and who has the key of David. What I open no one can shut, and what I shut no one can open. [8]I know your works. Look! I have set before you an open door that no one can shut. For you have a little strength and have obeyed My words and have not denied My name. [9]Watch what I do! Those of the synagogue of Satan who say they are Jews (they are not - they lie), watch! I will make them come and bow down at your feet and acknowledge that I love you. [10]Because you have obeyed what I said about loyalty, I will keep you from the hour of trial that will come upon the whole world to test those who live upon the earth. [11]Watch! I come quickly. Hold what you have, so that no one takes your crown. [12]If you overcome, I will make you a pillar in the temple of My God and you will never go out. I will write on you the name of My God and My new name and the name of the city of My God, the new Jerusalem. [13]If you have ears, then listen to what the Spirit says to the churches.

LAODICEA: YOU ARE INDIFFERENT TOWARD GOD. REPENT!

[14]"To the angel of the church in Laodicea write: Thus says the Amen, the faithful and true witness, the beginning of God's creation. [15]I know your works. You are neither cold nor hot. I wish you were cold or hot, [16]but because you are lukewarm and neither cold nor hot, I will spew you out of My mouth. [17]You say, 'I am rich! I have become wealthy and have no need of anything.' You cannot see that you are

wretched, miserable, poor, blind and naked. [18]I counsel you to buy from Me gold that is refined in the furnace. Then you will be rich. Buy white clothing from Me to wear so the shame of your nakedness is not seen. Buy medicine from Me to put on your eyes so you may see. [19]Those whom I love I chasten and instruct. Therefore be zealous and repent. [20]Look! I stand at the door and knock. If you hear My voice and open the door, I will come in to you and sit down to eat with you, and you with me. [21]To those who overcome I give the right to sit with Me on My heavenly throne, even as I overcame and sat down with My heavenly Parent on the throne. [22]If you have ears, then listen to what the Spirit says to the churches."

JOHN SEES GOD

[4:1]After this I looked and saw a door open in heaven. Then the voice that had first spoken to me and that sounded like a trumpet said, "Come up here. I will show you what must take place after this." [2]At once I was in the Spirit and saw a throne set in heaven with someone sitting on it. [3]The One who sat on it had the appearance of jasper and carnelian. An emerald-colored rainbow encircled the throne. [4]Around the throne were twenty-four other thrones, and on the thrones I saw twenty-four elders seated. They were clothed with white garments, and on their heads were crowns of gold. [5]From the throne came forth lightning and thunder and voices. Seven lamps, which are the seven Spirits of God, burned before the throne. [6]In front of the throne was something like a sea of glass, clear as crystal. In the middle, around the throne, were four living creatures, covered with eyes in front and in back. [7]The first living creature was like a lion, the second like an ox, the third had a face like a human and the fourth was like a flying eagle. [8]The four living creatures each had six wings and were full of eyes all around. Day and night without resting they sing, "Holy, holy, holy is God Almighty, who was, and is and is to come." [9]When the living creatures give glory and honor and thanks to the One who sits on the throne and who lives forever and ever, [10]the twenty-four elders fall down before the One who sits on the throne and worship the One who lives forever and ever. They lay their crowns before the throne, saying, [11]"You are worthy, O mighty God, to receive glory and honor and power! For You created all things, and by Your choice they are and were created."

THE BOOK SEALED WITH SEVEN SEALS

[5:1]I saw a book in the right hand of the One who sat on the throne. It had writing on the inside and on the back and was sealed with seven seals. [2]And I saw a mighty angel calling out with a loud voice, "Who is worthy to loosen the seals and open the book?" [3]No one in heaven, on earth or under the earth was able to open the book or look in it. [4]I wept profusely, because no one was found worthy to open the book or look in it. [5]Then one of the elders said to me, "Don't weep, for the Lion of the Tribe of Judah, the Root of David, has conquered and will open the book and its seven seals."

[6]As I looked and watched, I saw in the midst of the throne and the four beasts and the elders a Lamb, as if slain, standing with seven horns and seven eyes, which are the seven Spirits of God sent out into all the earth. [7]The Lamb came and took the book from the right hand of the One who sat on the throne. [8]When the Lamb had taken the book, the four living creatures and the twenty-four elders fell down before the Lamb.

Each of them had a harp and golden bowls full of incense, which are the prayers of the saints. [9]They sang a new song, "You are worthy to take the book and to open its seals, for You were slain. With Your blood You redeemed us for God from every race and clan and language and people and nation. [10]You made them a royal house and priests to our God, and they will reign upon the earth." [11]Then I saw and heard the voices of many angels all around the throne and the living creatures and the elders. Their number was ten thousand times ten thousand and thousands of thousands, [12]singing with a great sound, "Worthy is the Lamb who was slain to receive power and riches and wisdom and strength and honor and adoration." [13]Then I heard every creature in heaven and on earth and under the earth and in the sea, with everything in them, sing, "Adoration and honor and glory and power belong to the One who sits on the throne and to the Lamb forever and ever." [14]The four living creatures said, "Amen," and the twenty-four elders fell down and worshiped.

JESUS OPENS SIX OF THE SEVEN SEALS

[6:1]I watched as the Lamb opened the first of the seven seals. Then I heard one of the four living creatures say with a voice like thunder, "Come and see." [2]I looked and saw a white horse. Its rider was given a crown and went forth as a conqueror to conquer.

[3]When the Lamb opened the second seal, I heard the second living creature say, "Come and see," [4]and a red horse came out. Its rider was given a great sword and power to take peace from the earth so that people would kill one another.

[5]When the Lamb opened the third seal, I heard the third living creature say, "Come and see," and I saw a black horse. A balance was in the rider's hand. [6]Then I heard a voice from among the four living creatures say, "A measure of wheat for a day's wage, and three measures of barley for a day's wage! And do not harm the olive oil and the wine!"

[7]When the Lamb opened the fourth seal, I heard the voice of the fourth living creature say, "Come and see!" [8]I looked and saw a pale horse. Its rider's name was Death, and Hell followed close behind. Power was given to them over a fourth of the earth to kill by sword, hunger, death and the wild animals of the earth.

[9]When the Lamb opened the fifth seal, I saw under the altar the souls of those who were slain because they had faithfully proclaimed the message of God. [10]They cried out with a loud voice, "How long, O God, holy and true, before You judge and avenge our blood upon those who dwell upon the earth?" [11]White robes were given to each of them, and they were told to rest yet a little longer until the complete number of God's other servants and believers were killed.

[12]When the Lamb opened the sixth seal, I looked and saw a great earthquake. The sun became as black as sackcloth made of goat hair, the moon became like blood [13]and the stars of the sky fell to earth like a fig tree casting off its unripe figs when shaken by a mighty wind. [14]The skies went away like a scroll that is rolled up, and every mountain and island moved from its place. [15]The kings of the earth, the great, the rich, the commanders of thousands, the mighty, every slave and everyone free hid themselves in the dens and the rocks of the mountains. [16]They said to the mountains

and rocks, "Fall on us and hide us from the face of the One who sits on the throne and from the wrath of the Lamb! [17]For the great day of God's wrath has come, and who can stand!"

THE 144,000

[7:1]After these things, I saw four angels standing at the four corners of the earth holding back the four winds of the earth, so that the winds would not blow on the earth or on the sea or on any tree. [2]I saw another angel ascending from the east with the seal of the living God and crying out with a loud voice to the four angels who had been given the power to harm the earth and the sea, [3]"Do not harm the earth or the sea or the trees until we have sealed the servants of our God on their foreheads." [4]I heard the number of those who were sealed: 144,000 from all the tribes of the descendants of Israel. [5]12,000 from the tribe of Judah were sealed, 12,000 from Reuben, 12,000 from Gad, [6]12,000 from Asher, 12,000 from Naphtali, 12,000 from Manasseh, [7]12,000 from Simeon, 12,000 from Levi, 12,000 from Issachar, [8]12,000 from Zebulun, 12,000 from Joseph and 12,000 from Benjamin.

THE UNCOUNTABLE MULTITUDE OF THE REDEEMED BEFORE THE THRONE

[9]After this I looked and saw a great multitude, more than anyone could count, from every nation and race and clan and people and language, standing before the throne and before the Lamb. They were clothed with white robes and had palm branches in their hands. [10]They cried out with a loud voice, "Salvation belongs to our God who sits upon the throne, and to the Lamb." [11]All the angels stood around the throne and around the elders and the four living creatures. They fell down upon their faces before the throne and worshiped God, [12]saying, "Amen! Adoration and glory and wisdom and thanksgiving and honor and power and strength to our God forever and ever."

[13]Then one of the elders asked me, "Who are these in white robes, and where did they come from?" [14]I answered, "O sovereign, you must know." Then the elder said to me, "These are those who came out of the great tribulation. They have washed their robes and made them white in the blood of the Lamb. [15]Therefore they are before the throne of God and serve God day and night in the temple. The One who sits on the throne will take care of them. [16]They will never be hungry or thirsty anymore, nor will the sun shine on them, nor any heat. [17]For the Lamb who is in the midst of the throne will feed them and will lead them to springs of living water. And God will wipe away every tear from their eyes."

JESUS OPENS THE SEVENTH SEAL

[8:1]When the Lamb opened the seventh seal, there was silence in heaven for about half an hour. [2]I saw the seven angels who stand before God being given seven trumpets. [3]Another angel came and stood at the altar with a golden censer. This angel was given much incense to offer with the prayers of the saints upon the golden altar that was before the throne. [4]The smoke of the incense and the prayers of the saints ascended up before God out of the angel's hand. [5]Then the angel took the censer and filled it with fire from the altar and threw it upon the earth with a crash of thunder, bolts of lightning and an earthquake.

THE ANGELS BLOW SIX OF THE SEVEN TRUMPETS

[6]The seven angels who had the seven trumpets prepared to sound them. [7]The first angel sounded a trumpet, and hail and fire mingled with blood was thrown upon the earth. A third of the earth, a third of the trees and all the green plants were burned up.

[8]The second angel sounded a trumpet, and something like a great mountain burning with fire was thrown into the sea. A third of the sea became blood, [9]a third of the living creatures that were in the sea died and a third of the ships were destroyed.

[10]The third angel sounded a trumpet, and a great star burning like a torch fell from the sky upon a third of the rivers and upon the sources of the waters. [11]The name of the star is Wormwood. A third of the waters became wormwood. Many people died from the waters that had become poisoned.

[12]The fourth angel sounded a trumpet, and a third of the sun and a third of the moon and a third of the stars were struck. A third of the day was not light, and the night likewise. [13]Then I saw and heard an eagle flying through the sky, crying with a loud voice, "Woe! Woe! Woe to the inhabitants of the earth because of the remaining trumpet blasts from the three angels that are yet to sound!"

9:[1]The fifth angel sounded a trumpet, and I saw a star fall from the sky to the earth. The star was given the key to the bottomless pit. [2]The star opened the bottomless pit, and smoke rose out of the pit like the smoke from a great furnace. The sun and the air were darkened by the smoke from the pit. [3]Locusts came upon the earth out of the smoke, and power was given to them like the power of the scorpions of the earth. [4]They were commanded not to harm the grass of the earth, nor anything green, nor any tree, but only those humans who did not have the seal of God on their foreheads. [5]They were not allowed to kill, but only to torment for five months. Their torment was like the torment from a scorpion when it stings. [6]In those days people will seek death and will not find it. They will desire death, but death will flee from them. [7]The locusts looked like horses prepared for battle. They wore what looked like crowns on their heads, and their faces were like human faces. [8]They had hair like the hair of women, and their teeth were like lion's teeth. [9]They had breastplates like breastplates made of iron, and the sound of their wings was like the sound of many horses and chariots running to battle. [10]They had tails like scorpions, with stingers in their tails, and they had the power to harm humans for five months. [11]They had as ruler over them the angel of the bottomless pit, whose name in Hebrew is Abaddon and in Greek is Apollyon. [12]One woe is past. Watch! Two more woes are still to come.

[13]The sixth angel sounded a trumpet, and I heard a voice from the four horns of the golden altar that is before God [14]saying to the sixth angel who had the trumpet, "Loose the four angels who are bound at the great river Euphrates." [15]The four angels who had been prepared for this hour and day and month and year were loosed to slay a third of all humans. [16]The number of troops on horseback was two hundred million. I heard the number of them. [17]This is what the horses and their riders that I saw in the vision looked like: Their breastplates were fiery red, hyacinth blue and sulfur yellow. The heads of the horses were like the heads of lions, and out of their mouths came fire,

smoke and sulfur. [18]A third of all humans were killed by these three: by the fire and the smoke and the sulfur that came out of their mouths. [19]Their power was in their mouths and in their tails. Their tails were like snakes that had heads they could use to do harm. [20]The rest of the people who were not killed by these plagues did not repent of the works of their hands. They continued to worship demons and idols made of gold, silver, bronze, stone and wood, which can neither see nor hear nor walk. [21]Nor did they repent of their murders, their magic, their sex sins or their thefts.

THE ANGEL WITH THE LITTLE BOOK

[10:1]Then I saw another mighty angel coming down from heaven, clothed with a cloud, and above whose head was a rainbow. The angel's face was like the sun, and the angel's legs were like pillars of fire. [2]A little book was open in the angel's hand. The angel put one foot on the sea and the other foot on the earth [3]and cried out with a loud voice, as when a lion roars. When the angel cried out, seven thunders were heard. [4]When I heard the seven thunders, I was about to write, but I heard a voice from heaven say, "Seal up what the seven thunders uttered and do not write it." [5]Then the angel I had seen standing upon the sea and upon the earth lifted a hand up to heaven [6]and swore by the One who lives forever and ever who created heaven and earth and the sea and all that is in them, "There will be no more delay, [7]but in the days when the seventh angel blows the trumpet, the mystery of God will be fulfilled as declared to God's servants the prophets."

THE VISION CONTINUES. JOHN EATS THE LITTLE BOOK

[8]Then the voice I had heard from heaven spoke to me again and said, "Go, take the little book that is open in the hand of the angel who stands upon the sea and upon the earth." [9]I went to the angel and said, "Give me the little book." The angel said to me, "Take it and eat it. It will be bitter in your belly, but it will be sweet as honey in your mouth." [10]I took the little book from the angel's hand and ate it. It was sweet as honey in my mouth, but as soon as I had eaten it, it was bitter in my belly. [11]Then the angel said to me, "You must prophesy again about many peoples, nations, languages and rulers."

TWO PROPHETS PROPHESY FOR THREE AND A HALF YEARS

[11:1]Then I was given a reed like a measuring rod, and I was told, "Go and measure the temple of God and the altar. Count those who are worshiping there. [2]Leave out the court that is outside the temple. Do not measure it, for it has been given to the Gentiles. They will trample the holy city underfoot for forty-two months. [3]I will give power to my two witnesses, and they will prophesy for 1,260 days clothed in sackcloth." [4]These are the two olive trees and the two lampstands that stand before the God of the earth. [5]If anyone is inclined to harm them, fire will come out of their mouths and devour their enemies. Anyone trying to harm them will be killed in this way. [6]They have power to shut the sky so that it will not rain during the days of their prophecy. They also have power over the waters to turn them to blood and to strike the earth with any plague as often as they wish. [7]When they finish their testimony, the beast that comes up out of the bottomless pit will make war against them, overcome them and kill them. [8]Their dead bodies will lie in the street of the great city that is spiritually called Sodom and Egypt, where also their God was crucified. [9]For three and a half days people from every race, clan, language and nation will look at their dead bodies and not allow their bodies to be put in graves. [10]The people who live on the earth will rejoice over them and make merry and send gifts to one another, because these two prophets had tormented those who dwell on the earth.

[11]But after three and a half days a breath of life from God entered them and they stood on their feet. Great fear fell upon those who saw them. [12]They heard a loud voice from heaven say to them, "Come up here!" and they went up to heaven in a cloud. Their enemies saw it all. [13]That same hour there was a great earthquake. A tenth of the city fell, and seven thousand people were killed in the earthquake. The rest were terrified and gave glory to the God of heaven. [14]The second woe is past. Watch! The third is coming quickly.

THE SEVENTH TRUMPET

[15]The seventh angel sounded a trumpet. Loud voices in heaven said, "The realm of this world has become the realm of our God and of the Messiah. God shall reign forever and ever!" [16]Then the twenty-four elders who were sitting on their thrones fell face-down and worshiped God, [17]saying, "We thank You, O God Almighty, who is and who was, because You have taken Your great power and have begun to reign. [18]The nations were angry, but Your wrath has come. The time has come for the dead to be judged and for You to give a reward to Your servants, the prophets, and to the saints and to those who fear Your name, both small and great, and to destroy those who destroy the earth." [19]Then the temple of God was opened in heaven and the ark of God's covenant was seen in the temple. There were flashes of lightning, voices, thunderings, an earthquake and great hail.

A GODLY WOMAN GIVES BIRTH TO A MALE CHILD

12:1Then a great wonder appeared in heaven: A woman clothed with the sun, with the moon under her feet and a crown of twelve stars upon her head. [2]She was pregnant and was crying out with the pains of childbirth as she began to deliver. [3]Then another wonder appeared in heaven: A great red dragon with seven heads and ten horns and seven crowns upon its heads. [4]Its tail drew a third of the stars from heaven and threw them to the earth. The dragon stood in front of the woman who was ready to give birth, in order to devour her child as soon as it was born. [5]She gave birth to a male child, who is to rule all nations with a rod of iron. Her child was caught up to God and to God's throne. [6]The woman fled into the wilderness, where she had a place prepared by God, and they fed her there for 1,260 days.

[7]There was war in heaven, and Michael and Michael's angels fought against the dragon. The dragon and the dragon's angels fought, [8]but they were not strong enough. No longer was there a place for them in heaven, [9]and the great dragon was thrown out, that old serpent called the devil and Satan who deceives the whole world. Satan was thrown out to the earth, and Satan's angels were thrown out too. [10]Then I heard a loud voice in heaven saying, "Now salvation and power and the realm of our God and the authority of God's Messiah have come! For the accuser of our fellow believers is thrown down who accused them before our God day and night. [11]They

overcame the accuser by the blood of the Lamb and by the word of their testimony. They did not love their lives so much that they feared death. [12]Therefore rejoice you heavens and you who live in them. But woe to you, earth and sea! For the devil has come down to you in great wrath, knowing that the time is short.

[13]When the dragon saw that it had been thrown down to earth, it persecuted the woman who had given birth to the male child. [14]The woman was given two wings like those of a great eagle, so that she could fly to a place in the wilderness where she could be nourished for a time, times and half a time away from the presence of the serpent. [15]The serpent poured water out of its mouth like a flood after the woman to cause her to be carried away by the flood. [16]But the earth helped the woman and opened its mouth and swallowed the flood that the dragon had poured out of its mouth. [17]The dragon was enraged with the woman and went to make war on the remnant of her descendants who keep the commandments of God and have the testimony of Jesus.

A BEAST ARISES WHOM ALMOST ALL WILL WORSHIP

[13:1]As I stood on the sand by the sea, I saw a beast rise up out of the sea. It had seven heads and ten horns and ten crowns on its horns. On its horns were blasphemous names. [2]The beast that I saw was like a leopard. It had feet like a bear and a mouth like a lion's mouth. The dragon gave it power and a throne and great authority. [3]One of its heads looked like it had been wounded and had died, but its deadly wound was healed. All the world was amazed and followed the beast. [4]They worshiped the dragon who gave authority to the beast. They also worshiped the beast, saying, "Who is like the beast? Who is able to make war with the beast?" [5]The beast was given a mouth to speak great blasphemies and authority to continue for forty-two months. [6]It opened its mouth in blasphemy against God, and it blasphemed God's name and God's dwelling place and those who live in heaven. [7]It was allowed to make war with the saints and to overcome them. Authority was given to it over every race, clan, language and nation. [8]All those who live upon the earth whose names have not been written down from the creation of the world in the book of life of the Lamb who was slain will worship the beast. [9]If you have ears, then listen. [10]Those who are to be taken captive, to captivity they will go. Those who kill with the sword, with the sword they will be killed. This requires endurance and faith on the part of the saints.

THE MARK OF THE BEAST

[11]Then I saw another beast coming up out of the earth. It had two horns like a lamb, but it spoke like a dragon. [12]It exercised all the authority of the first beast in the presence of the first beast. It caused the earth and those who live on it to worship the first beast whose deadly wound was healed. [13]It did great miracles: It made lightning come down from the sky to the earth in the sight of the people [14]and deceived those who live on the earth with those miracles that it had the power to do in the sight of the first beast. It commanded those who live on the earth to make an image in honor of the beast who was wounded by the sword and yet lived. [15]It had power to give breath to the image of the beast, so that the image of the beast could speak and cause those who would not worship the image of the beast to be killed. [16]It made everyone - small

and great, rich and poor, free and slave - receive a mark on their right hand or on their forehead. [17]No one could buy or sell unless they had the mark of the name of the beast or the number of its name. [18]Here is wisdom: If anyone has wisdom, compute the number of the beast. It is the number of a human, and the number is 666.

THE LAMB WITH 144,000 ON MOUNT ZION

[14:1]Then I looked and saw the Lamb standing on Mount Zion. With the Lamb were 144,000 with the Lamb's name and the name of the Lamb's Parent written on their foreheads. [2]I heard a sound from heaven like the sound of many waters and like the sound of loud thunder. It was the sound of harpists playing their harps. [3]They sang a new song before the throne and the four living creatures and the elders. No one could learn the song but the 144,000 who had been purchased from the earth. [4]These are those who were not soiled by sex, for they are virgins. And these are those who follow the Lamb wherever the Lamb goes. These were redeemed from among humans as the firstfruits to God and to the Lamb. [5]In their mouth was found no deceit, for they are without fault.

ANGELS ANNOUNCE THE TIME OF JUDGMENT UPON THE EARTH

[6]Then I saw another angel flying through the sky with the everlasting gospel to announce to those who live on the earth and to every nation and race and clan and language and people [7]with a loud voice, "Fear God and give God glory, for the hour of judgment has come. Worship the One who made heaven and earth and sea and the springs of water." [8]Another angel followed, saying, "Babylon has fallen! The great Babylon that made all the nations drink its passionate and immoral wine!" [9]A third angel followed them, saying with a loud voice, "Those who worship the beast and its image and receive its mark on their forehead or on their hand [10]will also drink of the wine of the wrath of God that is poured out full strength into the cup of God's indignation. They will be tormented with fire and brimstone in the presence of the holy angels and in the presence of the Lamb. [11]The smoke of their torment will ascend forever and ever. They will have no rest day or night if they worship the beast and its image or if they receive the mark of its name. [12]This requires endurance on the part of the saints who keep the commandments of God and their faith in Jesus."

THE FATE OF THE REDEEMED

[13]Then I heard a voice from heaven say, "Write: Blessed are the dead who die in Jesus from now on." "Yes," says the Spirit, "for they will rest from their labors, and the things they have done will stay with them."

THE EARTH IS HARVESTED

[14]Then I looked and saw a white cloud. Sitting on the cloud was One like the Son of Humanity, wearing a golden crown and holding a sharp sickle. [15]Then another angel came out of the temple and called out with a loud voice to the One who sat on the cloud, "Thrust in Your sickle and reap, for the time has come to reap and the harvest of the earth is ripe." [16]The One who sat on the cloud swung a sickle on the earth, and the earth was reaped.

[17]Then another angel came out from the temple in heaven. That angel also had a sharp sickle. [18]Then an angel who had power over the fire came out from the altar and

called out with a loud voice to the angel who had the sharp sickle, "Thrust in your sharp sickle and gather the clusters from the vine upon the earth, for its grapes are fully ripe." [19]The angel swung the sickle upon the earth, gathered the grapes of the earth and threw them into the great winepress of the wrath of God. [20]The grapes were trampled in the winepress outside the city. Blood came out of the winepress as high as the horse's bridles and flowed out for two hundred miles.

THE VICTORS SING ON THE SEA OF GLASS

[15:1]I saw another great and astonishing sign: seven angels with the seven last plagues. With these plagues the wrath of God will end. [2]And I saw, as it were, a sea of glass mingled with fire. Standing on the sea were those who had been victorious over the beast and over its image and over the number of its name. They held the harps of God. [3]They were singing the song of Moses, the servant of God, and the song of the Lamb:

"Great and marvelous are Your works, great God Almighty.

Just and true are Your ways, Ruler of the ages.

[4]Who will not fear You, O God, and glorify Your name?

For You alone are holy.

All nations will come and worship before You,

for Your fairness has become apparent."

THE SEVEN BOWLS

[5]After this I looked and saw that the temple of the tabernacle of testimony in heaven was open. [6]The seven angels with the seven plagues came out of the temple clothed in pure bright linen, with golden sashes around their chests. [7]One of the four living creatures gave the seven angels seven golden bowls full of the wrath of God, who lives forever and ever. [8]Then the temple was filled with smoke from the glory of God and from God's power, and no one was able to enter the temple until the seven plagues of the seven angels were accomplished.

[16:1]Then I heard a loud voice from the temple say to the seven angels, "Go and pour out the seven bowls of the wrath of God upon the earth." [2]The first angel went and poured the first bowl out upon the earth. Then loathsome and painful sores broke out on those who had the mark of the beast and on those who worshiped its image.

[3]The second angel poured the second bowl out upon the sea. It became like the blood of the dead, and every living thing in the sea died.

[4]The third angel poured the third bowl upon the rivers and springs of waters, and they became blood. [5]I heard the angel of the waters say, "O Holy One, You are and were and will be. You are right to judge thus, [6]for they shed the blood of saints and prophets. You have given them blood to drink as they deserve." [7]I heard the altar say, "It is so, O mighty God. True and righteous are Your judgments."

[8]The fourth angel poured out the fourth bowl on the sun, and it was given power to scorch humans with fire. [9]Humans were scorched with great heat, and they blasphemed the name of God who had power over these plagues. But they did not repent or honor God.

^{10}The fifth angel poured out the fifth bowl on the throne of the beast. Its realm became dark, and its subjects gnawed their tongues in pain. ^{11}They blasphemed the God of heaven because of their pains and their sores, but they did not repent of their deeds.

^{12}The sixth angel poured out the sixth bowl on the great river Euphrates, and the water was dried up to prepare the way for the kings from the east. ^{13}Then I saw three unclean spirits in the shape of frogs come out of the mouth of the dragon and out of the mouth of the beast and out of the mouth of the false prophet. ^{14}They are the spirits of demons performing miracles, and they go out to the rulers of the whole world to gather them to the battle on the great day of God Almighty.

^{15}"Be ready, for I come like a thief. Blessed are those who stay awake and keep clothed, lest they go naked and everyone sees their shame."

^{16}The frog-like spirits gathered the rulers together to a place called, in the Hebrew language, Armageddon.

^{17}The seventh angel poured out the seventh bowl in the air. A loud voice came out of the temple from the throne saying, "It is done!" ^{18}Then there were voices and thunder and lightning and a great earthquake. It was the worst earthquake there has ever been since humans have been upon the earth. ^{19}The great city was divided into three parts, and the cities of the nations fell. Great Babylon was remembered before God and was given the cup of the wine of God's fierce wrath. ^{20}Every island fled and the mountains could not be found. ^{21}Great hailstones weighing as much as a hundred pounds fell out of the sky upon humans. They blasphemed God because of the plague, for the plague was exceedingly great.

THE BIG UNGODLY WOMAN ON THE RED ANIMAL

$^{17:1}$One of the seven angels who had the seven bowls came and said to me, "Come, I will show you the judgment of the huge unfaithful woman who sits on many waters. ^{2}The kings of the earth have practiced idolatry with her, and the inhabitants of the earth have been made drunk with the wine of her excesses."

^{3}The angel carried me away in the Spirit into the wilderness. There I saw a woman sitting on a scarlet beast covered with blasphemous names. It had seven heads and ten horns. ^{4}The woman was arrayed in purple and scarlet and glittered with gold, precious stones and pearls. She had a golden cup in her hand full of the disgusting filth of her idolatry. ^{5}On her forehead a name was written: MYSTERY BABYLON THE GREAT, THE MOTHER OF PORNOGRAPHY AND THE DISGUSTING THINGS OF THE EARTH. ^{6}I saw that the woman was drunk with the blood of the saints and with the blood of the martyrs of Jesus. I saw her, and I looked closely at her. And I wondered.

THE ANGEL EXPLAINS THE VISION

^{7}The angel said to me, "Why do you marvel? I will tell you the mystery of the woman and of the beast with seven heads and ten horns that carries her. ^{8}The beast that you saw was, is not and will come up out of the bottomless pit and go to destruction. Those who dwell on the earth whose names were not written in the book of life from the creation of the world will marvel when they see the beast who was, is not and is yet to come. [9]This is for the mind that has wisdom: The seven heads are seven hills on which the woman sits. [10]They are also seven rulers. Five have fallen, one is, and the other is yet to come. The ruler who comes must continue a short time. [11]The beast who was and is not, is in fact the eighth. This ruler belongs to the first seven and is going to be destroyed. [12]The ten horns you saw are ten rulers. They have not received a realm as yet but will receive authority as rulers for one hour with the beast. [13]These are of one accord and will give their power and authority to the beast. [14]They will make war with the Lamb. The Lamb will overcome them, because the Lamb is God of gods and Ruler of rulers. Those who are with the Lamb are the called, the chosen and the faithful."

[15]Then the angel said to me, "The waters you saw where the unfaithful woman sits are multitudes of peoples, nations and languages. [16]The beast and the ten horns you saw will hate the unfaithful woman and make her desolate and naked. They will eat her flesh and burn her with fire. [17]God has put it into their hearts one after another to agree to give their realms to the beast in order to carry out God's purpose until the words of God are fulfilled. [18]The woman you saw is that great city that reigns over the rulers of the earth."

THE DOOM SONG OF UNRIGHTEOUS BABYLON

[18:1]After this I saw another angel coming down from heaven. The angel had great authority. The earth was illuminated by this angel's brilliance. [2]The angel called out with a strong voice, "Babylon the great has fallen! She has fallen and become the dwelling place of demons, the jail for every foul spirit and a coop for every unclean and hateful bird. [3]For all nations have drunk eagerly of her lusts. The rulers of the earth have slept with her, and the merchants of the earth have become wealthy through the abundance of her power."

[4]Then I heard another voice from heaven say, "Come out of her, My people, so you do not participate in her sins, and so you do not receive her plagues. [5]For her sins are heaped up to heaven and God remembers her wrongs. [6]Give to her as she has given; repay her double according to her works. In the cup she mixed for others, mix for her double. [7]Give her as much torment and sorrow as the glory and power she gave herself. For she said in her heart, 'I sit as a queen! I am no widow; I will never see sorrow.' [8]Therefore in one day her plagues will come: death, mourning and famine. She will be utterly burned with fire, for strong is the One who judges her.

[9]"The rulers of the earth who were unfaithful with her and shared in her power will bewail her and lament for her when they see the smoke of her burning. [10]In fear of her torment, they will stand far off and say, 'Alas! Alas! Babylon that great city, that mighty city! In one hour your judgment has come!' [11]The merchants of the earth will weep over her, for no one buys their merchandise anymore: [12]merchandise of gold, silver, precious stones, pearls, linen, purple, silk, scarlet, fragrant wood, containers made from ivory, containers made from precious woods, bronze, iron, marble, [13]cinnamon, incense, perfumed oils, frankincense, wine, olive oil, flour, cattle, sheep, horses, chariots, slaves and human souls.

[14]"The merchants will say, 'The fruits that your soul lusted for have departed from you. Everything that was luxurious and lavish has been lost to you and you will find it no more.' [15]The merchants who were made rich by her will stand far off in fear of her torment. They will weep and wail [16]and say, 'Alas! Alas for the great city that was clothed in linen, purple and scarlet and glittered with gold, precious stones and pearls. [17]In one hour that great wealth has come to nothing.' Every ship captain and all who travel in ships and the sailors and as many as trade by sea will stand far off [18]as they watch the smoke of her burning and cry out, 'What city was ever like this great city?' [19]They will throw dust on their heads and weep and wail and cry out, 'Alas! Alas for the great city where all who had ships at sea were made rich by her wealth. In one hour she has lost it all.' [20]But rejoice over her, you in heaven and you saints and apostles and prophets, for God has punished her for you."

[21]Then a mighty angel picked up a stone like a great millstone and threw it into the sea, saying, "Thus with violence will the great city Babylon be thrown down and never be found again. [22]The sounds of harpists, musicians, flutists and trumpeters will never be heard in you again. No artisan of whatever craft will be found in you again, the sound of the millstone will never be heard in you again, [23]the light of a lamp will never shine in you again and the voices of the bride and the bridegroom will never be heard in you again. For your merchants were the great ones of the earth, and by your sorceries were all nations deceived. [24]In the great city was found the blood of prophets and saints and all those who were slain upon the earth."

HEAVEN REJOICES AT THE TRIUMPH OF GOOD OVER EVIL

[19:1]After this I heard the great sound of a vast multitude in heaven singing, "Hallelujah! Salvation and glory and honor and power to our God! [2]For true and righteous are God's judgments. God has judged the huge unfaithful woman who corrupted the earth with her immorality and has punished her for shedding the blood of God's servants." [3]Again they sang, "Hallelujah! Her smoke will rise forever and ever!" [4]The twenty-four elders and the four living creatures fell down and worshiped God, who was seated on the throne, saying, "Amen! Hallelujah!" [5]A voice came from the throne, saying, "Praise our God, all you servants of God and all you who fear God, both small and great."

THE SAINTS ARE ARRAYED IN WHITE FOR THE WEDDING OF THE LAMB

[6]Then I heard the voices of a vast multitude, like the sound of many waters, and like the sound of mighty thunderings, singing, "Hallelujah! For the great God Omnipotent reigns! [7]Let us be glad and rejoice and give honor to God, for the marriage of the Lamb has come and the bride has made herself ready!" [8]To her it was granted that she be arrayed in linen, clean and bright. The linen represents the righteousness of the saints. [9]The angel said to me, "Write, 'Blessed are those who are invited to the marriage supper of the Lamb.' This is the true message of God." [10]I fell at the angel's feet to worship, but the angel said to me, "Can't you see? I am your fellow servant and the fellow servant of those believers who hold to the testimony of Jesus. Worship God! For the testimony Jesus gave is the Spirit of prophecy."

THE ARMY ON WHITE HORSES

[11]Then I saw heaven open, and look, a white horse! The One who sits on it and who judges and makes war in righteousness is called Trustworthy and True. [12]Your eyes are flames of fire, and on Your head are many crowns. You have a name written that no one but You Yourself know. [13]You are dressed in a cloak dipped in blood, and Your name is THE WORD OF GOD. [14]The armies of heaven clothed in linen, white and clean, were following You on white horses. [15]Out of Your mouth comes a sharp sword with which You will strike the nations. You will rule them with a rod of iron, and You will tread the winepress of the fierce wrath of Almighty God. [16]On Your cloak and on Your thigh is written a name: RULER OF RULERS AND GOD OF GODS.

AN ANGEL CALLS THE BIRDS TO THE FEAST

[17]Then I saw an angel standing in the sun and calling out with a loud voice to all the birds flying in the air, "Come and gather to the great supper of God, [18]so that you may eat the flesh of kings and the flesh of commanders and the flesh of the strong and the flesh of horses and all those who sit on them, and the flesh of everyone free and slave, small and great."

THE BATTLE OF ARMAGEDDON

[19]Then I saw the beast and the rulers of the earth and their armies gathered together to make war against the One who sits on the horse and against God's army. [20]The beast was captured, and with it the false prophet who performed miracles in the beast's presence. By these miracles the false prophet had deceived those who had received the mark of the beast and worshiped its image. Both of them were thrown alive into the lake of fire burning with sulfur. [21]The rest were slain by the sword that came out of the mouth of the One who sat on the horse. All the birds gorged themselves on their flesh.

SATAN BOUND IN THE PIT FOR A THOUSAND YEARS

20:[1]Then I saw an angel come down from heaven with the key to the bottomless pit and holding a great chain. [2]The angel seized the dragon, that serpent of old who is the devil and Satan. Satan was bound for a thousand years, [3]thrown into the bottomless pit and locked up and sealed. Therefore the nations could not be deceived anymore until the thousand years were ended. After that Satan must be loosed for a little while.

GOD'S PRIESTS RULE WITH CHRIST FOR A THOUSAND YEARS

[4]Then I saw thrones, and the authority to judge was given to those who sat on them. And I saw the souls of those who were beheaded for witnessing for Jesus and for the word of God. They had not worshiped the beast or the image, nor had they received the mark on their foreheads. They lived and reigned with the Messiah for a thousand years. [5]The rest of the dead did not live again until the thousand years ended. This is the first resurrection. [6]Blessed and holy are those who have a part in the first resurrection. The second death has no power over them, but they will be priests of God and of God's Messiah and will reign with the Messiah for a thousand years.

SATAN RELEASED TO ATTACK THE SAINTS AT ZION

[7]When the thousand years are ended, Satan will be loosed from prison [8]and will go out to deceive the nations in the four corners of the earth. Gog and Magog will be gathered together for battle, and their number will be as the sand of the sea. [9]They will travel across the width of the earth and surround the camp of the saints and the beloved city. But fire will come down from heaven and consume them.

SATAN THROWN INTO THE LAKE OF FIRE

[10]Then the devil who had deceived them will be thrown into the lake of fire and brimstone where the beast and false prophet had been thrown. They will be tormented day and night forever and ever.

THE GREAT WHITE THRONE JUDGMENT

[11]Then I saw a great white throne. Earth and sky fled away from the presence of the One who was seated on it, and no place was found for them. [12]And I saw the dead, small and great, standing before the throne. The books were opened. Then another book was opened, which is the book of life. The dead were judged from what was written in the books according to what they had done. [13]The sea gave up the dead who were in it, Death and Hell gave up the dead who were in them, and all were judged according to what they had done. [14]Then Death and Hell were thrown into the lake of fire. This is the second death. [15]Anyone whose name was not found written in the book of life was thrown into the lake of fire.

THE GLORIOUS NEW JERUSALEM

[21:1]Then I saw a new sky and a new earth. The first sky, the first earth and the sea were no more. [2]And I saw the holy city, the new Jerusalem, coming down from God out of heaven, prepared like a bride adorned for her husband. [3]I heard a loud voice from heaven, saying, "Look! The tabernacle of God is among humans! God will live with them and they will be God's people. God will be with them in person and will be their God. [4]God will wipe away every tear from their eyes. There will be no more death or sorrow or crying or pain, for the former things have passed away."

WRITTEN PROMISES TO THE OVERCOMERS

[5]The One seated on the throne said, "Look! I make all things new! Write, for these words are trustworthy and true." [6]Then the One on the throne said to me, "It is done! I am the Alpha and the Omega, the beginning and the end. To the one who is thirsty I will give freely from the springs of the water of life. [7]Those who overcome will inherit all this. I will be their God and they will be My children. [8]But the faithless unbelievers, the detestable murderers, the immoral sorcerers and the lying idolaters will have their portion in the lake that burns with fire and brimstone. That is the second death."

FURTHER DESCRIPTION OF THE NEW JERUSALEM

[9]One of the seven angels who had the seven bowls full of the seven last plagues came and talked with me and said, "Come here and I will show you the bride, the wife of the Lamb." [10]The angel carried me away in the Spirit to a great high mountain and

showed me Jerusalem, the holy city, descending out of heaven from God, [11]radiant with the glory of God. It was luminous like a precious stone, like jasper or like ice. [12]It had a great high wall with twelve gates and had twelve angels at the gates. Names were written on them, and they are the names of the twelve tribes of the descendants of Israel. [13]On the east were three gates, on the north were three gates, on the south were three gates and on the west were three gates. [14]The wall of the city had twelve foundations, and on them were the names of the twelve apostles of the Lamb.

[15]The angel who talked with me had a golden reed to measure the city, its gate and its wall. [16]The city was laid out foursquare, the length as long as the width. The angel measured the city with the reed, and the length and the width and the height were all 1500 miles. [17]The angel measured the wall, and it was 144 cubits thick by the human measure the angel was using. [18]The wall was constructed of jasper, and the city was pure gold, like clear glass. [19]The foundations of the wall of the city were garnished with all kinds of precious stones. The first foundation was jasper, the second sapphire, the third agate, the fourth emerald, [20]the fifth sardonyx, the sixth carnelian, the seventh chrysolite, the eighth beryl, the ninth topaz, the tenth a golden-green gemstone, the eleventh jacinth and the twelfth amethyst. [21]The twelve gates were twelve pearls, each individual gate of one pearl. The streets of the city were pure gold and transparent like glass.

[22]I saw no temple in the city, for Almighty God and the Lamb are its temple. [23]The city had no need of the sun or the moon for light, because the glory of God illuminated it, and the Lamb is its light. [24]The nations will walk in its light, and the rulers of the earth will bring their glory into it. [25]Its gates will not be shut at all by day, and there will be no night there. [26]They will bring the glory and honor of the nations into it. [27]Nothing that is profane or disgusting, nor anyone who lies, may enter. Only those who are written in the Lamb's book of life may enter.

THE WATER OF LIFE FLOWS THROUGH THE CITY

22:1[1]Then the angel showed me the river of the water of life, clear as crystal, proceeding from the throne of God and the Lamb [2]through the middle of the street. On each side of the river was the tree of life bearing twelve harvests of fruit each month. The leaves of the tree are for the healing of the nations. [3]There will no longer be a curse. The throne of God and of the Lamb will be in the city, and God's servants will serve God. [4]They will see God's face, and God's name will be on their foreheads. [5]There will be no night there, and there will be no need for a lamp or the light of the sun. Almighty God will give them light, and they will reign forever and ever.

GOD ASSURES THAT THIS MESSAGE IS TO BE TRUSTED

[6]Then the angel said to me, "This message is trustworthy and true, for the mighty God of the spirits of the prophets sent an angel to show God's servants what must soon come to pass. [7]Watch! For I am coming soon. Blessed is the one who delights in the prophetic message in this book."

[8]I, John, am the one who saw and heard these things. When I saw and heard, I fell down to worship at the feet of the angel who showed me these things. [9]The angel said to me, "Can't you see? I am a fellow servant with you and your fellow believers the prophets, along with those who delight in the message of this book. Worship God!" [10]Then the angel said to me, "Do not seal up the prophetic message in this book, for the time is near. [11]Let those who do wrong continue to do wrong. Let those who are dirty continue to be dirty. Let those who do right continue to do right. Let those who are holy continue to be holy."

THE INVITATION

[12]"Watch! I am coming soon! My reward is with Me to give to everyone according to what they have done. [13]I am the Alpha and the Omega, the first and the last, the beginning and the end. [14]Blessed are those who wash their robes. They have the right to the tree of life and to enter the gates into the city. [15]Outside are dogs, sorcerers, pornographers, murderers, idolaters and all those who love to lie. [16]I, Jesus, have sent My angel to be a witness of these things in the churches. I am the root and the offspring of David, the bright morning star.

[17]"The Spirit and the Bride say, 'Come!' And let those who hear say, 'Come!' Let those who are thirsty come. And whoever will, let them take the water of life freely. [18]I warn everyone who hears the prophetic message in this book: If anyone adds anything to these things, God will add to that person the plagues that are written in this Book. [19]And if anyone takes anything away from the message in this Book of Prophecy, God will take away that person's part in the tree of life and the holy city which are written of in this Book. [20]The One who testifies to these things says, 'Yes! I am coming quickly.'"

Amen. Come mighty Jesus! [21]The grace of our Sovereign Jesus Christ be with you all. Amen.

FAMILY RECORDS

FAMILY RECORDS